CO-ED COMBAT

CO-ED COMBAT

The New Evidence
That Women Shouldn't Fight
the Nation's Wars

KINGSLEY BROWNE

SENTINEL

SENTINEL
Published by the Penguin Group
Penguin Group (USA) Inc., 375 Hudson Street,
New York, New York 10014, U.S.A.
Penguin Group (Canada), 90 Eglinton Avenue East, Suite 700, Toronto,
Ontario, Canada M4P 2Y3 (a division of Pearson Penguin Canada Inc.)
Penguin Books Ltd, 80 Strand, London WC2R 0RL, England
Penguin Ireland, 25 St. Stephen's Green, Dublin 2, Ireland
(a division of Penguin Books Ltd)
Penguin Books Australia Ltd, 250 Camberwell Road, Camberwell,
Victoria 3124, Australia (a division of Pearson Australia Group Pty Ltd)
Penguin Books India Pvt Ltd, 11 Community Centre,
Panchsheel Park, New Delhi – 110 017, India
Penguin Group (NZ), 67 Apollo Drive, Rosedale, North Shore 0745,
Auckland, New Zealand (a division of Pearson New Zealand Ltd.)
Penguin Books (South Africa) (Pty) Ltd, 24 Sturdee Avenue,
Rosebank, Johannesburg 2196, South Africa

Penguin Books Ltd, Registered Offices: 80 Strand, London WC2R oRL, England

First published in 2007 by Sentinel, a member of Penguin Group (USA) Inc.

1 3 5 7 9 10 8 6 4 2

Copyright © Kingsley Browne, 2007
All rights reserved
Page 351 constitutes an extension to this copyright page.

LIBRARY OF CONGRESS CATALOGING IN PUBLICATION DATA
Browne, Kingsley.
Co-ed combat : the new evidence that women shouldn't fight
the nation's wars / Kingsley Browne.
p. cm.
Includes bibliographical references and index.
ISBN 978-1-59523-043-0
1. Women soldiers. 2. Combat. I. Title.
UB416.B76 2007
355.0082'0973—dc22   2007019364

Printed in the United States of America
Set in Fairfield Light
Designed by Victoria Hartman

To Frances Anne Browne
United States Navy,
1943–1945

Preface and Acknowledgments

It may seem churlish to write a book questioning the placement of women in combat while they are in harm's way in both Iraq and Afghanistan. As I have attempted to make clear throughout this book, one may challenge the policy of sexual integration without disparaging the service of military women. Those who are serving now, and those who served in the past—not to mention those who will do so in the future—deserve the thanks of a grateful nation.

During the course of preparing this book, I have spoken with a number of current and former military personnel. My "sample" is what social scientists call a "convenience sample," which is "social-science speak" for "whoever I could snag." I make no claim that the views that were expressed to me are representative of military personnel generally. I have recounted some of their comments when I thought that they would be illustrative or otherwise interesting. Some preferred that their names not be used, some were happy to have their names used, while others were somewhere in between. Because of potentially serious repercussions that may befall military personnel who express doubts about sexual integration, I have chosen to err on the side of underdisclosure of identifying information and have not named any of the people with whom I spoke. They know who they are, and they know that they have my sincere thanks.

I have been assisted in numerous ways by others in this project. Naming names risks failing to acknowledge people who deserve thanks, so my apologies if I leave someone out. Several people have provided me with copies of papers not yet published or have answered questions about their work, including Alice Eagly, G. William Farthing, David Geary, Steven Neuberg, and Stephen Seiler. Others were kind enough to provide comments on drafts of some of my earlier work that served as the basis for portions of this book. They include Chris Bernard, Steve Colarelli, John Dolan, Patti Hausman, Owen Jones, Mike McIntyre, and Erin O'Hara. Thanks also to Elaine Donnelly of the Center for Military Readiness, who was more than generous in making documents available to me. Thanks also go to Robert Deaner and Alice Eagly for kindly reading draft chapters of this book in their areas of expertise. Special thanks must go to several people who suffered through multiple drafts of the entire book. These include Christina Beaton, April Bleske-Rechek, Helena Cronin, and Oliver Curry. I am immensely grateful to all.

I also owe a large debt of gratitude to my agent, Don Gastwirth, for his faith in me and for his tireless efforts on my behalf, and to my editor, Bernadette Malone Serton, who made this a far better book than it otherwise would have been.

Finally, this project would not have been possible without the unwavering support of my wife, Cynthia, who became a "book widow" for longer than I would have liked.

Contents

CO-ED COMBAT

1

Introduction

Wars may be fought with weapons, but they are won by men. It is the spirit of the men who follow and the man who leads that gains the victory.

—George S. Patton Jr.[1]

Facing its most serious test since the creation of the All-Volunteer Force in 1973, the United States is placing increasing numbers of women in combat situations, a move that poses substantial threats to military effectiveness. Women have served in combat aviation and on warships for over a decade, and some now call for integration of even the ground-combat arms of infantry, armor, and artillery. The desire to do the "right thing"—providing greater opportunities for women—has too often prevailed over the goal of doing the "smart thing"—forging the strongest military possible.

Sexual integration of the military jeopardizes the operation of the military in ways that are not fully appreciated. Integration remains a contentious issue both inside and outside the military, and the full consequences of even the integration that has occurred so far will not be felt until we face an enemy that more closely matches our own strength. When we face such a foe, policies that have rendered the military marginally weaker create a risk of disastrous consequences. The price will be paid in the lives of the nation's sons and daughters and in a reduction in the nation's ability to defend its interests.

Although military leaders were initially resistant to sexual integration, decades of political pressures and inculcation into the officer corps of the lesson that failure to support sexual integration will kill their careers have left a military leadership unwilling to admit that the emperor has no clothes. The media and Hollywood, always eager to promote the "girl power" agenda, gladly go along.

The push for sexual integration of combat forces rests on one of the central dogmas of twentieth-century social science—that men and women are largely interchangeable and that any differences that do exist are primarily, if not exclusively, a result of socialization. Whatever facial plausibility that belief system may once have possessed—and it was never very much—a burgeoning body of scientific evidence now reveals fundamental differences between the sexes. The relatively new field of evolutionary psychology has not only identified specific, and sometimes counterintuitive, ways that the sexes differ—not just as individuals but also as members of groups—it has also provided a comprehensive account of *why* they differ. Advances in knowledge about the influences of sex hormones on behavior have revealed *how* these differences come about. It is the purpose of this book to integrate this new evidence with the already rich literature examining the behavior of men in battle. This synthesis suggests that integration of women in combat will almost inevitably lead to a weaker military.

The Make-Believe World of Sexual Integration

In the 1997 movie *Starship Troopers*, the audience is treated to a vision of the sexually integrated military of the future.[2] The movie, based loosely on Robert Heinlein's 1959 novel, depicts a world unified under a single vaguely fascistic government that faces a threat from buglike creatures from the planet Klendathu.

We meet the protagonists as they are finishing high school in Buenos Aires, although they seem a better fit for *Beverly Hills 90210* than Argentina. Johnny Rico is a handsome football star who is smitten with the beautiful Carmen Ibanez. The also-beautiful Dizzy Flores is a football teammate of Johnny's—indeed, she is the quarterback—who is carrying a torch for him, though Johnny seems oblivious. The three decide to join the Federal Service, which is the only route to becoming a "citizen" rather than remaining a mere "civilian." Carmen is motivated by her desire to become a starship pilot, Johnny by his desire to be near Carmen, and Dizzy by her desire to be near Johnny. Carmen, who has brains behind her beauty, qualifies for the Fleet Academy to pursue her dream. Unfortunately, Johnny seems to lack the candlepower and, like Dizzy, is assigned to the Mobile Infantry, passing up an acceptance to Harvard, much to the chagrin of his parents.

Johnny and Dizzy go through a program of basic training that makes Marine boot camp look like a walk in the park. After the drill instructor intentionally breaks one man's arm, Dizzy accepts a challenge from him and, despite her diminutive stature, gets in a few solid licks before she is decked.

The movie's most famous scene is the "shower scene," which shows male and female recruits showering together unabashedly, making small talk about what led them to join the service. A room full of naked men and women joking around without any sexual tension might lead one to conclude that these humans have evolved to have very different psyches from those living today, who seem so vulnerable to the seductions of the flesh (or, alternatively, to suspect that the military is putting something in the food). Yet we see in a later scene that Johnny and Dizzy do indeed succumb to temptation. When their commanding officer discovers them—Dizzy now being embarrassed by her nudity in a way that she was not in the shower—he generously gives them an additional ten minutes to finish up, apparently unconcerned about fraternization between a squad leader and a subordinate.

What are we to make of the sexually integrated football team, in which small, feminine women seem to hit as hard as men? Or of the absence of lust in the group shower and the officially approved lust in quarters? Or of the service of women as mobile infantry, despite the fact that this space-age infantry faces challenges every bit as physically grueling as the infantry of today? Or of the almost matriarchal look of the fleet, with a female fleet commander and female pilots (perhaps implicitly suggesting what Heinlein claimed explicitly in his novel, that women make the best pilots)? What has changed?

It is not the bodies that have changed. Carmen, Dizzy, and many of the other women are soft and supple exemplars of femininity. Nor have the hormones changed, as the romantic and sexual attraction pervading the movie makes clear (other than the inexplicable asexuality of the shower scene). Nor is it the technology of warfare, as the mobile infantry of the Federation is no less blood-and-guts than the infantry of today. Indeed, unaccountably, the infantry of the future seems to lack armored ground vehicles and artillery. What has changed, it seems, is attitude.

The attitude on display in *Starship Troopers*—that ignoring sex differences renders them inconsequential—was very different from that initially faced by Lieutenant Jordan O'Neil, played by Demi Moore in the movie *G.I. Jane*, also released in 1997.[3] No G.I., she was a Navy intelligence analyst who, resentful that her boyfriend outranked her because of his combat service during the Gulf War, objected to the exclusion of women from combat. Her lack of combat experience, she believed, was impeding her quest for promotion. Fortunately for her, a female senator (Anne Bancroft) was itching to expand the role of women in the military and, as the price for confirmation of a nominee for secretary of the navy, the Navy agreed to a test case—a female candidate for the SEALs.

The Navy, of course, does not believe that O'Neil, or any woman, can pass the rigorous six-month SEAL basic training, which it describes as "the toughest training in the world."[4] It agrees to the test only because it assumes that she will fail. When she arrives at training, no one wants her there—not the base commander, not Command Master Chief John Urgayle (played by Viggo Mortensen) who directs the training, nor her fellow SEAL candidates. O'Neil is determined, however, and demands that she be given no special treatment. She shaves her head and insists on sharing the barracks with the men and satisfying the same physical standards. In her "spare time," she does one-handed push-ups to whip herself into even better shape.

Part of the SEAL training is simulated capture and interrogation. During an exercise, O'Neil and some others are captured. Urgayle begins abusing her, smashing her head into a post and behaving so brutally that the men all think he has gone too far. (In fact, he acts so brutally that in real life he would probably be court-martialed, a principal reason that the Navy refused to cooperate in the making of the film.) O'Neil, with her hands tied behind her back, head-butts Urgayle and then lands several blows with her feet, before being knocked to the ground. Bruised and bloody, she struggles to her feet and between clenched teeth utters the most applause-getting line of the movie: "Suck my dick!"

Now we know that O'Neil will make it; after all, what better indicator could there be that she "has what it takes"? At a bar later that night, her comrades show their acceptance of her by chanting "Suck my dick! Suck my dick!" After some unsuccessful political machinations intended to derail O'Neil's candidacy, she ultimately passes the course, but not before a brief diversion to Libya during which she saves Urgayle's life, leading him to accept her and to give her the Navy Cross he had been awarded for an earlier mission.

Thus, O'Neil succeeds largely by giving up her femininity, a price that the women in *Starship Troopers* did not have to pay. But her masculinization seems a bit artificial, as revealed in an interchange with a sympathetic female Navy psychiatrist, Lieutenant Blondell. One interview produced the following exchange:

BLONDELL: Lieutenant, why are you doing this?
O'NEIL: Do you ask the men the same question?
BLONDELL: As a matter of fact: yes, I do ask them.
O'NEIL: And what do they say?
BLONDELL: " 'Cause I get to blow shit up."
O'NEIL: Well, there you go.[5]

But, in fact, O'Neil was not driven by a desire to "blow shit up"; indeed, she showed little interest in such things. Instead, her motivation was to obtain a career-enhancing credential. Yet it is unlikely that *any* man has ever signed up for SEAL training as a route to promotion. There has to be a more primal drive than careerism to cause people to subject themselves to the rigors of the training and the danger of the missions they undertake.

In the end, it is not clear that O'Neil has accomplished much beyond her own personal triumph. Her acceptance does not reflect the acceptance of women but only of one incredibly driven woman who, in effect, turns herself into a man. The world of *Starship Troopers* has not yet arrived in *G.I. Jane*, because the belief that sex is a criterion relevant to combat service has not been extinguished, and the "attitude" that sex is easily ignored has not yet been widely embraced. The decade that has passed since these movies were released reveals that Hollywood's vision of the progress of sexual integration was seriously misguided. Not everyone, however, is ready to abandon it.

A *Starship Troopers* Military for the United States?

Will the science fiction of *Starship Troopers* become fact? Some people envision such a military for the United States, with women being fully integrated and fighting side-by-side with men as if sex does not matter. What is it that leads "integrationists"—that is, proponents of full integration of the combat arms—to believe that the military can—and should—take such an unprecedented step?

The argument that full integration would be effective seems to rest on four assumptions. The first is that the sexes do not differ substantially in combat-relevant ways, other than (perhaps) in physical strength, and that any differences that do exist are a result of socialization and can be eliminated through education and training. Therefore, the argument goes, it is sheer sexism to treat them differently. The second assumption is that modern warfare is so different from warfare experienced by our fathers and forefathers that millennia of experience limiting warfare to men provide no guidance for current policy. The third assumption is that there is nothing inherently "masculine" about war—that the association between men and warfare is mere happenstance and that combat neither calls for nor rewards masculinity. Women throughout history have played a role in armed conflict, the argument goes, and should today. The final assumption is that because the sexes are essentially interchangeable, the only obstacle to integration is "attitude"—an ideology of "masculinism" operating at a cognitive level—that causes men to resist inclusion of women into the "band of brothers." All that is required is an "attitude adjustment" to allow the military to eliminate the benighted sexism on display in *G.I. Jane* and to achieve the enlightened sex blindness of *Starship Troopers*.

Are Men and Women Really Interchangeable in Combat?

The primary purpose of this book is to examine the assumptions and arguments of integrationists. I shall argue that their assumptions are flawed, and, as a result, the costs and difficulties of sexual integration have been substantially underestimated. Indeed, full sexual integration would seriously undermine military effectiveness, which should be the sole touchstone of manpower policy.

The sexes differ on an array of physical and psychological dimensions. Many traits in which the sexes differ are critical in combat, including physical strength and endurance, physical aggressiveness, willingness to kill strangers, willingness to expose oneself to physical risk, and some cognitive abilities, such as the three-dimensional spatial ability that is so critical to the "situational awareness" of fighter pilots. These sex differences are increasingly recognized to have biological underpinnings. Recent scholarship in psychology, biology, and anthropology has refuted the mainstream intellectual view of the last half century that "gender differences" are mere social constructs and has confirmed the understanding of the "man on the street" that the psychologies of the two sexes differ in important ways.

The assumption that warfare has changed so much as to reverse the almost unanimous conclusion of human history that defense of the community should rest with men is based on a misunderstanding of the demands of modern warfare. The business of warfare is still killing and risking being killed, often at short ranges, as recent experience in Iraq and Afghanistan has repeatedly demonstrated. Many combat tasks have changed little from earlier times, and they continue to require physical strength and a warrior's ferocity, despite the remarkable wizardry of some modern weapons.

Warfare is a traditionally masculine enterprise that appeals specifically to the male psyche. Militaries have long recognized that fact and put it to work. Much of men's motivation to fight comes from their appreciation of the link between warfare and masculinity, and disruption of that link is likely to diminish their motivation.

Although a small number of women possess the array of physical and psychological traits required of war-fighters, the presence of even a few women in a combat unit can impair effectiveness in a variety of ways. An exclusive focus on individual traits of men and women neglects the critical importance of group dynamics in combat. Men fight for many reasons, but probably the most powerful one is the bonding—"male bonding"—with their comrades.

The prospect of integration raises a number of critical questions. Are men innately predisposed to resist introduction of women into certain all-male groups—even if the women possess as much strength, aggressiveness, and inclination to take risks as many men? Are men as willing to follow a woman into battle as they are a man? Perhaps for very fundamental reasons women do not evoke in men the same feelings of comradeship and "followership" that men do. Educating men that they "ought to" have those feelings would be difficult; actually creating those feelings is likely impossible.

Finally, beyond the question of how women fit in as comrades and leaders are questions relating to "femaleness" in itself. Will introduction of women impair effectiveness by causing men to be overprotective of women? Will it disrupt cohesion by creating competition among men for the attentions of women? Will it diminish the willingness of men to risk their lives and make the military less attractive to potential male "warriors"? Is it realistic to think that integration of men and women at the height of their reproductive lives can be structured in a way that is conducive to "good order and discipline" in the forced intimacy of the military? These questions address not the capacity of women as individuals but rather the social dynamic that results from mixing men and women under very trying conditions.

The Gradual Slide of Women into Combat Roles

About 15 percent of the American active-duty military is female, ranging from 6 percent in the Marines to 20 percent in the Air Force. As news stories from Iraq and Afghanistan remind us, women are playing an active role in the current war. Although claims that women face "the same risk" as men are far from the truth—as of the end of fiscal year 2006, women constituted 11 percent of all troops ever deployed to Iraq and Afghanistan but had suffered only 2 percent of the deaths—the fact remains that women in Iraq are playing an unprecedented role.[6]

Although women have long served in the military during wartime—indeed, 34,000 women served in World War I, and about 350,000 served in World War II[7]—the breadth of tasks performed by women in Iraq and Afghanistan is far broader than in these earlier wars, in which most women served far from the front. In Iraq and Afghanistan, women fly combat aircraft and act as drivers, interpreters, explosive-disposal specialists, military police, and a variety of other roles.[8]

The groundwork for this increased female participation was laid with the abolition of the draft and the creation of the All-Volunteer Force in 1973. During the draft era, despite the flourishing "women's movement," there was little call for the kind of equality that would require sisters to join brothers in the jungles of Vietnam. Although women were still barred from combat, they were admitted to the service academies in 1976. A number of other restrictions were lifted in the 1970s, allowing women to serve on noncombat ships and to fly airplanes in noncombat settings. Women were still excluded from all combat positions and from support positions where the risk of exposure to combat (or to capture) was as great as that faced by combat units (the "risk rule").[9]

Then came the Gulf War, the first large-scale deployment of women into a theater of war. By this time, women made up 11 percent of the active-duty force.[10] Unlike in earlier wars, women were much more involved in actual operations, although still barred from combat itself. They piloted aircraft, guarded bases, and repaired and fueled combat vehicles. Women drove trucks, operated heavy equipment, and worked in prisoner-of-war facilities, all in addition to the medical functions they had long performed.

Although the ground war lasted only about a hundred hours, it was preceded by a five-month buildup in the Gulf. Media reports reaching the American people of women's performance in the Gulf were virtually all positive. Predictions that the American people would be revolted by the idea of women coming back in body bags did not prove accurate, although relatively few personnel of either sex died in the Gulf (134 men and 13 women).

In the aftermath of the Gulf War, pressure to rethink limitations on women's military service increased. Congress repealed the statutory ban on women flying aircraft in combat in 1991, although it did not mandate that women be placed in such positions. In 1992, the Presidential Commission on the Assignment of Women in the Armed Forces studied the issue of sexual integration of combat positions. It recommended that Navy warships be opened to women—as the Navy had requested—but that combat aviation and ground combat remain closed, as the Army, Air Force, and Marines had requested.[11]

In 1993, the White House changed hands, and the Clinton administration was much more enthusiastic about integration than its predecessor.[12] The "risk rule" was abolished, and women were permitted to serve on warships and in combat aviation. The primary remaining "all-male preserve" was "direct ground combat," defined by Department of Defense regulations as

> engaging an enemy on the ground with individual or crew served weapons, while being exposed to hostile fire and to a high probability of direct physical contact with hostile force's personnel. Direct ground combat takes place well forward on the battlefield while locating and closing with the enemy to defeat them by fire, maneuver, or shock effect.

In addition to "direct ground combat," regulations require closure of positions to women if they would be required to physically "collocate" (that is, operate side-by-side) with ground-combat units.

The rapid repeal of legal barriers to women's service was due largely to a quirk of history: a large-scale war that produced only small-scale casualties. As one observer put it after the Gulf War, "If the war had lasted longer and the number of women killed in action had been greater . . . the public mood toward repealing the exclusions might be far less tolerant than it appears in Washington."[13]

The official position of the government continues to be that women should not serve in ground combat, a policy expressed directly by President Bush in January 2005.[14] Despite that pronouncement, the ban on women collocating with combat troops is seemingly violated on a regular basis in Iraq. Female troops sometimes accompany Army and Marine units on raids in case there are Iraqi women who need to be searched. When these raiding parties are attacked, the women participate in the action. Forward support companies containing women are also now being physically located with combat battalions. Although this practice seems to violate the rule against assigning women to units that collocate with ground combat units, the Pentagon contends that it is permissible because the women are *assigned* (on paper) to brigade support battalions—which are open to women—but they are merely *attached* to the ground-combat units. Yet the ground-combat policy is stated in terms of women's physical location, not simply in terms of bureaucratic record-keeping.

Sexual integration may already have had strategic consequences. It has been suggested that Osama bin Laden may have escaped in Tora Bora because of Defense Department policies on sexual integration, or, more accurately, the Army's disregard of them. According to Elaine Donnelly of the Center for Military Readiness, military planners proposed sending Reconnaissance, Surveillance, and Target Acquisition (RSTA) squadrons of Interim Brigade Combat Teams (now Stryker Brigade Combat Teams) to the Tora Bora area of Afghanistan in December 2001 to gather information (and fight, if need be).[15] Sources told her that the idea was rejected because the first of these units being trained at Fort Lewis, Washington, contained women, who could not legally be sent on combat operations. As the commander of Armor Command had written in a memo in August 2001, the RSTA squadron's Intelligence, Surveillance, and Reconnaissance

(ISR) components "will operate in direct contact with enemy forces with the imminent likelihood of combat throughout the Squadron battle-space," a mission meeting the DoD definition of "direct ground combat." If Donnelly's report is correct, then the Army's disregard of Defense Department regulations when it began training RSTA squadrons had substantial negative operational consequences.

Sexual Integration Should Be Subjected to Cost-Benefit Analysis

The final obstacle facing those arguing for full integration of women in the military is the exclusion of women from ground-combat arms. A sensible discussion of whether these positions should be opened to women—or whether some currently open positions should be closed to them—requires acknowledgment of both the benefits and the costs of integration. In performing this analysis, it is necessary to decide what kinds of costs and benefits "count" in the balancing. An underlying assumption (bias, if you will) of this book is that military effectiveness must be the touchstone of military manpower policy. Thus, something counts as a "benefit" if its net effect is to enhance military effectiveness (or if it furthers some other goal without impairing effectiveness), and a "cost" is something that interferes with effectiveness, whatever other benefits it might bring.

Advocates whose arguments rest on notions of equality and civil rights seem to believe that gains in those areas should be balanced against—and actually outweigh—any impairment of military effectiveness. Thus, one feminist economist writes: "If some women would choose to be soldiers, denying them this possibility . . . asks women to sacrifice whatever individual opportunities they expect to find in military service and whatever collective advantage they might gain by participating in it, for the sake of a common good."[16]

Well, yes, it does. Similarly, a feminist professor who has written widely on women in combat complains that the argument that the military "must not be used for social experimentation to the degradation of its warfighting capability" boils down to an argument that "national defense takes priority over rights and justice."[17] Again, depending upon one's definition of "rights and justice," yes, it may.

A Need for Candor

If men and women differ in relevant ways, a presumption in favor of sex neutrality is inappropriate. If the consensus view is that sexual integration is a bad thing if it degrades military effectiveness, then there must be candid discussions about whether it actually has that effect. Unfortunately, such discussions have proved difficult, for reasons both good and bad.

The good reasons first. Today, approximately 200,000 women serve in the active-duty forces of the United States, and another 140,000 serve in the reserve forces (including the National Guard).[18] Most of them, like most men, are highly dedicated to the service of their country, and their nation owes them a debt of gratitude. As of September 30, 2006, over 150,000 women had served in Iraq and Afghanistan, and 61 had died.[19] Many have performed bravely. Sergeant Leigh Ann Hester, for example, became the first woman to be awarded a Silver Star for combat for her performance in a firefight when the convoy guarded by her MP unit was attacked by insurgents.[20] Army Captain Kellie McCoy, commander of a headquarters company of an engineering battalion, was awarded a Bronze Star with combat "V" for her actions when the convoy she was leading was ambushed. Raising questions about sexual integration should not be seen as raising questions about the performance of the brave women now serving. One can simultaneously believe that women serving in Iraq, Afghanistan, and elsewhere are performing admirably and also that refusing to integrate women further—or even removing them from positions they now hold—is nonetheless a good idea.

The bad reason for the difficulty of candid discussion is even more powerful. Merely raising questions about sexual integration is likely to evoke a variety of ad hominem attacks against those who raise them, not to mention endangering the careers of military men impolitic enough to express reservations. By implicit convention, statements concerning women's service are typically stated in the most hyperbolic of positive terms. When the USS *Eisenhower* returned in 1995 from a six-month cruise with the first group of women to serve on a warship, for example, the ship's executive officer told *Time* magazine that the ship performed "as well as if not better than before women were aboard." In fact, he said, "if you took women off the ship now, it wouldn't feel right."[21] Perhaps he meant it, but could he have said anything else?

Integrationists and other celebrants of women's service seem unable to resist hyperbole. The newspaper in the town in which I live, editorializing in favor of the Vietnam Women's Memorial, asserted that women's sacrifice in Vietnam was "equal" to men's. Now, to say that female nurses performed admirably, that they were exposed to bloodshed and a degree of danger, and that their contributions to the war effort were extremely important is true. To suggest parity with men in sacrifice and suffering, however, is absurd. Over forty-seven thousand men were killed in action in Vietnam; one woman was. (Total deaths, including from accidents and disease, were fifty-eight thousand and eight, respectively.)[22]

Politicians, unsurprisingly, are no more inclined toward restraint than anyone else. After the Gulf War, then secretary of defense Dick Cheney announced that "women have made a major contribution to this effort," a statement that was both true and appropriate.[23] His next statement, however, was neither, as he went on to add, "We could not have won without them." Secretary Cheney's observation was echoed by Senator Patrick Leahy of Vermont, who asserted that "the recent victory against Saddam Hussein could not have been possible without women who served courageously in the Persian Gulf."[24] William Cohen, secretary of defense under President Clinton, asserted in a similar vein that "we cannot run a military without women."[25] (Although one might have supposed such statements to be modern phenomena, Woodrow Wilson stated in 1918 that World War I "could not have been fought . . . if it had not been for the services of the women.")[26]

None of these hyperbolic statements is remotely true. America's national security would have to be fragile indeed if the margin of victory in the Gulf had been so slight that the 6.8 percent of U.S. forces in the Gulf who were women—all noncombatants—made the difference between victory and defeat. But the Gulf War was not a close contest; in fact, it might more appropriately be considered a "walk over," despite the frequently overlooked fact that the war involved serious fighting, injury, loss of life, and heroism. There were more men in the U.S. military at the time of the Gulf War than there are total personnel—male and female—in today's armed forces. Thus, if all women suddenly decided that they would no longer join the military, the armed forces would not have to close up shop; instead, they would have to make adjustments, albeit some large ones. Either way, however, the U.S. military would continue to be the strongest in the world.

One might dismiss the statements of politicians as public-relations bloviation, or perhaps even less charitably, the patronizing statements of male politicians emanating from a misplaced sense of chivalry and no-blesse oblige. Such statements have consequences, however, whether or not they are meant to be taken seriously. People who believe that victory in the Gulf War hinged on the presence of women may well have different views about sexual integration than those whose assessment is more real-istic. People who believe that the military cannot run without women are likely to accept costs of integration that others would think unwise.

THE MILITARY PRESENTS unique challenges both to the individual and to the group, and the impact of integration and the consequences of its failure are orders of magnitude more serious than was the case with the very successful integration of the civilian workforce. Those challenges become more obvious when the physical and psychological differences between the sexes are considered.

PART I

SEX DIFFERENCES
AND THEIR ORIGINS

The belief that men and women are fundamentally the same—which is an underlying assumption of many integrationist arguments—has been a powerful one for much of the last century. Biologist Anne Fausto-Sterling, for example, describes her vision of a just society, a society that resembles the world of *Starship Troopers* more than it does our own: "In this world of the future men and women would fully share political and financial power [and] be represented equally, according to their equal abilities, in all walks of life."[1] Equality, under this view, not only assumes that men and women have "equal abilities," it requires it; otherwise, they could not be equally represented in all walks of life. Even a child knows, of course, that men and women do not have "equal abilities," as they learn early, for example, that if they need something heavy lifted, they should go to Daddy rather than Mommy. Few adults would maintain that women are as strong as men, and most assume— at least when it does not matter—that the difference is due to biology. When it matters, however, as it does to proponents of women in combat, arguments that physical differences are not that large, that they are due to socialization, and that they can be eliminated through training are pushed to the fore.

The assumption that men and women possess identical minds is pervasive in both the social sciences and the public-policy literature, despite well-known stereotypes of men being more aggressive, risk-taking, and the like. A central feature of the sex-differences debate is the contrast between views of "ordinary" men and women from all backgrounds and educational levels, on the one hand—who are likely to say "of course males and females are different"—and the views of many social scientists and policymakers involved in "gender issues," on the other hand, with the latter telling the former not to believe their lying eyes. This denial of sex differences brings to mind a comment of George Orwell, writing at the end of World War II about the misguided views of intellectuals on the progress of the war: "One has to belong to the intelligentsia to believe things like that: no ordinary man could be such a fool."[2]

Despite the common contention that differences between the sexes are due mostly, if not entirely, to socialization, a large and ever-growing body of literature demonstrates that the development of not just physical sex differences but also psychological ones is due in large part to the action of sex hormones. Although socialization can have important effects, it is acting on brains that are already sexually differentiated.

If human males and females were psychologically identical, they would be unique among mammals. Evolutionary processes have shaped the minds of men and women to be different, just as they have shaped different minds in bulls and cows, stallions and mares, and lions and lionesses. Males in all of these species are larger, stronger, and more aggressive toward members of their own species than females. Males compete among themselves for access to females, and those who succeed pass on more of their genes to the next generation. Females in all of these species nurture and nurse their offspring, and those who succeed pass on more of *their* genes.

The next two chapters will detail a number of differences between the sexes that affect their relative suitability for combat. Chapters 4 and 5 will then examine how and why these differences have come about.

2

Physical Sex Differences
in Size, Strength, and Speed:
Separating Fact from Myth

Everybody knows that the "gender gap" between men and women runners in the Olympics is narrowing. Everybody is wrong.

—Steve Sailer and Stephen Seiler, 1997[1]

What do college and professional football, soccer, basketball, golf, tennis, and hockey have in common with Olympic running, jumping, swimming, diving, skiing, and ice skating? The answer is that they all require a high level of physical ability and all are structured such that men and women do not compete against each other. Occasionally a female may play on a male team, especially in noncontact sports,[2] but when males attempt to play on female teams, it is widely viewed as unfair.

One must question a system that rigorously segregates the sexes in sports but is willing to integrate them in the military where the stakes are so much higher—with lives and not just trophies on the line. If sex differences are small or if physical capacity is not relevant to combat performance, then perhaps it would make sense, but, as we will see, neither is the case.

A remnant of the single-sex-team approach does survive in the military in the different physical standards applied to men and women. Lower standards for women are a frequent source of complaint among military men. The different expectations begin with standards at entry and continue throughout the military career. For example, at the time of enlistment, a seventeen-year-old female is expected to do thirteen push-ups, compared to thirty-five for males, while for forty-one-year-olds, the numbers are six and twenty-four, respectively. A seventeen-year-old girl is expected to run two miles in nineteen minutes, forty-two seconds or less, which is twelve seconds more than a forty-one-year-old man gets.[3] A forty-one-year-old woman has to "run" two miles in twenty-four minutes and six seconds, almost five minutes more than a man receives. Only in combat, it seems, will demands on the sexes be equal, but there they will be compelling.

Measuring the Size of Differences

Much of the argument for sexual integration of combat forces rests upon a misunderstanding of the significant differences between the sexes— their magnitude, their origins, and their malleability. Before delving into the relevant differences, it is necessary to define what is meant by "significant differences," a term that might mean one of two things. The first is simply that the difference between male and female samples in a particular study is "statistically significant." In other words, the observed difference is unlikely to have occurred simply because of the "luck of the draw" and would be expected to be replicated in a different random sample of males and females. Even a statistically significant difference might be of little practical significance, if it is small in magnitude.

The term "significant difference" might also refer to its *practical* significance, which usually turns on its size. A common statistic used to characterize the magnitude of differences between groups is *effect size* (denoted as d). Effect size is the number of "standard deviations" separating the male and female means (averages). So, an effect size of 1 indicates that the male mean exceeds the female mean by one standard deviation, which in turn indicates that the average male scores higher than 84 percent of females (so that among those exceeding the male mean, the sex ratio is about 3 to 1). An effect size of 2 means that the average male scores higher than 98 percent of females, with a sex ratio of 25 to 1 among those exceeding the male mean. If the effect size is only 0.5, in contrast, then the average male will score higher than 69 percent of females, with a sex ratio of about 3 to 2 among those exceeding the male mean. By convention, effect sizes of 0.2 are labeled "small," those of 0.5 are labeled "moderate," and those of 0.8 or above are labeled "large."[4]

A way to visualize different effect sizes is to think of the scores of each of the sexes as falling along their own bell-shaped curve. Most scores of males and females will cluster around the center of their respective distribution. The effect size affects the extent of overlap of the male and female curves. If the effect size is zero, for example, then the apex of the two curves will be in exactly the same place. As the effect size increases, the high points of the curves diverge, so that with a small *d,* the two curves look like a mountain with two peaks, and as it gets larger, the saddle between the two peaks gets lower and lower, until finally the curves look like two separate mountains with a broad valley between them.

Most physical differences between the sexes are very large, ranging from 1.5 to 4 standard deviations, meaning that there is very little overlap. On many psychological measures, in contrast, the sexes differ little, although on some of the psychological traits discussed in the next chapter, effect sizes range from around 0.5 to perhaps as much as 1.5. Thus, there tends to be substantially more overlap on psychological traits than on physical ones.

MYTH: *The Sexes Do Not Differ That Much in Physical Strength.*

Most people acknowledge that men and women differ in physical strength, but advocates of integration often downplay the difference by pointing out that some women are stronger than some men. In fact, however, there is very little overlap between the sexes. Women have only one-half to two-thirds the upper-body strength of men,[5] and in many studies, the effect size separating males and females is on the order of 2 to 3. The probability that a randomly selected man will have greater upper-body strength than a randomly selected woman is well over 95 percent. (If there were no overlap at all between the groups, of course, then the probability would be 100 percent.) For comparison purposes, the effect size for height is generally a little less than 2, so the likelihood that a randomly selected man will be taller than a randomly selected woman is about 92 percent.[6] In other words, the sexes are more different in strength than they are in height.

Most of the sex difference in strength is due to differences in the amount of muscle tissue, a difference attributable primarily to sex hormones.[7] Testosterone increases muscle mass and is also associated with a reduction in body fat, especially subcutaneous fat and deep intramuscular stores of fat, of which men have less than women. As many male beer drinkers have learned to their sorrow, however, testosterone does not decrease abdominal fat. Rather, it is estrogen that inhibits deposition of fat in the abdomen, although it increases it in the breasts, thighs, and buttocks.[8] Thus, the greater musculature of men and the higher proportion of body fat in women are both traceable to sex hormones.

Despite the small overlap in physical strength between the sexes, some integrationists want to set the bar so high that strength differences hardly matter. Linda Bird Francke, for example, criticizes the "presumption" that "all men are stronger than all women," although she does not identify anyone who has actually articulated that presumption.[9] Joshua Goldstein looks at the glass and sees it 10 percent full. Examining data concerning lifting capacity, he notes that "even the most pronounced gender differences regarding height and strength alike appear to show a nontrivial overlap of bell-curves."[10] One can quibble about what is trivial and what is nontrivial, but the overlap was between the strongest 10 percent of women and the weakest 10 percent of men. Trivial or nontrivial, the overlap is very small.

MYTH: *Muscular Strength Is the Only Relevant Physical Sex Difference.*

In dismissing objections to placing women in combat, many integrationists reject the importance of muscular strength and then assume that they have dealt with the issue of physical sex differences. The sexes differ not only in strength, however, but in a host of other attributes, such as speed, aerobic and anaerobic capacity, endurance, throwing speed and accuracy, height, weight, bone mass, and amount of oxygen-carrying hemoglobin in their blood. These differences in physical capacity should be of major concern to advocates of sexual integration.

Men run substantially faster than women at all distances, from the 100-meter sprint through ultra-long distance races, with men's world-record speeds at the various distances ranging from 7 to 12 percent faster than women's for commonly run distances.[11] These differences may not sound great, but when the fastest man crosses the finish line in the marathon, the fastest woman is more than two miles behind him.

The reasons for the male edge in sprinting and in long-distance running differ. Sex differences in sprinting result primarily from differences in the amount of leg muscle. The male advantage in long-distance running, in contrast, is due primarily to men's greater aerobic capacity, which in turn is attributable to their larger hearts, higher hemoglobin concentrations, and greater blood volume.[12] Men also have greater aerobic and muscular endurance.[13] In ultra-long-distance races (100 kilometers or more), for example, the male advantage is more than twice as great as it is in shorter distances. Testosterone again plays a role, as it stimulates production of the red blood cells that carry oxygen throughout the body.

Large sex differences also exist in speed and accuracy of throwing. These differences appear early in life, before children have the opportunity to accumulate much experience. The developmental pattern of these differences is quite different from that of other physical differences. Strength and speed, for example, show only moderate differences in childhood, although sex differences in strength are found even in newborns.[14] These differences become pronounced only at puberty.[15] The pattern for throwing is quite different and quite remarkable. At just three years of age, the effect size for throwing velocity is 1.5, and by age twelve it exceeds 3.5, the latter difference meaning that a person's sex can be predicted *with 95 percent accuracy* simply by measuring the speed with which the person can throw.[16] The sex difference in throwing *accuracy*—which is a product of both muscular coordination and spatial ability[17]—is similarly observable even in preschool-aged children.

The male advantage in throwing performance is believed by many evolutionists to derive from selective pressures acting on men for throwing projectile weapons, such as rocks and spears.[18] The ability to throw projectiles hard and accurately would have allowed men to kill animals at a greater distance and to kill larger ones. It would also have been a tremendous advantage in conflict between humans, as it still is when grenades must be thrown.

Myth: *Sex Differences in Physical Performance Can Be Overcome Through Training.*

A common explanation for sex differences in physical performance is that boys engage in more vigorous athletic activities than girls. Therefore, the argument goes, performance could be equalized through training. Although it is true that boys are more physically active than girls, training will not eliminate the difference; indeed, it may actually increase it.

Both sexes benefit from strength training, of course, and sometimes women gain more from training than men. A study of muscular strength before and after Army basic training, for example, found that women's upper-body strength as a percentage of men's increased from 57 percent to 60 percent, leading the researchers to conclude that "basic training brought the strength of the females closer to that of the males."[19] Although it is true that the average difference between the sexes decreased slightly with training, the *overlap* between the sexes also decreased. Training not only increases the strength of both groups, it also decreases the variability within the groups. Thus, despite the increase in female strength, the likelihood that a randomly selected man from this group would be stronger than a randomly selected woman increased from 97.5 percent to 98.5 percent.

Sex differences in strength exist even among the physically fit. A study of trained athletes (swimmers) found a male average in the bench press of 152 pounds compared with 87 pounds for women.[20] With this large a difference, the likelihood that a randomly selected man would be stronger than a randomly selected woman is over 99 percent.

The greater benefit from training that women sometimes experience results from a "catch up" effect, because young women tend to be less physically active than young men. When males and females both start out in good physical condition, women gain *less* than men from further conditioning, so that the gap between the sexes actually increases. A study of male and female cadets at West Point, who all started out in relatively good condition, found that although women's upper-body strength was initially 66 percent of men's, by the end of their first two years, it had dropped to below 60 percent.[21]

This is not to suggest that it is impossible to increase female strength substantially. The Army conducted a six-month study with forty-six female volunteers (mostly civilians) to determine the effects of intensive training.[22] Subjects trained for ninety minutes a day, five days a week. Prior to the training, only 24 percent of the women could lift one hundred pounds to a height of fifty-two inches, whereas after the training, 78 percent of the thirty-two women who completed the study could do so. "Women Can Train to Lift Like Men, Army Study Finds," shouted one headline.[23] No one ever doubted, of course, that out-of-shape women would benefit from rigorous physical training, and, contrary to the implication of the headline, they were not being compared to men.

Strangely, in her book advocating full integration of women into combat positions, Erin Solaro asserts with respect to the foregoing study, "I find it hard to believe that anyone who *likes* women could dispute" the results.[24] Solaro does not identify anyone who actually disputes the *results* of the study, however. She simply criticizes a commentator for questioning whether it makes sense to invest so much in training when one can "hire men off the street now who already have the physical strength." If efficiency is a legitimate goal of military manpower policy, and one would hope it is, that seems a legitimate point, a point captured by a female Army officer—an athlete herself—who told me that perhaps women could be trained for combat, "but at what cost?"

MYTH: *Female Athletes Are Catching Up to Men.*

In 1992, the journal *Nature* published a report by physiologists Brian Whipp and Susan Ward titled "Will Women Soon Outrun Men?" They demonstrated that since the 1920s, women's world records had been broken more frequently than those of men, an unsurprising finding in light of women's increased athletic participation. The controversial aspect of the paper was its projection that by 1998 women's marathon performance would equal men's and that by 2050 performance would be equal in all running events.

The most obvious problem with Whipp and Ward's thesis was the assumption that the increase in women's relative performance would continue indefinitely. If the authors extrapolated even further, women would eventually run twice as fast as men, and, at some point in the very distant future, they would exceed the speed of light.[25] One might as well chart the growth of a child and predict that when he reaches the age of sixty, he will be twenty-two feet tall.

Despite the obvious flaws in Whipp and Ward's analysis, their predictions were widely trumpeted by a credulous press. Science writer Natalie Angier exclaimed in the *New York Times* that "women's performance has been accelerating at two to three times the rate of the men's, and in an unerringly linear fashion."[26] This breathless reporting had predictable effects. In a poll taken before the 1996 Olympics, 66 percent agreed that "the day is coming when top female athletes will beat top males at the highest competitive levels."[27]

Even at the time, it was obvious that Whipp and Ward's projections would not come true. A *Runner's World* article of that same year noted that the improvement of women relative to men in the marathon had leveled off since 1985.[28] A 1997 study by Steve Sailer and Stephen Seiler made clear that not only was the "gender gap" in running not disappearing, it had actually been increasing. They pointed out that although the 1996 Summer Olympics were hailed as the "Women's Olympics," women's times in footraces were slower relative to men than in any Olympics since 1972. Subsequent research has revealed that sex differences in sprinting events—running, swimming, and speed skating—have continued to increase in the last decade; indeed, women's *absolute* performance in running has actually declined since the 1970s and 1980s.

What accounts for the halting and then reversal of the convergence of male and female speed? First, of course, there is a predictable "plateauing" effect. One would expect records to fall quickly as more women began competing seriously, but over time women would get closer and closer to their physiological maximum just as men have. Second, the 1990s saw substantial curtailment of the use of performance-enhancing steroids, which had been especially widespread among eastern European women in the 1970s and 1980s.[29] In those earlier two decades, East German women alone set forty-nine world records in the sprints and relays, at a time when male sprinting was overwhelmingly dominated by men of West African descent. As Sailer and Seiler pointed out, East German women won eight medals at the 1988 Olympics, but women from reunified Germany emerged from the 1992 and 1996 Olympics with a combined total of a single bronze medal.

Sex differences in physical performance are here to stay. As Constance Holden observed in *Science* magazine, the male advantage in athletics will endure, due to men's "steady supply of a performance drug that will never be banned: endogenous testosterone."[30]

Myth: *High Levels of Training Injuries in Women Can Be Overcome Through More Training.*

Related to differences in strength and bone mass is the high rate of injuries, especially stress fractures, suffered by women in physical training. Women are much more likely than men to be discharged from basic training due to injuries.[31] Although female Army parachutists jump under safer conditions than men—more likely to be in daylight, from a static line, and in a nontactical environment—they suffer more, and more serious, injuries. Female athletes likewise suffer more injuries than male athletes. Players in the WNBA, for example, have a higher rate of injuries than players in the NBA.[32] Women participating in sports that involve jumping, pivoting, and twisting are four to six times as likely as male athletes to tear the anterior cruciate ligament of their knees.

A British Ministry of Defence study reported a conclusion that some have misunderstood as undermining the significance of greater female injuries. It reported that "gender *per se*" is not the cause of sex differences in injuries; instead, "men and women of equal physical fitness suffer a similar incidence of musculoskeletal injury."[33] Erin Solaro cites this study to minimize the consistent finding of greater female injuries. Indeed, she is quite snide about the reaction of eminent military sociologist Charles Moskos, who, when told by her of this conclusion, responded, "I don't believe it."[34] Her description of his reaction seemed designed to show his close-mindedness.

Moskos was right to be skeptical. A careful reading of the Ministry of Defence report reveals that it was using the term "equal physical fitness" in a very precise sense: having identical muscular strength and aerobic capacity. Because there is very little overlap between the sexes on these measures, however, it is rare to find a woman whose "physical fitness" equals a man's. The British report concluded:

> The overwhelming majority of females applying to the Army or currently serving in the Army would be physically incapable of performing many of the tasks required by the Infantry and RAC [Royal Armoured Corps]. Among the remainder who might achieve the required standards, the risk of injury will be higher than among their male counterparts, as these individuals will be working at a higher percentage of their maximum capability, and their reserve capacity will be less.
>
> *However, there remains a tiny minority of women estimated at 0.1 percent of recruits and 1 percent of trained soldiers who could probably achieve the required standards and perform the job effectively without sustaining higher rates of injury.*

Had Solaro read Moskos the emphasized portion of the report, thereby providing some context for the conclusory assertion she repeated, it would have been clear that it was Solaro's "spin," rather than the report's conclusions, that justified Moskos's skepticism.

IN SUM, THE sexes differ dramatically in physical performance. Physical differences are not the only sex differences that bear on combat performance, however. Combat places not only heavy physical demands on its participants but also serious psychological ones, and, as we will see in the next chapter, the sexes are not equally equipped to meet those demands.

3

Sex Differences in Mind:

Separating Fact from Myth Again

The entire life strategy of males is a higher-risk, higher-stakes adventure than that of females.

—Richard D. Alexander[1]

Imagine that you are an anthropologist canvassing the diverse societies of the world. In each society, you present your informants with descriptions of two groups. Group One is described as "sentimental, submissive, sensitive, dependent, emotional, fearful, softhearted, and weak." Group Two is characterized as "adventurous, dominant, forceful, independent, strong, aggressive, autocratic, enterprising, active, courageous, and unemotional." You ask your informants to identify which group is male and which is female. How much variation in responses would you expect from society to society? If your answer is "none," your views are in harmony with the rest of the world, as made clear by a cross-cultural study of sex stereotypes.[2]

Are these "stereotypes" just misguided, or is there an underlying reality to them? It turns out that these stereotypes are, in fact, accurate—as psychological research shows most stereotypes to be.[3] To be sure, there is substantial overlap between the sexes, so that there are aggressive, courageous, and unemotional women, just as there are submissive, fearful, and emotional men. Still, the sexes differ *on average* on many of the key psychological traits required by combat. A critical question facing the military is whether it can accurately identify prior to combat the aggressive and courageous individuals. As discussed in chapter 9, the consensus seems to be "no."

ACCURATE STEREOTYPE: *Men Have Higher Risk Preference Than Women.*

The stereotype that females are more risk averse than males is an accurate one. Starting in childhood, boys expose themselves to more physical risks than girls do, as evidenced by the higher rate of accidental death among boys worldwide.[4] Sex differences in risk preference emerge early in childhood, earlier than can plausibly be attributed to differential socialization. A study of toddlers found that boys were significantly more likely to approach hazardous items (with an effect size of 0.8) and that boys were more likely to retrieve the item, rather than merely looking at it and pointing, as girls did.[5] A related study found that sex differences in attitudes toward risk were so large that the sex of 80 percent of children could be predicted from their attitudes alone.[6] Researchers analyzing 150 risk-taking studies covering subjects of all ages concluded that "males took risks even when it was clear that it was a bad idea," while females "seemed to be disinclined to take risks even in fairly innocuous situations or when it was a good idea."[7] The largest differences were in physical and intellectual risk-taking.

Risk affects males and females differently. Girls are usually willing to take risks—such as falling—only if they don't think they will get hurt, whereas boys will take risks if they don't think they will get *too* hurt.[8] The difference in risk-taking grows dramatically after puberty, so that men are overwhelmingly represented in risky employment, with well over 90 percent of workplace deaths in the United States being male. The highest-risk occupations—such as fisherman, logger, structural metal worker, coal miner, and roofer—are virtually all male.[9]

Men also participate disproportionately in high-risk recreational activities, such as car racing, skydiving, and hang gliding.[10] Indeed, the variable most predictive of engaging in high-risk recreational activities is sex. Men's driving style is also riskier, a pattern that begins in the teen years.[11] Risk-takers tend to be more socially aggressive, accept more dares, fight more frequently, and participate in more rough sports and physical activities, such as hunting, mountain climbing, and auto racing.[12]

A study of awards for heroism by the Carnegie Hero Fund Commission provides additional evidence of men's greater risk-taking. From 1989 through 1995, the commission recognized 676 acts of heroism, 92 percent of which were performed by men.[13] Most men were rescuing strangers, while most women were rescuing people they knew. The male disproportion is particularly noteworthy because many heroic acts, predominantly by men, are excluded from consideration for the Carnegie Medal. Acts by military personnel do not qualify, nor do those by on-duty police officers and firefighters "unless the rescues are clearly beyond the line of duty."[14]

Emotions affect the risk-taking behavior of the sexes differently. Anger increases risk-taking among men, for example, but does not do so for women.[15] On the other hand, disgust inhibits risk-taking among women, but it does not for men.

ACCURATE STEREOTYPE: *Women Are More Fearful Than Men.*

Risk-taking and fear are intimately related, and females from infancy experience greater fear than males. In adulthood, women experience more fear of a number of risks, such as animals, spiders, and crime, and they experience fear more intensely than men do.[16] Reactions to social risks also often show a sex difference. A recent British study, for example, found that female academics are more likely to suffer stage fright when presenting academic papers and are more prone to "freezing or becoming incoherent when lecturing."[17]

Sex differences in fear and risk perception have two components. Women are more likely to perceive risk in a situation than men are, and even when the sexes perceive the same level of risk, women have higher levels of fear and lower levels of confidence in their capacity to deal with the risk. For example, notwithstanding the fact that women are less frequently victimized by violent crime, they are more fearful of it than men.[18] Although one might suppose that women's heightened fear of crime is due to their special vulnerability to rape, it extends to other crimes, such as murder (of which they are actually at lower risk) and property crimes.

Sex differences in fear affect attitudes about war. Women were more likely than men, for example, to fear substantial casualties from the Gulf War and to believe that the death of U.S. troops was too high a price to pay for the expulsion of Iraq from Kuwait. Similarly, after the attacks of 9/11, men's estimates of the probability of further terrorist attacks were lower than women's, in large part because men reported more anger and less fear than women did.[19]

Many studies of fear suffer from the drawback that they ask subjects how afraid they would be if confronted with some hypothetical threat, so the studies are not measuring an actual fear response but rather the subjects' cognitive prediction of how they would feel under some imagined scenario. A recent study avoided this problem by looking at a real-life event.[20] For a three-week period in October 2002, the Washington, DC, area was terrorized by a series of random shootings. Fourteen incidents occurred, leaving ten people dead and three injured, most taking place in large parking lots or at gas stations. Women, far more than men, reported that they had cut back on everyday activities, such as shopping, driving, and filling their cars up with gasoline. These results tend to refute some common explanations for women's greater fear levels. The sniper's killing at a distance would not have triggered the fear of sexual assault, for example. Although some argue that men are less afraid of assault because their larger size makes them better able to cope with a violent assailant, men's size and strength provided no protection from the sniper's rifle. In fact, men were more likely to be targeted by the sniper than women, with nine of the thirteen victims being men.

ACCURATE STEREOTYPE: *Men Are More Physically Aggressive and Dominant Than Women.*

The well-known stereotype of men as more physically aggressive and more dominant than women has substantial basis. Psychologists often employ a narrow meaning of the term "aggression": the intentional infliction of harm on another. However, both psychologists and laymen sometimes employ a broader meaning, including not only harm-inflicting behavior, but also "assertiveness," "competitiveness," and "dominance-seeking,"[21] as in the terms "aggressive businessman" and "aggressive athlete." These traits, though not identical, are highly correlated and show consistent sex differences.[22] Like risk-taking, sex differences in aggression appear early in development, being present from about two years of age. Physical fights among schoolchildren overwhelmingly involve boys.[23]

Psychological studies regularly report substantial sex differences in aggression. The largest differences are in physical aggression (as opposed to verbal or "indirect" aggression), and the age cohorts showing the largest sex differences are ages eighteen to twenty-one and twenty-two to thirty—obviously prime demographics of combat soldiers. [24] As aggressive behavior becomes more violent, the sex difference increases, with the sex difference in criminal aggression being very large. Between 1976 and 2004, almost 90 percent of convicted murderers were male (as were over three-quarters of their victims).[25] In 2000, state and federal prisons held approximately 1.3 million inmates, of whom 93 percent were male. The sex disparity for violent crimes is even greater than that statistic would suggest, however, because a greater proportion of male prisoners had committed violent offenses.[26]

Men not only engage in more physical forms of attack, they also have more positive attitudes about aggression. They are more inclined to view it as an acceptable way of achieving one's ends, and they experience less guilt and anxiety about aggression than women do.[27]

The sexes also differ in dominance behaviors. Unlike "aggressiveness" narrowly defined, dominance does not entail a desire to cause harm but rather "to obtain power, influence, or valued prerogatives."[28] Aggression is one way to achieve dominance in certain settings, but in civilized society it may be more likely to land one in jail than in the executive suite. As Allan Mazur and Alan Booth have noted, "Sports, spelling bees, elections, criticism, competitions for promotion, and academic jousting all involve domination without aggression."

Throughout life, dominance behaviors are a larger part of the male repertoire than the female. Even among preschool children, boys are much more likely to engage in dominance-related activities, such as rough-and-tumble play. As early as nursery school, boys generally assume the dominant positions in mixed-sex groups.[29] In adulthood, sex differences in dominance-seeking have clear effects in the workplace, as men's occupational behavior is more likely to be oriented toward high wages and opportunities for promotion to high-status positions. Achievement of the highest corporate positions often requires a massive investment of time and energy. Even without the complication of families, women are less willing to make these investments than men, in large part because they do not value the payoff—being "top dog"—as much as men do.[30]

ACCURATE STEREOTYPE: *Women Are More Nurturant and Empathic Than Men.*

The popular stereotype of women as more empathic, more nurturant, and more interested in children also has ample foundation. Women are generally more concerned for the well-being of others and engage in more "prosocial" behaviors. In the words of psychologists Eleanor Maccoby and Carol Nagy Jacklin, "women throughout the world and throughout human history are perceived as the more nurturant sex, and are far more likely than men to perform the tasks that involve intimate care-taking of the young, the sick, and the infirm."[31]

Women score higher on most measures of empathy, which consists of, to paraphrase a former president of the United States, the ability to feel someone else's pain. This greater empathy may be responsible for the heightened guilt and anxiety that women feel about acting aggressively.[32]

The relationship of mothers and children, especially infants, tends to be more intense than that of fathers. Mothers experience more grief from the death of a newborn, and after divorce, noncustodial mothers are far more likely than noncustodial fathers to maintain close contact with their children.[33] Women are also more likely to elect to stay home with their children, even when high-quality care is available.[34]

The sexes also differ in the circumstances that attenuate empathy, as demonstrated by a study examining empathic responses with functional magnetic resonance imaging (fMRI) of the brain.[35] Subjects watched pairs of players playing a game, some players playing fairly and some unfairly. Players were then given electrical shocks. When a player who had played fairly was shocked, both male and female subjects showed activation of brain areas that respond to one's own pain and to the observation of pain in others. When an unfair player was shocked, however, the empathic response of men, but not of women, was substantially reduced. Areas of the brain associated with reward processing, on the other hand, showed enhanced activation in men, but not women, when the unfair player was shocked. These findings suggest that men's empathy may be more easily "switched off" and that they may derive greater psychic satisfaction from physical revenge.

What do empathy and nurturance have to do with combat performance? For one thing, they are negatively associated with aggressiveness.[36] We will see in subsequent chapters that empathy inhibits the willingness to kill. Men's diminished empathy for those who "deserve" punishment probably increases their willingness to kill the enemy. Moreover, the strength of the mother-infant bond may make the long deployments often required by military service more difficult for mothers than for fathers. In addition to causing greater psychic pain for women, these separations can undermine their performance.

MYTH: *Women Have Higher Pain Tolerance Than Men.*

Although it is commonly asserted that women have a higher tolerance for pain—a belief resting primarily on women's endurance of painful childbirth—a large body of data refutes this "old wives' tale." The fact is that women generally withstand pain less well than men.[37] A major review of pain studies found average effect sizes of greater than 0.5 for both pain threshold (the level at which a stimulus is perceived as painful) and pain tolerance (the level at which pain is no longer bearable).[38] So much has been written in the past few years on sex differences in pain that, in the words of one group of pain investigators, "it is quite impossible today to follow all the literature on the subject,"[39] but men's higher tolerance is a consistent finding.

Some may be tempted to argue that these findings simply reflect men's "macho" denial of pain. Observed sex differences are not limited to reports of subjective experience, however, but are also found in measurable physiological responses to pain. Women, for example, exhibit pain-related muscle reflexes at a lower level of stimulation, they show greater pupil dilation in response to painful pressure, and they have greater activation of pain-related brain regions during stimulation.[40] Sex differences are more robust for acute rather than chronic conditions, and they are greater for musculoskeletal pain than for visceral pain, with some studies finding women less sensitive to the latter pain than men.

Men's traditional roles as hunters and fighters would have led to high levels of musculoskeletal injuries, so that a mechanism to deal with the ensuing pain would be highly adaptive.[41] The need for combatants to endure pain is so obvious as scarcely to merit mention. In ideal circumstances, an injured soldier is withdrawn from the line and receives immediate medical care. His pain at that point is a matter of intense concern to himself and to his health-care providers but of no military importance. In many circumstances, however, the wounded soldier must continue to fight despite his wounds, and the more pain he is experiencing, the less able he is to fight effectively.

MYTH: *Sex Differences Are Not Large Enough to Have Real-World Effects.*

Individually, sex differences in risk-taking, fear, aggressiveness, dominance, and so forth are substantial, but not nearly of the magnitude of physical sex differences, so there is substantial overlap between the sexes. As a result, one could argue that they are not large enough to have real-world effects and certainly not large enough to warrant excluding women from combat. Although the magnitude of the difference in any given psychological trait is not by itself sufficient to warrant women's exclusion—or at least would not be if these traits could be measured reliably in potential soldiers—two factors suggest that existing studies may *underestimate* sex differences.

First, to the extent that these traits vary independently of each other, the number of women possessing all of these traits to the extent of the average man is very small. As mentioned previously, for a trait with an effect size of 1, there will be a sex ratio of over 3 to 1 among those scoring as high as the average man. If two *independent* traits are involved, however, the sex ratio among those scoring as high as the average man on *both* will be about 10 to 1, and if three independent traits are involved, the ratio will be 30 to 1. Because traits such as fear, aggressiveness, dominance, and risk-taking are positively correlated, however, the sex ratio would not be as dramatically skewed by considering multiple traits. Because they are not perfectly correlated, however, the larger the combination of traits considered, the more unbalanced the sex ratio will be among those possessing high levels of all of them.

The second reason that these academic studies may underestimate combat-relevant sex differences is that in most of them the relevant emotions have not been activated. It is one thing to ask city dwellers how afraid they are of bears; it is quite another thing to put them in a bear-filled forest at night and observe their emotional and behavioral response. Men and women might *reason* very similarly about hypothetical situations—which may be reflected in their scores on various tests—but *feel* very differently about them.

A more accurate measure would be to consider real-life situations in which individuals have a choice whether to engage in activities that involve a combination of relevant traits—such as fear, risk-taking, and physical aggressiveness. For example, who are the people who foil robberies, chase down purse snatchers and carjackers, and rescue others from criminal assaults? A study of individuals intervening to thwart violent crimes, such as muggings, armed robberies, and bank holdups, found that only one of thirty-two individuals in the sample was a woman.[42]

Another look at the Carnegie awards provides strong evidence of large sex differences in actual behavior. Between 1998 and July 2006, over 90 percent of the almost eight hundred awards went to males. (No individual awards were conferred for heroism arising out of the attacks of September 11, 2001— overwhelmingly displayed by men—as the commission honored the heroes of 9/11 as a group).[43] Most of the awards during this period were for rescues and attempted rescues of people from either drowning or fires, but eighty-two went to people responding to an assault, of which ten went to women. The patterns here are telling. In attempting a rescue, men were much more likely to engage the assailant physically. Only four of the ten women engaged the perpetrator physically, compared to sixty-five of seventy-two men. Of the forty-seven rescuers responding to an assailant armed with a gun, five were women, none of whom physically engaged the assailant, compared with thirty-five of the forty-two men. Ten people were killed while aiding assault victims, all of them men. Men were also substantially more likely to come to the aid of strangers. In sum, as in responses to the DC sniper, men and women respond very differently in response to real and immediate threats to their well-being.

MYTH: *The Sexes Do Not Differ in Cognitive Abilities.*

As Harvard University president Lawrence Summers discovered, after suggesting that innate sex differences *might* contribute to women's low representation in certain scientific fields, a fixed dogma in large segments of academia denies the existence of cognitive sex differences. After Summers's statement, he issued multiple apologies and pledged $50 million of Harvard's money to increase faculty diversity,[44] but that was not enough to save his job. Apparently signaling its rejection of his odious thoughts, Harvard fired Summers and replaced him with the first female president in its 371-year history. Yet thousands of mainstream studies attest to the kinds of differences Summers was adverting to, as reflected in the book *Sex Differences in Cognitive Abilities* (now in its third edition) by psychologist Diane Halpern, past president of the American Psychological Association.[45]

Although most combat-relevant psychological differences relate to temperament and personality, some cognitive sex differences may affect the average suitability of men and women for certain military tasks even where the need for brawn has, in fact, been replaced by a need for brains. Just as in the civilian sector—where men substantially outnumber women in many technical fields[46]—they will do so in the military as well. Some cognitive differences will be discussed in greater detail in chapter 7, which considers sexual integration of aviation.

One of the largest sex differences, at least partially cognitive in nature, was described previously: throwing accuracy and, more generally, targeting accuracy. Targeting a moving object requires a high degree of spatial ability, and at least some of the sex differences in throwing accuracy result from differences in spatial skills.

Apart from targeting, the largest and most consistently found spatial sex difference favoring males is on tests of mental rotation. A typical test requires a subject to imagine what a three-dimensional figure would look like if it were flipped over or rotated in a particular way. A review of a large number of studies found an average effect size of 0.66 in adults, but depending upon the sample, the sex difference sometimes exceeds a full standard deviation. Mental rotation is correlated with a variety of other abilities, such as mechanical ability, map reading, way-finding, mathematical reasoning, and success as a pilot,[47] all abilities showing a decided male advantage.

IN SUM, THERE is convincing evidence that men and women differ in a number of important combat-relevant physical, temperamental, cognitive, and behavioral traits. Most of these traits would have been important to the primitive warrior, as they often still are to the modern warrior: physical strength, aggressiveness, willingness to take risks, ability to throw accurately, and ability to navigate through strange territory. Moreover, given the technical nature of some modern warfare, mathematical and mechanical ability has become increasingly important to many military functions. (I have not discussed women's greater verbal abilities, as verbal skills are seldom decisive in a firefight.) Now that we have canvassed some of the differences between men and women, we can ask where those differences came from. How and why did these differences arise? Are they mere products of differential socialization? Can we just educate people out of them, or do they have deeper origins?

4

How Did Sex Differences Come About?

Pure Socialization, or Do Hormones Play a Role?

There is increasing convergence of evidence across methods showing the masculinizing effects of prenatal androgens, especially
at high doses of androgens and especially for sex-typed interests,
spatial ability, and aspects of personality.

—Celina Cohen-Bendahan, Cornelieke van de Beek,
and Sheri A. Berenbaum[1]

August 22, 1965: Winnipeg, Manitoba.
Janet Reimer gives birth to a set of identical twins, Bruce and Brian.
When they are seven months old, a medical condition requires that the
twins be circumcised. Bruce goes first. The doctor uses a cautery machine
that burns the edges of the incision as it cuts to prevent bleeding.
Whether through equipment malfunction or human error, "a wisp of
smoke" curls up from Bruce's groin and "an aroma as of cooking meat fills
the air."[2] Bruce's penis is burned beyond repair.

Bruce's parents take him to Dr. John Money, a noted sex researcher at
Johns Hopkins University. Money believes that humans are born "neutral"
and that "gender identity"—meaning one's felt sense of which sex one belongs to—is a product of rearing. Money recommends that Bruce undergo
sex-change surgery—including castration—to be followed when he is
older by hormonal treatments. Surgically constructing a vagina is much
easier, he says, than constructing a functioning penis. The parents agree.
Money tells the parents that "Brenda" should not be told that she was not
born a girl and that she should be encouraged in feminine pursuits.

In 1972, Money delivers a paper to the American Association for the
Advancement of Science portraying the case as an unabashed success.

Brian was described as interested in "cars and gas pumps and tools," while Brenda's interest was in "dolls, a doll house, and a doll carriage." The case is seized upon by "women's liberationists" as proof that sex differences are a result not of biology but of social expectations. The case is enshrined in numerous textbooks as the "John/Joan" case to demonstrate that any inborn sex differences that might exist can be overcome by learning. Sex-reassignment surgery becomes standard treatment for infants with ambiguous or injured genitalia.

The problem with the rosy picture painted by Money is that it is wildly inaccurate. Brenda has been uncooperative from the beginning, and her parents' attempts to reinforce her feminine behavior are largely unsuccessful. When she is put in a frilly white dress shortly before her second birthday, she tries to rip it off, and she insists on standing to urinate. When she is fourteen, the girls finally refuse to allow her to use the girls' bathroom and threaten to kill her if she persists.

Throughout childhood, Brenda feels that she is "different." She says that "every day I was teased, every day I was threatened." In her fantasies, she sees herself "as this big guy, lots of muscles and a slick car and hav[ing] all kinds of friends." Her goal is to be a mechanic.

At age fourteen, Brenda simply refuses to live as a girl and intentionally gains weight to hide the breasts that resulted from hormone shots. Finally, Brenda's father tells her what happened to Bruce as an infant. "All of a sudden," David, as he is later called, says "everything clicked. For the first time things made sense and I understood who and what I was."

The road back to anatomical malehood is a difficult one. A double mastectomy is required to remove his breasts, and David begins taking male hormone shots. Difficult surgical procedures are required to reconstruct a penis.

At age twenty-five, David marries a woman and adopts her three children. In 2004, at age thirty-eight, he saws off the barrel of a shotgun, drives to a grocery-store parking lot, puts the gun to his head, and ends his tormented life.

MYTH: *Sex Differences Are Due Mostly to Socialization.*

People from a broad variety of perspectives agree that many of the previously described sex differences exist, but they often disagree sharply over causes. Are they simply products of socialization, as so many would argue? Are men stronger because society values strength and activity in males and encourages them to engage in sports? Are men dominance-seeking risk-takers because they have been taught to behave like little soldiers and business tycoons? Do men have greater spatial ability than women because they get practice in video games and sports? Are women more interested in babies because they were given dolls as children and taught that a woman's place is in the home? Or is there something more fundamental, as implied by the case of David Reimer?

The influence of social forces is far less clear-cut than often assumed.[3] Many differences, such as in toy choices and playmate preferences, appear before children can identify their own sex or the sex of others.[4] Even if infants or toddlers have some implicit sense of sex earlier than currently appreciated, it is hard to imagine how society could inculcate in these young minds the idea that they should have the preferences associated with their sex. To say that children pick up "subtle but pervasive cues" from the world around them is an incomplete answer, because it begs the central question: why do these "subtle" cues affect children so strongly when conscious attempts to direct them in the other direction seem to fail? Many things must be laboriously taught to children, whether academic tasks such as arithmetic, reading, and writing, or just day-to-day activities like closing the door, cleaning up their rooms, and being nice to baby sister. It requires a mind strongly "biologically prepared" to classify by sex and assimilate sex roles—just like the mind is biologically prepared to learn language—for these ideas to be absorbed so readily.

The debate over causes, it should be emphasized, is not between those who attribute sex differences entirely to culture and those who attribute them entirely to biology. Rather, the difference is between those who attribute differences wholly to culture (with biology either playing no role or a trivial one) and those who believe that biology and culture are closely intertwined. The fundamental question is whether the human mind is inherently "sexually monomorphic" or "sexually dimorphic." In the absence of differential social inputs, would the minds of males and females operate identically or would they still differ? All of the evidence points to a sexually dimorphic mind. In fact, "social influences" are products of a society itself composed of—and created by—people with sexually dimorphic minds. These influences, in turn, act on the sexually dimorphic minds of individuals.

MYTH: *Parents Create Sex Differences by Treating Boys and Girls Differently.*

Social constructionists generally assume that the arrow of causation points invariably from the parent to the child: parents treat their sons and daughters differently, thereby causing them to be different. At least part— and a substantial part—of the differential treatment accorded boys and girls, however, is a result of differences in the children themselves. The assumption that causation runs from parent to child is so strong that most people never consider the opposite possibility. Sociologist Christine Williams, for example, attributes women's "greater desire and need for emotional intimacy" to the greater frequency with which parents caress and hold their infant daughters. However, psychologist Joyce Benenson and colleagues have found that individuals blind to the sex of newborns rate female infants substantially more "cuddly" than male infants.[5] This finding might cause one to doubt that later emotional sex differences were caused by the parents' differential cuddling of boys and girls. It seems more likely that parents cuddle more with particularly "cuddly" infants, and "cuddly" infants are more likely to be girls than boys.

Another setting in which the causal arrow is often misperceived is in play styles. When parents treat boys and girls differently, whether by roughhousing more with boys or giving children sex-typed toys, social constructionists assume that later physical activity levels and toy preferences of the children were created by the parents. But some children, from a very early age, like roughhousing and others do not, and boys tend to be more receptive to it than girls. Persisting in roughhouse play with children who shrink from it is less likely to teach them to enjoy it than it is to cause them to recoil from their tormentors. Similarly, although parents may be less likely to give a doll to a son than to a daughter, a son is also less likely to play with it than a daughter if they do. In fact, parents' gifts are more likely to be sex-typed when they purchase toys that were specifically requested by the child than when parents select the toys themselves.[6] Failure to appreciate that parents *respond* to differences in their children leads to a substantial overestimation of the effect of socialization.

MYTH: *Sex Differences Are a Consequence of "Sexist" Western Culture.*

Many social constructionists attribute sex differences to features specific to our culture (such as Barbie dolls or television shows). The cross-cultural ubiquity of consistent sex differences suggests, however, that idiosyncrasies of Western culture are unlikely to be responsible. Sex differences in temperamental and cognitive traits are found throughout the world, and across the globe people hold the same stereotypes of men and women.[7]

Not only are the sex differences seen in Western societies replicated in non-Western societies, but many are observed in other mammal species as well. The greater male dominance-seeking, risk-taking, and aggressiveness in humans is the usual pattern among mammals, and greater male spatial ability is found in a number of mammal species.[8] Female nurturance toward infants is practically definitional in mammals. Sex-differentiated toy preferences, so commonly attributed to socialization, are exhibited even by young monkeys. Yes, boy monkeys like "boys' toys" and girl monkeys like "girls' toys," even in the absence of social expectations and television commercials.[9] Likewise, the preference for same-sex playmates seen in children is also found in young monkeys, suggesting an innate bias toward such play rather than merely a response to social pressures.[10]

MYTH: *Sociological Explanations Can Account for Cross-Cultural Uniformity.*

Sociological explanations, as mentioned previously, have difficulty accounting for cross-cultural uniformity. Biologist Anne Fausto-Sterling suggests, for example, that a kind of "founder effect" may be responsible. Perhaps, she says, "the entire population of the world all evolved from a small progenitor stock and these behaviors have been faithfully passed down from generation to generation a thousand times over."[11] Her argument ignores two important questions. The first is how this progenitor group initially assigned sex roles, although her argument implies that it was simply arbitrary. The second question is how one can square the faithfulness with which this "cultural artifact" has been transmitted with its being an arbitrary choice. This faithfulness surely says something important about the human mind.

Attempting to remedy the flaws of the sociocultural view, psychologists Alice Eagly and Wendy Wood advocate what they call a "biosocial" approach.[12] They argue that sex roles developed because of two underlying biological facts: men's greater size and women's childbearing and nursing. Social roles grow out of these differences, they argue, because society "assigns" roles to the sex that can do a task most efficiently. Hunting is assigned to the stronger and more mobile sex and child-rearing to the sex that lactates. The psychological correlates of these roles, such as the risk-taking and physical aggressiveness of male hunters and nurturance of female caregivers, are assumed to reflect socialization of individuals into their assigned roles rather than innate tendencies.

Although having the virtue of explaining cross-cultural uniformities in a more satisfying manner than the strong social-constructionist view, the biosocial theory leaves fundamental questions unanswered. First, the theory explains why—assuming a sexual division of labor—tasks would be allocated as they are, but it does not explain why there is a division of labor by sex in the first place. That is, why have societies "assigned" tasks by sex and not simply given them to whichever individuals could do them? Second, it does not explain where the physical sex differences come from. The female role in gestation and lactation is of ancient origin, of course, dating back to the dawn of mammals some two hundred million years ago. The origin of the male advantage in size and strength is perhaps not as obvious, but in most species it seems to be an evolved consequence of male-male competition. Eagly and Wood's biosocial view simply takes greater male size and strength in humans as a given and *assumes* that—unlike the case in all other mammals—they have no innate psychological correlates. The third unanswered question is why this role specialization has not had genetic consequences. Even if it started as a cultural adaptation, over thousands of generations natural selection should have "codified" these rules in the genes, rewarding those males and females who performed their "assigned tasks" particularly well. Finally, and perhaps most critically, the biosocial theory resembles other social-constructionist explanations in ignoring the important and now widely recognized effects of sex hormones on psychological functioning.

FACT: *Sex Hormones Play a Large Role in a Host of Sex Differences.*

The pure-socialization argument can be seen to have serious, if not fatal, weaknesses. By itself, that would be reason to treat it with skepticism. More direct evidence exists, however, supporting its competitor—the view that biological factors are important influences on the development of human sex differences. Any explanation of sex differences must take into account, in some way, the vast literature on hormones and behavior.

Although the sexes share most genes, males have some genetic material that females do not: a Y chromosome, which contains a critical gene called *Sry*. This gene codes for the development of testes, which secrete male sex hormones or "androgens," the most important of which is testosterone. These hormones cause the fetus's brain as well as its body to develop in a male direction. Differential hormonal exposure throughout postnatal life—especially from the onset of puberty—enhances the difference. Androgens produce a male mind oriented more toward risk, aggression, competition, and dominance, just as they produce a male anatomy that is larger, hairier, and more muscular.[13]

Androgens work their magic on the brain in two different ways. During a critical period of brain development in the second trimester of pregnancy, and also perhaps in a period shortly after birth, they exert an "organizing" effect—producing "permanent changes in the wiring and sensitivity of the brain"[14] that are largely irreversible—leading to masculinization of the brain. Later in life, especially at and after puberty, circulating hormones influence behavior more directly, what is called the "activational" effect.

Evidence for organizing effects of androgens comes from a variety of sources, including what have been called "experiments of nature." In a condition known as congenital adrenal hyperplasia (CAH), for example, the fetal adrenal gland produces excessive levels of androgens during the critical period of brain development. Girls with CAH have a more masculine behavioral pattern, tending to be tomboys who are more likely to play with boys and with "boys' toys" and are less interested in infants and marriage than unaffected girls.[15] They also score substantially higher on "detachment," a trait inversely related to empathy and nurturance, and on measures of direct aggression.[16] They also perform better than unaffected girls on targeting tasks and have more male-like occupational preferences.[17]

Developing female fetuses are also affected by their *mothers'* levels of circulating hormones during pregnancy. Psychologist Melissa Hines and colleagues found a linear relationship between maternal testosterone levels during pregnancy and masculine-typical behavior in daughters at age three and a half.[18] Sociologist J. Richard Udry and colleagues demonstrated a similar relationship between maternal testosterone levels during pregnancy and the daughter's *adult* behavior. In fact, the mother's testosterone levels during pregnancy are a better predictor of the daughter's adult behavior than are the daughter's own testosterone levels.[19] Fetal testosterone exposure also appears to have cognitive effects, as the spatial ability of seven-year-old girls correlates positively with the level of testosterone in amniotic fluid.[20]

Circulating hormones later in life also influence behavior and cognitive performance in stereotypical ways. Although testosterone is most often linked in the public mind with aggression, it is also related to a variety of other traits and behaviors, such as dominance-seeking, risk-taking, pain tolerance, and cognitive abilities. Estrogen influences at least some of these traits as well.

The relationship between circulating testosterone and aggression is not a simple one[21] and is not what psychologist John Archer refers to as the "mouse model," under which increasing levels of testosterone cause a linear increase in levels of aggressive behavior.[22] Instead, their relationship is better explained by what has been called the "challenge hypothesis." Under this view, testosterone is maintained at a relatively low level in the absence of some sort of competition. When presented with a challenge—either a sexual opportunity or a competitive challenge from another man—testosterone levels increase. Numerous studies have found, for example, that men's testosterone levels increase before a sports competition. After the competition is over, the winner's testosterone levels typically remain high for a while, while the loser's decline. These changes would be adaptive during confrontations. The winner's elevated testosterone prepares him to meet another challenge, while the loser's diminished levels disincline him to remain in a belligerent state.

Testosterone is related to other attributes and emotions associated with challenge. Testosterone levels have been found to be positively correlated with the trait of "sensation-seeking" in some studies.[23] Moreover, in nonhuman animals—and potentially in humans—low levels of testosterone are associated with enhanced fear.[24] Greater risk-taking and lower levels of fear would obviously tend to facilitate aggressive responses to challenges, including the challenges of combat.

Not only do testosterone levels decrease after defeat, they also decrease when a man enters into a long-term romantic relationship and again when he becomes a father, encouraging the paternal care that is more frequent and more intense among men with lower testosterone. The relationship between lower testosterone levels and connection with infants and children is probably partially responsible for the tendency of older fathers to be more involved with their children than younger fathers.

Aggressive behavior is also influenced by estrogen, though in the opposite direction. In elderly men suffering from dementia, for example, aggression levels are negatively correlated with estrogen levels, and estrogen therapy has been effective in decreasing physical aggression in dementia patients.[25] Moreover, women's risk-taking activities vary over the course of the menstrual cycle, declining during the ovulatory phase of the cycle, when estrogen levels are especially high.[26]

Differences in pain response are also partially due to sex hormones. Estrogen appears to increase pain sensitivity, and androgens appear to inhibit it. Pain in women varies with the hormonal fluctuations of the menstrual cycle, and estrogen-replacement therapy increases women's sensitivity to pain. Fortunately for women, pain thresholds increase during late pregnancy and spike just before birth. Low androgen levels are also associated with higher levels of musculoskeletal pain.[27]

FACT: *"Biological" and "Social" Factors Interact to Affect Behavior.*

Increasing evidence about the effects of hormonal and social influences on behavior makes clear that the nature/nurture dichotomy is misleading. Biological factors do not act in isolation from social ones, any more than social factors act without regard to biological ones. (Indeed, many biologists would suggest that social factors *are* biological factors.)[28] In fact, the extent to which an individual responds to socialization pressures is itself influenced by sex hormones. J. Richard Udry found that girls born to mothers with high testosterone levels during pregnancy are less responsive to feminine socialization.[29] Testosterone seems to "immunize" against such socialization, and the daughter remains relatively masculine. Females exposed to low levels of testosterone, on the other hand, are more variable in their femininity, depending upon the extent to which they have been socialized in a feminine direction.

FACT: *Sex Differences Cannot Simply Be Defined Out of Existence.*

Opponents of biological explanations often argue that we cannot say anything meaningful about biological contributions to sex differences because children do not grow up in a world in which the sexes are treated alike. Joshua Goldstein, for example, denies the significance of parents' stories about their toddler sons' acting like little boys without any special encouragement or even in the face of active discouragement. None of these parents, he says, "have really shielded their children from a gendered culture that is ubiquitous for children growing up in contemporary Western society."[30] Not surprisingly, Goldstein points to no "ungendered culture" where an experiment satisfactory to him could be conducted.

Goldstein's argument would categorically rule all biological explanations out of bounds, as he would require a laboratory experiment that could never be conducted. Naturally, no parents completely shield their children from the culture around them; if they did so, they would be guilty of serious neglect. Under Goldstein's view, we could learn whether sex differences are innate only by placing babies in closets from birth and shielding them from any human contact. If sex differences emerged then, however, we would doubtless be told that children's reactions to such inhumane and unnatural environments tell us nothing about *normal* children.

Goldstein's argument proves far too much. If we cannot know anything about biology until we can hold all environmental influences constant, then presumably we cannot know anything about social influences until we hold all biological influences—especially sex hormones—constant. Because social influences act on sexually differentiated individuals, we cannot state definitively that they have any effect at all. The implication of Goldstein's argument, then, is that we cannot know anything about biological *or* social influences. That, at least, makes the nature/nurture argument go away.

IN SUM, THERE is compelling evidence that physical and psychological sex differences are not simply products of differential socialization of males and females. Instead, they have biological underpinnings and are strongly influenced by sex hormones. Explaining *how* these differences have come about leads to a deeper question: *why* do males and females have these distinct bodies and brains? The answer, as we will see in the next chapter, is that the differences are evolved products of natural selection in humans, just as they are in all other species.

5

Evolutionary Origins of Sex Differences:
The "Why" Question

Man's greatest good fortune is to chase and defeat his enemy, seize his total possessions, leave his married women weeping and wailing, ride his gelding, use the bodies of his women as a nightshirt and support, gazing upon and kissing their rosy breasts, sucking their lips which are as sweet as the berries of their breasts.

—Genghis Khan[1]

In AD 1206, Temujin, leader of a tribe of horse people of the Central Asian steppe, first united the feuding Mongol tribes. He adopted the title "Genghis Khan," or "Universal Ruler," and embarked on the creation of the largest land empire the world has ever seen, stretching from China to eastern Europe. The Mongols were ruthless in their conquests, slaughtering entire populations of cities that refused to submit promptly to them.

Genghis Khan demonstrated with a vengeance the adage "To the victor belong the spoils." In 1202, after the defeat of the Tatars—who had poisoned his father when he was a child—he had all of the men killed and the women and children taken as slaves. Two sisters he took for himself, one of whom became a favorite wife.[2] Throughout his life, the most beautiful women of the empire were presented to him, and he is said to have had a harem of five hundred wives and concubines. It is also reported that during the western campaign against the Khwarazmian empire, "twelve thousand virgins" taken prisoner in China were selected for Genghis and accompanied his army.

A sentimental family man, Genghis was very attached to his children and grandchildren. When his grandson Mutugen was killed in 1221 at Bamiyan—a city in present-day Afghanistan known for the giant Buddha statues blown up by the Taliban in early 2001—Genghis ordered that the city be destroyed and that no living being—human or animal—remain alive and that no plunder be taken. On another occasion, when his son-in-law was killed at Nishapur in present-day Iran, he let his daughter decide the punishment. She ordered the death of all 1.75 million residents of the city and had the skulls piled in giant pyramids. He showed similar devotion in defending another of his daughters whom he had offered to an Onggirat prince after the prince had submitted voluntarily to his authority. The daughter not being the prince's type, however, the prince demurred, stating, "Your daughter looks like a frog and a tortoise. How can I accept her?" That impolitic comment cost the prince his life, perhaps adding a ninth to the *8 Simple Rules for Dating My Teenage Daughter*.

The conquests of Genghis Khan rearranged the world map in ways that reverberate today. Only recently, however, has one particular consequence of his conquests come to light. Genetic researchers examining populations in Asia identified a distinctive Y-chromosome lineage dating back approximately one thousand years. The Y chromosome is passed from father to son down the male line with little change, rather like a surname. Originating in Mongolia, this Y chromosome is distributed across a broad swath of Asia stretching from northeastern China to Uzbekistan. The researchers believe that Genghis Khan and his male relatives are the source of this chromosome, which is found in approximately 8 percent of males throughout a portion of Asia largely congruent with the boundary of the Mongol empire when Genghis died. Thus, approximately sixteen million men—or one in two hundred in the entire world—are in the lineage of the self-described "flail of God."[3]

Myth: *Natural Selection Could Not Have Created Human Sex Differences*

To those having only passing familiarity with evolutionary theory, it might seem odd that males and females would have evolved to be different psychologically. Males and females live side-by-side, after all, and are thus exposed to the same "hostile forces of nature" that Darwin identified as driving forces in evolution. When it comes to reproduction, however, males and females are often exposed to different selective pressures; in essence, they experience different environments. Darwin called selection based upon mating success "sexual selection," to contrast it with "natural" selection,[4] which he viewed as being based primarily upon survival. Today, however, sexual selection is generally considered a subset of natural selection.[5] Evolved sex differences—in both humans and other animals—are caused primarily by this subset of natural selection.[6]

The key factor driving sexual selection is the "relative parental investment of the sexes in their offspring," with the sex making the greater investment becoming a resource for which the other sex competes. Because members of the less investing sex (males in mammals) have a higher potential rate of reproduction, they can rejoin the mating pool more quickly than members of the other sex. In humans, for example, children in hunter-gatherer societies are typically not weaned until about age four, so that by the time of weaning, the mother has devoted approximately five years of intense physiological investment to her child. During this time, the father can increase his reproductive success through numerous partners in a way that the mother cannot, a fact having far-reaching physical and psychological implications.[7]

All sexually reproducing organisms must expend energy to reproduce, and their reproductive effort can be characterized as either "mating effort" or "parental effort." In the vast majority of mammal species, virtually all of a male's reproductive effort is mating effort.[8] Once he has impregnated a female, the male moves on, never to have anything further to do with his mates or his offspring. The male's reproductive strategy in such circumstances is to mate with as many females as possible. The female mammal, however, faced with the demands of bearing and nursing offspring, necessarily engages in more parental effort.

In humans, although men's minimum necessary investment is low relative to women's, the long period of offspring dependency creates substantial pressure for male postconception investment through provision of resources and protection to both mate and child. Unlike most female mammals, therefore, women's mating decisions are influenced not only by the male's genetic quality but also by his prospects for investing in her and her offspring. Therefore, attributes of a desirable mate include more than simply physical signs of good genes—such as symmetry and good health—but also status, generosity, resources (or prospects for acquiring them), and bravery.[9]

The nature of mammalian reproduction guarantees that males and females will have somewhat different reproductive "strategies," often described as a choice between quantity and quality.[10] Successful pursuit by males of the "quantity strategy" is complicated by the fact that other males pursue the same strategy, resulting in competition for mating opportunities.

Because a small number of males may be responsible for a disproportionate number of pregnancies—with the unfortunate consequence for many males that they do not reproduce at all—the stakes of the competition can be very high indeed. An evolved male tendency toward dominance and risk-taking is a response to those stakes. Few win the reproductive jackpot like Genghis Khan did, of course, but just one additional mate may double a man's reproductive output.

Anthropologists have demonstrated a strong link between status, access to women, and reproductive success.[11] Even in primitive societies producing little surplus and therefore little accumulation of resources, differences in status have reproductive implications. Napoleon Chagnon's study of the Yanomamö, a South American tribe known for bellicosity, found that being a *unokai*, or "revenge killer," is a mark of high status although not necessarily of greater resource control. That status yields valuable reproductive benefits, as *unokai* tend to have more wives and children than non-*unokai*.[12] Reproductive rewards can similarly flow from skill at hunting: bringing home a large animal and sharing it with others is a form of display that is often rewarded with sexual attention.[13]

Why Haven't the Same Forces Acted on Women?

If risk-taking and achievement of status have been the route to reproductive success for men, why have they not had the same consequences for women? The main reason is that women cannot increase their reproductive success through acquisition of multiple mates the way men can. A woman with six husbands does not reap the reproductive benefit that a man with six wives does. Achievement of status and political power is, in fact, often associated with *reduced* reproductive success in women.[14] Risk-taking and dominance-seeking are related to testosterone in both sexes, but higher testosterone levels in women appear to be associated with decreased fertility (although increased libido),[15] placing a natural limit on the ability of high-testosterone women to pass their traits on to the next generation.

In a provocative article titled "Staying Alive," psychologist Anne Campbell argues that the conventional picture of sex differences in risk-taking—that women avoid risk because they have little to gain reproductively[16]—though accurate, is incomplete.[17] She shows that not only do women have less to gain from risk-taking, they also have more to lose. In primitive societies, death of either parent impairs a child's chances of survival, but death of the mother does so to a greater extent. Thus, women face a "double whammy" compared to men: there is less potential benefit and more potential harm from their risk-taking. As a result, Campbell contends, women's minds have evolved to rate the costs of physical danger higher than men do, which explains the sex differences in fear and risk-taking previously discussed.

Also related to the intertwining of maternal and infant fates is the close bond between mothers and their infants.[18] The dependence that human infants have had on their mothers over evolutionary history has left an important legacy. The anxiety that separation often produces in both mother and infant is an understandable consequence of that dependence. Women's greater empathy probably evolved, in part, to keep them attuned to the mental states and needs of their infants, increasing their likelihood of survival. Among men, however, concern for the feelings of others might have been disadvantageous in their contests with other men for dominance.[19]

Are Humans a Product of Special Creation?

The rejection of biological explanations of human behavior by social constructionists presents a bit of an irony.[20] They deny evolutionary explanations of human nature, arguing that biology provides little insight when the choice is between evolution and social construction. When the choice is between evolution and biblical creationism, however, they are firm believers that humans are a product of the same natural forces that produced all other living beings, having only scorn for those who argue for creationism. As philosopher Michael Levin has noted, however, "from a methodological point of view, belief in the special creation of the human species is entailed by *any refusal to apply evolutionary theory to man.*"[21] Thus, social constructionism might fairly be called "social creationism"— a belief that culture explains culture without any need to understand the nature of the organisms that make up the culture. In 1932, famed anthropologist George P. Murdock described the "practical unanimity" of social scientists in their belief that culture is "independent of the laws of biology and psychology." To his credit, Murdock himself later repudiated that view—labeling it "mythology"[22]— but it has been slow to die, and it lives on among those who believe that in structuring our combat forces we are free to ignore inconvenient differences between the sexes.

THIS PART HAS attempted to show that the sexes differ in many ways and that the differences so commonly attributed to socialization have fundamental biological causes. They cannot be educated—or wished—away; they are facts of life that must be dealt with to construct an effective military. The relevance of many of the traits in which the sexes differ becomes apparent when one considers the demands of warfare, the subject of the next part.

PART II

MODERN
WARFARE

$\mathbf{M}$uch of the enthusiasm for placing women in combat flows from a perception that warfare has changed so much that traditional warrior qualities—strength, daring, and ferocity—have been replaced by brains and technical expertise. Whatever deficits women might have in the traditional martial virtues, the argument goes, they are on a much more level playing field today. If women can drive bulldozers, they can drive tanks. If women can fly airliners, they can fly fighter planes. If women can fire rifles, they can be infantrymen.

War has been a characteristic of human societies for a very long time. Our ancient male ancestors were fighting one another for millennia, just as modern-day chimpanzees raid—and wipe out—rival communities.[1] Primitive warfare placed a premium on physical strength, involving as it did clubs, spears, and bows and arrows, and it required a psyche that allowed its participants to engage the enemy at close quarters, both risking death and killing at a face-to-face level. Because primitive warfare was so frequent and populations relatively small, the proportion of primitive populations killed in warfare was often several times the proportion killed in the massive, but episodic, wars of the past century.[2] The selective pressures acting on men have no doubt been very strong, and men have had a very long time to adapt to warfare.

The need for strength, endurance, risk-taking, and ferocity has not diminished. The infantryman of today goes into battle carrying more weight than the infantryman of World War II, and far more than primitive warriors ever carried. Hand-to-hand combat, though seldom the method of first resort, is the last resort of any war-fighter. Guns jam, positions get overrun, or someone jumps on your back as you enter a building to clear it. Planes crash, and tanks become disabled. You get captured and must overpower your captor.

Nobody wants a "fair fight"—that is, a fight in which the two sides are evenly matched. Indeed, as many soldiers and Marines will tell you, if you find yourself in a fair fight, someone screwed up.[3] American military doctrine calls for the application of overwhelming force, but "fair fights"—or worse—can occur even when we are fighting an enemy that is, on the whole, massively outgunned. If we were to fight a more equally matched foe, the pressures on individual war-fighters would increase substantially.

Although combat aviation, which was the first venue in which American servicewomen saw combat, has been viewed as a "special case"—a form of warfare in which the machine has largely replaced the man and where men's traditional advantage has been neutralized—combat aviation is not such a special case after all. Although it usually does not require tremendous strength—except when things go wrong—it still requires traits that men are more likely than women to possess.

War is still hell.

6

The Nature of Modern Warfare

War is cruelty and you cannot refine it.

—General William T. Sherman[1]

The belief in push-button war is fundamentally a fallacy. But it is not a new fallacy. It is simply an age-old fallacy in modern dress.

—S. L. A. Marshall[2]

Television commentators could pontificate from their climate-controlled studios about technology and the "revolution in military affairs," but out on the battlefield that night, long history marched unchanged into the twenty-first century. Strong men hauled heavy loads over rough ground. There was nothing relative about it—no second chances and no excuses. It was elemental and dangerous. It was exactly why I'd joined the Marines.

—Nathaniel Fick[3]

On the march into Baghdad. Brian Chontosh was a platoon leader rolling up Highway 1 in a humvee, when all hell broke loose. Ambush city.

The young Marines were being cut to ribbons. Mortars, machine guns, rocket propelled grenades. And the kid out of Churchville was in charge. It was do or die and it was up to him.

So he moved to the side of his column, looking for a way to lead his men to safety. As he tried to poke a hole through the Iraqi line, his humvee came under direct enemy machine gun fire.

It was fish in a barrel, and the Marines were the fish.

And Brian Chontosh gave the order to attack. He told his driver to floor the humvee directly at the machine gun emplacement that was firing at them. And he had the guy on top with the .50 cal unload on them.

Within moments there were Iraqis slumped across the machine gun and Chontosh was still advancing, ordering his driver now to take the humvee directly into the Iraqi trench that was attacking his Marines. Over into the battlement the humvee went and out the door Brian Chontosh bailed, carrying an M-16 and a Beretta and 228 years of Marine Corps pride.

And he ran down the trench. With its mortars and riflemen, machine guns and grenadiers. And he killed them all.

He fought with the M-16 until it was out of ammo. Then he fought with the Beretta until it was out of ammo. Then he picked up a dead man's AK-47 and fought with that until it was out of ammo. Then he picked up another dead man's AK-47 and fought with that until it was out of ammo.

At one point he even fired a discarded Iraqi RPG [rocket-propelled grenade] into an enemy cluster, sending attackers flying with its grenade explosion.

When he was done, Brian Chontosh had cleared 200 yards of entrenched Iraqis from his platoon's flank. He had killed more than 20 and wounded at least as many more.[4]

This description of Marine Brian Chontosh—awarded the Navy Cross for his actions—appeared on the Web site of Bob Lonsberry and was then widely circulated over the Internet. It was greeted with sufficient skepticism that Snopes.com, a Web site dedicated to confirming or debunking "urban legends," devoted a page to it and pronounced it "true," as in fact it is.[5] That Snopes was called upon to address the story as a potential urban legend reinforced Lonsberry's choice of title for his story, "Something That Didn't Make the News." This story is an example of a critical aspect of the current wars that is underreported—that they often involve raw and bloody combat, "up close and personal."

Combat Is Not a Video Game

Much of the momentum for sexual integration of the combat arms rests on the view that warfare is no longer the tough business that it was in times past. Because the soldier of today is a "technician" and battlefield prowess is "a matter of brains, not of brawn,"[6] the lessons of primitive warfare—or even that of any warfare prior to the late twentieth century—are thought to have nothing to teach us. Gerard De Groot has asserted, for example, that "modern weaponry no longer requires physical strength, rather only a resolve to kill." The *New York Times* criticizes the argument that "women would be ill-suited for hand-to-hand combat with men," arguing that "the vast majority of military jobs involve the use of sophisticated weaponry rather than close combat."[7] These arguments reflect a misunderstanding of the challenges that modern warfare presents.

Images from the first Gulf War misleadingly portrayed the war as the equivalent of a multibillion-dollar game of Nintendo that, at least for the allies, was no more dangerous than a daylight walk across Central Park. This view ignores the fact that the allies had more than half a million ground troops in the Gulf and that the ground war, although short, was massive in scale. Images from the current war in Iraq portray a different, but equally misleading, message—that coalition troops are passively waiting to be killed by unseen roadside bombs (when they are not busy abusing prisoners), roles that can be played equally well by men and women.

Combat Still Requires Hand-to-Hand Fighting

The largest and smallest conflicts may reasonably be expected to be "push-button wars." The minor conflict that involves the dispatch of one or two cruise missiles for a "pinprick" strike and the major conflict that is resolved with hundreds of ballistic missiles are very high-tech affairs. Most conflicts in between, however, are not. Vietnam, for example, was far from being a push-button war. In his classic book *Dispatches*, Michael Herr described the bloody 1965 battles in the Ia Drang valley, capturing a grim postbattle scene: "Americans and North Vietnamese stiff in one another's death embrace, their eyes wide open, their teeth bared or sunk deep into enemy flesh."[8]

The 1982 Falklands war between Britain and Argentina, though relatively small in scope, was also characterized by primal warfare. The Battles of Mount Longdon and Tumbledown Mountain, between British paratroopers and Argentine marines, saw the British attacking enemy positions with bayonets fixed and engaging in fierce and prolonged hand-to-hand combat.[9]

More recently, the British have maintained their fierce tradition in Iraq. In May 2004, Shiite militiamen under Moqtada al-Sadr ambushed two Land Rovers containing nine soldiers from the Argyll and Sutherland Highlanders near Amara in southern Iraq. After escaping a hail of small-arms fire and RPGs, the soldiers encountered a larger force of at least a hundred fighters. They called in reinforcements from the Princess of Wales's Royal Regiment. Forty soldiers arriving in armored vehicles found insurgents waiting in foxholes along the road. They dismounted and carried out a flanking maneuver, charging two hundred meters to the insurgents' position with fixed bayonets, taking three trenches in succession from the enemy.[10] In the words of one of the British soldiers:

> The look on their faces was utter shock. They were under the impression we were going to lie in our ditch, shoot from a distance and they would run away. I slashed people, rifle-butted them. I was punching and kicking. It was either me or them. It didn't seem real. Anybody can pull a trigger from a distance, but we got up close and personal.[11]

Followers of al-Sadr later accused the British of "mutilating" the bodies of the insurgents,[12] but there is no way to kill with a bayonet that is not at least a little messy. At the end of the four-hour battle, at least twenty-eight insurgents were dead, and two British soldiers were slightly wounded. *That* is the spirit of the bayonet.

The British have no monopoly on hand-to-hand combat in the current wars. In the mountains of Afghanistan in January 2002, for example, a team of Army Special Forces was raiding a compound harboring Taliban and al-Qaeda terrorists. Master Sergeant Anthony Pryor and another soldier were searching a building room by room. As they began entering one room, enemy fire caused Pryor's comrade to stop and return fire. As Pryor entered the room alone, he encountered an enemy fighter charging out of the room and assisted comrades in killing him. As he went farther into the room, he found two more fighters shooting at his comrades outside the compound, and Pryor dispatched them as well. Then, as he started to change the magazine in his weapon, a "larger-than-normal Afghan" sneaked up behind him and, in Pryor's words, "whopped me on the shoulder with something and crumpled me down," breaking his collar bone and dislocating his shoulder in the process. Then, "he jumped up on my back, broke my night-vision goggles off and started getting his fingers in my eyeballs. I pulled him over, and when I hit the ground, it popped my shoulder back in." Pryor then stood up and killed his attacker in a hand-to-hand struggle. As he was feeling around for his night-vision goggles, he later said, "the guys I'd already killed decided that they weren't dead yet." The enemy fighters lost the race to get to their weapons first. Pryor then rejoined the fighting outside. At the end of the battle, twenty-one enemy fighters had been killed, but Pryor, with his non-life-threatening injuries, represented the only American casualty.

At a later ceremony awarding Pryor the Silver Star, Major General Geoffrey Lambert, commander of the U.S. Army Special Forces Command, commented, "Think about a cold, black night; think about fighting four guys at the same time, and somebody jumps on your back and starts beating you with a board. Think about the problems you'd have to solve."[13] For an even greater challenge, think about how you'd solve those problems if you were a woman.

Today's infantryman must be proficient with hand grenades, yet many women cannot throw a grenade outside the blast radius—that is, far enough to avoid blowing themselves up. In basic training, women are required to throw practice grenades at a target twenty-five meters away, whereas the target for men is thirty-five meters away.[14] When Sergeant Leigh Ann Hester and her squad leader, Staff Sergeant Timothy Nein—both of whom were awarded the Silver Star for their courageous actions (although his was later upgraded to a Distinguished Service Cross)—were battling insurgents, Hester gave her grenade to Nein because he "had the better arm." She did, however, throw one about fifteen yards, which, depending upon cover, may be a little close for comfort given the fifteen-meter effective casualty-producing radius of the standard fragmentation grenade.[15] Even if two men had been involved, of course, one might have given a grenade to a comrade with a better arm, but the soldier with the better arm in a mixed-sex pair will almost always be the man. If both members of the pair are women, their ability to throw a grenade where it is needed will be substantially limited.

All Troops Must Be Prepared to Fight

Some argue that even if women cannot perform certain combat tasks, such as infantry service, there are many combat specialties that do not impose the same physical burdens. Even those in noninfantry positions, however, are often forced by circumstances to do the work of infantry. In northwestern Europe in 1944, the number of replacements needed substantially exceeded estimates, so antiaircraft and tank-destroyer units were inactivated and personnel were transferred to the infantry.[16] In October 1944, General Eisenhower imposed a 5 percent levy on all rear-echelon troops and had them rushed to the front,[17] so that "cooks, drivers, mechanics, clerks, and other rear-echelon personnel" flowed into the pipeline of infantry replacements.[18] When the Korean War erupted, Operation Flush Out was designed to get troops out of noncombat positions in Japan and into action in Korea as quickly as possible.[19] During the Tet offensive in Saigon, "cooks, clerks, and jerks" were called upon to defend Tan Son Nhut Air Base.[20] In the event of major attacks on base camps in Vietnam, some helicopter pilots were to fly helicopters away while others stayed behind to defend the camp.

Although support troops must occasionally be used in combat, they are less effective than combat troops and "will be destroyed more quickly," but the greater mobility of today's battlefield exposes more of them to combat than in the past.[21] A modern-day drill sergeant, when asked whether clerks should have to carry 70-pound backpacks and be able to drag 190-pound men out of an area, responded: "Who's defending your airfield? Your support weenies."[22] In March 2003, when a group of these "support weenies" took a wrong turn, the world learned the name of Jessica Lynch. The poor showing that support troops made in the early days of the Iraq War, in comparison with the performance of support troops in prior wars, has been attributed to the "dumbing down" of mixed-sex basic training over the prior decade and has since resulted in enhancement of that training.[23]

Over a half century ago, in his classic study *Men Against Fire*, S. L. A. Marshall—official historian of the European Theater of Operations in World War II—issued the warning about comforting notions of push-button war quoted at the beginning of this chapter. Apt at the time it was issued, this warning is equally appropriate today, a time when many seem to believe that technology has transformed the rules of warfare. But overestimation of the advantage provided by technology was a consistent feature of warfare in the twentieth century. Even in the twenty-first century, we were wrong to believe that the "sustaining power of tyranny" in Iraq would be overcome by the "shock and awe" of a few days of bombs and cruise missiles.[24]

Combat Requires Strength,
Not Just "Resolve to Kill"

The view that sex differences in strength are no longer important is widespread, but wrong. Although most soldiers will not engage in hand-to-hand combat—and the military makes every effort to avoid the evenly matched contests that hand-to-hand combat implies—such combat is the last resort of all warriors, whether they are infantry riflemen, tank drivers, or fighter pilots, and it can be the last resort of those occupying support positions, whether signalmen, clerks, cooks, or truck drivers. Moreover, hand-to-hand combat is not the only combat task requiring strength. Many others do, as well, whether the lifting of heavy artillery shells, damage control tasks on a warship, carrying a machine gun, pulling the lever operating the ejection seat of a fighter plane, or manually cranking down an airplane's landing gear in an emergency.

Many infantry tasks impose physical demands far beyond just fighting. Even the prosaic task of digging "fighting holes" and "ranger graves" imposes a substantial obstacle to women. Indeed, it presents such a challenge that a British study purportedly designed to test whether women could perform combat tasks—but apparently in fact designed to prove that they could—excluded the task of digging themselves into hard ground under fire. As one Defence Ministry source put it: "The girls could not do it. So they decided to reduce the level of the tests for everybody, which kept it gender neutral but meant that of course the girls did OK."[25] In combat conditions, wearing of protective clothing to guard against chemical and biological weapons is sometimes required, as in the early days of the war in Iraq. Such clothing increases the energy costs of physical tasks, and those costs are substantially greater burdens on women than on men.[26]

Physical demands can be reduced in training, but combat will impose the demands it imposes without regard to sex. At the Marine Corps Officer Candidate School at Quantico, Virginia, the bars on the obstacle course are two feet lower for women, and there are "assist sticks" nailed into the obstacle-course climbing walls.[27] In combat, however, we cannot count on the enemy leaving step stools at the base of walls to allow female troops to succeed equally. Ilario Pantano tells of a raid on a compound in Iraq that was surrounded by a six-foot wall, which he described as "not tall by standards of the OCS obstacle course." He and his men, "teeter[ing] under our loads of ordnance," went over the wall in a "tumbling rush."[28] In real life, one must not only clear obstacles without "assist sticks" but also do it in full "battle rattle" and be prepared to fight once on the other side.

There can be a huge difference between performing a task in training and doing it in combat. Sustained combat is a physically arduous activity, often requiring immense stamina. It is not enough to know how to do something; one must also be able to do it over and over in adverse conditions. Israeli women serve as tank instructors, for example, but they are not eligible for combat assignments in the Armored Corps.[29] As an armored brigade commander noted, his brigade had allowed two female instructors to join male crewmen in advanced training, but the women quit, complaining of exhaustion. In the words of an Israeli tank commander, "The girls are great as instructors, but they are too weak. After loading just a few shells, they are wiped."

Many Noncombat Tasks Also Require Strength

The need for strength is not limited to combat roles. A study conducted in the early 1980s found that all Army men in heavy-lifting Military Occupational Specialties (MOSs) were qualified for their jobs, but only about 15 percent of women were. The military has been reluctant to impose strength requirements widely. Training has changed to accommodate weaker females. For example, training runs are now performed in running shoes rather than combat boots to prevent the high level of stress fractures among women. Increasing women's strength has often taken a backseat to the more palatable chore of making the job easier. Thus, the task of stretcher carrier in the Navy, formerly a two-man job, is now a four-person job. Problem solved—unless only two people are available to carry the stretcher.

Adverse conditions often interfere with the neat system of classifying jobs into MOSs. Although women may be able to drive a truck as well as men, if the truck gets a flat tire, then the driver needs to be able to handle the seventy-pound tires. Lives may depend upon the task being done quickly. In the Gulf War, male officers had to perform heavy lifting when they should have been tending to their command responsibilities, because their female enlisted subordinates were too weak to do it.[30] Although "lifting" might not be in the job description, when you have to "bug out," you have to bug out.

If a ship gets struck by a bomb, missile, or mine, all hands may have to turn to the tasks of damage control, such as firefighting, flood limitation, and evacuation of the wounded. Analyst James Dunnigan has described damage control as "the most dangerous, unpredictable, and chaotic" of the Navy's combat operations.[31] Sex differences in ability to engage in such tasks are huge. A 1985 study found that "while clear majorities of women (more than 90 percent in some cases) failed to meet the physical standards for eight critical shipboard tasks, virtually all the men passed (in most cases 100 percent)."[32] One percent of women but 96 percent of men, for example, could carry water pumps to the scene of a fire or flooded compartment. As one former Navy officer with damage-control experience sardonically noted, "When your air-conditioned seat in front of a radar console is a smoking hole in the deck, you grab some shoring or a pump and apply some serious strength and stamina to the problem at hand."[33] If the ship has a crew that is 20 percent women, the damage-control enterprise starts off in nearly the same position it would be in if the initial emergency rendered 20 percent of the crew incapable of assistance.

When the USS *Cole* was attacked by terrorists in October 2000— killing seventeen sailors—the demands on the crew were intense.[34] Uninjured sailors carried the wounded to the corpsmen. Hearing screams and voices from inside the chiefs' mess, sailors ripped through a bulkhead to enter the room full of injured and dead. Others had to go below to shore up leaks, struggling to drive wedging material into holes. The ship's gangplank, normally lifted by a crane, was lowered manually by about fifty sailors. It was three days before it was clear that the ship would not sink, and it took a week to remove all of the bodies.

In 1988, the guided missile frigate USS *Samuel B. Roberts* was assigned to duty escorting oil tankers in the Persian Gulf when it struck an Iranian mine. It came closer than any other U.S. ship since the Korean War to be sunk due to hostile action.[35] The ship was saved only by the dedication, bravery, and strength of its officers and men. Sailors of all specialties— radiomen, mess specialists, and myriad other ratings that ordinarily do not require great strength—turned to fighting the fire and flooding that resulted from the mine. Because the captain was concerned that shells in one of the magazines would "cook off"—a phenomenon that had sunk several ships during World War II—he ordered the magazine cleared of ammunition. A "bucket brigade" of fifty sailors—20 percent of the ship's crew—passed the fifty-pound 76mm shells from man to man. Although the regular job duties of many of these sailors did not require heavy lifting, if they had been unable to perform when necessary, the *Roberts* would almost certainly have sunk.

One advocate of women in combat acknowledges that physical strength "does matter occasionally, as when technology fails to function properly."[36] Because such circumstances "are the exception and not the norm," however, she argues that they "are not a legitimate ground for a blanket prohibition on using women in combat roles, including direct or ground combat." What is combat, however, but one "exceptional circumstance" after another? Even if the likelihood of having to perform a task is relatively low, an inability to do it when needed is potentially fatal.

The Need for Interoperability

The requirement of "interoperability"—the need for each individual in a team, especially a combat team, to be able to carry out a range of tasks in his unit—was stressed in the British Defence Ministry's report on the effect of removing the ban on women in ground combat. Simply tailoring the strength requirement to a specific MOS—as many integrationists urge—is bound to have fatal consequences. Although some jobs—even noncombat jobs—require large amounts of physical strength, many do not. For example, the specific duties of individuals in communications or intelligence may ordinarily require little strength at all. It might seem irrational to impose strength requirements (or a sex restriction) on those performing the latter tasks, just as it would be in office settings in peacetime. In the field, however, and even more so in combat, there is an ever-present possibility of serious physical challenges.

A recent Israeli study recommended that women continue to be excluded from infantry, armor, and artillery units because of their weakness. According to Donald Sensing, a retired Army officer, "None of this is surprising to any man or woman who has served in line units in the American military."[37] He recounted that when he was a fire-support officer for an armor brigade in Germany, the entire intelligence section of the brigade tactical operations center (TOC) was for a time made up of women. Sensing had high praise for the female personnel but viewed their physical weakness as a substantial handicap.

When setting up the TOC, four large tracked vehicles were arranged so that a common work area could be erected between them. Each of the four sections—fire support, operations, engineering, and intelligence—was responsible for its part of the work area. The three male sections got the job done in about ten minutes, but it took the female intelligence section twice that long. The women could finish more quickly only if one of the other sections could spare one or two soldiers, "but this was usually not possible because of mission requirements."

Now, perhaps in Germany at the time, it was not terribly important that it took twice as long to set up the TOC. This was, after all, just training. But during the "real thing," ten minutes can be a very long time; indeed, it can be a lifetime. Sensing's experience led him to conclude that "women should not be assigned to infantry, armor or artillery units at any level at or below brigade."

Sensing is not alone in his complaints. Indeed, despite rave reviews in the media of women's performance in the first Gulf War, many participants, especially—but not only—men, believed that women's relative weakness impeded the mission and that men had to work harder because of women's limitations.[38] Stephanie Gutmann reports that "men in many units took over tearing down tents or loading boxes because most of the women simply couldn't or wouldn't do these chores as fast."[39] In the Iraq War, Kayla Williams, who served as a sergeant in a military intelligence company, recounted in her memoirs that when they were in the field, they were supposed to dig a three-foot-deep "survivability position." About a foot down, they ran into a layer of hard salt. "Luckily," she said, the men took over and dug the positions for the women.[40]

Female lack of strength is often masked by the emphasis on "teamwork." Teamwork, of course, is critical in military units; there is no "Army of One." But invocation of teamwork should not be allowed to obscure individual performance deficits or to excuse those who cannot do their share. When male soldiers have to neglect their own duties to assist female comrades who cannot perform their tasks, unit effectiveness diminishes, and people may die as a result.

The Soldier's Load

The large sex difference in strength—or perhaps more accurately, women's relative weakness—has led some to argue that equipment should be redesigned to eliminate the need for strength. If the effectiveness of equipment can be retained with lower weight, then such a change would benefit both men and women; if nothing else, it may allow more ammunition to be carried. Equipment modification, like any other change, however, should be judged first by its effect on combat effectiveness, not its effect on combat integration.

What does the soldier of today carry? To start with, just what he wears, but the body armor itself, with front and back ceramic plates, weighs about twenty-six pounds, and even more if optional pieces are added. When allegations surfaced that the body armor of soldiers in Iraq and Afghanistan was not providing as much protection as some thought it should, many soldiers and Marines made clear that they did not want more armor because of its effect on mobility.[41]

Add to the body armor an M-16 rifle or its carbine sibling, the M-4, weighing seven to nine pounds. But the weapon is worthless without ammunition, so the soldier must also carry eight to twelve thirty-round magazines at approximately two pounds apiece. Add a helmet, which weighs three to four pounds, and the load is over sixty pounds already. But he also needs a radio and night-vision goggles, not to mention the food and especially water necessary to function in the 125-degree heat of the Iraqi desert. And don't forget the batteries for the high-tech gear and maybe a few grenades. Backpackers know what it is like to carry packs weighing fifty or sixty pounds. Imagine carrying that weight for several miles and then coming under fire, having to avoid it or attack toward it. Then imagine doubling the weight.

Reducing the weight carried by the soldier is an obvious response, but if you were a soldier, what would you leave behind to lighten your load? You might be tempted to leave your night-vision goggles behind if it is a daytime operation. A group of Rangers did just that in Somalia in 1993, and, as Mark Bowden's *Blackhawk Down* revealed, they had a pretty rough time of it in consequence.[42] You could leave some ammunition behind instead, but running out of ammunition in a firefight can ruin your whole day.

The Next War?

It is often said (mostly unfairly) that generals prepare to fight the last war. It could be said with greater fairness that advocates of women in combat are even more guilty of that mistake, using the last war (or the current war), rather than all imagined future ones, to design policy. In the 1990s, the recurrent refrain was that because "peacekeeping operations" were the primary business of the modern military, any disadvantages that women might have in combat were no longer relevant. Today, the argument is that women are essential to the military, because they are needed in Iraq to assist in searching Iraqi women.

Apart from a short burst in the first few weeks of the wars in Iraq and Afghanistan, the conflicts have been relatively low in intensity, as wars go, although they have had periods of high intensity for the participants. Wars against organized armies that actually want to stand and fight impose greater challenges. Conflicts with North Korea, China, Russia, or even Iran are likely to involve much more intense and prolonged fighting. The military must plan for the hardest war it will fight, not the easiest. As one analyst has written, "Defense planning geared to fit a world shaped by the trends identified today is almost certain to rest on shaky assumptions."[43]

The most recent wars—the wars that have fueled the push to place women in combat—have in common that the United States controlled the timing. In both wars against Iraq, the United States had months to build up in-theater forces before commencement of hostilities. It is not always that way. When North Korea invaded South Korea in June 1950, for example, the United States had no combat units in Korea and had to throw units into battle on a piecemeal basis as they arrived from Japan. It took a month before a defensive line—the Pusan Perimeter—could be established to stop the relentless offensive of North Korea. Only in September, with the amphibious landing at Inchon, was the pressure on the Pusan Perimeter relieved. Until that time, U.S. forces were vastly outnumbered and were fighting mostly for time.[44] That kind of war must play a role in manpower planning as much as a war in which the enemy generously grants us time to build up our forces.

No Front Lines?

One commonly raised argument against the combat exclusion is that excluding women from the front lines does not protect them, because the fluidity of today's battlefield means that rear-echelon positions are no longer safe.[45] Thus, the argument goes, the distinction between the front lines and the rear echelon is arbitrary.

The "consistency" argument cuts both ways. An equally consistent response to the absence of safe rear areas would be not to open frontline positions to women but to close the rear-echelon positions. If all troops in Iraq face the prospect of combat, it is not illogical to declare Iraq a combat zone, and if women are to be excluded from combat, then arguably they should be excluded from the entire war zone.

In the current war, it is often said that women are "in combat" already, and, in a sense, of course, they are.[46] Women face "combat risks"—risks of being shot, mortared, or blown up by an improvised explosive device (IED)—and they also engage in protection of convoys and other defensive actions. Being in "harm's way" is not necessarily the same thing as being in combat, however. Many combat troops, for example, do not agree that women in Iraq are "in combat." Combat typically involves seeking out the enemy and closing with him for purposes of killing him. In contrast, when manning a gun on a Humvee while guarding a convoy, the hope is that the convoy will not be attacked, in other words, that the enemy will *not* be engaged. Making a related point, an Army lieutenant just back from Iraq pointed out to the *Army Times* that although female gunners on convoys might encounter hostile fire, those incidents generally last only a few minutes. "The men of the infantry are not so lucky," he said. "We own an area, and if we receive contact in that area during our sometimes 24 hours of patrolling, we have to stay and fight it out."[47]

Perhaps we have gotten accustomed to the thought of female soldiers holding their own in the company of their male comrades. But if women are to be combat soldiers and if we really believe the "women warrior" story, surely we need to be able to imagine female soldiers operating outside the comfortable protection of large numbers of men. Perhaps one can visualize a charge "over the top" at the Somme in which one in twenty soldiers is a woman, or a D-Day landing or a "Thunder Run" into Baghdad with a similar proportion of women. But can one imagine a charge toward the enemy trenches by an all-female army? Or the landing of thousands of women, but no men, on the beaches of Normandy? Or any other large battle? The answer is, I think, no, because the women would not have men to protect them and to perform essential functions that they are unable to perform. Until one can imagine such a circumstance, the "warrior's mantle" cannot, contra anthropologist David Jones, be considered "a woman's birthright as surely as it is a man's."[48] Indeed, until one can imagine large all-female combat units, arguably it does not belong to women at all.

What About Peacekeeping?

In the 1980s, and even more so in the 1990s, one of the most common arguments for sexual integration was that the military's primary function is no longer to engage in war but rather to perform peacekeeping tasks.[49] Because the military's "true" function is now more akin to that of policeman, the argument went, women are made for the job because they have proven themselves adept at preventing confrontations from turning violent.

To the extent that it reflected a belief that the central function of the military is no longer "to fight and win the nation's wars," the view was shortsighted at the time and, as recent events have shown, simply wrong. Manpower policies in pursuit of goals other than war-fighting ability are likely to have adverse consequences for military readiness and perhaps even lead to more wars by signaling weakness.

Men and women may react differently to peacekeeping missions. A study of peacekeeping in Somalia conducted by sociologists Laura Miller and Charles Moskos found two divergent patterns.[50] One reflected a "warrior strategy," according to which soldiers treated all Somalis as potential enemies. The other pattern—a "humanitarian strategy"—led soldiers to avoid the use of force and to seek cultural and political explanations for Somali behavior. Women were more likely to reflect the humanitarian approach and men the warrior approach. A study of Dutch peacekeepers in the Balkans similarly found that infantry soldiers, intensively trained as they are for combat, are less likely to adopt the humanitarian approach than other soldiers. Indeed, many of them argued that the peacekeeping mission was not masculine enough and that it was causing the Dutch army to become too feminine.[51]

The tension between war-fighting and humanitarian missions can be stark. Humanitarian missions require cooperation with the local population and a measure of empathy for it. War, on the other hand, requires the soldier to view the "other" as an enemy and to be sufficiently detached emotionally as to be capable of killing him. In peacekeeping situations, one must switch from humanitarian to warrior mode and then back again. Significantly, advocates of the "woman as peacekeeper" argument do not argue that women are better at switching between these two roles, only that women excel at the humanitarian role. If one sex is better at making the switch between helping and killing and then back to helping, however, it is probably men. Their greater ability to compartmentalize, their ability to kill with less emotion, and their greater ability to be friendly with those against whom they were recently fighting (see chapter 13) would predictably make it easier for men, rather than women, to assume the dual role of humanitarian *and* warrior.

WARFARE OF THE twenty-first century, like that of the twentieth and the nineteenth and as far back into history and prehistory as one cares to go, is bloody and brutal. This is most self-evidently true of ground combat. Even combat aviation, however, can present many of the same challenges. The risks of being shot down and having to fight on the ground or becoming a prisoner are ones all aircrew face. The next chapter will examine in more detail the suggestion that aviation is somehow special and an obvious candidate for sexual integration.

7

The "Special Case" of Aviation

The game [of air combat] is far from a contact sport. Rather the players are increasingly surrounded by high technology. The instruments of violence and their successful implementation require brain versus brawn. This is a playing field where men and women are more clearly equivalent. Are the facts that men can run faster and lift more weight relevant to whether women should be [in] combat units?

—Patricia Shields, Landon Curry, and Janet Nichols[1]

Satrapa has a bad ear from flying, as well as a neck injury. The high noise and physical stress are to blame. ACM [Air Combat Maneuvers] is a contact sport.

—Robert Wilcox[2]

April 1, 2001, 9:55 A.M. Over international waters in the South China Sea, seventy miles south-southeast of Hainan Island, China.[3] A Navy EP-3E ARIES II reconnaissance plane commanded by Lieutenant Shane Osborn is finishing the last leg of its routine mission before beginning the long return flight to Okinawa. The EP-3E is a four-engine turboprop airplane, and its twenty-four-person crew is the largest of any U.S. military aircraft. Bulging with sensor pods and bristling with antennae, its mission is the collection of signals intelligence.

Suddenly, a pair of Chinese Navy J–8 II ("Finback") fighter planes appears off to the right. They are not an unexpected sight, as Chinese fighters typically intercept U.S. reconnaissance flights, but they have become increasingly aggressive. They are even more so than usual this morning, with one of them—piloted by People's Liberation Army Air Force pilot

Wang Wei—getting closer and closer, ultimately closing to within ten feet. This is too close for comfort, and Osborn feels his T-shirt becoming damp. The Finbacks are not stable at the slow speeds at which the EP-3E cruises, and Wang is no Blue Angel. When the fighter drops off, a wave of relief floods through the crew, but Wang then closes a few more times.

On his last approach, Wang comes too close. He pitches up to maintain his low speed, and one of the EP-3E's propellers strikes his plane at the junction of the vertical stabilizer and the fuselage, sounding "like a monster chain saw hacking metal." The propeller cuts the Finback in two. The fighter's nose flips up and strikes the nose of the American plane, knocking off the large fiberglass nose cone containing the weather radar. The immediate decompression of the cabin is deafening.

The EP-3E immediately flips over into a nearly completely inverted dive. "This guy just fucking killed us," Osborn thinks, as he is looking *up* at the sea below and observing that his plane is falling almost as fast as the wreckage of the Finback. The lumbering EP-3E, which is a converted Lockheed L-188 Electra passenger airliner, has never been rolled and never recovered from an inverted dive.

Using "every ounce of strength" in his muscular frame, Osborn struggles to bring the wings level. Gradually, he is able to gain airspeed and recover from the roll. The plane has fallen almost 8,000 feet from its original altitude of 22,500 feet in about thirty seconds and is still losing altitude. Cranking the three remaining engines up to maximum power, Osborn gains speed and is able to level the plane out at about 8,000 feet.

The only acceptable option, Osborn concludes, is to attempt to land the plane at Lingshui air base on Hainan Island. Osborn repeatedly radios for permission to make an emergency landing but receives no response. Crew members in the rear gather classified documents and place them in jettison boxes, and they smash laptop computers with a fire ax, making certain to destroy their hard drives. Then, boxes and laptops are thrown out of the open hatch into the sea.

Having received no permission to land, Osborn has no choice but to land without it. He is able to land safely, and now he and his crew are at the center of the first major international incident of the presidency of George W. Bush.

Following protracted negotiations between the American and Chinese governments, the Americans are released, having spent eleven days in captivity. Osborn is awarded the Distinguished Flying Cross for his re-markable efforts in saving the plane and the crew.

WOMEN HAVE SERVED in combat aviation for over a decade. Many who acknowledge that differences in physical strength may warrant continued exclusion of women from ground combat nonetheless believe that women's participation in combat aviation poses substantially less risk.[4] This belief rests on the assumptions that the only sex differences that are relevant to combat involve physical strength, which is not an issue in aviation, and that the kind of "unit cohesion" so important in ground combat is less important in air combat.[5]

As Shane Osborn's experience reveals, strength is not irrelevant to modern aviation. Although it is not usually an issue in flying modern air-planes under ordinary circumstances, when things go wrong the situation can change dramatically. In the words of the principal investigator of a study of strength requirements of aviators, "If they lose hydraulics or an engine or two engines, it gets really tough to fly the plane."[6] It is in the na-ture of combat for things to go very wrong. After the encounter with the Chinese fighter, Shane Osborn had to physically "wrestle" the plane down, "using brute strength in the absence of most other ways of controlling the plane."[7] Could a female pilot have successfully landed the plane, thereby preserving twenty-four American lives? It is possible, but very unlikely.

During the "Thunder Run" into Baghdad in spring 2003, Air Force Major Jim Ewald had an experience not unlike Osborn's. Flying his A-10 "Warthog," whose mission is close air support of ground troops, Ewald dropped down low trying to confirm enemy presence and avoid attacking friendlies or civilians. His plane was then hit by a surface-to-air missile, causing it, in the euphemism of aviation, to "depart controlled flight." Ewald was able to regain control, but, having lost hydraulics, "he fought to keep the plane under control, straining his arm and leg muscles."[8] He flew toward American lines, and as he went through emergency procedures, he saw pieces of his burning engine break off and fall away. With the engine and control now lost, Ewald ejected from the plane, landing in a field and hiding, not knowing whether he was in friendly or enemy territory. One can imagine his relief when he heard: "Hey, pilot dude! Come out. We're Amer-icans!" Would a female pilot have been able to regain control and maintain it long enough to return to American lines? It is impossible to know for sure, but one can say with confidence that it is substantially less likely.

Aircrew Face the Risk of Being Shot Down and Captured

As the experience of Jim Ewald demonstrates, an airplane pilot is just one missile away from being an infantryman but lacking most of an infantryman's gear. Because helicopters can be taken down by small-arms fire and rocket-propelled grenades, the helicopter pilot is even closer. Once that happens, the physical demands of survival, let alone combat, can become immense.

The illusion that combat flying is similar to a video game encourages the view that women can fit easily into the role, but sometimes the reality is far removed from the high-tech image. About 90 percent of the prisoners of war held by North Vietnam were downed pilots and aircrew. An example of what a flyer might face is provided by the case of Air Force Lieutenant Lance Sijan, vividly captured in *Into the Mouth of the Cat*. Sijan was shot down over Laos in 1967. In Malcolm McConnell's words, "In the short time it took him to parachute to earth, he would travel from the relative security of the twentieth century's most advanced military technology to a jungle where the rules and conduct of combat had not undergone any major alteration since Neolithic times."[9]

Despite serious injuries, including a compound fracture of his tibia and a broken hand, Sijan evaded capture for forty-six days in enemy-controlled territory. After his capture, again despite his grievous injuries, he overpowered a guard and escaped into the jungle. Captured once again, he was taken to Hoa Lo prison (the "Hanoi Hilton") in North Vietnam, where he resisted torture for two weeks until he died of his injuries. He was awarded the Medal of Honor posthumously in 1976, the first Air Force Academy graduate to be so honored.

While Sijan's story is particularly compelling, his fate is one potentially faced by all pilots. Two other former POWs were awarded the Medal of Honor the same day. One was Admiral James Stockdale, who was imprisoned for eight years. He was the ranking POW at the Hanoi Hilton and was most responsible for maintaining the command structure in the prison. Stockdale was also subjected to repeated torture, and he inflicted near-mortal wounds upon himself to prevent the North Vietnamese from using him in propaganda pictures. Stockdale later served as Ross Perot's running mate in the 1992 presidential campaign.

The third POW honored that day was Air Force Colonel George "Bud" Day, one of the most highly decorated servicemen of the century. The first part of Day's story is much like Sijan's.[10] After being shot down over North Vietnam, he was immediately captured. Five days later, despite his injuries, he managed to escape and navigate his way fifty kilometers to South Vietnam, aided by his experience as a Marine in World War II. Then, just a mile or so from a Marine camp and twelve days after he had escaped, he was recaptured by North Vietnamese soldiers, being shot twice in the process. Thus began six years of captivity and repeated torture.

More recently, Scott O'Grady was flying his multimillion-dollar F-16 five miles above Bosnia but in short order found himself on the ground with bugs as one of his major sources of food, being pursued by enemy soldiers intent on his capture or death.[11] The protection afforded by a multimillion-dollar fighter plane can be ephemeral indeed.

Combat Aviation Is a High-Risk Affair

In addition to the strength demands that it can sometimes impose, combat aviation often requires the same combination of readiness to kill and willingness to face physical danger required of the infantryman. Consider the life of a scout helicopter pilot in Vietnam: repeated low-level missions over enemy concentrations, taking heavy ground fire, day after day.[12] Indeed, drawing fire was an important part of the scout helicopter's function, because it was a way of locating the enemy.

Flying jet fighters presents many of the same challenges, even though the flying is at higher altitude and higher speed and pilots may never get within visual range of their opponents. Many seem to believe that, because most encounters between modern fighter aircraft are often decided by long-range missiles without the pilots ever having visually observed their enemies, the immediacy is removed from combat. It was this same belief in the primacy of missiles and obsolescence of close-in fighting that led the Air Force after the Korean War to stop teaching dogfighting skills, a decision that led to many combat deaths in Vietnam. That decision was ultimately repudiated, as reflected in the establishment of the Navy's Top Gun school and the Air Force Aggressor Program.[13]

A willingness to close with the enemy is still required, however, even if "closing" may no longer be quite so close. Moreover, the era of close-range air combat is not over, and the modern pilot "must be prepared to oppose the enemy face to face and at close quarters, just as his grandfathers did in the skies above Flanders."[14] Either close up or at a distance, the individual attributes of pilots are critical—according to some, even more important than technological advantages, for "superior aircraft and inferior pilots generally equal defeat."[15] Although better aircraft provide an edge to the pilot, "the advantage has historically been marginal at best."[16]

The "Right Stuff"

Two critical questions must be considered in analyzing the desirability of including women in combat aviation. First, what is it that makes a good combat pilot? Second, is it reasonable to believe that there are many potentially outstanding female pilots? A complete answer to the former question leads to a negative answer to the latter.

The services devote tremendous resources to the selection and training of pilots; indeed, "probably no occupation benefits more from personnel selection technology than that of military pilot."[17] Nonetheless, the services never know until the shooting starts who is going to excel in combat, perhaps because, in the words of one pair of researchers, "psychology may have been pursuing the right stuff but with the wrong scales."

Although combat aircraft are extremely complicated machines, it is not just technical competence that separates the average from the superior pilot. A number of temperamental and cognitive traits are important to a pilot's success, and the gulf between the combat pilot and even the average *man* is large. A study of Navy jet pilots showed them to have "greater manifest needs in the areas of Heterosexuality, Dominance, Change, Achievement, and Exhibition, while expressing lower manifest needs in the areas of Nurturance, Abasement, Deference, Order and Succorance" than the average man.[18] Effect sizes between pilots and the average man ranged from 0.8 to 1.4. Given that these attributes are highly differentiated by sex, one can only conclude that the temperamental difference between the average fighter pilot and the average *woman* is huge.

Pilots are a special breed. According to Captain Frank Dully, then commander of the Naval Aerospace Medical Institute in Pensacola, pilots tend to be distant, perceiving emotions and attachments as signs of weakness.[19] Although difficult on the home life, this quality is beneficial to the job because it allows the pilots to stay cool and focused on the mission. Pilots tend to "compartmentalize" and not be distracted, for example, by concerns about their wives or children: "Feelings screw things up," Dully says. "On a mission, he's only to be thinking of safety, flying, and getting the job done." One set of investigators, recognizing sex differences in the ability to set aside emotions, has suggested that "men may need to become desensitized to crying during combat training"[20] (and presumably during combat as well).

Combat pilots are differentiated from the general public not only by temperamental traits but also by cognitive profiles. The successful pilot is high in what is called "situational awareness"—often referred to as a "sixth sense"—which has been defined as "the ability of the pilot to keep track of events and foresee occurrences in the fast-moving, dynamic scenario of air warfare."[21] Situational awareness is the ability to know where you are; where your opponent is; where the ground is; what the state of your aircraft is; what your opponent is going to do next; and when, where, and how you can get the enemy in your sights and kill him. Most aircraft accidents are due to pilot error, and the most prevalent errors involve a failure of situational awareness.[22]

The identity of all of the components of situational awareness is unknown; indeed "there is little agreement about what SA is."[23] Spatial ability is a major contributor, however, especially understanding relationships "between dynamic objects in three-dimensional space."[24] Because spatial abilities, of all cognitive abilities, most distinguish the sexes, especially at the high end, it is predictable that far fewer women than men are competitive on this dimension.

Sex differences on standardized tests bear out the above prediction. Men outperform women on virtually all components of the Air Force Officer Qualification Test (AFOQT).[25] Even when the comparison is limited to pilot trainees—who have been prescreened on such factors as physical and medical fitness, academic performance, aptitude test scores, and previous flying experience—significant differences remain. Similar differences exist on the Basic Attributes Test (BAT), another test used for pilot selection. The BAT consists of five tests that measure psychomotor coordination, short-term memory, and attitudes toward risk-taking.[26] The tests are Two-Handed Coordination, Complex Coordination, Item Recognition,

Time Sharing, and Activities Interest Inventory. The largest differences are found on a composite of the two coordination tests (effect size of 1.68) and for Time Sharing (effect size of 1.04). Time-sharing is the ability to shift attention between different tasks, and is a component of situational awareness that is positively associated with flight performance.[27]

Thus, combat pilots are differentiated by at least two patterns. Their cognitive pattern is characteristic of engineers, but their temperamental pattern is often more akin to that of mountain climbers. Indeed, there are even personality differences among pilots of different kinds of military aircraft.[28] Because the cognitive and temperamental patterns vary somewhat independently, the number of individuals who will satisfy both is very small, and, one suspects, vanishingly so for females.

"Aces" and "Turkeys"

The ability to fly aircraft successfully in combat is one that not many people have. Indeed, it is an ability that not even all combat pilots have.[29] Mike Spick has observed: "The gulf between the average fighter pilot and the successful one is very wide. In fact it is arguable that there are almost no average fighter pilots; just aces and turkeys; killers and victims."[30] In the words of legendary naval aviator Joe "Hoser" Satrapa, fighter pilots fall into two categories: "those who are going to shoot and those who secretly and desperately know they will be shot at; the hunters and the hunted."[31] In every armed conflict from World War I through Vietnam, 4 to 5 percent of pilots have accounted for about 40 percent of kills.[32] As one Air Force pilot stated, "Most guys can master the mechanics of the systems, but it's instinctive to be able to assimilate all the data, get a big picture, and react offensively. Not a lot of guys can do that."[33] Analogously, almost anyone can drive a car, but few can drive competitively in the Daytona 500.

The belief that technology is a "great equalizer" that renders personal qualities less important is woefully misguided. Admiral James Stockdale wrote that his experience as a squadron and wing commander in Vietnam led him to conclude that high-performance fighter aircraft resulted in "*illuminating* the difference between the courageous and the timid, not fuzzing it up."[34] Advances in the technology of airplanes were met with advances in the technology of air defenses, increasingly polarizing the mass of warriors, "with the heavy end of the fighting load being taken over by proportionately fewer and fewer of the best," an observation that is probably equally true of ground combat.

Ideally, one would have only "aces" and "killers," leaving the "turkeys" and "victims" to another career path. The difficulty lies in the absence of an effective way to separate the aces and turkeys prior to combat. Unfortunately, many who will end up being turkeys do not know what they are getting into. They may have the intelligence and know-how to fly the plane well, but they ultimately lack the "fighting spirit" that they will need in combat. "Competent" flying is not enough. There are, as fighter pilots like to say, "no points for second place."[35]

THE "SPECIAL CASE" of aviation is not so special after all. As with warfare generally, recent experience gives an unrealistic picture of its demands. In both wars against Iraq, air defenses were largely neutralized, and Saddam Hussein helpfully buried his own airplanes in the sand (or had them flown to Iran) prior to the Gulf War. The air campaign in Kosovo was conducted at a minimum altitude of fifteen thousand feet to avoid many of the Serbs' air defenses, although two planes were nonetheless downed, including an F-117 fighter, the first stealth aircraft to be shot down in combat.[36] Still, given the more than thirty-eight thousand sorties, the losses were slight.

American pilots have not opposed an air force with top-quality aircraft and pilots since Vietnam, and the air war over Vietnam imposed extreme demands on pilots both in the air and in North Vietnamese prisons. Aerial combat imposes much greater demands than the pounding of ground targets. Moreover, the relative safety that flyers enjoy when they have total air supremacy cannot be counted on. During the Battle of Midway, for example, fifty-one American torpedo bombers attacked the Japanese fleet; only seven returned.[37] The pilots of those planes knew what they were up against, but they also knew that the outcome of the war might turn on their efforts. Would commanders have been as willing to send so many female pilots into the jaws of death? Perhaps.

The central question for the military is whether it is more likely to maximize the number of top pilots by having flying billets open to women— with the concomitant pressure to have them succeed—or by filling them with men. Put another way, how many female "aces" are there likely to be and at what cost in dollars, morale, and human lives?

PART III

THE MANLINESS
OF WAR

The previously discussed differences affecting combat capability are average differences, not categorical distinctions between men and women. Not many women are as strong as most men, but some are. Not many women are as physically aggressive and willing to take risks as most men, but some are. In theory, therefore, if not in practice, one might develop a method for screening those individuals with the "right stuff" for the particular combat task, obviating the need to use sex as a proxy.

There is one trait for which sex is not a proxy, however, and that is maleness itself. No matter how many masculine traits a woman might have, she is still not a man. Does this matter? There is reason to think that it does. Warfare throughout the world is associated with men, not merely with individuals of either sex who possess masculine traits.

War triggers something primal in many men and can be intensely appealing. The danger, destruction, and even the killing of war can create what some describe as an addiction, suggesting that it stimulates some pleasure center deep within the brain of at least some men. Indeed, the link between war and sexuality suggests the existence of some primitive connection between war and sex itself.

Militaries have long recognized the link between manliness and war and have harnessed it to great effect. Men's concern about not measuring up as a man is one of the greatest fears and most powerful motivators of fighting men. This fear is positively motivating, but it is not one to move women. Most other fears are negatively motivating, and women are likely to have them in greater measure than men, suggesting very large sex differences in the effect of fear on combat performance.

8

War as a Traditionally Masculine Pursuit

And the talk slid north, and the talk slid south,
With the sliding puffs from the hookah-mouth.
Four things greater than all things are,—
Women and Horses and Power and War.

—*Rudyard Kipling*[1]

Warfare has always been, with only very limited exceptions, the work of men. No modern society relies, and virtually no premodern society relied, on women as combat soldiers. Not only is warfare a male occupation, in many ways it has been viewed as the quintessential "manly" pursuit. Unlike, say, the manufacture of musical instruments—a task that also tends cross-culturally to be performed by men[2]—warfare has often been the defining feature of masculinity for a culture.

Courage and manhood are inextricably intertwined. In many primitive societies, for example, a male was not entitled to full status as a man until he distinguished himself in warfare, usually by killing an enemy. In some areas of Oceania, a man could not marry until he had taken an enemy head.[3] Women were often among the "spoils" of primitive warfare and sometimes one of its primary goals.

Just as war has been associated with men, peace has been associated with women. Although the Shoshone girl Sacagawea is often erroneously referred to as Lewis and Clark's "guide," her most significant contribution to that epic journey was to reassure Indians who might have been wary of the explorers' intentions. William Clark wrote in his journal: "The wife of [Charbonneau] our interpreter we find recon[c]iles all the Indians, as to our friendly intentions. A woman with a party of men is a token of peace." Similarly, when Australian prospector Michael Leahy made the first contact with New Guinea highlanders in the early 1920s, his lowland native guide was relieved to see that the highlanders were accompanied by women and told Leahy "that there would be no fight." Psychological research supports the association of women and peace, revealing that the presence of sexually attractive women has a pacifying effect on men.[4]

The link between warfare and manliness persists to the modern age. Samuel Stouffer's classic study of soldiers in World War II concluded that the core code by which members of combat units judged one another was "Be a man." The shared conception of masculinity included "courage, endurance and toughness, lack of squeamishness when confronted with shocking or distasteful stimuli, avoidance of display of weakness in general, reticence about emotional or idealistic matters, and sexual competency."[5]

Even in the Dutch army—the product of a self-consciously, and proudly, sexually egalitarian nation—the "strong masculine image" of the combat soldier prevents women from being well accepted. Despite the fact that prior to the current conflicts in Afghanistan and Iraq the Dutch army had not seen combat since 1948, anthropologist Liora Sion found in her study of Dutch peacekeepers in the Balkans (1999–2000) that infantry soldiers rejected not only the idea of women serving in infantry units but also in the military at large. Men were concerned, she said, that "it would hurt their self-image as combat soldiers, an image that was already damaged by the peacekeeping missions that they saw as 'not masculine enough.' "[6]

Warfare and Masculine Men

Combat rewards masculinity. A study of combat performance in the Korean War found that more masculine men were judged by their peers to be more effective fighters than less masculine men. The attributes of effective fighters ranged from calmness under fire to "the highest kind of daring and bravery," while the attributes of ineffective fighters included firing at imaginary objects, failing to fire, and running away under fire. The five main factors distinguishing good fighters were (in decreasing order of importance): leadership, masculinity, intelligence, sense of humor, and emotional stability.[7]

Cynthia Gimbel and Alan Booth found, long after the Vietnam War, a positive correlation between testosterone levels and extent of combat exposure among Vietnam veterans.[8] They found that testosterone had a positive effect on assignment to the combat arms, and that among those in the combat arms, it had a positive effect on the extent of combat exposure they experienced. These findings suggest that Army assignment policies somehow managed to select soldiers for combat who may have been better combatants and more resistant to the trauma of combat.

Women Warriors of Other Times and Places

Certain stock examples of women's prowess as warriors inevitably appear in response to expressions of doubt about women's combat service. A favorite group is the Amazons, mythical female warriors living in an all-female society, so committed to warfare that they removed one of their breasts to facilitate the use of the bow (or the javelin, depending upon the telling).[9] Having more historical basis were the reputedly fierce warrior women of the West African kingdom of Dahomey in the nineteenth century. Although called the "king's wives," these women were taken as teenagers to the king and were the ones the king chose not to marry. They were then intensively trained in the art of war and led a secluded life, forbidden to have sexual relations or marry. As Israeli military historian Martin van Creveld notes, "To become warriors they had to surrender their womanhood, turn into men, and despise women."[10] A society that shuns conscription would surely shun creating a caste of female slave warriors.

War leaders, such as Boudica—who ultimately led a Celtic army to its slaughter at the hands of the Romans—and Joan of Arc are often invoked in the discussion. Their significance, however, is not that they were fierce warriors or even brilliant commanders but rather that they—by force of personality or grace of God, depending upon one's tastes—rallied their people to fight. That these extraordinary women were able to do so sheds little light on whether ordinary women would enhance the effectiveness of modern combat forces.

Women have also played a role in most modern unconventional armed struggles. Their role in these movements is often a subordinate one, however, and in most cases their primary functions are medical services, communications, intelligence, and cooking.[11] Guerrillas, unlike regular soldiers, seldom engage in sustained conflict, tending to stage hit-and-run attacks and often expending most of their energy avoiding the enemy. In virtually all cases, after the fighting is over and a formal military structure is established, women are removed from combat positions.

For many people, the "trump card" in this argument is the use of female soldiers in Israel and the Soviet Union, but neither example provides strong support for integration.

Contrary to widespread belief, women have not traditionally been integrated in Israeli combat forces. In the struggle for independence against the British, women served in the Palmach, an underground paramilitary arm of Haganah. They were especially useful in undercover missions, surveillance missions, and smuggling weapons, because British soldiers were reluctant to search them. When the Palmach undertook large missions, however, such as retaliatory raids against Arab villages or blowing up bridges, women did not generally participate. The number of women who actually employed weapons was "very small" and female combat deaths were few. After a mixed-sex patrol was wiped out by Bedouin in the Negev Desert in 1947 and their bodies mutilated, Haganah ordered that women be taken out of combat. Although sometimes violated because of practical exigencies, the order laid the groundwork for what would happen upon independence. After Israel achieved statehood and established the Israeli Defense Force in 1948, it barred women from combat positions.[12] Although Israel has long drafted women, it did not draft them for combat.

As for the Soviet Union, approximately 800,000 women volunteered for military service during World War II. Given the massive size of the Red Army, however, this amounted to only about 3 percent of the total force, roughly equivalent to the percentage of women in the U.S. military at the time.[13] According to Joshua Goldstein, only "a few thousand were combatants" although sources are "distressingly vague" about the actual number.[14] The Soviets had two female bomber regiments and one female fighter regiment, totaling about a thousand female pilots, less than 1 percent of the Soviet total. For the most part they flew obsolete aircraft, and reports of their effectiveness are mixed. Although some of the female pilots were said to be very good, and there are reports about the Germans' fear of them—particularly the regiment known as the "Night Witches"—there is also some suggestion that they were viewed as expendable by the Soviets and used primarily for their propaganda value.[15]

The Soviet Union's move was one of desperation. Hitler's invasion of the Soviet Union in June 1941 created a massive Soviet manpower need. Many Soviet women served bravely, as did numerous German fifteen-year-old boys and fifty-year-old men, who were preferred by the Germans to women when their manpower needs became acute. The lessons of these examples are not extendable to the wisdom of such practices when the country is not in extremis. If the United States were invaded by a highly trained army that caused massive casualties and threatened the very existence of the nation—the situation facing the Soviet Union in 1941 and Germany in 1945—public sentiment and military necessity would support the participation in combat not only of women but also of many other currently excluded groups. If the choice comes down to a seventy-year-old with a rifle or nobody at all, the former would be the preferable option. That hardly shows that armies should routinely recruit from the septuagenarian set.

The question is not whether there are conceivable circumstances in which it would make military sense to include women in combat; there clearly are. The question is whether it makes military sense to put women in combat roles when there are enough men to fill them. These historical examples may tell us something, but they certainly do not support the extravagant claim described earlier that "history . . . demonstrates that the warrior's mantle is a woman's birthright as surely as it is a man's."[16]

A Critique of the Link Between
Warfare and Masculinity

The long-standing link between warfare and masculinity has recently been challenged. One feminist professor criticizes the "androcentrism" of the military; another finds it difficult "to pinpoint why it is that the army is more male than the university." Madeline Morris, a Duke Law School professor and former Special Assistant to the Secretary of the Army, has elaborated the position to the greatest extent, arguing for transition to an "ungendered" vision of warrior, "from a masculinist vision of unalloyed aggressivity to an ungendered vision of aggressivity with compassion."[17] She is critical of "standards of masculinity that emphasize dominance, assertiveness, aggressiveness, independence, self-sufficiency, and willingness to take risks, and that reject characteristics such as compassion, understanding, and sensitivity." These masculine attitudes, she says, contribute to the "rape culture" of the military (a strange assertion given the lower rate of rape in the military than in the civilian world). Unfortunately for her argument, however, the objectionable traits—dominance, assertiveness, aggressiveness, independence, self-sufficiency, and willingness to take risks—are also highly desirable, if not essential, in a combat soldier.

Although Morris believes that enhancing the "compassion, understanding, and sensitivity" of military personnel would decrease levels of both rape and war atrocities, these traits can be fatal (as insensitive as it might be to say so). Retired Major General Robert H. Scales has noted that in war, "the American soldier's humanity occasionally gets him killed,"[18] a problem we should be reluctant to exacerbate.

Military training must overcome the reluctance to kill that is commonly exhibited by members of Western societies. Imbuing the soldier with "compassion, understanding, and sensitivity" would enhance the difficulty of doing so. One can imagine a soldier as the enemy approaches. He reflects on the fact that the enemy soldier is a human being just like himself—with a mother and father, perhaps a wife and children. He thinks about the fact that the enemy soldier bears no moral blame; he is just doing his duty, too. In that brief moment of psychic connection with the enemy, the soldier gets his brains blown out.

Including women in combat forces might reduce rapes and war atrocities, although, as Morris acknowledges, Soviet soldiers in World War II were sometimes assisted by female comrades in their widespread rape.[19] Some measures to reduce wartime atrocities might come at the cost of combat effectiveness, however, since the same psychological traits that cause men to be willing to kill in battle may dispose them in extreme circumstances to overdoing it. A study of men who committed atrocities in Vietnam found that they were "three times as likely as the others to win medals and they tended to have killed legitimately more than those who did not commit atrocities."[20] One might take Morris's argument even further and argue that the military should be staffed *entirely* with women (or, better yet, female social workers), although such a course might have some undesirable side effects.

Morris acknowledges that idealization of masculine characteristics is "highly functional in an organization whose raison d'être is combat," but she contends that "there is *no reason* that the high valuation of those attributes cannot be retained while simultaneously dissociating them from masculine gender."[21] According to Morris, there is "much to be gained and little to be lost by changing this aspect of military culture."

Is it really correct to say that there is "no reason" that stereotypically male traits cannot be dissociated from maleness? Is it also correct to say that there is much to be gained by changing this aspect of military culture or that there is little to be lost? Is it even possible to change the military culture in this way and end up with an effective military? The answer to these questions turns on whether the age-old linkage between war and masculinity is functional, which requires an analysis of both what soldiers fear and why they fight.

9

What Men Fear

I don't believe there is any man who, in his heart of hearts, wouldn't rather be called brave than have any other virtue attributed to him.

—Lord Slim[1]

The study of battle is . . . always a study of fear and usually of courage.

—John Keegan[2]

Northeastern France, July 1, 1916. Nineteen British army divisions, along with three French divisions—the bulk of the French army being occupied at Verdun, 125 miles to the southeast—are preparing to attack along the Somme River. Their goal is to retake territory held by Germany since 1914. British guns have pounded German positions with upwards of two million artillery shells, but the German dugouts, many as much as thirty feet deep, are largely impervious to artillery. Although the attack had been scheduled for June 29, inclement weather forces a two-day delay, giving the attacking soldiers additional time to focus on their fears of what lies ahead.

At 7:30 in the morning, the attack begins, and soldiers begin pouring out of the trenches, "over the top" into no-man's-land. Unprotected soldiers being no match for dug-in machine guns, the result is entirely predictable. By day's end, twenty thousand British soldiers lay dead, with twice that many wounded, most on ground held by the British at the outset of the attack—the most deadly day, before or since, in British military history. When the Battle of the Somme ends (or, perhaps more accurately, "peters out") in November, combined casualties exceed one million, but the battle lines have changed by only a few miles.[3]

Fear in Battle

What were the fears that filled these soldiers' hearts before the attack and that threatened terrorized immobilization or panicked retreat? One might suppose that they focused primarily on the impending danger of being killed and perhaps, secondarily, of being wounded. A number of other possible evils also occupy the soldier, however, evils that often loom larger than even death itself.

FEAR OF COWARDICE

Soldiers facing the enemy for the first time often fear the enemy's strength of arms less than they fear their own weakness of spirit. John Dollard's classic study of fear among Spanish Civil War veterans found that the most common fear of men about to experience their first action was that they would turn out to be cowards. Although most of these veterans were poorly trained, Dollard's findings are consistent with reports from more highly trained troops. Many members of the British parachute battalions that fought so well in the Falklands reported that fear of "bottling out"—of showing cowardice—was their greatest prebattle concern. Commenting on the American soldier in World War II, Samuel Stouffer and colleagues noted that combat is a "dare," and "one never knew for sure that he could take it until he had demonstrated that he could."[4] Showing cowardice in battle brought not just censure for cowardice itself; even more powerfully, "to fail to measure up as a soldier in courage and endurance was to risk the charge of not being a man."

James M. McPherson found that fear of cowardice was a common theme in letters written by soldiers on both sides of the American Civil War. "Death before dishonor," he says, is a phrase that recurs too frequently to count. "And," he adds, "they really seem to have meant it." A Texas infantry captain wrote his wife that if he ever "showed the white feather in battle," he hoped "that some friend will immediately shoot me so that the disgrace shall not attach either to my wife or children."[5]

Combat memoirs paint a similar picture. Eugene Sledge recalled that the Marines fighting with him in the Pacific never reflected on the fact that they might be killed or crippled: "The only thing that we seemed to be truly concerned about was that we might be too afraid to do our jobs under fire. An apprehension nagged at each of us that he might appear to be 'yellow' if he were afraid." Before shipping out for southern France from Italy, Audie Murphy, the most highly decorated American soldier in World War II, suffered from malaria and a 105-degree fever. He declined the obviously rational course of reporting to the infirmary because, he reported, he "lacked the guts to take being thought a coward."[6]

Why do so many men fear cowardice even more than their own deaths? Primarily because of the "desire to appear a man amongst men," and battle is the "acid test." As British historian Richard Holmes puts it, "There are occasions when this desire to preserve status is quite literally stronger than the fear of death."[7]

The "status" that the soldier seeks is not a hierarchical status—in fact, it is unrelated to formal military rank—but rather a kind of "membership" status. The soldier's small unit becomes what sociologists call a "reference group"—a group "in which he wants to be counted as an individual, which include the individuals whose opinions make a difference for him, whose standards and goals are his."[8] Unlike situations in which men compete against one another for the top positions, as in tribal or corporate politics,[9] men in combat units seek acceptance into the "band of brothers"; they seek acknowledgment of other men that they are a valuable part of the group. As military historian John Keegan has observed of the soldier, "It is the admiration of other soldiers that satisfies him—if he can win it."[10]

The importance of group membership to the individual—and the importance of the individual to the group—is highlighted by traditional "drumming out" ceremonies. A soldier adjudged guilty of cowardly or disloyal behavior, especially in wartime, was subjected to rituals emphasizing that he no longer belonged. Cutting off his insignia of rank or of unit membership and breaking the sword of an officer in front of his men were common acts symbolic of the miscreant's exclusion from the group.[11] A soldier who served in Iraq told me that a member of his unit—during a mission in which they had "handcuffed some bad guys" but were not under fire—simply sat down and said, "I'm not going any farther; I quit." His superiors sent him back to camp on a helicopter, but not before taking his rifle and his knife, and ripping the rank insignia off his uniform, leaving him nothing but his body armor and helmet. When the rest of the men returned after the mission, they were not "kind and understanding." In fact, the sergeant major called him a "bitch." "And he was," said the soldier. "He failed. He failed himself, and he failed everyone around him. He's a wuss. There's nothing more dishonorable than that to me."

Men are correct in their belief that others are watching to see if they measure up, and they are correct to believe that when they do not, it is their manhood that is impugned. Journalist Evan Wright describes an exchange between two Marines:

> [Colbert] and Person spot a Marine, whom they both know and despise, taking a leak outside the Humvee. "That's that fucking pussy," Person says. "He was crying when we left Camp Pendleton." He adds in a pitying baby voice, "He didn't want to go to Iraq."
>
> Colbert looks at him. "When we were at the airport flying out here he lost his gear. He was trying to get out of coming here."
>
> "Yeah," Person says. "He was at the airport on the phones, calling senators and stuff to try to get them to pull strings. Fucking pussy wimp."
>
> "A scared little bitch," Colbert says. He and Person stare together at the Marine they deem cowardly, bonding in their mutual contempt.

"The judgment of the pack," Wright concludes, "is relentless and unmerciful."[12]

Most men do not strive, however, to be the bravest of the brave. S. L. A. Marshall observed that "the majority are unwilling to take extraordinary risks and do not aspire to a hero's role, but they are equally unwilling that they should be considered the least worthy among those present."[13] In modern warfare, the aspiring hero is not typically admired by his comrades, and the negative definition of the "hero" role by many soldiers tends to discourage the overly risky and aggressive behavior that may cause enemy fire to rain down. Mistrust of the aspiring hero underlies the infantry maxim "Never share a foxhole with anyone braver than you."[14] (Although if you use the term "foxhole" to a Marine drill instructor, you may get the response: "Foxes dig holes to hide in. Marines dig fighting holes to kill the enemy from. Are you planning to hide in your hole or use it as a weapon to kill the enemy?").[15]

FEAR OF DEATH AND WOUNDING

The fear of cowardice that figures so prominently among those yet to undergo their baptism by fire diminishes with combat experience. Soldiers who have found that they can cope with the pressures of combat gain confidence in themselves in future engagements. Dollard's study of the Spanish Civil War found that as soldiers gained combat experience, their fear of being cowards dropped from most to least prominent of the five common fears studied. The fear of death remained constant among green troops and veterans, and the difference was made up by a substantial increase in the fear of crippling or disfiguring wounds and fear of capture and torture. Of greatest concern—more than the fear of death—were injuries to the abdomen, eyes, brain, and genitals.[16]

The increasing significance attached to disfiguring wounds is a predictable result of battlefield experience. Although men know even prior to combat that being wounded can be messy, knowing that one might be seriously wounded is quite different from the vivid mental picture created by seeing a comrade with half his face blown away by a shell fragment, moaning in agony and begging to be killed. Philip Caputo wrote of the combat soldier in Vietnam: "The infantryman knows that any moment the ground he is walking on can erupt and kill him; kill him if he's lucky. If he's unlucky, he will be turned into a blind, deaf, emasculated, legless shell."[17] The more combat experience he has, the more such images the soldier carries with him, so it is not surprising that the dead may be considered the lucky ones.

FEAR OF KILLING

Fear of killing is also sometimes identified as stronger than the fear of death. Men willing to expose themselves to great physical risk are sometimes unwilling, or at least extremely hesitant, to kill. S. L. A. Marshall reported that fear of killing was the most common cause of battle failure in the soldier, followed closely by fear of failure.[18]

Whether or not it is fair to describe soldiers' reluctance to kill as "fear," the initial hesitance of most individuals to engage in lethal violence, though a blessing in peacetime, is an obvious impediment to combat performance. According to ethologist Irenäus Eibl-Eibesfeldt, "In all cultures there is a marked inhibition against killing a fellow human being, and if it is desired to ignore it, as in war, for instance, special indoctrination is necessary if the sympathetic appeal of common humanity is to be disregarded." Thus, military training is intended not only to teach soldiers the mechanics of killing but also to inculcate a willingness to kill. Demonizing the enemy, though offensive to civilian sensibilities, is an effective way to diminish the reluctance to kill, although it may simultaneously facilitate atrocities. During its invasion of China, the Japanese army inured soldiers to killing by having them practice on captured Chinese.[19]

It is commonly believed that soldiers in World War II exhibited a widespread reluctance to kill, as manifested in their failure to fire their weapons in combat. S. L. A. Marshall reported—purportedly based on some four hundred group interviews with rifle companies—that only 15 percent of soldiers in battle actually fired their weapons.[20] The "default of fire," as he called it, of the other 85 percent was not attributed to cowardice. The men were brave enough and did not run away; they were simply unwilling to kill. Marshall's conclusions were influential and resulted in changes in infantry procedures, including the use of more realistic targets in training and the issuance of fire commands in combat.

Despite their influence, substantial doubt has been cast on Marshall's findings.[21] No supporting statistics were found in his notes, and his assistant did not recall the subject of nonfiring soldiers ever coming up in the interviews with rifle companies or in his private conversations with Marshall. Moreover, infantry soldiers and officers were virtually unanimous in their belief that many more men than Marshall asserted had fired their weapons. Nonetheless, other studies suggest that some number—and it is probably a substantial number, though less than Marshall claimed—fail to fire.[22]

Killing by soldiers is facilitated by what has been called *pseudospeciation*, a process that entails the psychological categorization of other individuals into a class that denies their common humanity.[23] Once opponents have been so classified, a process made easier by racial, cultural, or ideological differences,[24] it is as acceptable to kill them as it is to kill hunted prey. Although this process may be decried, Richard Holmes has noted that "without the depersonalization of the enemy during training, battle would become impossible to sustain."

A MEDLEY OF FEARS

The answer to the question set forth at the outset of this chapter—what were the soldiers feeling as they waited to go over the top at the Somme?—is that they experienced a variety of fears. Those who were members of "Pals" or "Chums" battalions—units of volunteers who had never before faced combat—were likely preoccupied with worry that they would not withstand the test of combat and would humiliate themselves in front of their mates, a particular worry for men serving with others from their hometowns. Veterans of earlier fighting on the western front or the disaster at Gallipoli had far fewer such doubts. Their mettle had been tested already, and most knew that they were not cowards or that, if they were, they could conceal the fact. They had, however, experienced the carnage of combat firsthand and had witnessed the awesome destructive power of machine guns and artillery, an experience that caused disfiguring or fatal injuries to loom large in their minds. Both experienced and inexperienced soldiers—especially those who had never killed—may also have dreaded the prospect of killing another human being, but, if they lived long enough, they probably outgrew that feeling.

The fears of these men are not in themselves of importance, as fear, in itself, is of no military moment. The critical importance of fear lies in its outward manifestations—its effects on the behavior of the soldier and of his comrades. The central question is therefore not what fears these men entertained, but rather what impact these fears had on their combat behavior.

Fear and Combat Motivation

Fear is often adaptive, as, like physical pain, it encourages avoidance of harmful stimuli. What is adaptive for the individual is not necessarily useful for the institution, however. What the military needs, in the words of one British researcher, are "personnel that are willing to forego concrete guarantees of self-preservation, somehow 'short circuiting' their otherwise natural human bias towards risk aversion."[25]

The various fears faced by soldiers often work at cross-purposes. The soldier's fear of "not measuring up" is positively motivating. It inspires men to act despite their fear of injury or death, since, by not acting, a man stands to lose "the one thing that he is likely to value more highly than life—his reputation as a man among other men."[26] As far back as Demosthenes, it has been recognized that shame is "the most powerful compulsion on the actions of free men."[27] Thus, soldiers often stand and fight because it would be more costly to them, in the currency that they value most, to turn tail to save their lives.

Fear of injury and death are negatively motivating, as fear restrains aggressive behavior.[28] An exclusive focus on the potential consequences of enemy fire, rather than on accomplishment of the mission, can be debilitating, placing a high premium on the ability to "compartmentalize," concentrating on the mission at hand rather than on the assortment of unpleasant outcomes that potentially lie ahead.

Reluctance to kill is, by definition, negatively motivating. The primary function of the soldier in battle is to close with and kill the enemy. If he has reservations—whether moral or otherwise—about killing the enemy, he will be less likely to further the mission. His disinclination to fire may or may not threaten his own well-being. If it causes him to fail to act in self-defense, it is personally dangerous to him. If it simply causes him not to call attention to himself, it may reduce his risk of being fired upon, to the detriment of his comrades.

Although the negative effect of fear to the mission is obvious, excessive fear is often dangerous to the combatant himself. John Keegan has noted that "soldiers die in largest numbers when they run, because it is when they turn their backs to the enemy that they are least able to defend themselves." Mike Spick has similarly noted that pilots may endanger themselves "through being overcautious at a time when daring and controlled aggression would not only have had a better chance of success, but would have been the safer course." Spick's emphasis on *controlled* aggression is worth emphasizing. The effective combatant is not indiscriminately aggressive. Starting fights in garrison or abusing prisoners are both acts of aggression, but they are not necessarily, or even probably, positively related to effective combat behavior.[29]

Sex Differences in the Various Fears

Fear in battle has been studied extensively, but the literature has necessarily focused on men. Men and women are likely to respond differently to the perils of combat, however, in part because of temperamental sex differences. What we know of these differences, combined with what we know about men's combat motivation, may allow us to make some predictions about sex differences in battlefield behavior.

To be sure, as long as we have a volunteer army, soldiers will not be random samples of either women or men. Female soldiers—particularly ones who elected to serve in the combat arms—would probably be more "male-like" in their psychologies than the average woman. A self-selection effect operates on men as well, although the deviation of the female soldier from the average woman is doubtless greater than that of the male soldier from the average man. Nonetheless, substantial sex differences between the average female soldier and the average male soldier persist.

EXPOSURE TO RISK

Women's greater fear of death and injury and greater aversion to physical risks are likely to affect their combat performance negatively. As Anne

Campbell showed, women have evolved to see less potential gain and more potential loss from exposing themselves to physical risks. A study of survivors of London air raids during World War II found that women were substantially more fearful of being injured or killed than men even though they faced no greater risk.[30] Women are also more likely to suffer posttraumatic stress disorder (PTSD) following violent assaults, even nonsexual ones.[31] Thus, if men going into battle are concerned with death and disfiguring injuries, as they are, women will be even more so.

Women are likely to suffer more psychic pain than men from injuries that do occur. A female Army sergeant who lost a hand to an IED noted that male amputees are more likely than women to go around without their prosthetic limbs.[32] There is no cultural value attached to battle scars for women. For a man, a battle scar might have the cachet of a dueling scar; for a woman, it is just disfiguring.

Being in a war zone is considerably more stressful to women than to men. A study of male and female support troops in the Gulf War, none of whom had seen combat, found that women reported significantly more psychological stress than men, especially stress in anticipation of combat.[33]

Women's lesser pain tolerance also implies that women are likely to be less effective fighters than men after being wounded. Thus, it is predictable that fear of death and injury, as well as injuries themselves, will have a greater negative impact on women's combat motivation than on men's.

WILLINGNESS TO KILL: "NATURAL BORN NEUTRALIZERS"?

The sexes also differ in willingness to kill. Women are far less likely than men to kill strangers, in part because of their greater empathy. The psychological process of pseudospeciation, which allows—or even encourages—soldiers to kill, is the antithesis of compassion and sensitivity. Indeed, it is a mechanism that precludes empathy, for only by categorizing the enemy as someone not entitled to a full measure of compassion is it possible for most people to kill without experiencing the guilt that typically accompanies taking the life of a fellow human being.

The infantry soldier who told me about the soldier who had "quit" saw substantial combat in Iraq, and he provided some support for the suggestion that men and women differ in attitudes toward killing. Based on his experience, he said:

Guys tend to get used to it faster. Guys are more logical thinking about things and they brainwash easy to where—no lie, guys do, they brainwash easy—it's more in our nature to kill and . . . to not have any feelings about it, but for some odd reason when a woman kills, she tends to become emotional about it and gets upset about it. I get upset about it sometimes, but I look at it in more of a logical perspective— they were going to get me or they were going to get my boss, and they had to die.

Empathy not only engenders a reluctance to kill, it also increases the psychological cost of killing if that reluctance is overcome. Combat troops often experience guilt over having killed during war, empathizing with their victims in leisure even if they did not in the heat of battle. Having engaged in conduct inconsistent with their personal natures, many soldiers have a difficult time living with what they have done, in extreme cases resulting in PTSD.[34] The fact that women are likely to feel greater empathy for the enemy than men, coupled with the fact that they are also more likely to experience PTSD, suggests that not only are women less likely to kill but also they are likely to pay a heavier psychic cost for it when they do. This cost will be borne not only by themselves but also by their children, born and unborn, as maternal depression and anxiety are very strong negative predictors of a child's well-being.[35]

Reports from Iraq suggest that, indeed, women are suffering PTSD at approximately twice the rate as men, despite the fact that they are exposed to considerably less combat danger. Moreover, the form of PTSD that they suffer tends to be more severe than that suffered by men. As a sign of the times, a book has been created for children of such women titled "Why Is Mommy Like She Is?"[36] One disadvantage that women have compared with men is that wives monitor the health and health-care activities of husbands more than husbands do for wives. Thus, no matter how well intentioned, husbands are unlikely to be as attuned to their wives' needs, or as likely to ensure that their wives get the care they need, as wives are of their husbands' needs.[37]

The apparent greater distaste for killing exhibited by women was displayed by a female Army helicopter pilot who shot insurgents on the ground. When interviewed, the pilot, Chief Warrant Officer Mariko Kraft, asked: "Do you have to say 'kill' in the paper? Can't you say neutralize? I don't want folks back home to think we enjoy killing people. It is a part of our job we don't enjoy." The story noted that "her sensitivity stands out in an army in which male soldiers talk of 'smoking,' 'wasting,' or 'whacking' the enemy."[38]

A female helicopter pilot similarly discovered that she reacted very differently to combat than her male comrades did: "Everyone was like, 'Yeah, get them' and I was having trouble with that really aggressive attitude," she recalls. "People were saying, 'Yeah, let's go level that whole area.' And I was saying, 'There's no reason to go level 50 homes'—it just wasn't necessary."[39]

A twenty-nine-year-old female gunner with an Army National Guard unit—who "like[s] knives and smokes cigars"—said that she thinks that women do not fire their guns as much because they are more cautious: "Men are more aggressive and trigger-happy. We have a lot of younger guys—eighteen-, nineteen-year old guys—who can't wait to get their first kill. Women don't look at death that way. We would rather solve the situation. If somebody has to die, then nobody really wins."[40]

A nice sentiment, perhaps, but if we are to win a war, then people must die. Dead enemy soldiers are not "collateral damage" and are not simply a distasteful side effect of war. As an Army officer who served as a company commander in Iraq advised in *Infantry* magazine, "In the end, U.S. Soldiers must meet the enemy—specifically terrorists—face-to-face, hand-to-hand and kill them."[41]

Although we may take some comfort in the fact that killing causes anguish in some of our soldiers—that they are not crazed killers consumed by blood lust—reluctance to kill may have adverse consequences. It may lead to hesitation when swift action is necessary, and it may lead to adverse psychological consequences, such as PTSD. Three months after the ambush that netted Leigh Ann Hester a Silver Star for bravery, she said, "I think about March 20 at least a couple times a day, every day, and I probably will for the rest of my life. It's taken its toll. Every night I'm lucky if I don't see the picture of it in my mind before I go to sleep, and then, even if I don't, I'm dreaming about what we did."[42]

A MAN AMONG MEN?

What of sex differences in the powerfully motivating fear of "not measuring up"? The quotation about bravery at the head of this chapter by Field Marshal William Slim—commander of British troops in Burma during World War II and later Chief of the Imperial General Staff—is not much of an exaggeration, if an exaggeration at all. Because women do not feel a man's need to be considered a "man among men," it is predictable that they would be less likely to expose themselves to the risk of death to achieve that respect.

Women have far less incentive than men to take risks to avoid being thought cowards. To label a woman a "coward" is a far lesser insult than labeling a man one, so much so that the word is seldom applied to women. This disparity arises not because women are physically braver than men but because they are not and are not expected to be—a fact that demonstrates the validity of Aristotle's observation that "a man would be thought a coward if he had no more courage than a courageous woman." As William Ian Miller has pointed out, it will not be the award of Medals of Honor to women that shows that women have become "official players at aggressive combat courage," because it will be suspected that the medals were awarded on the basis of sex. Instead, Miller argues, "we will know women have made it when it is fully believed that they can be subject to a court-martial for cowardly conduct,"[43] a prospect that seems very remote indeed.

Even if women did not experience more fear of death than men (although, as we have seen, they do), their incentives for overcoming that fear are considerably smaller. In short, if the need to prove one's manliness is an essential motivator of the soldier, what motivates women?

A SOLDIER AMONG SOLDIERS?

Advocates of the social-role theory of sex argue that the same motivational goals could be achieved by "decoupling" the role of soldier from the role of man.[44] Rather than encouraging the soldier to be a "man among men," an exhortation that would not resonate with women, the soldier should aspire to be a "soldier among soldiers." That prescription rests on the assumption that one's identity as a man runs no deeper than one's identity as the occupant of a job, so that the prescription "be a soldier," though no longer meaning "be a man," would have an equivalent effect.

If combat is no longer a "manly" pursuit, then failure at it is no longer a failure of manhood. In the words of David Marlowe, then chief of military psychiatry at the Walter Reed Army Institute of Research: "The soldier's world is characterized by a stereotypical masculinity. His language is profane, his professed sexuality crude and direct; his maleness is his armor, the measure of his competence, capability, and confidence in himself."[45]

If that "armor" is stripped away, it is predictable that some of the soldier's "competence, capability, and confidence in himself" will be stripped away as well. Separating the performance of the combat job from the soldier's feeling of self-worth as a man may take away much of the stigma for failure and much of the motivation for success. If all that is at stake is an individual's performance of a job rather than his fundamental manhood, why should he risk his life? No mere "job" is worth dying for.

Defining Bravery Down

Inclusion of women in combat units may result in a "defining down" of acceptable combat behavior. It is often assumed that placing women in combat units with men will cause them to behave in a more male-like way, incorporating the "warrior spirit" more typical of the male soldier. The combination of training and self-selection would no doubt have some effect in that direction, so that the average female soldier will be a more aggressive risk-taker than the average woman. Sexual integration may also result in a reverse effect for men, however, with the behavior of men in integrated groups becoming less aggressive and more risk-averse than that of men in all-male groups.

Group expectations are a critical factor in combat performance. A reduction in those expectations will almost inevitably lead to a reduction in performance. As Elmar Dinter has noted: "We should never forget that the average soldier would really like to run away from the fighting. The group prevents him from doing this. If group morality allows for an 'honourable' means of flight, it will be accepted gratefully." Commenting on the poor performance of some British units during the German spring offensive of 1918, historian Martin Middlebrook noted, "The real limit of a Western soldier's resistance is that point at which he feels his individual honor is satisfied." The location of that point depends heavily on the expectations of the group to which he belongs.[46]

The fact that it is group morality that keeps men in combat suggests that if expectations of risk-taking and coping with fear are reduced for some, as is a likely outcome of sexual integration, then the pressure to behave bravely will be diminished for all. Advocates of women in combat who argue that men should be tolerant of such things as women's crying[47] should understand that they are potentially setting the stage for a substantial breakdown in discipline and resultant decline in combat effectiveness. Outward manifestations of fear are contagious. A survey of combat troops in Italy in 1944 found that most men had seen "a man's nerves 'crack up,' "and half of those reported that witnessing the event made them nervous and feel like "cracking up" themselves.[48] Lessening of group expectations for a subset of unit members, combined with the norm of equality within units, threatens a decrease in performance of individuals and therefore of the group.

A possible example of this dynamic occurred in 2004 in Iraq. A mixed-sex platoon of South Carolina reservists refused a direct order to drive a convoy to deliver fuel, arguing that it was a "suicide mission" because their trucks were not armored and also that the fuel was contaminated. The incident came to light when Specialist Amber McClenny left the following message on her mother's answering machine: "Hi Mom. This is Amber. This is a real, real big emergency. I need you to contact someone. I mean raise pure hell. We had broken down trucks, non-armored vehicles and we were carrying contaminated fuel." When told to deliver the fuel, McClenny responded, "No, no way in the world." Another soldier e-mailed his mother, asking about the potential consequences if he disobeyed his commanding officer and "had to get physical."[49]

In all, about twenty soldiers refused the order, of whom at least five were women. News reports are unclear about how the group reached its decision, including who instigated the refusal. Although it may be unfair to speculate, one could easily see how the sex composition of the group might have contributed to this incident. Expressions of unwillingness by one or more of the women could give cover to the men to go along. As Elmar Dinter argued, soldiers, especially support troops, often do not want to expose themselves to risk and would like to run away. By supporting the women who did not want to take on the mission (if this is what happened), the male soldiers could convert (in their minds) a cowardly refusal to take on a dangerous mission into a brave willingness to accept discipline in order to "protect" the women. In the event, of course, their refusal did not reduce the risk of the assignment; it merely shifted it to soldiers of a Montana National Guard unit—which had no more armor than the South Carolina unit—who carried out the mission without injuries.[50]

Remarkably, no courts-martial ensued. McClenny was demoted from specialist to private first class and a number of others received similar punishments. Because the Article 15 proceedings brought against the soldiers are deemed "personnel actions," the Army has not released the details.[51]

A similar incident occurred during the 1989 Panama invasion, with a happier result for the drivers. CBS News reported that two female truck drivers had tearfully refused to drive troops to the scene of fighting, prompting an Army investigation. Two days into the investigation—and several days before it was completed—the Army announced that the women had acted appropriately. According to Army spokesmen, the two women were "exhausted" after driving under fire for nine hours and had asked to be relieved because they feared they might endanger the lives of their passengers. According to officers of the infantry battalion whose soldiers were supposed to be transported, however, the women had not been driving under fire for nine hours. They had come under fire briefly in the first hour of the invasion and then spent eight hours waiting for their next mission, at one point having to be rousted from their barracks and made to stay with their trucks. According to Brian Mitchell:

> Only after they were told where they would be driving did one of the women object. When she began to cry, the second woman said she didn't want to go, either. The men at the scene had no doubt but that the women were afraid, not tired. . . . When they broke down in tears, the NCO replaced them with male drivers.[52]

Nonetheless, according to an Army official, these two women "performed superbly."

If the Army viewed the actions of these drivers as praiseworthy, one must fear for the performance of the Army in the face of sustained combat. The conditions in Panama (an eight- or nine-hour shift of mostly sitting around) were in stark contrast to the conditions facing American troops during the breakout from Normandy in August and September of 1944. There, drivers of the "Red Ball Express" were on the road twenty hours a day moving fuel, food, and ammunition to the ever-eastward-shifting front lines.[53] Perhaps those soldiers would have called their mothers to complain if they possessed the means, but it is doubtful, and it is also doubtful that any such complaints would have been seriously entertained.

The Panama episode revealed, if only unwittingly, the Army's low estimation of women's courage. If these drivers had been men, there is little chance that their performance would have been labeled "superb." Indeed, they almost certainly would have been disciplined, if not court-martialed. Similarly, the refusal to drive in Iraq was a major breach of discipline that would almost certainly have resulted in jail time or dishonorable discharges had some of the refuseniks not been women.

To expect less of some members of a unit is to expect less of all. A double standard for courage will ultimately result in a single standard, and that standard will be the lower one.

Selection of Effective Fighters

The fact that more men than women possess the traits of the effective soldier does not mean that all men would be better than all women. Some women possess more physical courage and willingness to kill than some men. One might argue, therefore, that combat personnel should be selected on the basis of these traits rather than using sex as a proxy. The problems with such an approach are twofold.

First, unlike strength, which can be easily and cheaply screened for, future courage under fire cannot be readily measured. A consistent theme in the combat-behavior literature is that one never knows who is going to be an effective soldier until the shooting starts, and the identity of the good fighters often turns out to be a surprise.[54] In the words of one set of military psychologists, "All research work done to predict stress tolerance of soldiers under war conditions has to be an illusion in terms of the present methodological possibilities."[55] In his book *Fighting Spirit,* F. M. Richardson commented that "soldiers know from experience that it is so difficult as to be well-nigh impossible to foretell which men will do well in battle and which will fail."[56] Individualized predictions of combat performance are therefore not a practical way to select personnel.

The second reason that sex-blind selection of soldiers on the basis of their own individual traits is unworkable relates not to the individual but to the group. The historic linkage between warfare and masculinity has important consequences, because men are willing to risk their lives to satisfy their notions of manhood. As Charles Moskos has noted, one of the only ways to convince men in combat to do "an essentially irrational thing—put themselves in a position where they are likely to get killed"— is to appeal to their masculinity.[57] Recruiting slogans such as "The Marine Corps Builds Men" are designed to operate on a young male mind that already associates masculinity with toughness.[58]

. . .

THE LINK BETWEEN the military and masculinity creates a special appeal for men because it provides an opportunity largely lacking in modern society—the opportunity to prove their manhood. That is part of the appeal of war for men, but it is not all of it. As we will see in the next chapter, despite fashionable claims that "no one wants to go to war," war holds many attractions for men.

10

Why Men Love War

What are these secret attractions of war, the ones that have persisted in the West despite revolutionary changes in the methods of warfare? I believe that they are: the delight in seeing, the delight in comradeship, the delight in destruction. Some fighters know one appeal, and not the others, some experience all three, and some may, of course, feel other appeals that I do not know.

—J. Glenn Gray[1]

With rare exceptions—people who might be considered mentally ill in another context—soldiers who participate in combat find it extremely unnatural and horrible. . . . Contrary to the idea that war thrills men, expresses innate masculinity, or gives men a fulfilling occupation, all evidence indicates that war is something that societies impose on men, who most often need to be dragged kicking and screaming into it, constantly brainwashed and disciplined once there, and rewarded and honored afterwards.

—Joshua Goldstein[2]

November 16, 1864–December 21, 1864, from Atlanta to Savannah, Georgia.
General William Tecumseh Sherman leads an army of sixty-two thousand troops out of Atlanta, having captured the city in September. Sherman's army is, in the words of Victor Davis Hanson, "possessed of a lethal destructive power unmatched by any other infantry force in the history of conflict, lightning quick, absolutely unstoppable."[3] Sherman's goal is the Atlantic coast.

Having culled the unfit from his army, Sherman plans to make ten to fifteen miles per day. His army is traveling light, with an atypically small supply train. Every day, parties of foragers—"bummers"—explore the countryside searching for provisions and livestock, and soldiers devote much energy to ripping up railroad tracks to deny the Confederacy their use. Sherman's strategy is risky, because if he is delayed by a protracted battle, his troops would quickly run out of provisions. Thus, he tends to avoid fortified cities such as Augusta and Macon, which hold substantial Confederate garrisons.

Sherman's army, increasingly expert at "fire and ruin," sweeps through Georgia leaving devastation—largely of property rather than human carnage—in its wake. Sherman's goal is not to kill Confederate soldiers, but to destroy the economic base of the Confederacy and demoralize its plantation class, letting them taste the misery of the war for which he holds them responsible. Soldiers are instructed to distinguish in their pillage between the rich, who are generally hostile to the Union, and the poor, many of whom are not.

By the time Sherman reaches Savannah, the tally of his own dead stands at only about one hundred—most of whom were caught in the act of pillage and executed—but the cost they had inflicted on Georgia was staggering, by Sherman's estimation approximately $100 million in property damage. "Never before," says Hanson, "had an army wrought such havoc in such a brief period at such small loss to itself."

WAR IS "HELL," as Sherman said, but it is not pure hell for all men all the time. In fact, despite denials such as that of Joshua Goldstein quoted above, many men enjoy war and "there are few soldiers for whom military service does not have, albeit in rosy retrospect, some attractions."[4] "The honor and romanticism involved in fighting a war," Darryl Henderson writes, "often appeal to the young soldier who experiences the need for asserting manliness or toughness."

Many soldiers look back at their combat service as the happiest time of their lives. After leaving the Marines, having seen extensive combat in Afghanistan and Iraq, Nathaniel Fick wrote: "At age twenty-six, I feared I had already lived the best years of my life. Never again would I enjoy the sense of purpose and belonging that I had felt in the Marines." Andrew Exum expressed much the same thought upon leaving the Army after his service in Afghanistan, observing that his "greatest fear at the age of twenty-five is that my best years are already behind me" and that he would "never find an opportunity to do so much, to be a part of something so significant as what we did in the aftermath of September 11."[5]

If there were not some countervailing appeal to war, the horror—and there is plenty of that—would be unbearable. But appeal there is. The ambivalence of professional soldiers is revealed in Robert E. Lee's famous observation, made while overlooking the Union dead at Fredericksburg: "It is well that war is so terrible or we would become too fond of it." George S. Patton expressed similar fascination. Overlooking a "scarred and scorched landscape of war" in France, he exclaimed, "Could anything be more magnificent?!" Then, as an artillery battery opened up, he proclaimed in a louder voice, "Compared to war, all other forms of human endeavor shrink to insignificance. God, how I love it!"[6]

This is not to say, of course, that all men enjoy combat or the prospect of it. If they did, there would be little need for wartime conscription. From the privileged position of a prosperous society, however, the question that needs answering is why anyone would abandon the relative security of home and find satisfaction in an endeavor involving so much risk, privation, and pain.

Many Men Eagerly Go to War and Like It

Despite frequent claims that few people want to go to war—a view often expressed when arguments are raised that so few women would want to join combat units that their inclusion would not be worth the cost—the eagerness of many men to go to war and their positive reactions to it are well known. In the early stages of World War I, Americans crossed the border into Canada to join the Canadian army before the "fun" was over. Audie Murphy was one of untold numbers who described being afraid that the war would be over before he got into it. Eugene Sledge wrote that his family had urged him in 1942 to stay in college to obtain a commission, but "prompted by a deep feeling of uneasiness that the war might end before I could get overseas in combat, I wanted to enlist in the Marine Corps as soon as possible." Sledge then signed up for an officer training program, but, like half of his detachment, intentionally flunked out of school to get into the war sooner as an enlisted man.[7]

Many men want more than just to wear the uniform; they long to be in the thick of the fighting. Alvin Kernan wrote that he resigned from aviator training because the glut of aviators in training meant that it would take him another year to get his wings, and he wanted to get back to the war. Samuel Hynes recounts the positive effect on Marine aviators of a kamikaze raid late in the war: "We took it as a sign that the war was still with us, that we still had an enemy, and went to bed heartened by the incident."[8]

This rosy perspective is not limited to men who are on the winning side. It is hard to imagine a more unpleasant experience than serving in the German army on the Russian front. Guy Sajer recounts almost inconceivable hardships and brutality—from men urinating on their hands and the hands of their comrades to warm them and cauterize their cuts; to a pattern of atrocities on both sides; to extraordinarily heavy casualties. Yet, he wrote, "Even now, looking back on everything that happened, I cannot regret having belonged to a combat unit. We discovered a sense of comradeship which I have never found again, inexplicable and steady, through thick and thin."[9]

Although the Vietnam War was unpopular at home (and often in the field), the common assumption that most, or all, of those who fought there hated the experience is belied by the testimony of many participants. Philip Caputo in his classic memoir, *A Rumor of War*, wrote that he never answered truthfully when asked how he felt going into combat for the first time because he did not want to appear to be "some sort of war-lover." In fact, he said, "I felt happier than I ever had."[10] Men in the current war have experienced similar feelings. Evan Wright describes the Marines' exhilaration on the eve of the attack into Iraq: "When formations ends, Marines jump up and down, laughing and throwing each other around in the dust. Two different men run past me, shouting exactly the same phrase, 'This is like Christmas!' "[11]

A 1980 Veterans Administration study suggests that Caputo's perspective on his Vietnam experience is not an idiosyncratic one. That study found that "71 percent of those polled said that they were 'glad' to have gone to Vietnam; 74 percent claimed to have 'enjoyed' their tour there; 66 percent expressed a willingness to serve again."[12] Although the flight of many American draft dodgers and deserters to Canada is well known, less well known is the fact that even more Canadians—some thirty thousand—voluntarily enlisted in the U.S. armed forces and saw service in Vietnam.[13]

The appeal of combat for many men is not simply born of either igno-
rance before experiencing it or the rose-colored glasses of nostalgia. Mark
Bowden describes the decision of a young Ranger to reenlist. He made the
decision while crouched in a street in Mogadishu behind a rock too small
to provide him cover and with bullets snapping over his head and hitting
around him. Although one might suppose that a man in his situation
would be committing himself to the priesthood—or at least a life free of
sin—should he escape alive, this Ranger decided that the experience was
so rewarding that he would commit to another four years of service.

War memoirs no doubt present readers with a biased survey of opinion.
They are written by those who live to tell the tale, and they are hardly a
random sample of even the survivors. Those for whom wartime service
was a positive experience are presumably more likely to write about it than
those who would prefer never to think about it again. Many soldiers no
doubt share Paul Fussell's opinion that their experience produced a prolonged "attenuation of innocence and optimism,"[14] but, unlike Fussell,
most would rather not devote the energy to re-creating unpleasant memories that writing a memoir demands.

Soldiers Are Not "Victims" of Coercion

Although Joshua Goldstein argues that men "need to be dragged kicking
and screaming" into war, coercion cannot account for men's putting themselves in the position of having to fight after the draft ended. Political sci-
entist Judith Hicks Stiehm has argued that in addition to coercion, men
get into combat through "step-by-step ensnarement."[15] Men know that
even if they are in uniform, they are unlikely to serve in combat, she argues, and then once in uniform they are subjected to indoctrination into
the military view of "how 'men' should act." This explanation cannot account for the enlistment of support troops at a time when dispatches from
Iraq are full of stories about such troops being involved in firefights.

Even more fundamentally, the progressive-entrapment analysis does
not account for the enlistment of those who actually bear the brunt of the
fighting—the ground-combat troops, especially infantry. Those who go
into the infantry volunteer for it; they are not placed there against their
will. Even before September 11, it was obvious that ground troops might
be sent into harm's way, whether in a large-scale operation, such as Desert

Storm, or smaller-scale deployments, such as those in Panama, Somalia, and the Balkans. Virtually all of today's combat troops either enlisted or re-enlisted since the fighting in Afghanistan and Iraq began. Yet the Army (almost always) and Marines (always) have met their enlistment targets since those wars began.

Soldiers who enlist today are neither coerced nor entrapped. Many enlist for the personal challenge, including the testing of their manhood. Nathaniel Fick joined the Marines in 1998 after college, eschewing the law school or medical school route of so many of his Dartmouth classmates. He wrote: "None of it appealed to me. I wanted to go on a great adventure, to prove myself, to serve my country. I wanted to do something so hard that no one could ever talk shit to me." He elected to join the Marines because at a time when the Army, Navy, and Air Force were promising education, training, and skills, the Marine Corps asked, "Do you have what it takes?" Fick was on a six-month deployment to the Indian Ocean and the Persian Gulf on September 11, 2001, and it is clear that he did not feel entrapped. Instead, he believed that his Marines were in an enviable position. As he told his men, "You're it, fellas. A hundred million American men would like to be in your shoes right now. We have the honor of fighting back."[16]

Expressing similar motivations for joining, Andrew Exum commented, "I wanted to be a killer. I wanted to be something elite, like a Navy SEAL or Army Ranger. I wanted to be something I could brag about when I got old." As Robert Scales has noted, "close-combat soldiers do not choose to join the services for the money or to get an education."[17] These men are not entrapped, progressively or otherwise.

What Do Men Love About War?

As the Glenn Gray quotation at the beginning of the chapter noted, war holds a number of attractions for men. Samuel Hynes, who became an English professor after his service in the Marines, not only wrote his own memoir but also conducted a study of the memoirs of others. In that study, he mused about the attractions of war: "What is it, exactly, that war lovers love? Not the killing and the violence, I think, but the excitement, the drama, and the danger—life lived at a high level of intensity, like a complicated, fatal game (or a Wagnerian opera)."[18]

When Demi Moore's character in *G.I. Jane* claimed that wanting to "blow shit up" was her motivation for joining the SEALs, we already knew enough about her character to realize that she was not telling the truth. She wanted a combat assignment to further her career, which, according to James Dunnigan, is the principal motivation of women seeking to serve in combat units.[19] For many men, however, the pleasure of "breaking things and killing people" is intense. Evan Wright describes a Marine's reaction to surviving an ambush and his comparison of the experience to a video game: "I was just thinking one thing when we drove into that ambush," he enthuses. "Grand Theft Auto: Vice City. I felt like I was living it when I seen the flames coming out of the windows, the blown-up car in the street, guys crawling around shooting at us. It was fucking cool."[20]

The delight in destruction should not be underestimated. Victor Davis Hanson may have done just that in attributing the morale of Sherman's soldiers to their belief in the Union cause. "The usual wages of regret and shame that accompany the soldier as arsonist and thief," he says, "are absent when the immediate, quite visible aim of such terror is to free the oppressed."[21] This statement may overestimate men's negative reactions to their arson and theft and hence the extent to which they require rationalization. Belief in their cause certainly helps overcome the natural reservation that civilized men feel about harming others, but that reservation gives way easily. Indeed, one imagines that Sherman's march to the sea was actually "fun" for most of its participants. Young men like to destroy things and set fires, and they enjoy roaming the countryside with the rules of civilization lifted. Add to that a splash of danger—not a lot, but just enough to heighten the senses—and one has the recipe for a jolly good time.

Describing himself as a lad of seventeen—who had lied about his age to join the British army at the outbreak of World War I—Charles Carrington sounds like just the sort of young man who would have joined Sherman enthusiastically. A half century after the Great War, he wrote, "I have wondered whether the boy I re-discovered was anything more than a juvenile delinquent, whose characteristics were a love for ganging-up with the other boys, a craving to demonstrate his manliness, and a delight in antisocial violence."[22] A boy such as he, "ripe for mischief," in Carrington's words, "was, and thought himself, lucky when in August his errant purpose was directed towards a task that was socially acceptable."

Many men describe their attraction to combat in terms that sound like an addiction. James Estep, commander of an airmobile rifle company, explains his decision to volunteer for a *third* tour of duty in Vietnam. He wrote: "Why? I asked myself. Why go back again? . . . You know the answer . . . [Y]ou like the pace of combat, like that awareness of life that only it seems to induce. You like to feel that sudden surge of adrenaline when confronting the unexpected; you like the lack of routine, the opportunity to innovate, the hunting of animals who do indeed shoot back, the stark terror and brilliant splendor of a firefight."

Nathaniel Fick expressly invokes the idea of addiction. He writes that "the adrenaline rush of combat and the heady thrill of being the law were addicting us," but notes that he was aware enough of his feelings "to be concerned that I was starting to enjoy it." One of Fick's Marines told Evan Wright: "You really can't top it. Combat is the supreme adrenaline rush. You take rounds. Shoot back, shit starts blowing up. It's sensory overload. It's the one thing that's not overrated in the military."[23]

Winston Churchill once wrote of the thrill of escaping fire unhurt: "Nothing in life is so exhilarating as to be shot at without result." One of Fick's men expressed the same thought in the aftermath of a bloody battle: "I feel invincible. I had rounds skipping in the dirt right next to me, a BMP [Iraqi armored vehicle] shooting straight at us, Cobras lighting stuff up all around, a five-hundred-pound bomb blow up almost on top of us, and nothing hit me. Maybe it's karma."[24]

The Dark Side?

Sometimes there is a darker side. Some men find that they not only like the camaraderie, excitement, and freedom in a combat zone, but also, contrary to Hynes, that they actually like to kill. Frederick Downs, a platoon leader in Vietnam, candidly acknowledged what many are loath to admit:

> It turned out that most of us liked to kill other men. Some of the guys would shoot at a dink much as they would at a target. Some of the men didn't like to kill a dink up close. The closer the killing, the more personal it became.
>
> Others in the platoon liked to kill close in. A few even liked to torture the dinks if they had a prisoner or cut the dead bodies with knives in a frenzy of aggression. A few didn't like to kill at all and wouldn't fire their weapons except to protect their buddies.[25]

Characterizing the enemy as "dinks" no doubt facilitated the killing.

Downs's description of the soldier's zest for killing is not anomalous, as such reports are common in the combat literature. Joanna Bourke relates the deep pleasure that many men experience in killing—from the British soldier who described his first bayoneting of a German as "gorgeously satisfying" to the French trench mortar officer who, after scoring a direct hit on the enemy and seeing "bodies or parts of bodies go up in the air" and hearing "the desperate yelling of the wounded or the runaways," pronounced the event "one of the happiest moments of my life." A Marine general recently captured the sentiment of many fighting men when he remarked, "It's fun to shoot some people," an ill-advisedly candid comment that prompted counseling about his "choice of words."[26]

In a famous article in *Esquire* magazine having the same title as this chapter, William Broyles wrote that "one of the most troubling reasons men love war is the love of destruction, the thrill of killing." Writing in the same magazine almost half a century earlier, Ernest Hemingway described the thrill of combat: "Certainly there is no hunting like the hunting of man and those who have hunted armed men long enough and liked it, never really care for anything else thereafter. You will meet them doing various things with resolve, but their interest rarely holds because after the other thing ordinary life is as flat as the taste of wine when the taste buds have been burned off your tongue." Marine sniper Jack Coughlin expressed much the same sentiment, noting that he does not hunt animals, although he has no moral objections to the sport: "I just see no thrill, or challenge, in shooting an animal. Once you hunt men, nothing else can compare."[27]

This attraction to killing is deeply disturbing to those having responsibility for the spiritual side of fighting men. Evan Wright describes the battalion chaplain's complaint that some Marines sought counseling from him because they felt guilty about not having had the chance to shoot. "The zeal these young men have for killing surprises me," the chaplain said, and "it instills in me a sense of disbelief and rage."[28]

Although society asks men to kill and wants them to come home emotionally unscarred, it nonetheless seems suspicious of those who participate in combat without sufficient anguish. When Nathaniel Fick left the Marines, he applied to graduate school. He received a call from one school saying that they liked his application but that a member of the admissions committee had concerns about Fick after reading Evan Wright's story in *Rolling Stone* magazine. In that story, Wright had quoted Fick as saying before a mission, "The bad news is, we won't get much sleep tonight; the good news is, we get to kill people." The university official noted that a retired Army officer on staff "warned me that there are people who enjoy killing, and they aren't nice to be around." Fick declined the opportunity to explain his comment.[29]

Not only do civilians find the appeal of killing inexplicable, so do some soldiers after they return from battle. Glenn Gray tells of a Pacific war veteran whose unit had unexpectedly flushed out a Japanese soldier on an island that had been mostly cleared of enemy troops. As the Japanese soldier ran frantically for safety, the American soldiers found the spectacle enormously funny and kept missing because of the poor aim produced by their laughter. They eventually killed him, and the incident cheered the soldiers and provided fodder for jokes for some time. After the war, this veteran could no longer remember why the soldiers found the incident humorous, believing in retrospect—with most detached observers—that their behavior was nothing but cruel.[30] Sometimes, it seems, you really did have to be there.

The lot of the combat soldier is a difficult one, and sometimes extraordinarily so. What is it, then, that accounts for the strange appeal of an enterprise that can be so painful and destructive and that is so contrary to "civilized" mores and norms? The answer, it seems, lies deep in the male psyche.

Sexuality and Warfare

William Broyles captured much of the source of war's appeal when he noted that men's love of war "stems from the union, deep in the core of our being, between sex and destruction, beauty and horror, love and death." Many men find something deeply sexual about war itself, a link that has been frequently commented upon but that produces profound discomfort among some, as it seems to evoke images of the pathological sexual thrills of a serial killer.

The link between warfare and sexuality persists in the modern age. Alvin Kernan wrote that when he returned on leave to Wyoming after service in the Pacific during World War II, "girls who would never speak to me before were now willing to dally and to charm" and that "chastity seemed to have been cast aside in the Rocky Mountains for the duration." Glenn

Gray reported that the uniform affected not only the women who saw it but also the men who wore it, remembering that "when we were in uniform almost any girl who was faintly attractive had an erotic appeal for us."[31]

The goals of soldiers are frequently phrased in sexual terms. The phrase "get some!"—which Evan Wright refers to as the "unofficial Marine Corps cheer"—is used to spur men on who are going into battle. As Wright describes: "Get some! expresses, in two simple words, the excitement, the fear, the feelings of power and the erotic-tinged thrill that come from confronting the extreme physical and emotional challenges posed by death, which is, of course, what war is all about. Nearly every Marine I've met is hoping this war with Iraq will be his chance to get some."[32]

The phrase "Get some!" is more than pure metaphor, as the feelings evoked by battle are sometimes overtly sexual. As one Vietnam veteran reported, "I enjoyed the shooting and killing. I was literally turned on when I saw a gook shot." During a brief lull in combat operations in Mogadishu, Mark Bowden reported, one Ranger suggested that it would be a good time for a "combat jack," as there was a running competition for masturbating in exotic locations. Evan Wright recounted a similar focus in conversations among the Marines, with attempts to tally who had masturbated the most since the invasion began. He quotes one Marine as saying that after one ambush, "I get into my hole, and I had to go three times, bam, bam, bam! Couldn't stop. Hadn't happened like that since I was seventeen. I thought something was broken." Another Marine reported a "funny combat stress reaction": "When we rolled back from the bridge the first time, I had a chubb. It wouldn't go away. Maybe it was 'cause I didn't get to shoot my SAW [squad automatic weapon]."[33]

The machinery of death can be arousing as well. After watching helicopters "vomit destruction," a Marine commented, "I used to get a kind of semi-chubb when Cobras went past. After today, seeing those birds overhead makes me so hard I could hammer nails."[34]

In an unusual (for the time) invocation of Darwinian principles, Glenn Gray provided an explanation for the linkage of sex and war. He argued that because war poses a special threat to the survival of the species, humans reproduce more rapidly to make up for the killing. "As individuals," he says, "we have no freedom to do otherwise, since the needs of the species are imperious."[35]

Most modern evolutionists would cringe at Gray's "for the good of the species" argument, as the broad concept of "group selection"—that natural selection favors traits that are good for the species but not for the individual bearing them—has been largely discredited. The difficulty with the group-selection argument is that there is no known mechanism by which such a trait could evolve. A famous, yet spurious, example of group selection are the lemmings that march dutifully into the sea when food is scarce. One can immediately see that a lemming gene for altruistic suicide would have difficulty gaining a foothold in the population, as the gene would die with the individual who carried it into the sea, leaving behind those lemmings who had the "let George do it" gene.

Although Gray's group-selection logic is flawed, the notion that natural selection created a link between sex and war is quite plausible. The reproductive rewards to men from war have been previously mentioned, and the prevalence of wartime rape is discussed in a later chapter. The sexual opportunities available in wartime could easily cause a deep psychological connection between war and sexuality in men, similar to the mechanism that causes many men to feel sexual attraction toward women over whom they have power.[36] Moreover, uncertainty of the future is typically associated with acceleration of reproduction—the "why wait?" argument—a phenomenon probably responsible for the lower age of first childbirth in inner-city populations.[37] Danger also diminishes selectivity in mate choice, not only in humans but in other animals as well.[38] That would explain why women in wartime may be less chaste, and women's preference for brave, strong men would explain why their chastity may be more vulnerable to men in uniform.

The focus of soldiers on sex is reflected in the ubiquitous World War II "pinup pictures" and the paintings of scantily clad women on the fuselages of airplanes. Such displays were widely believed to contribute to soldiers' morale. All of this "sex stuff" is distasteful to some today, however, especially female officers. Although "cheesecake" pictures and shows featuring attractive women have always appealed to men in war zones, some people seem to have a visceral distaste for "boys being boys," at least "if ladies are present." In Iraq, for example, a female Air Force captain complained about a performance by a group called "The Purrfect Angelz," who perform in hot pants and halter tops. Their Web site describes them as "a stunning group of dancers, singers, fire twirlers, aerial artists, and acrobats." The captain complained that "the show only appeals to men, and in my mind has the potential to increase sexual advances toward female soldiers afterward."[39] Because of her complaints, including an e-mail to the *Sacramento Bee*, the location of the show was changed.

Men can be forgiven for thinking that some women simply resent their having fun. A retired female Navy captain complained to *Bee* reporters that "they're trying to appeal to the 18-to-25-year-old males, forgetting that there are a lot of women there. I don't think it's good for women in the military to have to put up with this kind of thing." She also complained that she had to endure USO shows with the Dallas Cowboys cheerleaders twenty years earlier. One senses that she would not have been too happy with Bob Hope's USO shows with the "Golddiggers" in Vietnam either, or even his World War II shows.[40] On his 1944 South Pacific tour, Hope traveled more than thirty thousand miles and gave over 150 performances. A young "skimpily clad" dancer named Patty Thomas was a part of the show. Hope would stand next her and crack, "I just want you boys to remember what you're fighting for." That was back when one could have a sense of humor about such things.

Preserving the Masculinity of War

At bottom, what appeals to many men about war is its masculinity. Being a combat soldier "represents one of the last all-male adventures left in America,"[41] and it is in its essence, and necessarily, masculine. It celebrates strength, aggressiveness, courage, and violence, and it counterposes these attributes with their opposites, which are effeminate, if not feminine. Those who can't hack it, as pointed out in the last chapter, are simply "pussies."

The environment of the combat soldier is not one that women, no matter how strong and brave, can enter without changing its basic nature. Evan Wright describes the spare time of the Recon Marines:

> At night they fight constantly. They judo-flip each other headfirst into the plywood floor of the tent. They strong-arm their buddies into headlocks and punch bruises into each other's ribs. They lie in wait for one another in the shadows and leap out swinging Ka-Bar knives, flecking their buddies' rib cages with little nicks from the knife tips, or dragging their blades lightly across a victim's throat, playfully simulating a clean kill. They do it to keep each other in shape; they do it for fun; they do it to establish dominance.[42]

Is there any likelihood that these activities, which clearly contribute both to cohesion and to combat skills, would, or even could, continue in a sexually integrated environment?

THE TASK FACING the military is difficult enough even with male soldiers. Andrew Exum has noted the difficulty the Army already has training young men how to be warriors, "not in the Nintendo sense of the word, but in the visceral, primitive sense." What has always been a difficult task is made more so, he says, "by a society in which young men are taught to apologize for their testosterone and aggressiveness." Today, the military, especially the infantry, "remains one of the last places where that most endangered of species, the alpha male, can feel at home."[43] But for how much longer? In all-male combat arms, the military can train men to ignore the denigration of masculinity they have lived with throughout their lives and "get in touch with their inner beast." Can the military really do that in integrated combat units—simultaneously celebrating and encouraging the masculinity of the soldier while embracing (only figuratively, of course) the "woman warrior"?

PART IV

MEN AND WOMEN
IN GROUPS

Much of the optimism about the potential effects of sexual integration derives from the assumption that appropriate criteria can select women who possess warrior attributes and that women so selected would then function like men. Realism about the physical and psychological differences between the sexes suggests that the number of women so chosen is likely to be small. Those few women, however, are thought entitled to be judged on their individual merit. We saw in the last section that maleness itself may be an important warrior attribute, as soldiers' concerns about proving their manhood are important motivators. The view that sex-neutral selection criteria can create an effective fighting force also neglects something even more fundamental.

Individuals do not fight wars; groups do. Combat is an intensely cooperative enterprise, and the effectiveness of a combat force is not simply the sum of the attributes of individuals but rather a product of how the group works together. In other words, the group can be either more or less than the sum of its parts. Even a strong and aggressive woman may not add to the effectiveness of the group the way an equivalent man would—and may in fact detract from it—if she is not accepted and not trusted because she is a woman.

Group dynamics are critical to combat effectiveness. Men fight for many reasons, but if any reason could be labeled primary, it is that they fight for their comrades with whom they have bonded. This bond, often characterized as "male bonding," is a powerful one, and women cannot partake of these bonds the way men can.

Beyond the "horizontal cohesion" of bonds among combat comrades, there are bonds of "vertical cohesion" between leaders and followers. Leadership is a group endeavor. It is not measured by the traits or behaviors of the leader but by the behavior of the follower. Thus, the question is not whether women exhibit leadership behavior, but whether they evoke "followership" in men to the same extent as male leaders. There is reason to believe that, at least in dangerous endeavors, they do not.

The assumption that men can be "educated" to accept women into their "band of brothers" with proper leadership rests on the view that their resistance is a consequence of the "sexist" culture of the military and the greater society. Throughout the world, however, men have traditionally excluded women from groups organized around dangerous activities. From childhood, the sexes tend to segregate by sex, and male and female groups differ in structure and activities. Male groups are characterized by competition and hierarchy, female groups by equality. Male groups are larger and more resistant to disruption by conflict than female groups. Male groups thrive on competition and even conflict, while female groups are often ripped apart by them.

There is much reason to think that sex differences in group dynamics have an underlying biological basis. Men's antipathy toward female comrades in arms may run much deeper than mere "attitudes" operating at a cognitive level. Although socially derived attitudes may be amenable to change through cognitive input, the forces that cause men to band together in same-sex groups operate not on a cognitive level but on an emotional one, suggesting that "education" may have little effect. If so, men's lack of acceptance of women will be a permanent feature of the military.

11

The Bond of Brothers:
All for One and One for All

We few, we happy few, we band of brothers;
For he to-day that sheds his blood with me
Shall be my brother; be he ne'er so vile,
This day shall gentle his condition;
And gentlemen in England, now a-bed,
Shall think themselves accurs'd they were not here;
And hold their manhoods cheap whiles any speaks
That fought with us upon Saint Crispin's day.

—William Shakespeare[1]

Greater love hath no man than this, that a man lay down his life
for his friends.

—John 15:13

October 25, 1415: Outside the northern French village of Agincourt.
Imagine yourself an archer in the army of Henry V on this autumn morning. You are in the front line, facing the army of Charles VI massed a few
hundred yards across a field recently sown with winter wheat. You sense,
as does everyone on both sides, that the English forces are substantially
outnumbered—which is why your king was hoping to avoid a head-on
battle—but you may not realize that there are at least four Frenchmen for
every Englishman. You know that when the order to loose arrows is given,
it will be followed immediately by a French charge. A cloud of arrows soon
fills the air, and the French men-at-arms, both mounted and unmounted,
charge toward your lines in full armor. Every human instinct tells you to
turn tail and run, but you stand fast. When the battle is over, a scant three

hours later, seven to ten thousand Frenchmen lie dead at the cost of fewer than one hundred Englishmen.[2]

January 22, 1879: South Africa.
Fast forward a few centuries and shift location. You are a soldier at the small supply station and hospital at Rorke's Drift in Natal province. The garrison has just learned that much of the regiment, almost two thousand souls, has been wiped out by a force of twenty thousand Zulus at Isandhlwana across the border in Zululand. But it gets worse. A fresh Zulu army of four thousand warriors under the command of the Zulu king's brother is only a few miles from Rorke's Drift. Had the colonial cavalrymen and native African riflemen remained, the garrison would have had over four hundred defenders, but because they fled the total force numbers only 139. Eighty of these are healthy riflemen; the remainder are bedridden or cooks, orderlies, and teamsters. Despite the ominous situation, there is, in the words of Victor Davis Hanson, "scarcely any chance that they would flee, despite the odds and the macabre battle to come."[3] Sixteen hours after the battle began, the Zulus withdraw, with as many as one thousand warriors lying dead or mortally wounded at the cost to the British of fifteen dead and twelve wounded.

HOW COULD THESE lopsided outcomes occur? There is no single cause, of course. At Agincourt, the terrain favored the English, the English had a more unified command, their longbows were more effective than the French crossbows, and many of the French dead were killed after being taken prisoner. At Rorke's Drift, however, the terrain favored the Zulus, and the Zulus had far more rifles than the British, although they lacked the marksmanship and fire discipline to exploit that advantage fully. The British had the advantage of greater discipline and organization than the Zulus, a discipline characteristic of Western armies, and they were blessed with exceptionally able, though largely untested, leaders.

The stories of Agincourt and Rorke's Drift are particularly dramatic, but victory of numerically inferior forces is a frequent occurrence in the history of warfare. Every battle has its own story—leadership, terrain, technology, surprise, luck, and so many other variables—but a constant in war is the human psyche. We know from chapter 9 that most of the men on both sides in these battles would have experienced fear. How were they nonetheless able to stand together as cohesive groups rather than yielding to the "every man for himself" impulse that so often ends in a rout?

The Human Element

It is commonplace today to emphasize the quantitative and technological aspects of war—which side has more and better missiles, aircraft, ships, and tanks, and who has the greater number of men under arms. Material factors are important, of course, but it is wrong to think that they are necessarily determinative.

The importance of the "moral" factor in combat has long been recognized. Xenophon observed two and a half millennia ago that "not numbers or strength brings victory in war; but whichever army goes into battle stronger in soul, their enemies generally cannot withstand them." Over two millennia later, Napoleon gave voice to the same thought in his famous observation that "in war the moral is to the material as three to one."[4] This is not to suggest that numbers mean nothing, as captured in the wry aphorism variously attributed to both Lenin and Stalin that "quantity has a quality all its own."

OVERCOMING FEAR

Management of fear—rather than its elimination—is the key to combat effectiveness.[5] Fear, and even the cowardice that consists of giving in to that fear, requires little explanation. The desire for self-preservation is easily understood from an evolutionary perspective, but one does not need a Ph.D. in evolutionary biology or formal instruction about "the selfish gene" to explain a soldier's reluctance to advance in the face of hostile fire, where the risk, and sometimes the virtual certainty, of death awaits. The more interesting question is what force is strong enough to motivate men to overcome this fear and close with the enemy or to hold fast to a position in the face of an enemy advance? In the words of Ardant du Picq, how does one achieve "the temporary domination of will over instinct"?[6]

The effect of fear varies to some extent with the individual and the circumstances. A few men simply, and possibly pathologically, do not experience fear on the battlefield, perhaps exhibiting the courage that Lord Moran characterized as having "its roots in a vacant mind."[7] Most men, however, do experience fear, but what separates the brave from the rest is the ability to act despite that fear. A number of influences act on the soldier, from coercion, to the "manly honor" explored in chapter 9, to patriotism. As we will see, however, perhaps the primary motivator of men is their commitment to their group.

Coercion, "Cause and Country," and Hatred

Men often fight not because they do not fear the enemy but because they fear something else even more. This "something else" is often their own superiors, as most armies employ means to make it difficult for soldiers to retreat. During World War II, Soviet officers were authorized to shoot their men on the spot, a circumstance that led Stalin to remark that "it takes a very brave man to not be a hero in the Red Army."[8] After the "major-combat phase" of operations in Iraq, captured Iraqi soldiers almost universally reported that it was fear that kept them going—not fear of the coalition forces facing them, but of the Baath Party and the Fedayeen Saddam death squads behind them.[9]

Soldiers may also be motivated by a belief in the rightness of their cause,[10] although ideology and patriotism are less important than many war movies and much wartime propaganda might lead one to believe. Hatred of the enemy and a desire for vengeance also may motivate the soldier, and militaries often foster that emotion. Japanese soldiers were told before the invasion of Malaya to think of themselves "as an avenger come at last face to face with your father's murderer."[11] Hatred is especially powerful if it is based upon personal experience. Philip Caputo wrote of his own motivations for transferring back to a line company in Vietnam from a rear-echelon position. Part of it was boredom, part of it was the "magnetism of combat," but part of it was "a hatred buried so deep that I could not then admit its existence." This hatred had nothing to do with the enemy's politics and everything to do with their brutal killing of some of his men.[12]

For Self and Comrades

Fear of superiors, belief in cause, and hatred of the enemy may be important influences on soldiers, and their relative importance may differ depending upon whether the question is why men sign up for war or why they fight when under fire. Many students of combat motivation believe that none of these factors is the primary motivator of men in battle, however. There is a broad consensus among those who have observed and studied the behavior of men in combat—and among those who have been in battle—that they fight primarily for their survival, for their immediate comrades, and for their standing in the eyes of those comrades.

In an often-quoted remark, S. L. A. Marshall observed: "I hold it to be one of the simplest truths of war that the thing which enables an infantry soldier to keep going with his weapons is the near presence or the presumed presence of a comrade." Darryl Henderson has similarly observed that "the only force strong enough to make the soldier willing to advance under fire is his loyalty to the small group and that group's expectations that he will advance."[13]

Group Cohesion

The bond that holds groups of fighting men together is widely viewed by students of the military as critical to combat effectiveness. Writers often use the term "cohesion" to describe the bonding of "primary groups" of soldiers, although the concept is admittedly nebulous. One widely accepted definition is "the bonding together of members of an organization/unit in such a way as to sustain their will and commitment to each other, their unit, and the mission."[14] This force, which leads individuals to value the group more than they value themselves and inclines them to further group objectives at substantial peril to themselves, is a combination of trust and reciprocal obligation.[15]

A striking feature of men's wartime memoirs is the deep emotional connection they display toward their comrades, a connection often compared favorably in strength to the male-female bond. Philip Caputo observed that "the communion between men is as profound as any between lovers." Indeed, it is more so, he says, as "it does not demand for its sustenance the reciprocity, the pledges of affection, the endless reassurances required by the love of men and women." Samuel Hynes spoke similarly of "an intimacy among us so close that I find it difficult to put a name to it."[16]

The relationship between a man and his small group defies easy understanding because it is based not on logic but on emotion. The soldier's "brothers," whom he may not have known a year earlier, are worth his life. In the bloody 1944 battle for Peleliu in the Carolines alone, six Marines earned the Medal of Honor for covering grenades with their bodies to save their comrades.[17] These actions were not aberrations and have been repeated several times in the war in Iraq.[18] In April 2004, in the town of Husaybah, for example, Corporal Jason Dunham was attacked by the driver of a vehicle that was to be searched. The man grabbed Dunham by the throat, and they began wrestling on the ground. The man then released a grenade. Dunham threw his helmet over the grenade and himself over his helmet to absorb the blast of the grenade to save his buddies. In January 2007, President Bush awarded the Medal of Honor to Dunham posthumously.[19] The behavior of such men is impossible to understand for people who believe that the duties of a soldier can be captured in a written job description, that aptitude for soldiering can be adequately assessed using scores on a paper-and-pencil test, and that military service is just a job.

Cohesion Is Not Just Friendship

The bond among men at arms is paradoxical. It is intense but at the same time ephemeral. Unlike the male-female bond, which can endure—though not always easily—long periods of separation, the bond among fighting men is transitory, usually lasting only as long as the group is together. Charles Moskos found, for example, that once a squad member left Vietnam to return home, he seldom contacted those remaining behind and they seldom contacted him.[20] Thus, it is wrong to characterize the bond that cements a cohesive group as "friendship," as some do,[21] although friendship is often part of the relationship between some members. Indeed, it is not necessary that all members of the group even like each other.

Men and women's same-sex relationships are not the same, as will be discussed in chapter 13. Men's tend to be broad and shallow, and women's tend to be narrow and deep. Men have a lower threshold for creating large cooperative groups and can maintain them with lower levels of investment. The flip side of that tendency explains the lack of persistence of the groups after its members physically separate. Describing same-sex friendships, Michael Gurian has written: "Male friendship is fragile in ways female friendship is not because male friendship is not talk-dependent. It is proximity-and-activity-dependent. . . . As a result, it is harder to sustain than female friendship. When the war, task, work, or life-period of friendship is over, the friendship is generally over."

The dynamic identified by Gurian that makes male relationships "fragile" may be exactly what allows the group bonding to occur in the first place and may contribute to the widely held belief that the "bonding" that cements soldiers is in fact "male bonding." Male relationships are sustained by proximity and shared tasks and experiences; they are made stronger if the experience is a difficult and dangerous one. A man's ability to work in a common endeavor with his comrades is not dependent upon his affection toward individual unit members, and male groups can be sustained even in the presence of internal conflict. What is required among the members is not affection, but trust.

Female relationships are fragile in a different way from men's. What sustains female relationships resembles what Caputo asserted is not necessary within combat units—"the pledges of affection" and "endless reassurances," if not explicit, at least implicit in the form of one-on-one emotional investment. Female friendships are emotionally deeper and more subject to disruption by conflicts. As psychologist David Geary and anthropologist Michael Flinn have pointed out, if male coalitions required the same level of investment as female groups, they could not be sustained at their often large size.[22]

Creation of the Bond

The bond between men at arms is one of the primary objects of military training. It does not form spontaneously whenever men are put together; rather, the military goes to great lengths to foster it. The military structure deemphasizes individualism, and the soldier is "constantly reminded of his responsibilities to his buddies, to his leaders, to the squad, to the platoon, and ultimately to the people and the nation or party through the structure of his immediate unit." Questioning the military's current emphasis on "diversity," which highlights difference rather than similarity, John Luddy has argued that "in achieving victory, individuals generally mean nothing but units almost always mean everything." He noted that when he was an officer candidate, the worst thing a drill instructor could say was: "Candidate, do you want to be an individual?"[23]

The mere fact of membership in the unit does not entitle one to the benefits of primary-group membership, as individual replacements in combat units have discovered to their discomfort. The practice of replacing individuals as "spare parts" in combat units was a major failing of

American manpower practices in World War II, Korea, and Vietnam. The "new guy" (or "FNG," as he was often not so affectionately called) came in as an outsider who lacked the social support of the group and often did not live long enough to gain it.[24]

Hardship and the Bond

The more rigorous the shared experience, the greater the cohesion, which accounts for much of the difficulty of traditional basic training, as well as the hazing that has long been a common feature of military organizations. Although sometimes brutal and too often done to excess, hazing is a means for senior members of the group to establish dominance and to induce new members into "letting go of their old identities with and loyalties to former groups and organizations and taking on new identities."[25] Hazing has traditionally been a mostly male experience, and because women have less experience with it, they often believe that they are being singled out and view it as sex-based harassment. Male midshipmen at the Naval Academy are more likely than women to believe that physical hazing and severe verbal hazing should be permitted.[26] Part of the difference seems to be that women are more likely to view "plebe year" as a "leadership development tool," while men are more likely to view it as an initiation rite.

The greater the perceived difference between the newcomer and the group (whether the difference is sex, race, background, age, education, religion, or anything else), the more the newcomer is likely to be tested. In mostly male environments, therefore, women either tend to undergo more hazing than men or, more commonly, "they are protected from hazing and thereby are not given a chance to prove themselves and thus gain true membership."[27]

Even when subjected to the same hazing as men, women often respond differently. They tend to become angry, a reaction that often elicits more hazing. Women are also more likely to seek assistance from their superiors, continuing a tactic that begins in childhood, with girls being more likely than boys to complain to adults about peer conflicts. This is often a poor strategy in the face of hazing, because it is perceived as disloyal to the group and may create a permanent alienation from it.

Hazing has gotten a bad reputation, and it deserves much of it, as those who engage in it are easily swept up into cruel excesses. On the other hand, it may produce substantial benefits and perhaps even save lives. Admiral James Stockdale believed that it was of great benefit to him in his years of captivity in North Vietnam. Reflecting on the old "plebe year" practices of the Naval Academy, Stockdale recalled that the midshipmen were "constantly subjected to personal stresses that some might think of as pointless harassment." He viewed that year of stress, however, as "of great personal survival value to me." Shortly after he returned from Vietnam, at an Academy reunion, one of his former prison-mates told him gleefully of great changes: "They've practically done away with the plebe year at the academy, and they've got computers in the basement of Bancroft Hall." Stockdale's reaction was "Hell, if there was anything that helped us get through those eight years it was plebe year, and if anything screwed up that war, it was computers."[28]

How Large Is the Small Group?

Groups cemented by primary-group cohesion tend to be small. S. L. A. Marshall has described the narrowness of the combat soldier's vision: "In battle, you may draw a small circle around a soldier, including within it only those persons and objects which he sees or which he believes will influence his immediate fortunes. These primarily will determine whether he rallies or fails, advances or falls back." Expressing that same thought, Charles Carrington described the importance of small-unit cohesion even in a very large-scale conflict: the trench warfare of World War I, which involved hundreds of thousands of men dug into opposing trenches. Nonetheless, he noted, "A corporal and six men in a trench were like shipwrecked sailors on a raft, completely committed to their social grouping."[29] Virtually everyone else was "them"—whether the enemy, the platoon in the next trench that had drawn the fire of enemy gunners, or "the bloody munition-makers at home who were earning high wages and seducing your girl-friend."

Loyalty to the Group

Attachment to the primary group can be very strong. Audie Murphy declined a battlefield commission because under division rules he would have to transfer to a different platoon,[30] and he was unwilling to be separated from his men. Only after the rule was changed in response to acute personnel shortages would he accept the promotion.

The desire of wounded men to rejoin their outfits is a common feature of warfare. Many wounded men went AWOL during World War II to return to their former units rather than waiting around in a replacement depot to be shipped off to a unit of strangers.[31] William Manchester describes being wounded on Okinawa and escaping the hospital, in violation of orders, to rejoin his men. Calling it "an act of love," he wrote that his men "were closer to me than I can say, closer than any friends had been or ever would be."[32]

This is not to imply that most combatants necessarily want to be where they are. Typically, many, if not most, yearn to go home. But they want to go home having done their duty in a way that is acceptable to the group. Nonetheless, many soldiers in both Vietnam and Iraq voluntarily returned to the combat zone after their first tour of duty was complete or after they were wounded.

Understanding this common feeling of wounded soldiers toward their comrades may make sense of some of the anger expressed by veterans toward John Kerry during the 2004 presidential campaign. There are many disputed issues of fact in the "Swift Boat" controversy, but a number of relevant facts are not in dispute. Senator Kerry received three Purple Hearts for very minor wounds that resulted in little or no loss of duty time. He then invoked an obscure Navy regulation authorizing an early return for anyone who had received three Purple Hearts, allowing him to leave Vietnam after just four months, cutting his Vietnam service eight months short. Then in his presidential campaign, he made his Vietnam service a centerpiece of his candidacy, announcing that he was "reporting for duty" and invoking the "band of brothers" theme by showcasing a photograph of himself with a number of other men, many of whom apparently did not feel that they were in the same brotherhood.

Group Cohesion and Military Effectiveness

High levels of cohesion are associated with substantial benefits both to the individual and the group. Members of cohesive groups express less anxiety about physical dangers, and individuals who have strong group identification can withstand more physical pain.[33] Acts of heroism are also more likely to emerge from highly cohesive units than from less cohesive units.[34] Squads exhibiting high cohesion have been found to perform at a higher level than other squads,[35] although the direction of causation is subject to some debate.

One of the leading contributors to group cohesion is a set of "common attitudes, values, and beliefs." Indeed, psychiatrist Peter Watson reports that psychological homogeneity within a squad is associated with greater combat effectiveness.[36] Traditionally, part of that shared value for combat troops has been the bond of masculinity, which women simply cannot share.

Perhaps the greatest benefit of high levels of cohesion is the psychic inoculation, temporary though it may be, that it provides. Members of cohesive units rate higher in physical and emotional well-being, and they suffer fewer psychiatric casualties than members of less cohesive units.[37] Psychiatric casualties are a major source of incapacity in battle, whether the "shell shock" of the First World War, the "battle fatigue" of World War II, or today's "combat stress reaction" or PTSD. In World War II, typically 10 percent of a fighting force was psychologically disabled within the first few hours.[38] Although psychiatric casualties were once viewed as a mark of personal weakness, study of the almost one million psychiatric casualties of World War II led to the view that it is "a normal and natural consequence of extended combat, staved off by some better than others only by virtue of supportive relationships to their unit and leaders."[39] Indeed, it is now believed that virtually all combatants will suffer it if they stay in combat long enough. Thus, the notion that "battle-hardened veterans" are inured to battle and inoculated from combat stress reaction is wrong; in a very real sense they are "fighting against the clock."

Cohesion Through Competition

Integrating combat units may limit the way that unit commanders can foster cohesion. Writing in the journal *Infantry*, Army Captain Thomas Greer described his approach to building cohesion in his rifle company in Korea. His goal was to prepare his men to be ready to provide "that extra 10 percent that will be required when the shots are for real."[40] Soldiers, he reasoned, are born competitors, and they need a sense of accomplishment. The device he chose was competition among various groups in a variety of "physically and mentally taxing" events. These included a physical-training test, a written test over information in field manuals, foot marches, and "combat runs" up a mountain in full gear that also included live-fire exercises. Enlisted men, NCOs, and officers all participated.

This was not just the self-esteem boosting so prevalent in the schools today—or even in basic training—in which everybody is a "winner." Instead, the competitions were designed to show the men "what it is like to give their all and still come up short," an experience that could "spark healthy discussion." Greer found that if the events were not hard enough, the soldiers would complain. He was sensitive to the fact that too much emphasis on competition could create dissension, and he attempted to ensure that everything was "kept in perspective and the rewards do not outshine the events."

Integration of women would probably adversely affect such competitions, which by their nature cannot be subject to different standards depending upon whether—and how many—women are in the various groups. How would a machine-gun crew feel about always coming in last because the woman takes 50 percent longer to complete the full-gear combat run, and how would that cause them to feel about military women? Finally, how much pressure would the company commander face to terminate the competition?

Cohesion Outside of the Infantry

Most of the writing on cohesion centers on infantry. There is less consensus about the relevance of cohesion in other contexts. Martin Binkin has argued that interdependence is most crucial, and therefore the need for bonding most prominent, in ground combat, but it is less important in air and naval combat, which, he says, "depend more on individual performance or are inherently less dangerous."[41] He acknowledges, however, that this is a contentious point.

Many students of the military do not believe that the need for cohesion is limited to the infantry. If rigorous training, shared dangers, and interdependence are key to the origins of cohesion and its necessity, there is little reason to think that its function would be so circumscribed. The high degree of interdependence and danger within aircraft crews and among members of a squadron, in tank and helicopter crews, and in many ship-board positions suggests that bonding may be critical in these positions as well. According to a report of the U.S. Army Research Institute for the Behavioral and Social Sciences, "Aircrews are typically small, experience high risks, and rely upon interdependent input from team members and the quality of this cohesive teamwork can determine mission success."[42] Although in many of these settings the possibility of individual retreat does not exist, the immobilization created by uncontrolled fear is always a danger, as the functional equivalent of cowering in a foxhole exists in virtually all combat settings.

In a remarkably courageous statement, given the political climate, twenty-one of twenty-three Navy Top Gun instructors signed a letter to the Presidential Commission opposing women in combat aviation. They asserted that they did not believe that the essential bonding could occur in the presence of women.[43] Among aviators, it was the Navy lieutenants and Marine captains—those whose lives are most clearly on the line—who most vehemently opposed sexual integration, a finding consistent with a report of the Center for Strategic and International Studies, which found greater concern about sexual integration among less senior personnel, whose lives are most directly imperiled by reductions in combat efficiency.[44]

The Ambivalent Findings of Social Science

Although the importance of cohesion to military performance has been, in the words of military psychologist Frederick Manning, "a staple of military doctrine for 2,500 years,"[45] the evidence from social science remains equivocal.[46] As one leading researcher on military cohesion put it, "There is little consensus concerning the who, what, where, when, how, and why of cohesion."[47]

Discussions of cohesion in the literature tend to fall into one of two categories: descriptions of an almost mystical force that is of central importance in combat, and descriptions of a dry sociological construct that is difficult to understand, let alone measure, and not obviously related to any particular outcome. Many students of the military—including military personnel, authors of combat memoirs, and some academics—tend toward the former view, while most social scientists seem inclined toward the latter.

Most sociological and psychological studies have been conducted on civilians (often college students), and those that have been conducted on military subjects have concentrated primarily on peacetime tasks. These studies have generally found that "social cohesion"—which is sometimes described as "interpersonal attraction"—is not positively correlated with group performance, while "task cohesion"—shared commitment to achieving goals—is correlated, albeit moderately, with performance.[48] Though no doubt ignorant of these studies, soldiers appear to be aware of the difference between these forms of interpersonal relationship, as soldiers in effective units often choose different colleagues for combat tasks than they select to accompany on leave.[49] Given the tendency of females to select their friends when picking teams for sports—rather than choosing the best player, as boys do[50]—that same tendency might not be true for women.

There is some question about the generalizability of most of the social-science literature to the combat setting. Social-science studies rejecting the relationship of performance and "social cohesion"[51]—defined as how much members of the group like each other and want to spend their social time together—are not measuring the kind of cohesion that military writers are describing. As Glenn Gray noted, "Comrades are loyal to each other spontaneously and without any need for reasons. Men may learn to be loyal . . . even to those they dislike."[52] Fredrick Manning and Terrence Fullerton argue that definitions of cohesion used in the social-science literature simply do not capture the concept of military importance.[53]

Difficulties in defining and measuring cohesion are hardly surprising given the limits of social science. Bonding among men is an emotional phenomenon, rather than a product of conscious thought, making it difficult to define and measure scientifically. It is no less real for being difficult to measure, however, any more than our inability to formulate a universally accepted definition of romantic love or a method for measuring it in a laboratory should cause us to question its importance, let alone its existence.

Whatever the formal definition of the concept, those who study men in battle nearly universally believe that the phenomenon exists in some form and is important to military effectiveness. This view is shared by military personnel, as most of them—not just members of combat units—believe that bonding, and specifically *male* bonding, is necessary for effective combat units.[54]

The Increasing Importance of Cohesion

As the technology of war develops, cohesion becomes more critical but also more difficult to achieve. In Napoleon's day, soldiers acted under the watchful eyes of their superiors, and they stood shoulder to shoulder with their comrades, drawing strength from their physical presence. Today, however, direct control of troops has become more difficult and soldiers operate more independently. Because the soldier is no longer bound to his job through strict discipline and drill, the military must, in the words of Darryl Henderson, "gain control of the individual soldier through the process of internalizing values and codes of behavior that cause the soldier to act as a reliable member of his unit in combat."[55] Urban warfare, such as that conducted in Iraq, negates some of the technological edge of modern armies and requires dispersal into small groups, magnifying the importance of the individual soldier and group cohesion. Indeed, according to retired Major General Robert Scales, "The isolation inherent in urban fighting . . . requires a degree of small-unit cohesion never before seen in the American military."[56]

Ironically, a feature of modern warfare that is often viewed as morale-enhancing can have adverse effects on cohesion. The easy communication between the war zone and home that is made possible by modern technology is a two-edged sword. Psychiatrist Peter Bourne found in his study of battle stress in Vietnam that frequent communication with the United States tended to de-emphasize the primary group as a source for dependence and emotional support.[57] A parachute officer who served in the Falklands War recalled that receiving mail from home was unsettling, because it reminded him that he had two personas: an expendable "cog in a military machine," and a husband and father upon whom a family depended.[58] He needed constantly to remind himself that his military role must remain dominant.

Although reassurance that everything is fine at home may sometimes enhance the soldiers' morale, soldiers may learn of petty problems in phone calls or e-mails that would never make it into a letter, or they may have unsatisfying exchanges because their families, though supportive, lack an understanding of what the soldier is going through. An unmarried infantryman who served in Iraq told me that he seldom called home, "because I didn't really want to think about home because I didn't want to get homesick." Although he served in an all-male unit, his observations on base led him to conclude that men and women react differently to events back home. As he said, "A lot of men find it really easy to dis-attach from the stuff at home but a lot of women don't. They have a hard time—a lot harder time—doing it, and they get caught up in the whole 'I'm away from home; I'm lost; I don't know what to do' thing." In a combat situation, he added, they "can't be thinking like that."

What About Women?

This chapter has often used the terms "soldiers" and "men" interchangeably, a rhetorical device that begs one of the central questions of this book—whether the same psychological processes that cause cohesive groups of men to form will operate the same, or at least as well, in forming mixed-sex groups. This book has already suggested a number of reasons for thinking they will not.

There are a few empirical studies of performance of sexually integrated noncombat units, which have produced inconsistent results. Psychologist Leora Rosen and colleagues have conducted a number of studies of cohesion, often finding some negative effects of integration. One study, based on 1988 data, found a significant negative correlation between the percentage of women in a group and cohesion of male junior enlisted men, but a study conducted in 1995 disclosed no such relationship.[59] A review of five separate studies—three on deployments in the Persian Gulf, Somalia, and Haiti, in addition to two garrison studies—found in four of the five studies that the more women in the unit, the lower the cohesion. The researchers concluded that "overall patterns indicate a consistent negative relationship" between the percentage of women and unit cohesion.[60] In the deployment studies, the negative impact of women correlated with the extent of physical danger. It was most pronounced in Somalia, where the risk of coming under fire was greatest; only moderate in the Persian Gulf, where the risk was somewhat less; and neutral to mildly positive in Haiti, where the risk was virtually nil.

Rosen and colleagues found that the dynamics of cohesion differ between the field and garrison. They found that increased time in the field was positively correlated with "group hypermasculinity"—defined as "expressions of extreme, exaggerated, or stereotypic masculine attributes and behaviors"—in both all-male groups and mixed-sex groups.[61] In mixed-sex groups, field duty time was associated with *decreased* acceptance of women. The researchers attributed this association to the fact that the field environment "is likely to emphasize 'warrior' values of toughness, independence, and aggression." In male-only groups, hypermasculinity was associated with both increased vertical and horizontal cohesion and readiness. They concluded that military effectiveness was positively associated with a culture of hypermasculinity and that "ungendered professionalism," which has positive effects in the garrison environment, "may be difficult to maintain in the field where a warrior culture is likely to develop, a culture that may be necessary for the successful accomplishment of the mission."

A GAO (General Accounting Office, now Government Accountability Office) study of the performance of women in the Gulf War found that a sizeable minority expressed the view that women did not perform as well as men. Overall, however, it noted that comments in focus groups were "notably positive," not surprising in an environment where expressing negative feelings can be career-threatening if not career-terminating. Use of focus groups reduces the likelihood of adverse reports about women, because, as Laura Miller found in her study of attitudes of Army personnel, many men do not feel free to give candid answers.[62] Many women are probably also reluctant to report negative opinions, less because they fear discipline, as the men do, than because of peer pressure from those who would view them as "traitors to their sex."

The Center for Strategic and International Studies also reported fairly negative conclusions about sexual integration.[63] It found "significant perception problems" about the performance of female personnel and expressed surprise that a significant percentage of women admitted skepticism about the performance of female service personnel. The study also reported that focus group discussions revealed more concern about female job performance and the impact of sexual integration on unit cohesion than many prior studies had suggested.

The 1997 RAND study by anthropologist Margaret Harrell and sociologist Laura Miller found that "gender integration is perceived to have a relatively small effect on readiness, cohesion, and morale in the units we studied,"[64] although such effect as was found was negative. That report minimized the effects of sexual integration by attributing the problems it found to "leadership" or "training" rather than to integration itself. The study's attribution of problems to these other influences illustrates a form of sleight of hand by which any problem can be redefined as something other than what it really is.

Men's Objection to Female Combat Comrades Runs Very Deep

Men's objection to female combat comrades is strong and widespread. Polls of military personnel demonstrate substantial opposition to women in combat, with varying views depending upon branch and combat arm. The Presidential Commission reported that across all services, 69 percent of men in air combat units opposed allowing women to enter those units.[65] The commission's survey of retired generals and admirals revealed that between 76 percent and 90 percent opposed the assignment of women to the different combat specialties. I spoke with a Marine platoon commander who had done a survey of his Marine Reserve infantry company for a course he was taking. He found that 89 percent of the approximately two hundred men opposed the opening of ground combat to women.

Many poll results reflect a kind of parochialism, with respondents reporting more favorable attitudes toward integration of arms other than their own. For example, more Navy personnel, both male and female, believe that women should be excluded from submarines than believe that they should be excluded from infantry. With Marines, the pattern is just the opposite, with more Marines of both sexes believing that women should be excluded from infantry than believing they should be excluded from submarines.[66] The more familiar individuals are with the duties of a particular combat arm, it seems, the less inclined they are to believe that women should participate.

Similarly, service members who have served in infantry, armor, and artillery are more opposed to inclusion of women in ground-combat arms than those who have not.[67] Even in the Air Force, the service with the most women, a third of male pilots expressed the view that women should not fly in combat, their primary concerns being that women would destroy unit cohesion, that they are more emotional and less aggressive than men, and that they are a distraction to male aircrew members.[68]

Reported statistics may understate men's opposition. Laura Miller found that most of the men who favored opening combat roles to women on the same terms as men favored it only because they believed that women would fail. These men, whom Miller labeled "hostile proponents" of women in combat, also believed that inclusion and ultimate failure of women was necessary to obtain closure on the issue.[69]

Resistance to women in combat does not necessarily reflect opposition to women in the military more generally. Many men who are favorably inclined toward working with women in noncombat units nonetheless believe that women should not serve in combat.[70] Most men I spoke with who expressed negative attitudes toward women in combat—and that was most of the men I interviewed—also expressed positive views of women in noncombat positions. Thus, it is inaccurate to attribute men's opposition to misogynistic attitudes.

Even if a majority of men can be convinced that inclusion of women in combat units is a good thing, cohesion and morale are not decided by majority vote. If a bare majority thinks there is not a morale problem, and a substantial minority thinks there is, the minority is right. In a study of the attitudes of male pilots toward women as fighter pilots, Patricia Shields and her colleagues acknowledged that "male pilot acceptance of women as fighter pilots is important if women are to become members and leaders of effective fighter squadrons."[71] They then reported that their survey of male pilots "indicates indecision, or at worst marginal disagreement," about female integration. In their survey, however, the most common response was "strongly disagree" with integration. If half of a group strongly favors integration and half is strongly opposed, the numbers do not indicate neutrality. Instead, they show substantial opposition, which in the context of combat suggests substantial risk.

BEYOND THE QUESTION of men's willingness to accept female comrades in arms is an even more difficult question. Will men be willing to be led into combat by a woman? As we will see in the next chapter, acceptance of women as combat leaders would require overcoming substantial obstacles.

12

Who Men Follow:

Leadership and Followership in Combat

The test of a leader lies in the reaction and response of his followers. . . . He must make his influence felt by example and the instillment of confidence in his followers. . . . His worth as a leader is measured by the achievements of the led. This is the ultimate test of his effectiveness.

—General Omar N. Bradley[1]

June 4, 1945: Oroku Peninsula, Okinawa. William Manchester, a twenty-three-year-old sergeant with the Sixth Marine Division, has just come ashore and is pinned down with his men behind a seawall. A lieutenant newly assigned to the platoon proclaims that he is going to take the men "over the top" and conduct a frontal assault against the enemy. Manchester tells him that they must wait until units on the Japanese flank take out the Japanese machine guns and that if the lieutenant orders the men to follow him, they will not obey. "You're not on some fucking parade ground," Manchester tells him, "You can't just pump your fist up and down and expect the men to spring up."

Undaunted, the lieutenant orders the men to follow him over the wall. Despite the lieutenant's rank, the men remain in place. He then jumps atop the wall, breathes deeply, and yells, "Follow me!" No one moves, except for the Japanese machine gunner who stitches the lieutenant "from forehead to crotch."[2]

THE FOUNDATION OF military discipline is that leaders lead and followers follow. It is erroneous to assume, however, that leadership follows as a matter of course from the command structure. Leadership, under this misguided view, means no more than that superiors issue orders and subordinates follow them; it's as simple as that. In fact, subordinates follow orders only some of the time, and it is not easy to get them to follow certain orders, especially ones likely to result in their deaths. Combat leadership requires, as Manchester's experience revealed, something more than brass bits on one's collar.

The kind of leadership discussed in this chapter is intentionally quite narrow. It does not include leadership in the civilian world or even throughout the military. Rather, it focuses exclusively on leadership in actual combat. Much of the military—to a greater or lesser extent—may parallel the civilian world more than it does the world of combat, especially in peacetime. Even in time of war, only a small but crucial part of the military is at the "sharp end of the spear." It is that small part to which this discussion pertains.

S. L. A. Marshall observed that "the qualifying test of an officer is the judgment placed upon his soldierly abilities by those who serve under him," and if they "do not deem him fit to command, he cannot train them to obey." Combat leadership depends critically upon personality and is not something that simply inheres in a "role" into which one is slotted.[3] Indeed, in the heat of combat, leadership may emerge independent of rank. As one veteran of the North African campaign in World War II told interviewers, "men turn to the officer for leadership, and if he doesn't give it to them then they look to the strongest personality who steps forward and becomes a leader—maybe a staff sergeant if the platoon leader is a weak leader." In the aftermath of the attack on the USS *Cole*, the ship's executive officer noted that junior sailors were actually leading their seniors "just by the force of their personality and their background."[4]

The Varieties of Leader Power

Combat leaders can call upon a number of bases of power, to greater or lesser effect. They can exact compliance through punishment and reward. They can also obtain compliance using "expert power," whereby the soldier complies with the leader's orders because the leader is perceived as having superior knowledge and ability. The most effective form of power for a combat leader, however, is "referent power," which depends upon the soldier's intense identification with a respected leader. In Darryl Henderson's words,

"The leader approaches the stature of beloved and respected parent or of the charismatic leader who demonstrates consistently the Weberian quality of 'Grace,' or the ability to consistently handle difficult situations well."[5]

"Followership" behavior, at least in dangerous contexts, rests to a large extent on an emotional bond with the leader—sometimes called "hierarchical" or "vertical" cohesion, in contrast to the "horizontal" cohesion of compatriots—rather than the mere fact that the follower is, say, a corporal and the platoon leader is a second lieutenant.[6] Successful combat leaders, as opposed to simple managers, evoke the followership of their subordinates; they do not simply command it. James Calvert—then executive officer of a World War II submarine, later rising to command of the Pacific fleet—recognized this quality in his submarine's cook and took the unprecedented step of naming him Chief of the Boat, the top warrant officer on the submarine. As Calvert recalled in his memoirs, "Watson had that magical ingredient called *leadership ability,* which is so hard to define and yet so immediately recognizable."[7]

A striking pattern in combat memoirs is the reverence that many of the authors felt for their commanding officers. Eugene Sledge reflected on his company commander, Marine Captain Andy "Ack Ack" Haldane:

> Although he insisted on strict discipline, the captain was a quiet man who gave orders without shouting. He had a rare combination of intelligence, courage, self-confidence, and compassion that commanded our respect and admiration. We were thankful that Ack Ack was our skipper, felt more secure in it, and felt sorry for other companies not so fortunate. While some officers on Pavuvu thought it necessary to strut or order us around to impress us with their status, Haldane quietly told us what to do. We loved him for it and did the best job we knew how.[8]

When Haldane was later killed on Peleliu, his men were devastated. His death "was like losing a parent we depended upon for security—not our physical security, because we knew that was a commodity beyond our reach in combat, but our mental security." Although Haldane was apparently a remarkable man, he was one of many such men who have led their troops and earned, in the process, their lasting devotion.

Sledge's invocation of the parental role for a commander is a common image. If combat soldiers are "brothers," the combat leader is a "father" even if he is no older—and sometimes even younger—than the men he leads. He is an authoritarian figure to whom the soldier looks for leadership and protection, and he becomes the "old man," even though he may be in his twenties. As Roy Grinker and John Spiegel observed in their study of World War II aircrews, "whether he is a good or bad father is reflected in the morale of the unit."[9]

Leadership and Risk-Taking

Willingness to expose oneself to danger is a critical attribute of effective combat leaders, although, as William Manchester's lieutenant demonstrated, it is not a sufficient one. The effective leader is one who leads by example—one who says "Follow me" and then shares equitably the risk of death. As military analyst James Dunnigan has observed, "Officers who stay to the rear find their troops following them in that direction, also."[10] There must be no question about the leader's courage because such questions weaken the identification of the follower with the leader and disincline him to risk his own life.[11] According to Darryl Henderson, "Leaders of front-line units must be viewed as 'men of steel' professionally equal to meeting all tasks demanded by the situation."[12]

Bravery of commanders is widely recognized as inspirational to their men. Philip Caputo recounted the awe in which he held Marine General Lew Walt, recipient of three Navy Crosses and one of the few generals, Caputo believed, who considered it his job to lead from the front "and not from a cushy command post so far removed from the action that it was almost desertion." Many successful generals recognize the confidence that exposing themselves to danger engenders in their troops. George S. Patton, as Victor Davis Hanson has noted, "deliberately exposed himself to hostile fire to create élan among his troops—and reassure himself that he had not lost his nerve."[13] This attribute of combat leadership is required up the chain of command, from squad leaders to general officers.

Philosopher Glenn Gray vividly described the positive effect that coolness in the face of danger can have on those who observe it. Recalling his amphibious landing in southern France, he described the gratitude he felt toward a captain who was standing by the edge of the landing craft calmly smoking a cigarette as Gray hid under his jeep. Gray said that he "longed to creep through the gear, clasp him around the knees, and look up to him worshipfully."[14]

Sex and Leadership

In prior chapters, we have considered whether women can join the "band of brothers" without impairing its effectiveness. When women are included, does it become a "band of brothers and sisters" or does it remain a band of brothers that includes women who play the role of brother? There is another question, perhaps even more difficult, and that is whether this band, however characterized, can be *led* by a woman.

Many women have proven themselves effective leaders in the civilian sector, but military leadership—specifically, combat leadership—calls for a somewhat different set of attributes. For example, although physical fitness is not generally perceived as an important attribute in civilian leaders, it is a significant predictor of both attainment of leadership positions and effectiveness of leadership in the military.[15] Likewise, the personality trait of dominance—which men tend to display more than women—is an important predictor of military leadership. Unlike in most civilian settings, the combat leader must be prepared to lead his subordinates in situations where the likelihood of death is very real.

If the combat leader is the "father," what is the role of the female combat leader? A mother, a female father, an androgynous "parent," a big sister? None of these roles seems to work. If the power of the leader comes from the soldier's identification with him, there is reason to doubt that a woman can instill the same feelings in combat soldiers who, regardless of policies on sexual integration, will continue to be mostly men. Put bluntly, would a young man, trying to prove his manhood, be as likely to follow a woman into combat as he would to follow a man?

Sex Differences in Leadership

In at least some contexts, women may not evoke followership behavior (in either men or women) to the same extent that men do.[16] As we will see in the next chapter, even in early childhood, girls find it difficult to influence boys. In the civilian sector, women supervisors are usually trusted less by both men and women, and both sexes tend to prefer male supervisors to female supervisors, with women's preference for a male supervisor often being stronger than men's.[17] Both male and female subordinates have a more negative reaction to imposition of discipline by female superiors than by male superiors.[18]

Men and women in military training associate men with leaderlike qualities, such as leadership, self-confidence, dedication, and physical fitness.[19] Although having experience being led by female commanders might be expected to change the masculine stereotyping of military leadership, in fact the opposite seems to occur. A recent study at the Air Force Academy found that increased experience and seniority actually seem to increase stereotyping.[20]

Studies of leadership have found substantial sex differences. Men tend to emerge more frequently in initially leaderless groups when leadership is defined by contribution to the group's task, while women tended to emerge more frequently as "social leaders."[21] Men are especially likely to emerge as leaders for masculine-typed tasks. Military tasks are, of course, quintessentially "masculine" tasks. Even though military groups tend to be the diametric opposite of leaderless given the clearly understood hierarchy of formal rank, it must be remembered that when the designated leader is weak, leadership can emerge independent of rank.

Men and women often exhibit different leadership styles. Men are more likely to adopt an autocratic or directive style and women a more democratic or participatory style.[22] That tendency is weakened in settings that are highly male dominated, where women may adopt the more "masculine" leadership style. Yet psychologist Alice Eagly and her colleagues have found that although men and women tend to be evaluated equally favorably when they adopt a democratic style of leadership, women who adopt an authoritarian style of leadership tend to be devalued as leaders. As Eagly and Linda Carli have reported, "behaviors that convey dominance, negative assertion, self promotion, or a lack of warmth conflict with the communal demands of the female gender role and therefore interfere with female influence."[23]

Military women may be in a bind. The leadership role calls for an authoritarian style, but when women act accordingly, they tend to be negatively evaluated and therefore less effective. Reconstructing combat leadership in a more democratic form is not an option, as authoritarian leadership can be critical to primary groups operating in situations that bring forth needs for "paternal protection." As sociologist Edward Shils—who served in the Psychological Warfare Division during World War II—suggested, "Primary-group solidarity might well be disintegrated by democratic leadership."[24]

Sex Bias in Evaluation of Military Leadership?

Women tend not to be perceived by men (and often even by women) as military leaders, and this perception is not simply based on "sexist attitudes." Even men who profess egalitarian views, for example, often display visible signs of negative feelings toward female leaders.[25]

Perceptions of a lack of leadership on the part of women have led the service academies to alter their leadership evaluations. Prior to introduction of women into the Naval Academy in 1976, an important source of leadership ratings for midshipmen was ratings by peers. These peer ratings were thought to be important measures of leadership potential. Indeed, studies on the Israeli Defense Forces found that peers are often better judges of leadership ability than are superiors.[26] Nonetheless, after women were admitted to Annapolis, peer ratings were discontinued because women consistently received lower ratings than men.[27] This change lost to the Academy an important source of input on leadership ability.

The experience at Annapolis (as well as at West Point, which went through a similar experience[28]) is subject to varying interpretations. Men may have simply resented their female peers and rated them unfairly, although it is not clear exactly what an "unfair rating" means. Does it mean that men rated women as being low in leadership ability even though they knew the women were good leaders, or does it mean that the men rated women as low in leadership ability because they would have been reluctant to follow them even if the women displayed the same leadership behaviors that a highly rated male midshipman would display? The former would clearly be an unfair (and inaccurate) rating; the latter would be an accurate rating even if it is in some sense "unfair" that women are rated poorly even if they engage in the same behaviors as highly rated men. It could be viewed as equally unfair—as well as immeasurably more hazardous to life, limb, and mission success—if women are rated high in leadership ability because they display the same behaviors as successful male leaders even if men are not willing to follow them.

This is not just a semantic difference. Leadership entails more than objectively measurable skills and behaviors; it involves a number of intangibles—most important, the ability to evoke followership behavior in others. The quotation at the outset of the chapter from Omar Bradley—field commander of the American Army in northwestern Europe in 1944–

1945—makes the central point: the measure of a leader lies not in the leader's behavior but in the behavior of his subordinates. If potential followers will not follow a leader for whatever reason, the leader cannot be effective. Whether blame is assigned to the failed follower or the failed leader is immaterial. If the mission is not being accomplished, the unit is ineffective.

Recent Incidents in the Integrated Military

A couple of widely publicized incidents in the current conflict in Iraq arguably raise questions about female leadership. The first involved the refusal of a mixed-sex platoon of truck drivers to follow a direct order to drive a convoy to deliver fuel, because it was a "suicide mission" (see chapter 9). The company commander was a woman, and she was relieved of command, much to the apparent delight of a number of her subordinates, although there were conflicting reports about whether the move was "voluntary" or disciplinary.[29]

The second incident involved the well-known abuse of detainees at Abu Ghraib prison in Iraq. A number of soldiers in a military-police battalion participated in the sexual humiliation of detainees, and the involvement of women in the abuse was a widely discussed feature of the scandal.[30] A lack of leadership among lower-level enlisted personnel is not surprising, but their activities may be a reflection of the leadership of their brigade commander, who was a female general.

Brigadier General Janis Karpinski was the commander of the 800th Military Police Brigade, which was responsible for detention facilities in Iraq, including Abu Ghraib prison. Investigations revealed that her command was essentially dysfunctional in terms of supervision and training and that she seldom visited the prison. She was relieved of her command and demoted to colonel.[31]

Karpinski contended that she was blamed because of her sex and because she was a reserve officer. Others believed that if her sex played any role in the events, it was in her being selected for the initial assignment.[32] Where the exact truth lies is difficult to determine. There can be little doubt, however, that she was an ineffective leader. Notwithstanding lengthy investigations and reports detailing her command failings, she told the *Times* of London, "I don't know what I could have done differently" and told the BBC that she was a "convenient scapegoat."[33] Her willingness to point the finger of blame at everyone but herself—both up and down the chain of command, to both the domestic and foreign press[34]—provides ample support for the finding that she was an ineffective commander.

After her demotion, Karpinski's conduct eliminated any benefit of the doubt that even the most charitable people might have given her. "Testifying" before the self-appointed Commission of Inquiry for Crimes against Humanity Committed by the Bush Administration, Karpinski asserted that Lieutenant General Ricardo Sanchez, commander of coalition ground forces in Iraq, had orchestrated a cover-up of the deaths of female soldiers.[35] Several women, Karpinski claimed, had died of dehydration in their sleep because they were unwilling to drink liquids late in the day out of fear that they would be raped on the way to the latrine at night. According to Karpsinki, Sanchez's top deputy had demanded in 2003 that the death certificate of a female master sergeant be altered because it had listed "dehydration" as the cause of death.

If this story were true, it would be the strongest argument yet for excluding women from combat, if not from the military altogether. It is such a fanciful tale, however, that only someone whose hatred of the military (or contempt for women) had completely blinded him to reason could credit it for even a moment. Death from dehydration, even in desert heat, takes longer than "overnight," particularly if the affected individuals can drink all they want during the day. Moreover, a number of ways to avoid being attacked on the way to the latrine seem rather obvious. One would be to urinate in a container, such as a widemouthed water bottle; even if it is a little bit messy and against the rules, it beats dying. Another would be to go to the latrine armed; soldiers are, after all, issued weapons. Another would be for female soldiers to go to the latrine in groups, a behavior hardly unheard of even in civilian circles.

The story also implies a broad conspiracy, involving far more than just top leaders. These women have superiors and male friends, but everyone was supposedly too cowed to say anything as their female comrades dropped like desiccated flies. Moreover, master sergeant is almost the highest-ranking NCO in the Army. One does not achieve that rank without being able to do some fairly sophisticated problem-solving and without a substantial amount of self-confidence. As it turns out, no female master sergeants died in Iraq in 2003.[36] In sum, Karpinski's story gives one far more faith in the military's disciplinary process than it does in its promotion process.

Any linkage between these incidents and sex must necessarily be speculative. Were the truck drivers who refused to deliver fuel emboldened by the fact that their company commander was a woman? Were the MPs at Abu Ghraib less disciplined because their brigade commander was a woman? Was Janice Karpinski promoted to general based upon her sex rather than her qualifications? Was her lack of leadership related to her sex? These questions are worthy of more attention than they have received.

If these incidents were reflections of bad leadership, as they appear to be, it must also be noted that there is no shortage of bad male leaders. It is therefore unfair to suggest that these incidents are necessarily representative of women. However, proponents of women in combat have no problem at all with taking anecdotes of good performance by women and generalizing to all women. What is needed is reliable information about where the "center of gravity" lies.

Military Leadership: Can It Be Taught?

This question was posed by General Maxwell Taylor, whose service record included command of the 101st Airborne Division in World War II, as well as service as Commander in Chief, Far East, during the Korean War, and later as Chairman of the Joint Chiefs of Staff.[37] He expressed doubt that the essential inspirational qualities were teachable, although some relevant skills, such as communication, are.

A large industry of leadership trainers challenges the common belief that "leaders are born and not made." Even if leadership qualities are innate, there is plenty of room for training to bring out the best in natural leaders. The U.S. military probably devotes more resources to leadership training than any other organization in human history, yet it does not provide such training at random. Instead, it focuses that training on individuals who are thought to possess leadership potential.

True combat leadership (or the lack thereof) becomes apparent only when the shooting starts.[38] After the fighting began on Guadalcanal in 1942, a regimental commander expressed the view that his greatest problem was weak leaders. "The good leaders seem to get killed," he complained, and "the poor leaders get the men killed." "If you can find out who the good patrol leaders are before you hit the combat zone," he said, "you have found out something."[39]

Military "leadership" and "command" are not the same thing as "management."[40] Even in the civilian sector, as organizational behavior researcher Nigel Nicholson has observed, "the most important attribute for leadership is the desire to lead." While "managerial skills and competencies can be trained into a person," he says, "the passion to run an organization cannot."[41] This observation is even more true of the passion to lead men into combat.

Canadian venture capitalist Brent Holliday captured the essence of the problem facing people in leadership positions where they do not belong:

> Here's the thing about being a leader. . . . Your employees have a small neural connection from their nose to their brain that never, ever fails. They can smell it when you are not a leader. Independently at first, then in small groups in the hallways, employees have a basic instinctual capability to ferret out those who are merely trying tactics from the latest book and those who can truly lead. It's not that they can do better in most cases. Oftentimes they cannot articulate what a person is doing right or wrong. It's just that there is near universality in identifying and rallying around born leaders.[42]

Holliday laments (tongue in cheek) the failure so far to develop a blood test for the leadership gene, which would result in the saving of "tons of money and tons of anguish" squandered by "those who try to lead but fail miserably at it."

The sensitivity of those around the water cooler to weak business leaders is nothing compared to the sensitivity of combat troops to weak military leaders. A weak civilian leader may cause reduced profits and ultimately the loss of jobs, but the followers' reaction may just be scorn or apathy. A weak combat leader is likely to cause the death of his men, and those exposed to death are often exquisitely sensitive to the vulnerability created by their leaders' weaknesses.

SOME MEN ARE born to lead in combat, but most are not. Perhaps some women are also born to lead in combat. It remains an open question—subject to substantial doubt—how many women actually are. It is equally open to doubt how many men are born to *follow* women into combat.

13

The Evolved Nature of Male Bonding:
Is Men's Aversion to Female Comrades in Arms Intractable?

I couldn't think of a logical reason, a logical argument, for defending a policy of excluding women from combat assignments [but] I haven't changed my mind. . . . I still think it is not a good idea for me to have to order women into combat. . . . So I take some solace here in thinking that not all human problems yield to strict logic. There are other factors, human factors, and some judgment here. The fact that my position doesn't really meet everybody's strict evidence standards for logic doesn't bother me all that much.

—General Merrill McPeak[1]

The suggestion that integration of women into combat positions compromises military readiness is usually dismissed as being—if true at all—true only in the transition period until "male attitudes" are fully "adjusted." The assumption seems to be that these negative "attitudes" toward female comrades (or leaders) operate at a cognitive level, so that through education and proper leadership they will disappear. However, if these "attitudes" actually reflect deeply rooted predispositions, the period of transition may never end.

All-male groups are common throughout the world—whether secret societies, warrior groups, street gangs, or college fraternities. They are often involved with the use of force, which is virtually a male monopoly. In his seminal work *Men in Groups*, Lionel Tiger suggested that exclusion of women reflects not simply "formalized hostility" to them but in part a "positive valence" between men. He argued that men tend to bond most strongly in situations involving power, force, and dangerous work, and they consciously and emotionally exclude females from these groups.[2] An evolved tendency to exclude women from such groups would suggest that men's discomfort with female comrades and leaders may be an enduring feature of an integrated military.

Same-Sex Groups in Children

Even in early childhood, boys and girls are seldom indifferent to the sex of their playmates. By the time they are between three and four, most of their interactions are with others of the same sex. As children age, the tendency toward same-sex play increases. The more choice children have in selecting their playmates—as in schools, where there are large numbers of children—the more sex segregation will occur.[3] Psychologist Eleanor Maccoby has suggested that the aversion that girls have to playing with boys results from the difficulty girls have influencing them. Like boys, girls are more influenced by same-sex feedback than opposite-sex feedback, but the tendency among girls is not as strong.[4]

BOYS' GROUPS ARE LARGER AND MORE HIERARCHICAL

The characteristic size of same-sex groups differs between the sexes, as boys' groups tend to be considerably larger than those of girls. Referring to groups of girls, Anne Campbell notes that "groups that do form are likely to be cliquish (exclusive, intimate, intense) and small (usually pairs or threesomes)."[5]

The internal structure of groups also differs by sex. Boys establish relatively clear and stable dominance hierarchies; that is, they largely agree about who is on top, and these rankings tend to persist over time. Boys' hierarchies emerge quickly, often during their first interaction. The central determinant of dominance in these groups is "toughness"—both physical strength and unwillingness to back down.[6] Dominance hierarchies among girls, by contrast, are less clear and less stable, and there is considerably less agreement concerning the rankings of individual girls. Status among girls, at least among older children, tends to be linked to physical attractiveness and friendship with popular girls. Girls' groups are considerably more egalitarian in orientation than those of boys.[7]

BOYS AND GIRLS ENGAGE IN DIFFERENT KINDS OF PLAY

Not surprisingly, in their largely sex-segregated groups, the play of boys and girls is typically different. Boys tend to engage in more rough-and-tumble play than girls, to play in more public spaces, and to play (and roam) farther from the watchful eyes of adults. Although children of both sexes "police" the cross-sex behavior of other children, boys who play with girls and with girls' toys are subject to much harsher peer penalties than are girls who engage in cross-sex activities. The preference of boys for same-sex comrades increases the farther they roam from home. Once two or more groups of boys form, they typically engage each other in some kind of competition.[8]

In contrast to boys, girls' play involves much less role specialization and less coordination of activities, and girls spend considerably more time talking about problems and providing emotional support, activities that can occur only in very small groups. Boys are also more likely to engage in activities initiated by their peer group, while girls are more likely to select activities that are structured by adults. This tendency is reflected in the common tendency of males to organize spontaneous "pick up" team games, while female sports participation is much more heavily weighted toward organized leagues.[9]

Boys find participation in all-male groups to be an emotionally rewarding experience. As psychologists Carol Martin and Richard Fabes report from their study of preschool children:

> The more boys played with other boys, the more positive emotions they were observed to express over time. Thus, although play among boys is rough and dominance oriented, boys appear to find this active type of play increasingly interesting and compelling. . . . That many boys find this type of interaction pleasing and exciting is consistent with other research suggesting that boys respond with aroused interest and a matching response when another boy makes a bid to initiate rough play, whereas girls do not.[10]

In short, there is something about this rough same-sex play that is deeply satisfying to boys.

Dynamics in Groups of Children and Adults

Strong parallels exist between groups of children and adults that may have implications for sexual integration of combat groups. Males exhibit a lower threshold for forming cooperative relationships than females, and relationships among males are maintainable with a lower level of investment. Competition within the group tends to be a very different experience for males and females, and the sexes differ substantially in the effect of conflict on group stability.

FOR MALES, COMPETITION AND COOPERATION ARE MORE COMPATIBLE

It is frequently asserted that men's tendency toward competition and women's tendency toward cooperation make women more effective in groups, but data do not support that assertion.[11] Competition can either enhance group effectiveness or impair it, depending upon the composition of the group.

When men come together, there is, to be sure, a period in which jockeying for status occurs until the hierarchy gets worked out, but once it does—and it usually happens relatively quickly—the groups tend to function effectively in competition with other groups. As Eleanor Maccoby has noted, "Among boys, cooperation and competition are by no means antithetical, but are woven into the same web of social relationships."[12] She notes that even among friends, "boys take pleasure in competing to see who can do a task best or quickest, who can lift the heaviest weight, who can run faster or farther." A substantial portion of free-play activities among grade-school boys involves direct competition with other boys, while among girls direct competition is almost entirely absent.

For girls, competition with friends is often a negative emotional experience, probably because of their more egalitarian nature. Psychologists Joyce Benenson and Joy Schinazi found that girls react negatively to outperforming their friends. They often believe that their friends will think less of them if they outperform them, and they may also anticipate that another girl would not make a good friend if the girl has already achieved more. Boys, in contrast, actively seek out same-sex peers of higher status.

Benenson and Schinazi suggest that their results may shed light on some otherwise perplexing behavior of women at work—the difficulty women have "in forming hierarchical relationships with other women." As they note, across a variety of professions, men and women both report that "women are the first to attack a woman who gets promoted."[13] A recent study confirmed this suggestion, finding that women are more likely than men to view female candidates as less qualified than male candidates, to predict poor performance from them, and to be prejudiced against the idea of a female leader, a phenomenon sometimes labeled the Queen Bee syndrome.[14] Benenson and Schinazi suggest that women's more democratic leadership style may derive from a preference for egalitarian outcomes. "Females expect equality in their relationships," they argue, "whereas males are more comfortable with hierarchies." One consequence is that men's friendships are not as vulnerable to disruption by one friend's success.

Benenson and Schinazi's analysis may have implications for the military, a most hierarchical organization. Women's greater egalitarian tendencies may make them resentful of a hierarchy that automatically places some individuals above others. Men, on the other hand, having grown up in more hierarchical groups—and being more accepting of hierarchy—may find military organizations more immediately congenial. The female resistance to hierarchy was on display in a female sergeant's complaint in Iraq: "Some things we do are very degrading to women, like cleaning the [excrement] and digging foxholes. Sometimes women do the hard work and men sit around flossing because they have rank on us. I don't like disrespect, like the way males talk to you when they outrank you. That ticks me off."[15] In contrast, men are more likely to understand on an intuitive level that "shit runs downhill" and to view the fact that "rank has its privileges" as a motivation for promotion rather than as a basis for resentment.

Other anecdotal accounts also suggest that women do not respect the hierarchy to the extent that men do, even low-ranking men. An Army enlisted man told me that when a new female private comes into the unit, she will often start chatting casually with male officers. If an NCO observed a male private doing that, the soldier told me, the private would be quickly reminded that one salutes smartly and avoids familiarity with officers, and the lesson would likely be reinforced by an order to drop and do push-ups.

If the sexes differ in their responses to hierarchy, the military should take special care in ensuring that women understand the reasons for it.[16] Hierarchy is essential to the operation of the military, and a failure to accept its legitimacy could have grave consequences in dangerous situations.

MALE GROUPS CAN TOLERATE MORE CONFLICT THAN FEMALE GROUPS

Despite the greater conflict that occurs in boys' groups, conflict is less disruptive to relationships than it is in girls' groups. In a well-known study of childhood play, Janet Lever found that when boys played games, there were repeated disputes over the rules. Nonetheless, none of the games she observed were terminated because of these disputes. Indeed, she reported, the boys seemed to enjoy the rule disputes as much as they enjoyed the game. When girls quarreled over the rules, however, the games were likely to terminate, perhaps foreshadowing what primatologist Sarah Hrdy has referred to as "the well documented problem that unrelated women have working together over a long period of time."[17]

Males and females tend to have very different ways of dealing with conflict. As anthropologist Helen Fisher writes: "Because women generally seek consensus and harmony with those around them, they have much more difficulty working with people they dislike or disagree with. Women, more than men, tend to distance themselves from their rivals. Men, for example, will join one another for a drink after a divisive meeting in the office; women flee." Fisher notes that women are more likely to remember slights and to become visibly upset, including crying, when people disagree with them. Men shrug off verbal attacks and move on. "Not women," Fisher adds. "Women hold grudges." When women feel snubbed, they will often stop talking to the source of their offense, while men are more likely to confront the offender directly.[18]

Kayla Williams provides an unattractive example of this dynamic. She did not like her superior, a female staff sergeant, and described an episode with her in Iraq as follows:

> We didn't speak for days, except when absolutely required. And when we did speak, I would not stand at ease with her even at her order. I told her: "Sergeant, I believe it is more appropriate for me to maintain military bearing with you at all times." There was nothing she could do about it. I was demonstrating that I would respect her rank, but that was all—the ultimate show of disrespect. When she tried to open a conversation about my attitude, I shut it down. I knew that I could not be faulted for my bearing, since it was completely correct.[19]

Williams also describes, somewhat triumphantly, a later incident in which she caused the sergeant to cry.

From childhood, friendships among males are more resistant to termination because of conflict.[20] This greater resilience is probably due to the phenomenon described by Fisher. Females are more likely to hold a grudge, whereas males are more likely to reconcile using joking and other tactics.[21] The direct confrontation mode of males is more likely to result in reconciliation than the shunning and ostracism used by females. It is difficult for two people to make up when they refuse to speak to each other.

David Geary and Mark Flinn have suggested that males' greater tolerance for conflict is related to the larger groups in which they operate.[22] Such tolerance is necessary, they argue; otherwise their large coalitions, within which competition for dominance occurs, could not survive.

Evolutionary Origins of Male Coalitions

What might have caused an evolved tendency of males to aggregate in same-sex coalitions characterized by clear dominance hierarchies? The answer seems to lie, at least in part, in the sexual division of labor. A universal feature of human societies is the division of labor by sex.[23] All societies have recognized separate dimensions of "men's work" and "women's work," although the content of the categories varies by culture.[24] Some divisions are relatively constant, however, so that big-game hunting and warfare are virtually everywhere the domain of men.[25]

In our evolutionary past, as now, male-male coalitions were probably associated with resources best obtained or protected by groups of individuals.[26] Dominance hierarchies mute conflict within groups, because once individuals know their place in it, competition subsides (at least until the next revolution).[27] Ancestral men tended to cooperate with male relatives and nonrelatives at times and compete with them at other times, resulting in relatively fluid coalitions.[28] Women, in contrast, often worked with sisters and cowives in groups that were seldom powerful outside the domestic sphere, so that evolutionary pressures to develop a strong and specialized coalitional psychology were weaker.[29]

The taking-things-personally and grudge-holding that Helen Fisher has identified as core characteristics of female conflict would have been supremely maladaptive in males. The aggregation of men in large groups—and their shifting coalitions—would be impossible in groups composed of men who bear grudges and refuse to speak to each other (let alone cooperate). Fisher notes that we share this sex difference in grudge-holding with our chimpanzee cousins, as "female chimpanzees also nurse their grievances [whereas] male chimps tend to make peace with one another within hours after a fight."[30]

EVOLUTIONARY PRESSURES HAVE AFFECTED MEN'S PREFERENCES IN COMRADES

Lionel Tiger argued that male-male bonds are of the same biological order for defensive, food-gathering, and social-order-maintenance purposes as the male-female bond is for reproductive purposes.[31] The suggestion that men's choice of comrades is analogous to their choices of mates may seem bold initially but on reflection is rather unsurprising. Selection of associates for dangerous activities can strongly affect one's reproductive prospects. Just as the reproductive consequences of mate choice have led to men's innate biases in mate selection, the survival consequences of choice of comrades in arms have likely led to innate biases in their selection as well.

Given the importance of associates other than mates, it would be surprising if mate preferences were the only affiliative preferences to have evolved. Both warfare and hunting large game are dangerous enterprises that require substantial coordination among participants. Because warriors and hunters are vulnerable to the faults and failures of members of their party, they are rarely indifferent to the character of their comrades. Just as indicators of prowess as a warrior and hunter—strength, courage, and dominance—are attractive to women seeking mates, they are desirable to men seeking comrades in arms. Men who were as willing to stand shoulder to shoulder on the hunt or in battle with weak and cowardly men—or with women—as they were with strong and brave men would likely have found themselves disadvantaged over time.

Supporting the existence of a male preference for comrades who would have been good hunters or fighters is the finding that men have a preference for same-sex friends who are physical risk-takers.[32] Both men and women prefer those who are willing to take "heroic" physical risks—such as rescuing someone endangered by a fire—although men's preference for such friends is much stronger than women's. Even with respect to "nonheroic" risks, however—such as dangerous sports—men prefer risk-takers, in contrast to women's preference for same-sex friends who avoid such risks. Men's preference for risk-taking comrades makes sense if men have evolved preferences for those adept at hunting and warfare, as both enterprises often reward the bold (although not necessarily the "overly bold" or reckless) and penalize the timid.

Women *leading* men in combat (or in any other dangerous endeavor) would also have been unusual, and it is likely that male and female psyches have not evolved in a way that makes the vertical cohesion between female leader and male follower any more likely—and perhaps even less likely—than the horizontal cohesion, or bonding, that occurs within groups of soldiers. Men's desire for a "man of steel" as a leader would certainly have been adaptive in a day when most combat was face-to-face and at close range, and it probably remains so today. Men have never faced adaptive pressures to follow women into battle, so their psyches may not make that an easy behavior to evoke.

Is Men's Resistance to Women Intractable?

Large numbers of military men, especially those in the combat arms, have strong negative opinions about inclusion of women in combat units. Some men may identify specific reasons—women's lesser strength, men's protectiveness toward women, issues of sexual distractions, and so forth. Some simply say that it does not "feel right." A naval aviator captured this ambivalence by saying that he "logically" was comfortable with having women serve in combat next to men, "but my gut tells me something else."[33] This aviator was making the same point that General McPeak—then Air Force Chief of Staff—was making at the outset of this chapter: their heads tell them one thing, but their hearts tell them something very different.

The emotion of the exclusionary impulse raises special issues for the military, because it suggests that overcoming it through cognitive inputs may be difficult. If men's positions are not based on logic, then logical persuasion is unlikely to be terribly effective in reversing them. Visceral responses that are a product of evolutionary history are often not very responsive to cognitive input and can be difficult to extinguish.

EMOTION VERSUS REASON

Both emotion and reason evolved not because there is any inherent benefit in feeling and thinking, and neither feelings nor thoughts are themselves acted on by natural selection. Instead, it is the behaviors that these feelings and thoughts produce that provide the means for selection to act. When people act on the basis of their feelings, they are not necessarily acting irrationally, but rather, in the words of psychologist Victor Johnston, on the basis of "what is, or was, in their best biological interest."[34]

Simply because male soldiers cannot articulate a compelling reason not to trust women does not mean that no good reason exists. Sometimes we have good reasons for feeling something that we cannot quite "put our finger on." A woman who experiences a visceral foreboding about a man, for example, should not be encouraged to allow herself to be alone with him simply because she can identify no objective basis for her fear. Women have evolved to be very sensitive to sexual threats,[35] and they should probably listen to their intuition in such circumstances. There are, one hopes, few fathers who would encourage their daughters to spend time alone with a man who gives them "the creeps" simply because they cannot point to any objective sign that he poses a threat. Even if we are quite sure a woman is wrong about a man, the "wrongness" of her emotional response does not mean that she is not experiencing it or that her response would not interfere with her trusting him. Just as important, we assume that she may have subconsciously picked up on some danger sign that she should trust.

The Importance of Trust in Human Relations

"Trust," says John Howland, a Naval Academy graduate and former naval officer, "is the coin of the realm within a combat unit."[36] Yet, for a variety of reasons, men do not trust women to "have their back." An absence of trust, then, can be a major impediment to women's acceptance into combat organizations.

Trust is critical to all sorts of relationships. Psychologist Catherine Cottrell and her colleagues have examined affiliation choices in a variety of group and relationship types, such as romantic partners, family members, work-group members, and athletic-team members. Not surprisingly, they found that different traits are important in different kinds of groups; for example, intellectual ability is important to university study groups and athletic ability is important in selecting athletic-team members. Their results indicated that across group types, however, "trustworthiness" was of paramount value, more important, in fact, than cooperativeness. Interpersonal trust, they suggest, "may be foundational to the development and maintenance of all close relationships."[37]

Combat compatriots must have trust in both the willingness and the ability of their comrades to satisfy their obligations. The earnest assurance "I've got your back" is worth little in the absence of the physical courage, toughness, and skill to deliver on the promise. Conversely, all the courage and strength in the world is worth little to a soldier's comrades if he is unwilling to risk death in support of them. No matter how much faith a man might have in the good intentions of a female comrade, it is not reassuring for him to have to wonder, "If I'm hit, am I going to die because the girl next to me can't carry me to safety?"

The need for trust increases with danger. This tendency may explain the increasing strength of the same-sex preference among boys as their groups roam farther from home, as well as the increasing preference of men for male comrades when the group faces greater danger. The especially negative attitudes to sexual integration expressed by men in combat specialties may be a consequence of this tendency, as may be the cool reception of women in dangerous civilian occupations.[38]

THE DECISION TO TRUST

The decision whether to trust another person as a combat compatriot—or a comrade in other dangerous enterprises—is a consequential one that would have recurred over evolutionary time. Psychologists Martie Haselton and David Funder have suggested that "an evolved propensity for accurate personality judgment" would very likely have arisen for traits important to survival and reproduction.[39] One might therefore suppose that men make judgments—even if at a less than conscious level—about whom to trust in combat based on evolved psychological mechanisms. The preference of men for risk-taking same-sex friends likely reflects such a mechanism. The soldier would be attuned to more than risk-taking, however, as risk-taking without the means of making the risk work out is a negative indicator of worth of a comrade. The fact that the two most important attributes of soldiers judged to be effective fighters by their peers are "leadership" and "masculinity" suggests—as does common sense—that those attributes are also important ones engendering a soldier's feelings of trust.

A study of soldiers in the Korean War found strong indications that men somehow pick up on signals from other men indicating their combat capability. Immediately after combat ended, about three hundred men were classified as either "fighters" or "nonfighters" by their peers, judgments that were validated through independent verifications of the combat incidents that were the basis for the classification. These men were placed in groups of fifteen to eighteen men each, such that no group member knew any other member of his group. Those designated "fighters" and "nonfighters" were mixed together, but nobody knew about these designations or the purpose of the study. Each group then lived together behind the lines for a week of psychological testing. At the end of that week, soldiers were asked to identify the two men they would most (and least) like to have next to them in combat or leading them in combat. Fighters overwhelmingly chose other fighters as most suitable, both as combat comrades and leaders, and nonfighters chose fighters as the most suitable combat leaders. Fighters and nonfighters alike identified nonfighters as least suitable as comrades and leaders. The researchers concluded, "Obviously some observable manifestation [connected] with fighter status served as the basis for these judgments."[40]

In making their judgments, men are going to be particularly attentive to individuals who pose threats to the combat unit. Catherine Cottrell and Steven Neuberg have recently shown that rather than being an undifferentiated negative attitude toward a group, prejudice is a much more nuanced phenomenon. The negative emotion that a particular group elicits turns on the nature of the perceived threat. They suggest that people who are highly dependent upon their groups are "especially attuned to potential threats to reciprocity," and their vigilance is "accompanied by psychological responses that function to minimize—or even eliminate—recognized threats and their detrimental effects."[41] These results are consistent with the fact that men can simultaneously have positive views of women in noncombat positions yet have strongly negative views about their service in combat, as it is in the latter case that women pose the greatest risk to the group's well-being.

Trust decisions are, in the words of David Messick and Roderick Kramer, "fast, shallow, and context-sensitive."[42] By "shallow" they mean that the decision is not the product of "deep or systematic processing." We do not ordinarily agonize over the decision and try to reason it through; it just comes to us, based on "rules of thumb" of which we are largely unaware, and it comes rapidly. We have all no doubt had the experience of trusting and distrusting people upon first meeting. In most cases, we do not deviate from our initial judgments—especially judgments of initial distrust—either because of the accuracy of our first impressions or our attachment to them even in the face of contrary evidence.

TRUST AND ERROR MANAGEMENT THEORY

The uncertainty involved in making judgments about whom to trust— decisions that are more visceral than cognitive—means that these judgments are prone to error. One contribution that evolutionary psychologists have made to the study of decision making is the demonstration that errors are not likely to be random. Instead, they tend to be biased in one direction or another, depending on their average fitness costs.

An extensive body of research over the past several decades has demonstrated that people tend to make systematic errors in reaching judgments under uncertainty.[43] These biases were often attributed to quirky design flaws in the human mind. Evolutionary psychologists were puzzled by these apparent engineering "mistakes," however, and began thinking about why they would occur.

One important insight researchers reached was that natural selection would not be predicted to design the mind to minimize the *number* of errors—that is, to attain accuracy in the abstract—but rather to minimize the *fitness cost* of errors. In making dichotomous judgments, such as whether to trust or not, two kinds of errors are possible: false positives and false negatives. In most situations of any moment, the costs of the two kinds of errors will not be equal. A smoke detector is an example where a false positive (a false alarm) is not as bad as a false negative (failure of the alarm to go off when there actually is a fire). In criminal law, on the other hand, false negatives are generally preferred to false positives, so we require the prosecutor to prove guilt "beyond a reasonable doubt." Ideally, of course, one would like to reduce the probability of both kinds of error to zero, but in the absence of perfection, reducing the probability of one inevitably increases the likelihood of the other.

This insight about asymmetry in the costs of errors led to the development of what has been called "error-management theory," associated most prominently with psychologists Martie Haselton and David Buss.[44] Error-management theory proposes that many of the regular biases observed in human decision making result from asymmetry between the costs of the two kinds of errors. Haselton and Buss's initial paper on error-management theory demonstrated both kinds of biases in mating behavior. They found that men tend to *overestimate* women's sexual interest in them (probably not a major shock to most readers, especially female ones) and that women tend to *underestimate* men's willingness to commit. In these contexts, men are biased toward false positives—inferring sexual interest that does not exist—and women toward false negatives—failing to pick up on commitment intentions that do exist. Haselton and Buss make a compelling case that these errors would be less costly than their opposites— men failing to pick up on genuine sexual interest and women incorrectly perceiving that a man will commit to her.

What insights does error-management theory provide about men's willingness to accept women into combat organizations? The decision of whom to trust in coalitions organized to mete out violence is one that would have recurred with great frequency over evolutionary time, and it is one that is fraught with very serious fitness consequences. Moreover, it is a judgment that likely carries with it asymmetric costs of error. Declining to trust a potential comrade who in fact would have performed well would tend to be less costly than trusting a comrade who performs poorly.

One would suppose, then, that the default position is not to trust potential combat comrades. Although soldiers are likely to be attentive to both positive and negative indicators of combat capability, they are probably more attentive to the latter than the former. That is one of the central reasons that units train together—to develop trust—and probably the primary reason that the "FNG" is not trusted. There is no reason to trust him until he has proved himself. Because the proximate triggers that lead to such trust are ones that are associated with men and masculinity, it may not be possible to overcome the hurdle of initial distrust of a female comrade.

How Easily Could an Evolved Aversion To Female Comrades Be Overcome?

If men's aversion to female comrades is an evolved biological response rather than a product of social learning, it may be difficult to overcome. This would likely be true even if the reasons that selection favored the aversion have disappeared. That is, even if integrationists were correct in their argument that changes in the nature of warfare have made women equally competent comrades, the factors that trigger trust are ones that evolved over the course of evolutionary history, not necessarily ones that are important today.

Human decision-making processes are designed to be attentive to the kinds of information that were available in the environment in which the mind evolved.[45] Thus, good grades at a military academy or impressive performance on a paper-and-pencil personality test—even if truly valid predictors of combat capability—are likely to carry far less weight with potential comrades than features that have traditionally been important, such as strength, courage, dominance, and masculinity (or their correlates). So, even if there is a logical reason to trust women, women may not embody the proximal triggers of that trust, meaning that men will not trust them despite their fitness for combat.

People's capacity to overcome emotional responses based on cognitive input is limited. The male preference for beautiful young women, for example, evolved because youth and beauty are indicators of fertility. The fact that a man knows that a beautiful young woman is on the pill does not dampen his desire to have sex with her. Conversely, if a man were to learn that a woman who is fifty has been blessed, through the miracle of modern medicine, with the fertility of a twenty-five-year-old notwithstanding her age-appropriate appearance, he is unlikely to be as physically attracted to her as if she were an infertile twenty-five-year-old. The extent of his attraction in both cases is based not on knowledge about her fertility but by the extent to which she possesses traits that were associated with fertility over the course of evolutionary history. Thus, telling men that, despite appearances, women are actually fierce combatants—or requiring them to affirm that belief—is unlikely to be effective in fostering the trust necessary in cohesive combat units.

"Biologically prepared" emotions are not only easier to acquire but also harder to extinguish, as experience with biologically prepared fears, such as that of snakes, has shown.[46] Men's disinclination to trust female comrades may therefore be easily reinforced by a little bit of adverse experience but not easily extinguished by a lot of good experience. One hundred good tacos from the local taco stand may not be enough to outweigh the negative experience of food poisoning from one bad one. Sworn statements from a dozen health inspectors that the problem has been fixed may not be very effective in restoring one's hunger for tacos. Reason often cannot overcome emotion, a fact well known to people with irrational fears, many of whom know that the object of their fear is objectively nonthreatening but whose mental state does not allow them to let that fact affect their behavior.[47]

A Moral Bargain?

Recently, an argument has been made that the near-universal exclusion of women from combat is due to the high maternal mortality that women have faced throughout history. The combat exclusion, Erin Solaro argues, was "an attempt to balance risk for risk."[48] Placing women in combat during periods of high maternal mortality "would have violated a fundamental moral compact as old as our species." Now that infant mortality is much lower, she argues, the blanket exemption of women from combat—or from mandatory service if there were a draft—"is no longer moral" and should be eliminated. Our "moral emotions" have simply not caught up with "moral fact."

The linkage between maternal death rates and the exclusion of women from combat is flawed for a number of reasons. The first is the lack of any factual support for it. Solaro crunches some numbers and concludes that up until about 1960 maternal mortality exceeded combat deaths. Whether or not that factual conclusion is correct, she does not demonstrate any causal link between the two statistics. The fact that two things were happening at the same time is not strong evidence that one caused the other. Perhaps the combat exclusion resulted from men's feelings of inadequacy for failure to put a man on the moon, an inadequacy remedied in 1969, just four years before the creation of the All-Volunteer Force and expansion of women's military role. Coincidence? Perhaps.

The second major flaw is that her argument is unclear—and seemingly inconsistent—about whether it views the exclusion as being a conscious choice based on an explicit quid pro quo or whether it reflects an evolved psychological tendency of men to exclude women. Part of her argument makes it sound like the former, as in her assertion that "attitudes and practices often take generations to catch up with reality." On the other hand, her claim to be the first person to have recognized this "fundamental moral compact as old as our species," which elicits "deep moral revulsion" when violated, suggests that she believes this is all going on at a deeply unconscious level, which in turn implies that it must be part of the evolved psychology of men rather than a mere socialized attitude. Clearly, if one or the other of these explanations were correct, it would be the latter.

The argument that men's tendency to exclude women from warfare evolved to offset maternal mortality is far-fetched, as it seems to entail a claim that the propensity evolved to benefit women or the species as a whole, a "group-selectionist" argument of the kind discussed in chapter 10. Such an argument differs markedly from the argument presented in this book. My argument is straightforward: the psychological predisposition for men to prefer masculine comrades in arms and to resist inclusion of women in warfare evolved because it was in their survival interest—and therefore their reproductive interest—to do so. Similarly, women evolved risk-averse tendencies because it was in *their* reproductive interest to do so. The quid pro quo argument requires a more elaborate and fanciful explanation. Traits do not evolve as "moral bargains"; they evolve because they increase the reproductive fitness of the bearers of the genes producing those traits.

Finally, Solaro's argument assumes that evolved moral sentiments can be disregarded when the circumstances that led to their evolution have changed, perhaps with a lag time of a generation or two. Yet, as we have seen, evolved deep-seated emotions are not very susceptible to change through cognitive inputs, so even if the "bargain" has changed, our brains and emotions have not.

Potential Consequences of a Strong Aversion

Although the most obvious consequence of men's resistance to women is a disruption of unit cohesion and therefore combat effectiveness, more concrete effects may result as well. Men may turn on their own female comrades if they view them as a sufficient threat to their well-being. During the Vietnam War, hundreds of officers and NCOs fell victim to fraggings—that is, being killed by their own men. In 1971 alone, there were 333 confirmed incidents and another 158 possible ones.[49] While fragging in the strictest sense did not develop as a practice until the development of fragmentation grenades, "military leaders have always been at risk, living as they must among men used to violence in an atmosphere where life is cheap."[50] Many fraggings in Vietnam were responses to the perception that certain NCOs or officers (and even some enlisted men) were too gung ho and created excessive risk to the men involved.[51]

The objections that many men have to women are of a kind that would create a potential for fragging. Two of the most frequently heard complaints about women in the military are that women obtain favored treatment from superiors and that they are less combat capable and will not pull their weight in combat, thereby endangering the lives of male soldiers. In a combat situation, such perceptions may lead to deadly responses. In her study of sexual harassment in the Army, Laura Miller found that while only one group of men acknowledged that they themselves would "rape the women if you send them out to the tanks and foxholes with us," many men predicted that "other men" would harass, rape, and allow the killing of women who entered infantry or armor units.[52]

Evan Wright describes a platoon leader who, in the absence of strong discipline among the troops, would have been a prime candidate for fragging. Referred to as "Captain America," the excitable officer was prone to hysterics. The highly trained Recon Marines generally exhibited good fire discipline and chose their targets with care, but Captain America would fire out of his vehicle in the absence of targets, seemingly at random, and would scream things like "We're all going to die." It got to the point that the men would not take orders from him without clearing them with their sergeant first.

Even early in the campaign, Captain America's men were already fantasizing about his death. One Marine said, "All it takes is one dumb guy in charge to ruin everything. Every time he steps out of the vehicle, I pray he gets shot." It is a short step from hoping someone gets killed to thinking about doing it oneself. Sure enough, it was also not long before some of the Marines "begin fantasizing about capping [him], talking about it openly among themselves."[53] It is a giant moral step—but the history of war shows not always a large step in practice—from talking about killing your leader to actually doing it.

The male impulse to protect women (described at length in the next chapter) may weaken substantially if men perceive the women as endangering their lives. Although men may be willing to risk their lives for what they see as a good cause, few would view "gender equity" to be a cause worth dying for. Fraggings may seem grossly disproportionate to the situation, but a man who perceives his life to be in immediate peril may think it a wholly proportionate response. As Charles Anderson observed about fraggings in Vietnam, "every soldier, marine, sailor or airman who fragged a unit leader believed at the time of the incident that he acted with more than ample justification."[54] Fragging of women because they are perceived as a threat to the unit may be no more justified than the fraggings in Vietnam, but it is a not unpredictable reaction toward someone who is viewed as imperiling lives.

MEN SEEM TO be psychologically predisposed not to welcome women into combat groups, and the expectation that they will accommodate to women's presence may be overly optimistic. Although there are many logical reasons to reject integration of combat arms, much of men's resistance seems to have roots at the core of the male psyche. Military training, which already presents so many challenges, may face the ultimate challenge if it attempts to undo this tendency having origins deep in men's DNA. The military can force men to "accept" integration in the sense that soldiers must "accept" virtually anything their superiors impose upon them, but it cannot force men to trust women, and the absence of trust in battle can be deadly.

PART V

THREATS TO COHESION
AND EFFECTIVENESS
ARISING FROM
MIXING THE SEXES

Mixing the sexes together in an integrated combat force adds substantially to what Clausewitz described as the "friction" of war—"the force that makes the apparently easy so difficult."[1] The last section expressed doubt about women's ability to bond the way men do. The problems of sexual integration go deeper than that, however, because of the dynamics of interpersonal relationships between the sexes. Those relationships can impair cohesion and combat effectiveness in a number of ways.

Although a central tenet of much feminist thought is that males are predators of females, men have long played, and continue to play, a large role in protection of females. The male protective impulse toward women may have substantial negative effects in combat. Men are unlikely to be able to view their female comrades as "just another soldier" and are likely to take unwise risks in protecting them. Our enemies can exploit this protectiveness in a number of ways.

The sexual attraction that often exists between men and women, and the resulting sexual relationships, also threatens cohesion and effectiveness. Competition for the attentions of a woman can disrupt the cooperative nature of the unit, whether or not the woman has any interest in the men. A romantically involved couple—even assuming compliance with applicable restrictions on sexual activity—threatens cohesion because the bonds between the pair are likely to overshadow the bond of comrades that are so important to military effectiveness. Because of the skewed sex ratio in combat units, sexual jealousy and frustration are inevitable. When relationships end, the rancor associated with breakups will almost inevitably affect the harmony of the group.

The attractions between men and women—whether or not they are reciprocal—and the sexual activity that sometimes results have led to a series of sex scandals in the military. The resultant sensitivity about "gender issues" has resulted in a system of double standards and a climate of political correctness. Women are held to lower physical standards, and because even unfounded sexual harassment charges can terminate a career, men are often reluctant to impose discipline on women. In sexual misconduct cases, women are less likely than men to face discipline, even when their conduct was as egregious as men's. The climate of political correctness is so strong that revealing reservations about the performance of women in the military is likely to be a career-terminating event.

These problems are not necessarily the "fault" of women, but fault is not the issue. The issue is military effectiveness, and these problems are either inevitable or exceedingly likely in an integrated military, so they must all be counted as costs of integration.

14

Who Men Protect:
Women and Children First

To take your chance in the thick of a rush, with firing all about,
Is nothing so bad when you've cover to' and, an' leave an' likin'
    to shout:
But to stand an' be still to the Birken'ead drill is a damn' tough
    bullet to chew,
An' they done it, the Jollies—'Er Majesty's Jollies—soldier an'
    sailor too!
Their work was done when it 'adn't begun; they was younger
    nor me an' you;
Their choice it was plain between drownin' in 'heaps an' being'
    mopped by the screw,
So they stood an' was still to the Birken'ead drill, soldier an'
    sailor too!

—Rudyard Kipling[1]

*April 14, 1912, 11:40 P.M., 375 miles southeast of St. John's,
Newfoundland.*

Lookouts Frederick Fleet and Reginald Lee are high in the crow's nest of the RMS *Titanic,* on its maiden voyage between Southampton and New York, steaming at approximately twenty-one knots. The night is clear and moonless, and the sea calm. The lookouts are watchful, having been alerted to ice in the area. Suddenly, a dark mass appears before them. Fleet sounds the warning bell and notifies the bridge: "Iceberg right ahead." The officer of the watch orders the engines stopped and reversed and shouts to the helmsman "Hard a-starboard." Scarcely a half minute later, the vessel strikes it, but because of the evasive maneuver, the blow is merely a glancing one rather than a head-on collision. "That was a narrow shave," Fleet comments with relief to Lee, not realizing that ruptures along the riveted seams of the hull plates have inflicted a mortal wound on the ship.

Although the danger is not immediately apparent to passengers, Captain Edward Smith is told at midnight that the ship can stay afloat for just a couple of hours. He instructs the radio operators to send the international distress signal "CQD" (with which the operators occasionally intersperse the new "SOS" signal), and orders the lifeboats uncovered. Although the ship contains over twenty-two hundred passengers and crew, the lifeboats can hold barely half that number. Orders come down from the bridge that only women and children should be loaded into the lifeboats. As it happens, however, the first boat, with a sixty-five-passenger capacity, is lowered with only twenty-eight people aboard, including some men who are allowed in the boat when no other passengers are willing to forsake the warmth and apparent safety of the *Titanic* for a hard seat in a small boat on the cold open sea. As the precariousness of the situation becomes increasingly obvious, demand grows for spaces on the lifeboats, and available spaces are filled mostly with women and children: "Gentlemen passengers help the ladies board, then stand back, not boarding themselves."[2] Among those gentlemen is John Jacob Astor IV, one of the world's richest men, who, after assisting his pregnant young wife, Madeleine, into the boat, asks whether he might join her in light of her "delicate condition." When told that he could not, he kisses her good-bye, steps away, and lights a cigarette.

Shortly after 2:00 A.M., with the lifeboats away, Captain Smith returns to the bridge. Along the way, he tells crew members, "Well, boys, you've done your duty. Now every man for himself." At 2:20 A.M., the ship that had been described in the press as "practically unsinkable" breaks apart and begins its final two-and-a-half-mile journey to the bottom of the sea. The captain goes down with his ship.

Over fifteen hundred passengers and crew die this night, many succumbing to rapid hypothermia in the thirty-degree water. The deaths are far from random with respect to sex and age. Three out of four women on board survive, as do half the children. The men do not fare so well, however, as four out of five perish. Although much has been made of class differences in survival, women traveling in third class were more likely to survive than men traveling in first.

* * *

How is it that in the last hours of life, so many men were willing to step aside to preserve the lives of women and children? It seems that there was a strong expectation—largely satisfied—that men would not take spots that could be filled by women or children. One officer would later testify that the protection of women and children was not just an expectation but "a law of human nature."

Women and Children First

The "women and children first" norm is sometimes dated to the 1852 sinking of the *Birkenhead,* a British transport ship that struck an unmarked rock (now called Birkenhead Rock) off the coast of South Africa.[3] The ship had just three small lifeboats, which the ship's captain ordered filled with the wives and children of the troops aboard. After the boats were away, the captain ordered everyone aboard to abandon ship and make for the boats. The senior army officer on board recognized, however, that the boats would be swamped if that were to occur. He made an emotional plea to his men: "You will swamp the cutter containing the women and children; I implore you not to do this thing and I ask you all to stand fast." They did. "After the boats were safely away, the *Birkenhead* slipped off the rock and plunged to the bottom as the cargo of iron-disciplined troops stood at attention on her deck." In all, 445 men (out of the total of 638 people on board) perished, most either from drowning or from the feeding frenzy of man-eating sharks. (The area where the *Birkenhead* went down is now a popular spot for observing great white sharks by "cage diving.")[4] The marines aboard the *Birkenhead* were immortalized by Rudyard Kipling in "Soldier an' Sailor Too," quoted at the outset of the chapter.

Although deviations from the ideal have led some to label the "women and children first" rule a "myth," special efforts to save women and children were not uncommon even well before the *Birkenhead* disaster.[5] To be sure, however, even after the *Birkenhead,* there were instances of ships' crews saving themselves at the expense of women and children. Just two years after the *Birkenhead* went down, the American steamship *Arctic* collided with a French ship off Cape Race, Newfoundland. Despite orders of the captain to evacuate women and children first (and a U.S. statute mandating the same), many of the crew and many male passengers looked out for themselves, trampling women in their haste to take their places in the lifeboats. Of the approximately four hundred passengers and crew aboard, only eighty-six survived, of whom only twenty-two—all men—were passengers. Every one of the sixty women aboard succumbed to drowning, hypothermia, or sharks.

To say that the *Arctic* episode, and others like it, demonstrates the mythic quality of the "women and children first" norm is to neglect the public reaction to such events. The crew were publicly disgraced. As one letter to the *New York Daily Times* put it, the names of "these craven hearted (men?)" should be "conspicuously posted in every shipping office in the City" and be barred from service on ships so that "if at any future times our wives or children should be absent upon the broad Atlantic," the men would not be able to repeat their cowardly acts.

The Norm Survives

The sentiment that it is the duty of men to protect women—one of the central tenets of the medieval code of chivalry—may sound quaint when expressed. Yet the norm continues to operate today in many life-and-death situations. Consider, for example, the conflict in the former Yugoslavia. Reports from the Balkans often emphasized the killing of "innocent women and children," and humanitarian intervention was overwhelmingly directed toward evacuation of women and children. Despite the well-documented occurrence of mass rapes, however, women were not the primary civilian targets of violence.[6] Instead, as is typical in so many ethnic conflicts, it was adult men who were most commonly singled out for massacre. In the words of one student of international relations, "Male civilians were separated from women, children, and the elderly and executed while the latter were permitted to flee."[7] The men were "almost never given safe passage along with their families." Despite the policy of international agencies to give top priority to protection of the "especially vulnerable," it was primarily women and children who were evacuated. Despite the Geneva Conventions' prohibitions against adverse distinction on the basis of sex, protection agencies generally understand the prohibition to apply only to discrimination against women.

The strong expectation of male protectiveness toward women in American society cannot be denied. If a couple strolling along the street is attacked by a group of assailants, few would assert that it is the duty of the woman to protect the man; most would hold the man responsible for the woman's protection. A woman who ran away from the attack and left her companion behind—whether simply to avoid being injured or to seek assistance—would suffer little, if any, stigma. In contrast, a man who ran away from the attack, leaving his companion behind, would likely be branded a coward even if the only reason he left was to get help.

Some feminists go even further and not only deny the existence of a norm protecting women from violence but also assert that social norms actually *support* violence against women. As sociologist Richard Felson has persuasively shown, however, violence against women is deviant behavior that violates "a special norm protecting women from harm."[8] That violence against women does occur, he points out, does not mean that society approves of it. Instead, he musters an array of evidence demonstrating that society is far less tolerant of violence against women than against men. Women are much less likely than men to be targets of violence, and violence directed at women receives greater condemnation than violence directed toward men, by both observers and the judicial system, and is more likely to trigger assistance from bystanders. In experimental studies, subjects are less willing to deliver electric shocks to females than to males, and this tendency is enhanced in the presence of an audience and when the subjects are facing a mirror, both settings that tend to decrease the incidence of norm violations.

Although many feminists challenge the notion that men should protect women—with its implicit assumption that women's lives are somehow more important than men's (although one senses that their objection to that assumption is mostly rhetorical)—that is an assumption that is in many ways embraced not only by our culture but by most feminists as well. After all, the United States has a federal Violence Against Women Act—strongly pushed by feminists—and although its prohibitions are phrased in a sex-neutral way, the title of the act and the circumstances of its passage make clear that it is violence against women and not violence against men (or violence generally) that was the target. The sentiment expressed in the ubiquitous bumper sticker proclaiming, "There's NO excuse for violence against women" rests uneasily alongside the argument that women should be issued rifles and sent to the battlefield.

Many boys—and one would hope, against the evidence, all boys—are still taught that they should not hit girls. Writing in the *Minneapolis Star-Tribune*, columnist Katherine Kersten describes what seems to be an increasingly common phenomenon.[9] Minnesota law, although prohibiting boys from competing on girls' public-school athletic teams, allows girls to compete on boys' teams. Most schools do not have girls' wrestling teams at all because of lack of sufficient interest. As a result, a number of Minnesota high schools allow girls on the boys' team. Some Christian schools, as a matter of conscience, require their wrestlers to forfeit to female opponents.

Kersten describes a boy at a Christian high school who was matched against a girl. Although he did not want to wrestle her, he agreed to do so because his refusal would cause him to forfeit his chance to compete in the state tournament. Kersten writes:

> As the embarrassed boy walked out on the mat, spectators began to laugh. He quickly flipped the girl to her back, but couldn't bring himself to pin her, which required pushing directly on her chest. For about 40 seconds, the boy remained frozen. Finally his coach, in frustration, shouted, "Just do it!" The boy made his move, pinning the girl to the mat. But walking off, he looked defeated, not victorious. With hanging head, he strode—angry and humiliated—straight to the locker room.

Many would no doubt blame the boy's anguish on entrenched sexism. But don't we want boys to feel guilty for physically overpowering girls? Would we prefer that the boy walked off triumphantly and "high-fived" his teammates?

Male protectiveness toward women is so ubiquitous that it can be invisible. Frederica Mathewes-Green recounted the concern she felt when her daughter got a job delivering pizzas.[10] She was reassured when her daughter told her, "If they have any questions about the call, they won't send me. They'll send one of the guys." Mathewes-Green noted that risking their lives to protect women is a "part of the guy job description" that is taken for granted.

Mathewes-Green's conclusion about expectations of male protectiveness was illustrated by a newspaper story in the town in which I live. A man confronted four teenage boys who were tearing up his lawn in retaliation for the man's earlier intervention to prevent the boys from harassing two teenage girls.[11] The teenagers left the man unconscious in the middle of the road, suffering head trauma, a collapsed lung, and several broken bones. A seventeen-year-old girl came upon the victim and stopped her car so as to protect him from traffic, but she remained in the car with the windows up and the doors locked. Although she did not know how he came to be in the middle of the road, she was afraid that he might have been at-tacked and did not want to expose herself to the same fate. She got out of her car only when another passing motorist stopped to help.

A front-page headline proclaimed, "Young Hero Praised for Aid to Victim of Prank." Why was she lauded as a "hero"? It seems that she was viewed as having displayed extraordinary courage just by stopping. (To her credit, the girl demurred to the "hero" label.) But were her actions truly "extraordinary"?

Suppose that the sexes in the above scenario were reversed. The victim in the road is a woman, and a seventeen-year-old boy drives up and sits in his car with his doors locked, while, for all he knows, the woman in the road is bleeding to death. Would the boy be labeled a hero? It is highly doubtful. Indeed, if anything, he would be labeled a coward. After all, wasn't it his moral obligation to aid the woman? Yet when the female "res-cuer" did just the same thing, she was viewed as acting "above and beyond the call of duty," further illustrating Aristotle's observation about sex differ-ences in expectations of courage. Moreover, if the victim had been female, could anyone imagine the newspaper characterizing her as a victim of a "prank"? Indeed, she probably would have been labeled a hero for stand-ing up to four young toughs in defense of the girls.

Just as there is an expectation that men will protect women—and cen-sure when they do not—there is an expectation that men (or even boys, after a certain age) will not hide behind women for protection. Nonetheless, *New York Times* columnist Nicholas Kristof seemed quite pleased with himself for having done just that. He wrote that he asked a female soldier in Iraq to sit beside him "on the theory that befuddled snipers would hesitate to fire," thus letting "foreign chauvinism work for us."[12] As James Bowman wrote in his book *Honor: A History*, Kristof gave no indication that even "non-chauvinists" in the West might feel "some twinge of shame about hiding behind, if not the skirts, then the battle-dress of a woman."[13] One wonders whether Kristof would think it appropriate for a male *soldier* to similarly use a female com-rade as a "human shield."

Protectiveness and Concern About Female Casualties

Male soldiers share the traditional view that men are to be the protectors of women. A poll taken after the Gulf War found that two-thirds of military respondents believed that inclusion of women in combat units would lead to reduced effectiveness because of their protective impulses toward women.[14] A GAO study found that both men and women believe that men feel a need to protect women. The two most prevalent threats from which men were predicted to protect women were hostile fire and other men.[15] A Marine sergeant I interviewed told me that even if women were just as combat capable as men, he would be unalterably opposed to their participation because he was sure that he, and other men, would feel the need to protect them.

Inclusion of women in combat units may exacerbate an already well-recognized problem. It is always difficult for soldiers to continue a mission when comrades are wounded, and despite orders not to stop for the wounded, soldiers frequently disobey. Thus, the battle may be abandoned and the objective lost because of a single individual. As Richard Holmes has noted, "Few soldiers can remain deaf to the pleadings of a wounded man,"[16] and even fewer could do so if the pleas come from a woman.

Exploitation of Men's Protective Impulses

Much of warfare is psychological, and we can be sure that our enemies will exploit our protectiveness toward women, just as they exploit any other weaknesses that they can identify. They might use it strategically to undermine public support for war. They might use it tactically on the battlefield by taking advantage of men's protective impulses toward their female comrades. Finally, they might use it in the interrogation of prisoners of war.

STRATEGIC EXPLOITATION OF PROTECTIVENESS OF WOMEN

Our enemies know that the public reaction will be greater to female casualties and, especially, prisoners than to male ones. When fifteen British sailors and marines were recently taken prisoner by Iran in the Persian Gulf, sailor Faye Turney was the most public face of the hostages. The British press was incensed, a tabloid declaring it an "outrage" that a "young mum" would be "paraded like a trophy on TV." Even the British government pronounced it a "disgrace," asserting that it was "cold and callous to be doing this to a woman."[17]

The sexual composition of the military has been a factor in the strategy of the insurgents in Iraq. In June 2005, a suicide-bomb attack on a Marine truck took the lives of three female Marines (as well as three men). The Marines were on their way to man checkpoints around Fallujah, so that they could search Iraqi women for weapons and explosives.[18] The insurgents were apparently specifically targeting female troops in an attempt to undermine American morale.[19] The insurgents believe that increasing U.S. casualties is the way to break the nation's resolve, and they appear to believe that the nation is especially sensitive to female casualties. Intelligence reports shortly before the incident indicated that insurgents were going to start targeting female troops, hoping to capture them and display them on videotape.

The insurgents were probably correct that a large number of female casualties—and especially prisoners—would create more anguish than male casualties or prisoners. Whether targeting female troops would dampen or instead reinforce the resolve of American policymakers would probably depend on who the policymakers are at the time, but it is not self-evident that the insurgents' calculation about the American response was very astute, and they may have abandoned the strategy.

BATTLEFIELD USE OF MEN'S PROTECTIVENESS
TOWARD WOMEN

Men's protectiveness toward women can also be used on the battlefield. One way the Japanese attempted to demoralize and frighten Allied soldiers in the Pacific was to capture a soldier and then toss him back toward the opposing lines in pieces.[20] In the memoir of his experience as a helicopter pilot in Vietnam, Robert Mason describes a scene in which he objected to the killing of a North Vietnamese prisoner. One of the Americans argued that it was not murder; it was justice: "They cut off Sergeant Rocci's cock and stuck it in his mouth. And five of his men," said the voice. "After they spent the night slowly shoving knives into their guts. If you had been here to hear the screams . . . They screamed all night. This morning they were all dead, all gagged with their cocks."[21]

In Iraq, insurgents proudly torture and behead their captives. In June 2006, for example, two American soldiers were captured by insurgents in Yusufiya, south of Baghdad. When their bodies were recovered, there was evidence of "brutal torture," and at least one of them had been beheaded.[22]

These kinds of incidents are extraordinarily difficult on soldiers' comrades, and it is predictable that they would be even more so if the tortured soldiers are women. One question we as a society must face is whether we are willing to expose women to this kind of barbaric behavior.

Other tactics preferentially targeting women might also be employed. A common battlefield technique is to shoot to wound rather than to kill, because by wounding a soldier, you subtract not just him but also the soldiers who take him to the rear for medical attention. If men respond especially protectively toward their female comrades, the enemy might specifically target female soldiers on the theory that wounding them would cause more disruption. Another tactic is to wound a soldier so that a medic who comes to his assistance can be targeted as well. Now that some units are using female medics—in apparent violation of Defense Department policy—the enemy might combine these two tactics.

Prisoners of War

Threats of harm to other prisoners can be an effective way to extract information or other cooperation from POWs. The North Vietnamese commonly used this tactic,[23] and there is reason to believe that threats of harm to women would be especially effective. After the 1974 revolution in Portugal, the political police used recordings of women's screams to convince prisoners that their wives and girlfriends were being tortured nearby.[24] Such ploys have been used in the current war in Iraq. Shoshana Johnson, who was taken prisoner at the same time as Jessica Lynch, reported that her captors would open and close her cell door to give the male prisoners the impression that a guard had entered her cell. Such actions, she said, "can play a lot into the minds of the male soldiers."[25]

In the Air Force's Survival, Evasion, Resistance, and Escape (SERE) training, pilots are taught how to deal with being shot down. In SERE school, "captured" male pilots have acted much like Israeli soldiers did, with men trying to protect women pilots to the detriment of the unit—an impulse so ingrained that it comes out even in these simulations.

Male students are reported to be more concerned about the potential for sexual exploitation of female prisoners than the women are themselves. About three-quarters of male Air Force pilots in one study reported that they would be more protective of a female pilot. A study of male and female Army and Air Force aircrew revealed that both men and women were worried about the responses of men to maltreatment of women. A related study found that men had two different concerns; some were concerned that they would do anything to protect a female pilot, while others were angered by the thought that they might be "expected" to protect her.[26]

According to Linda Bird Francke, men should just get over it. She reports that women in SERE training perceived danger in men's reactions to threats of their sexual exploitation, because "if the enemy technique worked, the women prisoners would be subject to repetitive abuse."[27] This argument rests on an incorrect premise—that if the men did *not* react to sexual exploitation, female prisoners would be spared it. That premise rests in turn on the assumption that the sole motivation for rape is an instrumental one. That is, the raping soldier's motivations are not really sexual; instead, he is doing it only for the military advantage that it might bring—for "God and country," so to speak. While the slogan that "rape is not about sex" has been around a long time, it has been convincingly refuted.[28] Thus, there is every reason to believe that failure of male prisoners to react to abuse of female prisoners will not insulate women from it.

One of the central questions that must be addressed by any society that contemplates placing women in combat is what attitude society should have toward violence by and against women. Many feminists complain about the "male monopoly" on the use of physical force and believe that inclusion of women in combat will break down that monopoly.[29] But it must be understood that there is a certain symmetry in traditional arrangements. While the circumstances in which force could legitimately be employed by women were restricted, so were the circumstances in which force could legitimately be employed *against* them. One might think it a mark of civilization, not of oppression, that men protect women.

If women are considered proper combatants—and little boys play with G.I. Jane, as well as G.I. Joe, action figures—how do we continue to teach boys that it is unacceptable to hit girls even if the girls hit them first? If women are to be viewed as equivalent to men when it comes to violence, should we not view a man's punching a woman in a bar as morally equivalent to his punching another man?

No matter what the source of male protective behavior toward women, it can be diminished or heightened through either negative or positive reinforcement. The Air Force's response to male protectiveness in SERE training was to add a component desensitizing male pilots to violence against women.[30] Perhaps this indoctrination will work, but there must be some question about whether it is a good idea. Do we really want to desensitize men to violence against women? Surely, an increase in men's tolerance of violence against women must be counted as a cost—not a benefit—of sexual integration in the military.

15

Sexual Relationships and Attraction

To achieve tolerance and cooperation, the conflict over reproductive interests has to become subordinate to other interests.

—Jan A. R. A. M. Van Hooff and Carel P. Van Schaik[1]

You can't have an aircraft commander and a copilot get into a lover's quarrel at six hundred feet and crash their plane into the side of a building.

— Kelly Flinn[2]

One of the principal concerns about integration of women centers on their effects on cohesion. In part IV, the question was raised whether, all else being equal, women can share in the bonds that exist between men. Beyond that question, however, is the equally important question of whether women may disrupt the bonds already formed among men.

Although seemingly paradoxical—especially to those who view unit cohesion as a reflection of friendship—specific bonds between individuals may actually impair cohesion. Anthropologist Anna Simons found in her study of Army Special Forces troops that a close friendship between two individuals in a squad is viewed as harmful to the group because of the division of loyalties between the friendship and the unit.[3]

In a sexually integrated group, the risks are even greater. The relationship may be a sexual one—and therefore very powerful—which may lead not only to greater pair-versus-group conflict but also to conflicts related to sexual jealousy. In circumstances in which teamwork is essential, competition can lead to friction and loss of efficiency.[4] There is little that young men and women compete harder for than members of the opposite sex.

Military units generally, but cohesive combat units particularly, have strong norms of equality. Risks and rewards must be shared equally. In a small and isolated group with a skewed sex ratio, sex is a resource that cannot be shared equally and therefore almost always harms cohesion.

Sex Happens

When young men and women live together in close quarters, sexual and romantic relationships inevitably ensue. Two-thirds of service members polled after the Gulf War reported sexual activity in their integrated units. Over half believed that it had harmed morale and over a third believed that it had degraded unit readiness.[5]

The 1997 RAND study likewise found that dating and sexual relationships were perceived to reduce morale, especially on ships and on overseas deployments.[6] The "sexualization" of the atmosphere made it difficult for colleagues to regard one another as just coworkers, thereby undermining cohesion. One respondent complained that "the mess . . . at night [for] this unit looks more like a singles club or promenade deck than a mess hall." Another complaint was: "This place is like high school all over again. Everyone is dating others. To me this is not the military. We are here to do a job not meet our spouse. Guys seem more worried about getting a girl than doing their job."

The "high school" theme is a recurrent one, as those in charge of mixed-sex units often liken their task to being a counselor or principal at a high school,[7] and for good reason. A review of hundreds of disciplinary documents revealed that "instructors were kept busy policing the sexes at a time when their main task was to teach military skills."[8] The overwhelming view of drill sergeants was that "basic training has become primarily a baby-sitting exercise."

Stories of sexual problems are now emerging from Iraq. In 2005, the *New York Daily News* ran a story titled "Out of Control at Camp Crazy! Female Soldiers Dress Down & Get Dirty for Mud Romps."[9] The story described what looked like a drunken "out-of-control frat party" among MPs at Camp Bucca, a military prison in southern Iraq. Female soldiers were mud wrestling in their underwear, and sergeants were lending out their rooms for soldiers to have sex. Similar reports have come from other bases. A female Air Force Reserve sergeant who served at a supply base in Jordan was appalled by "tents that reeked of alcohol, smoke and vomit." Couples would stand cots on their sides to form an area for sex, and there were numerous illegal affairs involving enlisted personnel, noncommissioned officers, and officers.[10] Kayla Williams wrote of a female soldier who had performed oral sex on every man in her unit.[11] Iraq, she says, was "a massive frat party with weapons."

Sexual relationships can also result in jealousy and sexual frustration. The imbalance in the sex ratio means that some men will find girlfriends, but most will not (or some women will be very, very busy). As a former naval officer told me:

> One of the biggest things that used to upset me, and this was with women in general, was [romantic relationships] on ships. That obviously happens, and it's going to happen; it's human nature. But it's not very good for morale. You know you're on a ship for six months and your buddy has a girlfriend on the next deck. . . . Morale-wise, it's not a good idea. . . . It's not fair for a lot of guys. There's no time or place for it either. When you're at sea, you're basically working twenty-four hours a day except when you're sleeping.

He acknowledged that the "world's not fair," but this particular unfairness, he believed, strongly undermined morale.

In saying that "there's no time or place for it," this former officer obviously meant that there was no *legitimate* time or place. When it comes to sex, people can just about always find the time and place. On the aircraft carrier *Nimitz*, one couple was found having intercourse inside the air-intake ducts of an F-14 engine.[12] As an Army captain said about the numerous pregnancies in Bosnia, "They've locked us down so what else is there to do?" Among the favored locations for pitching woo in Bosnia were in the backs of Humvees, on deserted airstrips, in tents (conveniently co-ed), latrines, and even underground bunkers if one was willing to stand in ankle-deep icy water. "Where there's a will there's a way," the captain said,[13] and, he might have added, when it comes to sex, there's usually a will.

The skewed sex ratio not only creates competition for the "scarce resource" of women, it also results in some women being showered with a kind of attention they have never before experienced. As a female Army major commented, "Some of these women were probably never this popular at their former high schools and upon arriving to their new units . . . they are suddenly treated like the homecoming queen." Most of them cannot handle this newfound popularity, she says, and "if not cautious can earn a promiscuous reputation that once earned is hard to lose."[14] In Iraq, this syndrome is referred to as "Queen for a Year," and "even the unattractive girls start to act stuck-up."[15]

When sexual relationships occur between members of different ranks, the military chain of command may be compromised by the appearance of partiality, especially when the relationship occurs within the same chain of command. A romantic relationship between, say, a private and her squad leader creates many opportunities for favoritism, and even if no favoritism is extended, it is likely to be assumed. When relationships terminate, regardless of the ranks involved, the morale of both the individuals involved and the entire unit may suffer.

A "Military Incest Taboo"?

Recognizing the disruptive potential of sexual relationships, Madeline Morris has advocated a "military incest taboo" that would define members of sexually integrated units as "brothers and sisters between whom sexual relationships would be unacceptable."[16] This approach "would amount to a broadened fraternization policy, prohibiting not only inappropriate relationships between ranks but also sexual relationships regardless of rank within military units." Such an approach is unlikely to be effective.

Morris's proposal treats the incest taboo as an arbitrary social rule that can be extended at our whim to other contexts. Under this view, brothers and sisters abstain from sexual relations with each other because there is a rule against it; therefore, we can simply expand the group to which the rule applies. Freud notwithstanding, however, the primary reason that brothers and sisters do not engage in sexual relations is not that society has created a rule against it, but rather that brothers and sisters (and others who are reared together from an early age) are not ordinarily attracted to each other.[17] This phenomenon, known as the "Westermarck effect," is thought to be an evolved mechanism to avoid inbreeding. The notion that the incest taboo can be redefined arbitrarily and retain its force rests on an inadequate understanding of human psychology.

The military has a chance at successfully regulating behavior but not at regulating thoughts. The male and female soldiers who fall in love with each other but obey the strictures of the "incest taboo" pose little less risk to the group than a couple that consummates their love. The pair-versus-group conflict will continue to exist—perhaps in heightened form because of resentment over the limitation on their love—and to the extent that other members of the unit are aware of the mutual attraction, and they probably will be, they are likely to suspect that the couple is engaging in sexual relations anyway, with the same negative consequences to morale that would flow from a physically consummated relationship.

The suggestion that men should not consider their "sisters in arms" in a sexual way, but rather as "just friends" may be more than a little naive given what is known about opposite-sex friendships. Psychologists April Bleske-Rechek and David Buss found in their study of such friendships that men actually perceive sex to be an important motivation for embarking on a friendship.[18] Men, more than women, prefer sexual attractiveness in opposite-sex friends and desire to have sex with them. They are also more likely to terminate a friendship because of a lack of sex. Women, in contrast, are more likely to seek protection from their male friends and terminate friendships if it is not forthcoming. These results suggest that it is optimistic to assume that it is easy to maintain friendships at a platonic level, especially in the forced intimacy of many military settings.

The difficulty, from the man's point of view, of maintaining a purely platonic relationship, is captured in an exchange between Billy Crystal (Harry) and Meg Ryan (Sally) in the movie *When Harry Met Sally*. Harry tells Sally that they can never be friends, and Sally wants to know why not. Harry tells her, "Because no man can be friends with a woman that he finds attractive. He always wants to have sex with her." When Sally asks if a man can be friends with a woman he finds unattractive, Harry responds, "No, you pretty much want to nail them, too."[19]

Kayla Williams made a similar point in her memoir. A female soldier must toughen herself up, she said, not just to prepare for danger from the enemy but "to spend months awash in a sea of nervy, hyped-up guys who, when they're not thinking about getting killed, are thinking about getting laid." That perspective was also expressed by a female Dutch soldier on peacekeeping duty in the Balkans, who stated: "The men here think only about sex! During the entire deployment they make it clear. The men here are a bunch of horny dogs." A male NCO agreed, stating that a woman "causes a bit of diversion! And after two months I don't look at her eyes anymore but at her breasts. Every healthy man does it."[20]

Injecting women into combat groups alters the dynamic irrespective of sexual activity. Anna Simons characterizes the point as follows:

"Ultimately, this is the basic, undeniable, unresolvable problem: heterosexual men like women in ways they don't like other men. What they feel for women is not what they feel for men. How they think about women is not how they think about men. And what they see when they look at a woman is not another man."[21]

Introducing women into the group alters the group chemistry in subtle and complex ways. Simons observes that "as soon as the first soldier acts protective, defensive, flirtatious, or resentful, he initiates a dynamic which causes others to do the same, to do the opposite, or to do something else all in the name of setting themselves apart." A fully enforced ban on sexual relations would do little to alter this pattern.

The *New York Times* has argued that the claim that placing men and women in battle together would create a distraction "fails to recognize the discipline the military instills in its troops."[22] Oddly, though, when the topic is sexual harassment or rape in the military, the *Times* repeatedly lectures the military precisely for its failure to instill proper discipline.[23] The *Times* confuses what would be nice with what is practical given the limits of human nature.

Not All Sex Is Consensual

Unfortunately, not all of the sexual behavior that occurs in the military is consensual. Reports from Iraq indicate that there have been some number of sexual assaults, although accurate statistics are hard to come by. The *New York Times Magazine* recently ran a lengthy feature containing stories about a number of women who claimed to have been raped or otherwise sexually mistreated.[24] Such women are at an elevated risk of PTSD, as are women who were sexually assaulted prior to enlistment, and service women are more likely to have been raped prior to enlistment than their civilian peers. At least one of the accounts in the *Times* story turned out not to be true, as one woman—who claimed she was raped twice in the Navy and then injured in an IED attack in Iraq—was not in Iraq at all. In its subsequent correction, the *Times* noted that although it is now clear that she did not serve in Iraq, she "may have become convinced she did."

The *Times* cited a report indicating that almost one-third of a sample of female veterans seeking health care through the Veterans Administration said that they had been victims of rape or attempted rape. Over a third of those said they had been raped multiple times, and 14 percent said they had been gang-raped. Presumably, veterans seeking health care through the VA are not a representative sample of all veterans, so the overall statistics are undoubtedly substantially lower, but how much lower is hard to gauge.

Given the large number of male and female troops who have served in Iraq and Afghanistan, it would be very surprising if there were no sexual assaults. According to a female sociology professor quoted in the *Times* story, "When you take young women and drop them into that hypermasculine environment, the sex stuff just explodes." Because of the "he said, she said" nature of acquaintance-rape cases, many of the allegations of rape cannot be confirmed. Needless to say, an environment in which sexual assaults (and complaints of sexual assaults) are common is not an environment conducive to cohesion.

Is Big Brother Watching Her?

The argument that just as soldiers look on their male comrades as brothers, they should look on their female comrades as sisters neglects the fact that brothers and sisters are not interchangeable. The brother-and-sister metaphor is carried further by Erin Solaro, who suggests that these "brothers" should tell other men, "You disrespect or mistreat our sisters or betray their trust, you are not our brother."[25] This very suggestion highlights the nub of the problem. What Solaro is arguing is that men should play their traditional role toward their sisters—protecting them.

Men protect their sisters by fighting *for* them, not fighting *next to* them. Integrationists who argue that men should play their big brother/protector role vis-à-vis their own troops, all the while ridiculing the idea that they will experience any special protective urges on the battlefield, are attempting to have the argument both ways.

Would Romance Take Away the "Combat Edge"?

In his famous (or infamous) *Washingtonian* article, "Women Can't Fight," James Webb—now a senator from Virginia—described his experience as a Marine combat officer in Vietnam: "We became vicious and aggressive and debased, and reveled in it, because combat is all of those things and we were surviving."[26] While "vicious," "aggressive," and "debased" all have certain negative connotations, most people would choose these attributes over their opposites in soldiers who are defending them. If, as is often suggested, women are a civilizing influence on men, one might wonder whether the presence of women would take away some edge in combat. Is it true, as Webb suggested, that "men fight better without women around"?

There are a number of reasons for thinking that Webb's statement might be true. Combat requires a level of physical brutality found nowhere else. At the same time, men know that women tend to be more squeamish than they are and may tend to forgo some necessary brutality, especially after the "sensitization" training instilled in them by a military that seems to view offended women with more fear than an enemy armored division approaching with guns blazing.

Romantic relationships among troops are especially likely to sap them of aggressiveness. A man whose girlfriend is in the unit is likely to be more concerned with protecting her than with accomplishing the mission. People who doubt this is true should consider what they would do in an attack if their spouses were nearby. One can say, in the abstract, that the mission comes first, but putting that principle into operation in the presence of loved ones would require a level of "compartmentalization" exceeding the capacity of most people.

Another potential response by men in romantic relationships with their female comrades is physiological. Men in long-term committed romantic relationships tend to have lower levels of testosterone than unpaired men.[27] This pattern is consistent with the "challenge hypothesis," which suggests that testosterone levels rise in the context of reproductively relevant competition but decline in its absence. Reduction in testosterone levels of combat soldiers is probably not a good thing. High testosterone levels seem to be associated with greater aggressiveness, sensation-seeking, and pain tolerance, as well as lower levels of fear. Therefore, one might at least wonder whether being "embedded," so to speak, with girlfriends would have detrimental effects on the fierceness of fighting.

What About Prostitutes?

The military has often had an ambivalent attitude toward prostitution. On the one hand, it has recognized the "unabated sexual desires" of men who are away from home for many months, if not years.[28] On the other hand, it has recognized the health risks to soldiers and has provided both medical services for men who contract sexually transmitted diseases and discipline for those who use poor judgment.

What was once a primary sexual outlet for military men—often tolerated if discreet—has now been cut off. In late 2005, President Bush signed an executive order making patronizing a prostitute a specific offense under the Uniform Code of Military Justice (UCMJ). The stated reason for the change is that prostitution sometimes involves sexual slavery and that the new policy is intended to reduce sexual trafficking in women, a problem that has intensified since the breakup of the Soviet Union.[29]

When the Defense Department announced its new policy, it emphasized that the penalty for visiting a prostitute was now the same as the penalty for *being* a prostitute.[30] That seems a little odd. The consequences to "good order and discipline" of a man's visiting a prostitute off base in a legal brothel are quite a bit less severe than a woman's selling herself on payday to the guys in her unit.

Equating the patronizing of prostitutes with being one raises a dirty little secret of the military, and that is that prostitution by female personnel appears to be a widespread phenomenon, although the Pentagon's reticence on the subject makes it difficult to ascertain just how widespread. I have heard from numerous sources claiming personal knowledge (not as customers, they all assure me) of prostitution rings in the Army, Navy, Air Force, and Marines. I have heard it from officers who were responsible for discipline and from enlisted men who were aware of the women to go to. Not surprisingly, the military keeps these matters very quiet when it learns of them. They fit neither the military's desired image nor its story line about the unqualified success of sexual integration. They are usually dealt with in Article 15 proceedings, which are off the record, rather than in courts-martial.

Analyst James Dunnigan, comparing the prostitution ban to the 1914 ban on alcohol on Navy ships, commented that "it's a lot easier to keep whiskey off warships than it is to keep young soldiers away from young women."[31] He also reported that the new regulation had been slowed down because of concerns that it would hurt recruiting. He suggested that "even the senior commanders remember how they entertained themselves when they were young officers [and] some of them may realize that they might well have chosen another profession if their off-duty recreation was heavy on prayer services and light on sin." When it becomes clear to men that the traditional respite from the monastery is no longer available, the role of "warrior"—now "celibate warrior"—may no longer be as appealing.

A Parade of Sex Scandals

Intermixing of the sexes and the resultant sexual activity—both voluntary and coerced—have required the military to expend huge efforts policing sexual behavior. Even if the military performed this function well, it would be a cost of integration, but the military's response to the scandals is often worse than the behavior that created them.[32] A full exploration of the scandals that have faced the military would fill volumes, but a flavor of them is provided here.

TAILHOOK

The "granddaddy" of all sex scandals was the Tailhook fiasco, arising out of a convention of the Tailhook Association, a private association of Navy and Marine aviators, which gets its name from the hook on the rear of a plane that snags the arresting wire on an aircraft-carrier flight deck. The 1991 convention, the first since the dazzling success of the Gulf War, was characterized by what can only be called debauchery. It involved both consensual and nonconsensual sexual activity, the most famous of which was the "gauntlet," a double line of male aviators who groped women who had the fortune or misfortune, depending upon their preferences, of being in the third-floor hall of the Las Vegas Hilton. The out-of-control antics at the convention reflected poorly on many of the participants, both male and female, as well as on the Navy itself.

What followed was a series of investigations that have often been compared—and not unfairly—to "witch hunts," "inquisitions," and "Star Chamber" proceedings. Officers were asked questions about whether they masturbated and the kind of sex they engaged in with their wives or girl-friends. Some were falsely told that comrades had implicated them in misconduct, a common interrogation technique in civilian law enforcement, but a dangerous one to use in a widespread fishing expedition among comrades in arms. Sowing the seeds of distrust among squadron-mates, whose lives depend on each other, is a perilous course, and the technique contributed to the low morale already created by the investigation.

Despite the zeal of Navy prosecutors (or perhaps partly because of it), the net result of the Navy's prosecutions was not a single conviction at a court-martial. Of the 140 cases referred by the Pentagon Inspector General for disciplinary action, a majority (and almost all of the most serious ones) was dropped due to insufficient evidence. Twenty-eight were dealt with at nonjudicial "admiral's masts," with sanctions generally being fines and reprimands, and some officers received nonpunitive actions.[33]

Far from wishing to protect the accused officers, as some alleged, the mind-set of the naval prosecution was to get them at all costs. In the words of one Tailhook defense lawyer, a former Marine Corps prosecutor, "Anybody who said they were a victim, their words were taken as gospel, and anybody who happened to wear wings was a culprit. The insanity of this whole thing is a substantial percentage of people . . . identified as victims didn't regard themselves as victims." According to a PBS report, Tailhook terminated or damaged the careers of fourteen admirals and almost three hundred naval aviators.[34] It might have added that it made naval aviation an unpleasant place to be for thousands of others and led to an exodus of aviators from the Navy. It also caused the Navy to back away from its opposition to opening combat positions to women.

ABERDEEN PROVING GROUNDS

Following close on the heels of Tailhook came allegations by dozens of female trainees at Aberdeen Proving Grounds (and shortly thereafter at Fort Leonard Wood) that they had been subjected to rape and sexual harassment by, or had engaged in fraternization with, their drill sergeants.[35] Determined not to make the mistake that the Navy had made in the early days of the Tailhook scandal by giving the impression that it was not interested in getting to the bottom of things, the Army pulled out all the stops. It set up a worldwide "hot line" for service members to report sexual misconduct, anonymously if they desired, which yielded over eight thousand calls. As Charles Moskos noted, the hot lines "opened up a Pandora's box for those seeking revenge for whatever reason, and many good careers are being ruined needlessly."[36] The Army touted how quickly it had brought charges against some of the instructors as evidence of how seriously it took the complaints.[37] Several female soldiers subsequently took some of the wind out of the Army's sails by alleging that they had been pressured to make false charges of sexual assault.[38]

KELLY FLINN

A series of other high-profile scandals followed, such as the Kelly Flinn "adultery" case. Flinn was the Air Force's first female B-52 pilot, who was threatened with court-martial on charges arising out of sexual misconduct. She faced charges of adultery for having an affair with the civilian husband of a female airman, disobeying a direct order from a superior not to see him again (in fact, a week after that order, she took him to Georgia to meet her parents), lying under oath to investigators about the relationship, and fraternizing with an enlisted man (including an episode of sexual intercourse with him on her front lawn).[39]

The press and many in Congress came to Flinn's defense, with the *New York Times* characterizing her conduct as mere "lovesick blundering."[40] The Air Force saw it differently, however. As the Air Force Chief of Staff, General Ronald Fogleman, stated before the Senate Armed Services Committee, "This is not an issue of adultery. This is an issue about an officer, entrusted to fly nuclear weapons, who lied. That's what this is about."[41] In the end, Air Force Secretary Sheila Widnall offered Flinn a deal. Rather than the honorable discharge that Flinn was seeking or the court-martial that most of the brass wanted, Flinn could accept a "general discharge under honorable conditions."[42] Apparently realizing what a good deal she was offered, she accepted. In the years to come, other military personnel charged with adultery or fraternization would beg to be treated as "badly" as Kelly Flinn was.[43]

MIDSHIPMAN LAMAR OWENS

One would like to think that the crusading zeal has abated—that the lesson has been absorbed that oversensitivity to "gender issues" ultimately hurts rather than helps the cause of female integration—but two recent incidents at the Naval Academy demonstrate that the military has continued its ham-handed approach to allegations of sexual wrongdoing. One episode, involving an officer's off-color comment about a battleship, is described in the next chapter. The other episode was the prosecution of star quarterback Lamar Owens.

Owens was accused by a female midshipman of having raped her in Bancroft Hall, the Academy's residence hall, in January 2006. The case was a classic "he said, she said" acquaintance-rape case. Both parties agreed that sex had taken place. She said that it was nonconsensual; he said that it was consensual. The exact truth is hard to know, but what is crystal clear is that the prosecution's case was very weak.

The woman's story was that Owens had come to her room uninvited in the middle of the night and had sex with her against her will while she was "blacked out" from heavy drinking.[44] At the hearing to determine if there was enough evidence to proceed to court-martial, she was asked whether it was possible that she gave Owens her consent and because of her intoxication did not remember it. She responded, "I suppose," although she later added, "I wouldn't define it as consent if I can't remember it happening."[45] Her boyfriend testified that days after the incident she told him that she "might have" sent Owens an instant message inviting him to her room. Despite these devastating facts, which would make it virtually impossible for a jury to conclude beyond a reasonable doubt that Owens committed rape, Vice Admiral Rodney Rempt, Superintendent of the Naval Academy, nonetheless ordered the case to proceed to court-martial. Owens was acquitted of the rape charge in July 2006, although convicted of two lesser offenses for which the jury recommended "no penalty."

The judge was highly critical of e-mails that had been sent out at the superintendent's direction. One of the e-mails referred to the alleged victim as "the sexual assault victim," without indicating that the claim was an allegation yet to be proved. Another advised recipients to be wary of media accounts, stating that "the only story that gets to the media" is a false or misleading one told by defense attorneys.[46] The judge agreed that at least "the appearance of unlawful command influence" was created by the "rather damnable e-mails." According to the judge, the e-mails gave the impression that the admiral was more concerned with public relations and the reaction of Congress and the Pentagon than in ensuring that Owens got a fair trial. "This is almost like a trial by . . . public affairs," he said.

A few days after the Owens trial ended, Admiral Rempt is reported to have confirmed his political motivation. Explaining privately to a small group of alumni why he pursued charges against Owens, he is reported to have said, "I had no choice; if I did not, we'd have every feminist group and the ACLU after us."[47] If that story is accurate, it is an appalling indictment of Admiral Rempt.

SEXUAL ATTRACTIONS, TENSIONS, jealousies, and frustrations comprise much of the emotional repertoire of young men and women, and there is substantial evidence that these problems impair cohesion, morale, and readiness in an organization that depends critically on teamwork. Officers and NCOs must spend large amounts of time dealing with the turmoil that accompanies these sexual issues. As the commander of a Dutch peacekeeping unit in Bosnia said about women soldiers, "It is hard to choose between their contribution to the camp's life and the drama they create."[48] Time spent on sorting out these relationships is time that is not spent training for or executing the mission. Time spent "spinning" sex scandals is time not spent in defense of the country. These, also, are costs of sexual integration.

16

Double Standards and Political Correctness

It's becoming like Mao's cultural revolution. Everybody knows it's a system built on a thousand little lies, but everybody's waiting for someone that's high ranking who's not a complete moral coward to come out and say so.

—John Hillen[1]

Any officer who is not on-board for all women everywhere does not make Flag Rank.

—Active-Duty Naval Officer

One of the most significant obstacles to achieving a cohesive group is the belief that some members have privileges that others do not have or that rewards are allocated because of personal preferences or political considerations. The "we're all in this together" feeling essential to cohesive groups cannot persist when some are "more equal" than others.[2] Many men believe, with substantial justification, that women are "more equal" in the eyes of the military and civilian leadership. This perception is enhanced when integrationists insist out of one side of their mouths that women are equal to men in their capacity for combat, while at the same time insisting from the other side that women need special treatment and protections.

The 1997 RAND study confirmed a widespread belief that double standards exist for the two sexes.[3] The military has responded to many of these perceived problems by prohibiting their discussion. Statements that standards have been lowered, for example, as well as other "sexist remarks," are defined as "sexual harassment" and will subject the speaker to discipline.[4]

Lower Physical Standards

Lower physical standards for women are a perpetual source of resentment among men. Physical fitness grades are considered at promotion time and are important to careers. Men feel that they have to work very hard to "max" the fitness tests while women can meet their lower standards much more easily. As one female Army captain complained, "My fifty-one-year old father has to run faster and do more push-ups than I do to max/pass the APFT [Army Physical Fitness Test]." She noted that a "lame female in my age group still is allowed to virtually walk the two-mile run and still pass the test."[5]

Absurd complaints by women about physical training are taken remarkably seriously. In 2001, a female officer at U.S. Southern Command in Miami wrote an apparently anonymous letter to both Congress and the Pentagon complaining that a mandatory weekly training run for headquarters staff was demeaning to women because they could not run as fast as men.[6] Women could not keep up the required pace and would drop behind, and slower runners, she said, were being made fun of by faster runners. This weekly run, she claimed, created a "hostile work environment."

In a sane world, the complaining officer would have been told: "Grow up; this is the Army." This is not always a sane world, however. The run was canceled, much to the chagrin of those who thought this another example of an increasingly feminized military compromising its warrior culture to accommodate women. The matter was also referred to the Department of Defense Inspector General, who sent a number of agents to Miami to conduct interviews. *Two years* after the initial complaint, the Inspector General issued a report rejecting the claim of sex discrimination and concluding that a nine-minute-per-mile pace was not unreasonable in an informal staff run. Military men can be forgiven for believing that their concerns are not taken as seriously as concerns of women by commanders who believe that any claim, however trivial, must be investigated, often at the highest level.

Special Consideration for "Female Issues"

Some double standards involve special consideration for specifically female issues. The RAND study concluded that men's belief in double standards was enhanced by such things as "an unofficial Army policy" under which women were to receive showers every seventy-two hours while in the field. One need not invoke sexism to understand the resentment "among the men, who endure a heavier workload when the women, the vehicles, and the drivers return to base so that women can take showers." Another study recounted a complaint that, notwithstanding orders in the Gulf to use water only for drinking during times of shortage, female soldiers used it for bathing without apparent discipline.[7]

The RAND study also found that junior enlisted women often used "female problems" to get out of unattractive duties.[8] Several women told Laura Miller that they avoided certain duties by complaining of menstrual cramps. Others told her that they could hide contraband (such as candy) by placing tampons or underwear on top of the contents of their lockers or drawers because, once encountering these items, their superiors would be too embarrassed—or too afraid of harassment accusations—to look any further. Still others obtain special consideration by flirting with their superiors.[9]

Many men also resent the fact that women can avoid deployment—or often even their service contracts—simply by getting pregnant.[10] As discussed in the next chapter, there are widespread perceptions that many women intentionally become pregnant to avoid deployment.[11]

Perceptions That Women Do Not Do Their Share

Women are perceived by many men (and many women) as not contributing their share to today's military despite their demands for equal recognition. As one enlisted man complained to Laura Miller, "Today all you hear in the Army is that we are equal, but men do all the hard and heavy work whether it's combat or not."[12] Yet another told her: "The majority of females I know are not soldiers. They are employed. Anything strenuous is avoided with a passion. I would hate to serve with them during combat! I would end up doing my job and 2/3 of theirs just to stay alive."

These negative attitudes are not confined to enlisted men. One major told Miller that "if every soldier in the U.S. Army today had been trained at the same low level of expectation that female soldiers routinely are, the U.S. Army today would be either dead or in Prisoner of War camps."

Some women self-consciously use their sex to make their lives easier. Kayla Williams writes of women in Iraq:

> You could get things easier, and you could get out of things easier. For a girl there were lots of little things you could do to make your load while deployed a whole lot lighter. You could use your femaleness to great advantage. You could do less work, get more assistance, and receive more special favors. Getting supplies? Working on the trucks? It could be a cinch—if you wanted it to be. It didn't take much. A little went a long way. Some of us worked it to the bone. Who says the life of the Army girl has to be cruel?[13]

Many men feel that the presence of women imposes extra burdens on them. A sergeant in Mosul wrote to the *Army Times* that when insurgents placed a bounty on women, an order went out that women had to have male "battle buddies," requiring men to "stop what they were doing" to escort female soldiers. "Every time the chain of command puts a new policy into effect to protect our female soldiers," he said, "that requires more from the male soldiers, which means we're no longer equal."[14]

Requiring Men to Adapt to Women, Rather Than Vice Versa

The standard operating assumption seems to be that military men need to be educated out of their "masculinity," but it is not entirely facetious to suggest that perhaps women need to be educated out of their "femininity." The military was a largely male institution built upon masculine virtues of courage, stoicism, and toughness that instilled military bearing and skill in ways oriented toward the male psyche. When women's role in the military was expanded, one might have supposed that the attitude should have been, "Here is the military; adapt if you can!"

Instead of requiring women to adapt to the military and its men, however, the primary focus has been on requiring the military, and the men in it, to adapt to women. Even though women commonly say that they just want to be treated like everyone else—that is, like men—when they are treated that way, they often feel abused and complain. So, the result is that it is the military that must change. Women do not like yelling; okay, no more yelling. Women cannot handle the physical demands of basic training; okay, we'll make it easier. Women do not like sexual talk; okay, no more sexual talk. In other words, the female tail has been wagging the mostly male dog. Ironically, much of this response seems to be motivated by the propensity of men to protect women that so many advocates of sexual integration deny.

Resistance to Authority

The RAND study reported complaints that women were more inclined to resist leadership—to object to being told to do something their commander's way "because he said so"—a tendency that "undermines discipline and the rank authority system."[15] This finding is consistent with the earlier suggestion that women may fit less comfortably into hierarchical organizations. The RAND study, however, always eager to redefine a "gender problem" as something else, asserted that this apparent female resistance reflected a "generation gap," not a "gender gap."

The cause of the increasingly common resistance to leadership, the report asserted, is that the military is drawing from an undisciplined "generation that was never spanked." The trend only appeared to be related to sex "because women are overrepresented in the younger generation"; thus, "generational differences were occasionally reported as a gender problem." Contrary to the RAND report, however, women were not "overrepresented in the younger generation." They still made up only about 15 percent of the junior ranks, so if resistance to leadership was sex neutral, only one out of seven of the "resisters" would be female, hardly a basis for false impressions that the problem was related to sex.

Kayla Williams recounted her own resistance to authority, at one point saying to her platoon leader, a female lieutenant, "So why don't you go inside and do whatever it is that you do that makes you deserve so much more money than me." In another incident, the troops she is with hear firing in the distance, and everyone takes cover. Her female superior, Staff Sergeant Moss, tells her to "run ops," meaning to get in the truck and listen for enemy communications (their job is intelligence). "I ignore this," Williams says. "It cannot be happening. NCOs are not supposed to make their soldiers do anything they won't do themselves, so I think she can get up and pull ops herself if it's that important. . . ." Williams pretended not to hear Moss, and even though the enemy fire was weaker and more distant, she decided not to get up "until we are completely safe."[16] By then, presumably, the likelihood of intercepting actionable intelligence was much reduced.

Trainees, at least female ones, seem to learn early that there is little penalty for defying authority. A recent *Wall Street Journal* story about the softening of basic training described a female trainee who was caught writing letters home when she was supposed to be training. Her drill sergeant ordered her to crawl on her belly through the barracks and chant: "I will not write letters in the war room."[17] The private refused to comply with the order. That kind of insubordination should have resulted in either additional discipline or discharge for "failure to adapt." This trainee was simply transferred to another platoon. This is not only "not your father's Army," it is not so clear it is even your mother's.

The perception that "some are more equal than others" is extremely destructive of group cohesion, but female personnel are led to believe that they have moral authority to question their superiors. Madeline Morris points to the following statement of a female former Army officer as support for the view that integration of women has positive effects:

> It helps a lot to have females there, but especially if they have some rank. Like in Saudi, during the Persian Gulf War, my commander told me to "Act like a soldier, not like a girl." I confronted him and he backed off. So he got feedback, because there was a female there— but especially because I had enough rank and the confidence to confront him. Not everyone would have been in a position to do that.[18]

Thus, members of a small, and already suspect, group are thought to have a right empowering them to provide "feedback" to their superiors, questioning them, in this case, over a comment that is far milder than those that virtually every man must endure practically every day. The commander "backed off," probably not because he felt he was wrong but because he feared having career-destroying charges filed against him.

The RAND study also reported that male superiors were hesitant to discipline women, so "junior females were permitted to espouse these attitudes more freely than their male colleagues." Thus, it concluded, "gender is one of the ways in which subordinates are now reported to be challenging or even chastising their superiors." So, in what way, one might ask, is this *not* a "gender problem"?

Sexual Misconduct Charges and the "Gender Card"

The "gender card" is a potent weapon, and it accounts for some of the re-luctance to discipline women. According to personnel of both sexes, some women use complaints of sexual harassment, or a threat of such com-plaints, to avoid unpleasant tasks.[19] Some superiors are reluctant to push a woman hard during physical activities, because she has a "club" she could use against him if he did.[20] Moreover, a woman can complain of sexual harassment if she does not like her job and, even if the charges are unsubstantiated, she may be reassigned.

Men react predictably. A male Army warrant officer described his prescription for men working with female soldiers: "no humor, period; no being alone with a female soldier; not even the slightest hint of anything other than cold professionalism." An Army reserve officer said, "I never praise or chastise a female without someone else being present, preferably a female NCO."[21]

An organization based upon discipline cannot run effectively when some subordinates hold a club over their superiors. When superiors hold their positions at the sufferance of their female subordinates, the poor dis-cipline so often found in mixed-sex units is virtually inevitable.

Differential Treatment of Sexual Misconduct

The Tailhook investigation found numerous examples of misconduct by women.[22] Yet none of the Navy women involved was censured for their participation. Indeed, it was established Defense Department policy that the investigation would not include misconduct by female officers.[23]

In one particularly egregious case, Navy Lieutenant Cole Cowden was prosecuted for sexual assault and for conduct unbecoming an officer. Lieutenant Elizabeth Warnick claimed that Cowden, along with two other men, had attempted to gang-rape her at the 1990 Tailhook convention. Warnick later admitted under oath that she had lied about the attempted gang rape because she had had consensual sex with Cowden and was afraid that her fiancé would find out. Warnick's story was also apparently intended to deflect attention from her own misconduct at the 1991 convention, as she had been identified as being a willing participant in some of the rowdy behavior.[24] She apparently thought—correctly, as it turned out—that playing the victim would spare her conduct any scrutiny. Despite the fact that Warnick's attempt to destroy a fellow officer's career by false accusations of a serious felony was far more calculated than the exuberance that characterized most of the Tailhook activities, she received little, if any, discipline.

As events would show, the military did not learn much from the double standard of Tailhook. In many cases, an accused man is acquitted of criminal wrongdoing but then punished administratively for it, while the accuser, who may have violated the same rules as the accused, gets off unscathed because of immunity given her in exchange for her testimony or policies of "amnesty." Addressing this issue in the context of the investigation of sexual assaults at the Air Force Academy, the Pentagon Inspector General observed that this imbalance in treatment is "contrary to fundamental fairness."[25]

In the Lamar Owens case, the accuser and her witnesses had been granted immunity for underage drinking, drinking in Bancroft Hall, maintaining a party house off base, abusing prescription painkillers, having sex in Bancroft Hall, drinking on guard duty, being absent from the guard post, and sexual assault (it seems the accuser had sexually assaulted a male midshipman by grabbing his genitals in a bar).[26] Yet Owens is the one who was denied both a commission and a degree and required to pay the Navy more than $90,000 toward the cost of his education.

Such inequities can occur even in the absence of immunity. Several years ago at the Naval Academy, a male and female midshipman were found in the woman's room "after a long night of drinking and socializing."[27] The man admitted to consensual sex; the woman contended that she was heavily intoxicated and had no memory of having sex with the man but "suspected" that she may have been sexually assaulted. Because Academy rules forbid sex on campus, the man was expelled. The woman, by denying having engaged in consensual sex, had admitted no wrongdoing and therefore was not prosecuted. The man found himself working in a warehouse to pay off the $76,000 he owed the Navy for education costs, and the woman graduated to the fleet. The draconian punishment imposed for engaging in consensual sexual activity—termination of a naval career and repayment of tuition—creates large incentives for false claims of sexual assault.

Favored Assignments and Favorable Treatment

Women also receive favored treatment in assignments. Nowhere has this been more obvious than in combat aviation. With the post–cold war "drawdown" of the military, the number of flying billets was reduced, and competition for them was fierce. Women were moved ahead of men in response to pressures to train more female pilots.[28] At the Naval Academy, for example, women were given preference in claiming pilot billets over men with higher class standings. Only if women passed these positions by could they be claimed by men.[29]

The most famous female pilot so favored was Lieutenant Kara Hultgreen. Much has been written about the Hultgreen incident. Unfortunately much of it has been taken as critical of her, rather than of the Navy. (Hultgreen acted in admirable fashion at the 1991 Tailhook convention, when she responded to a man's grabbing her by decking him rather than by donning the victim's mantle.) Hultgreen was one of the first women to enter carrier aviation. She had originally been an A-6 Intruder pilot, and when that aircraft was phased out, she was selected to fly the F-14. In October 1994, she was killed in an abortive landing on the carrier USS *Abraham Lincoln*.

The Navy publicly maintained that Hultgreen was an above-average pilot whose death was attributable to a malfunctioning engine valve. It claimed that it had put nine experienced aviators on simulators in a similar situation and all but one had crashed. As details came out, however, the Navy's story was seen to have serious holes in it. First, it ignored the fact that the engine stall was itself precipitated by pilot error. Second, and more serious, was the fact that pilots in the simulator test were ordered not to use the standard procedures prescribed in such an emergency; in other words, the test "was configured to produce an almost automatic crash."[30]

The mere fact of Hultgreen's crashing was not particularly noteworthy, other than the personal tragedy of her death. Crashes during training flights occur regularly—most with male pilots, of course—and most of those crashes are caused by pilot error. What made the incident significant was the Navy's attempt to downplay pilot error as a cause and also the fact that training records that were leaked to the press indicated that Hultgreen had experienced serious problems in training and had been given more chances than men usually receive.[31] Indeed, many pilots were convinced that a man with her record would have washed out. The Hultgreen incident created a near-universal perception in the aviation community that standards were lowered for women.

The perception of lowered standards was reinforced by the case of Admiral Stanley Arthur. His nomination as Commander in Chief of Pacific Forces was blocked by a senatorial "hold" because he had upheld the dismissal from flight training of a female pilot who had claimed that she was failed in retaliation for filing a sexual harassment complaint. The treatment of Admiral Arthur, based entirely on his decision to support the grounding of a female pilot for substandard flying ability—a decision whose good faith was unchallenged—sent, in the words of Gregory Vistica, "a clear message—one not to be missed by many admirals."[32] After Admiral Arthur's experience, he wrote, "Any politically sensitive officer understood, rightly or wrongly, that women were to succeed as pilots—period."

One of the most egregious cases that came to light involved a female helicopter pilot who had failed a routine safety test. A subsequent review found that she had panicked on several occasions while carrying passengers. On one occasion, her copilot had to land the helicopter for her because she had become incapacitated. She was revived with oxygen on the ground and carried away on a stretcher. The admiral in charge of the Pacific Fleet's air forces overruled a safety panel's recommendation and allowed her to keep her wings. Not surprisingly, male pilots were outraged.

A study of Army and Air Force pilots found the same kinds of problems so apparent in the Navy. It reported an overwhelming belief on the part of men that women were given more time to complete tasks, more training, and more chances. Women themselves also felt that instructors were more lenient with them, and "they appreciated the special considerations."[33]

There is also a widespread perception among men that their superiors indulge women in requests that would go nowhere from a man. A former Navy officer told me of a female officer who was unhappy with her orders because she wanted to be assigned to the same base as her boyfriend: "She went to the CO's office and started crying, and he made some calls and got her orders changed." If a man had gone in and said that he did not like his orders—and few men would, he added—the response would have been, "I don't care. The Navy says that's where you're going; that's where you're going."

Preferential treatment is especially pernicious in the military. It undermines the equality that is so essential to group cohesion. Moreover, the consequences in the military of a less qualified person holding a position are more likely to be fatal than in the civilian world (with the exception, perhaps, of medicine). The stigma to the favored group that many have identified as resulting from preferential treatment is also more likely to have serious consequences. If you are a male pilot knowing that women are being passed through training under circumstances when men would not, how do you feel about being assigned to fly with a woman? Chances are, you would have less confidence in her because you know that she did not pass through as rigorous a selection process as the male pilots did (even though she may be just as good). Pilots trust each other with their lives. Anything that impairs that trust imperils their lives.

A Climate of Political Correctness

There is little that will terminate a military career faster than expressing doubts about sexual integration. Anita Blair, later Assistant Secretary of the Navy for Manpower and Reserve Affairs under the Bush administration, testified before Congress in 1999 that "the Army, Navy, and Air Force have declared gender-integration a success, and service members are strongly discouraged from even expressing concerns about gender-integration, much less criticizing any aspect of it."[34]

Because men do not feel themselves at liberty to make negative comments about sexual integration, studies that report men's support for it must be taken with a grain of salt. Laura Miller found in her study of attitudes of Army personnel that many men would initially recite the "party line" about the success of integration. Only when pressed would "their true feelings burst forth."[35] Other men would say nothing in mixed-sex groups, but they would privately indicate that they did not feel free to state their true opinions publicly, especially in the presence of female officers.

To the extent that the military has adopted a culture of double standards and political correctness—with all of the dishonesty that such phenomena entail—one must fear for the quality of the officer corps. People of integrity and honor do not operate well in such an environment, so there is a risk that the quality of the officer corps will decline as men of honor leave the service rather than participate in such behaviors and have their places taken by careerists all too eager to please.

Overreaction to Trivial Incidents: Lieutenant Bryan Black

At the same time that the Navy was prosecuting Midshipman Lamar Owens, a case was also proceeding against Lieutenant Bryan Black. Black was a Naval Academy oceanography instructor who, while observing the decommissioned battleship *Wisconsin* when in Norfolk, Virginia, on a field trip, said something to the effect that "battleships are just so freaking awesome, it gives me a hard-on just talking about it." Then, noticing a female midshipman, he is reported to have said, "Even [you] would get a hard-on, wouldn't you . . . oh, that's right, you can't do that, so I guess it would be tweaking your nipples." Black's comment to this warrior-in-training was certainly bad manners and worthy of a reprimand, but the Academy turned it into a court-martial offense.[36]

The day after the incident, Black apologized to the female midshipman, Samantha Foxton, and that had seemed to be the end of the matter. Unfortunately for Black, however, a female faculty member, who apparently nursed a strong dislike for him, conducted her own "investigation" and pushed the matter to higher levels. It turned out that not only had Black made the comment in Norfolk, but someone also reported that he had used vulgar language to characterize his ex-wife. What Black learned only later was that Foxton had been caught the day before the incident buying alcohol for underage enlisted personnel, suggesting that her initial complaint may have been an attempt to deflect attention from her own wrongdoing.

Although an investigation by a Judge Advocate General (JAG) Corps officer concluded that Black should be issued a "non-punitive letter of caution and counsel,"[37] Admiral Rempt rejected the recommendation and insisted instead on holding an admiral's mast, a hearing that could result in up to sixty days' confinement to quarters and a letter of reprimand, which would effectively terminate Black's career. The superintendent also announced that he was taking the unusual step of holding the usually private proceeding in the foyer of the administration building and inviting the faculty and staff to attend. Sensing—no doubt correctly—that the proceeding was to be a "show trial" to make an example out of him, Black invoked his right to refuse the admiral's mast and proceed by special court-martial.

Admiral Rempt's decision to disregard the recommendation of a nonpunitive letter was widely viewed as influenced by criticism he had received from the Academy's Board of Visitors that he was not making sufficient progress against sexual harassment. Ultimately, after holding the court-martial over Black's head for months, Admiral Rempt offered to downgrade the proceeding to an admiral's mast to be held before a different admiral "to avoid any perception of bias or any predetermined outcome." The hearing lasted an hour, and Black was given a "non-punitive letter of caution," which does not become a part of his military record, although a negative fitness report from the Academy could nonetheless block any promotion and lead to his forced dismissal.[38]

So ultimately the right result may have been reached, but at what cost in time and money? Black's original comment was made in September 2005, and the admiral's mast did not take place until September 2006. Black had been scheduled to deploy to Bahrain shortly after the complaint to support the fighting in Iraq, but his orders were changed because of the complaint, placing him in "limbo" for a full year.

What would have happened if the sexes had been reversed between Black and the midshipman? Probably nothing. There would likely have been no complaint even if a male midshipman had been offended. And can one really imagine a female officer being prosecuted for having made vulgar remarks about her ex-husband? It is extremely unlikely that any man would complain, and if he did, his complaint would have been ignored and he would have been made to feel like a fool for complaining.

The overreaction of the Academy does women no favors. The informative blog *CDR Salamander,* apparently hosted by an active-duty Navy commander, predicted that the response to the Black case, and presumably others like it, will be that "smart officers will gather their male buddies and ditch their female shipmates at the first chance they get on liberty or the weekends." Then, he added, "Wait, my male JOs [junior officers] already do that . . . those who aren't sleeping with them."[39]

Failure to Acknowledge "Bad News"

The Pentagon has all but announced that it will not release information reflecting negatively on women. Sara Lister, then Assistant Secretary of the Army for Manpower and Reserve Affairs, candidly stated that the Army does not publicly discuss strength and pregnancy issues because "those subjects quickly became fodder for conservatives seeking to limit women's role in the Army."[40]

The Defense Department's reluctance to report bad news is illustrated by the history of the 1997 RAND study on integration by Harrell and Miller, which has been mentioned throughout this book. Although the report as released identified a number of problems with sexual integration, it repeatedly discounted them and attributed them to something other than integration itself. The original draft of the RAND study was substantially more negative.[41] In testimony before a subcommittee of the House Armed Services Committee, Elaine Donnelly detailed a number of changes between the draft version of the report and the report ultimately released by the Pentagon. Even the title was changed to add an upbeat impression. The original title was the neutral, though descriptive, "Recent Gender Integration in the Military: Effects Upon Readiness, Cohesion and Morale." The principal title of the report as released was changed to add a little spin: "New Opportunities for Military Women."

According to Donnelly, a number of negative statements were removed from the draft, including the following:

- "Pregnant single women were perceived to be a long-term burden."
- "When women, especially single women, intentionally become pregnant to escape either unpleasant duties, a certain command, or a deployment, both men and women resent the additional burden they must shoulder as a consequence of their absence."
- "Some unit commanders appear to feel pressured to report success in the training, retaining, and promotion of women. Men who perceive this believe women are given more opportunities than men to work up to the standard."
- "Women agreed that false harassment complaints are a problem, and added that they undermine the ability of women who are truly harassed to have their complaint taken seriously. . . ."

Even the representativeness of the findings in the units chosen for study is subject to doubt, because unit commanders decided which individuals should be included and which should not. Harrell and Miller acknowledged that they might have been denied access to "individuals with objectionable views," but they said they had no reason to believe that this was the case.[42] If it were done right, of course, they would be given no such reason.

The notion that commanders would select individuals with favorable views is not fanciful. Laura Miller herself has reported that both men and women have complained to her that when commanders select personnel to meet with representatives of DACOWITS (Defense Advisory Committee on Women in the Services), they "typically sent soldiers whom they knew to possess a view compatible with that of the DACOWITS."[43]

A similar "spin" seemed to pervade a British army study conducted in 2000 testing the ability of women to serve in ground combat. The study concluded that women were as capable of serving in combat units as men based upon a series of physical trials. The army's director of infantry pointed out, however, that this result was obtained only by eliminating tasks from the study that women were not capable of performing. The field trials, he wrote, amounted to little more than "aggressive camping." His commentary on the report was apparently suppressed by his superiors.[44] Success is always possible, it seems; it just needs to be defined the right way.

The Message in the Media

The fact that expression of negative views about women is a career killer should be kept in mind when reading stories about women's performance in the military. Articles lauding the performance of women in the Iraq War are noteworthy for their almost universal absence of negative comment about women. This seems a little odd. Integrationists routinely speak of the entrenched sexism that makes women "second class" members of the military and of the widespread opposition to their presence, especially in combat zones. Yet the consistent message that the public receives from the media is that integration is a resounding success, that women are performing magnificently, and that these opinions are universally shared.

In May 2005, the *Washington Post* ran a lengthy front-page story on female personnel in Iraq titled "For Female GIs, Combat Is a Fact." Nowhere in the twenty-five-hundred-word story was there a hint of reservation.[45] The story was filled with assertions that women in Iraq are already "in combat" and that military personnel on the ground were chafing under existing restrictions on women's assignments. According to the story:

> Dozens of soldiers interviewed across Iraq—male and female, from lower enlisted ranks to senior officers—voiced frustration over restrictions on women mandated in Washington that they say make no sense in the war they are fighting. All said the policy should be

changed to allow, at a minimum, mixed-sex support units to be assigned to combat battalions. Many favored a far more radical step: letting qualified women join the infantry.

There are four possible explanations for this apparent unanimity. The first, and simplest, is that the story accurately reflects current opinion. The second is that the result is due to sampling error; that is, despite the fact that many people have reservations about women, the "luck of the draw" led to only supporters being questioned. The third possibility is that the author of the story simply chose not to include opinions that did not fit her story line—either by being selective in whom she talked to or by not including negative comments that she received. Fourth, some people with whom the author spoke may not have given her their candid opinion.

The first possibility—actual unanimity of opinion—is very unlikely. In response to stories like that in the *Washington Post,* a Marine infantry battalion commander fresh from the fighting in Iraq had the following reaction, in a private e-mail, to suggestions that women who are injured by IEDs are in combat and that sexual integration has been a resounding success. As to the suggestion that women injured in Iraq are "in combat," he responded, "No argument there." He continued:

> But the nature of what infantry units do, and particularly during times like what I've just experienced, is brutal, harsh, and requires a physical and emotional stamina that females, at least 99.9 percent of them, don't have. The other part of the story that never gets published is what I see first hand: the lack of discipline in most "mixed" units because you have men competing for the affections of the few females, and the pregnancy rates of deployed females. Those are the realities that get ignored in this discussion.

Needless to say, he made clear, as would virtually anyone in that circumstance, that his comments should not be attributed to him by name. From poll results, blog postings, and off-the-record discussions, it is clear that the absence of negative opinion in the story is not representative of soldiers' sentiments.

As for the "luck of the draw" explanation, that can be quickly ruled out. The probability of "dozens" of *randomly interviewed* subjects truthfully expressing unanimity about a policy over which there is substantial disagreement is very low.

That leaves the last two possibilities—either that the reporter chose not to elicit comment from opponents or that she did and they gave her less than candid responses. I do not know enough about the reporter to comment on any bias she might have, and it is always possible that she was playing word games, as her language could be interpreted to mean that all of the people who "voiced frustration" favored a policy change, not all of the people to whom she spoke. Regardless, no matter how diligent she was in attempting to sample a broad spectrum of opinion, she would be unlikely to elicit many negative opinions without providing clear and credible assurances of confidentiality. Because any savvy observer would know of the adverse career consequences for publicly expressing negative opinions about integration, a conscientious reporter might caution readers that the unanimity might be more apparent than real.

Are the Media Neutral Reporters?

There can be little doubt that the news media tend to support integration of women, and this is reflected in their stories. Laura Miller reports that the media gave extensive coverage to the debate over women in combat in the wake of the 1992 Presidential Commission report. Of the twenty-three stories in the *New York Times* and the thirty-nine stories in the *Los Angeles Times,* she found that "only two even suggested that some military women might not want to enter the combat arms."[46] Although military women testified on both sides of the issue before the commission, these papers quoted only women arguing for eliminating the combat exclusion. Moreover, the papers generally obtained comments from female officers, especially pilots, rather than the far more numerous enlisted ranks, where opposition to combat roles tends to be greater.

Although the papers are full of positive stories of women in Iraq and Afghanistan, stories that might reflect negatively on women get far less play. Such a story occurred quite early in the war in Afghanistan. In January 2002, two Marine helicopters were on a mission to resupply troops searching for Taliban and al-Qaeda forces, when one of the helicopters lost power because an engine clogged up with the powdery sand that plagued our forces there.[47] Because of the high altitude (about ninety-five hundred feet above sea level, although only two hundred feet or so above the ground), the heavily loaded helicopter lacked the power to maintain altitude with its remaining engines. The pilot, Captain Douglas Glasgow, was able to slow the descent somewhat and prevent the helicopter from nose-diving. Upon impact, the helicopter began burning, with its crew of seven inside. Two Marines were killed instantly, and the rest of the crew were injured and rendered unconscious. Upon regaining consciousness, three of them, including Glasgow, were able to get out of the helicopter on their own, but Glasgow went back in to free his copilot and another Marine, all while ammunition in the helicopter was cooking off.

The pilot of the lead helicopter, a female Marine captain, made a few passes over the crash site and decided that it was too risky to attempt to land. Assuming that everyone on board was dead, she headed back to base. Fortunately, an unmanned reconnaissance aircraft passed overhead, and its cameras recorded the "SOS" that Glasgow had crafted out of helicopter parts and other materials. About two and a half hours after the crash, the crew was rescued by Army helicopters.

A Marine report issued several months later lauded Captain Glasgow's courageous actions: "With complete disregard for his personal injuries and the extremely cold conditions, Capt. Glasgow continued to care for his crew and watched the area for enemy threats." The report was highly critical of the commander of the lead helicopter, however: "Had the lead aircrew flown as we train and complied with the on-scene commander checklist, they would have remained on the scene, probably seen the signaling of the mishap aircrew and engaged in tactical recovery of aircraft and pilots (TRAP) operations." Her failure to do so did not contribute to the two deaths, the report said, but it imperiled the survivors and prolonged their suffering.

It is unclear whether any action was taken against this pilot, as administrative actions are covered by the Privacy Act. This same pilot had made the news a few weeks earlier when she made a hard landing on an inclined slope on a mission to insert Special Forces troops, damaging the helicopter so it could not be flown. Perhaps it was this experience that led her to be unwilling to set her helicopter down when Glasgow's helicopter crashed.[48]

The national press was decidedly uninterested in this story. The report about her leaving the scene of the crash appears to have been reported in only two newspapers—the *Marine Corps Times,* for obvious reasons, and the *Los Angeles Times,* because the Marines were from a southern California base. If the sexes had been reversed, and the female pilot had rescued her crewmates and Glasgow had returned to base, the woman would have been lauded as a hero with her face adorning news magazines across the country, and her performance would have been treated as proof that women belong in combat. Glasgow, in contrast, would probably have been disgraced, labeled a coward, and court-martialed. Ironically, just a month before this incident, the woman had been interviewed from Afghanistan on CNN as part of its Christmas Eve coverage. Out of the sixteen hundred men and dozen women at the Marine base near Kandahar, CNN chose only her for a solo interview (although it subsequently jointly interviewed five male Marines for less time than the solo interview took).[49] She was considered newsworthy for simply being in Afghanistan, but her performance there—at least if not exemplary—was not.

What About Stories of Women's Gallant·Performance?

Stories from Iraq highlighting courageous performance by individual women—some of which have already been mentioned—are already beginning to skew the integration debate in an inappropriate way. Contrary to these stories, experience to date is not persuasive evidence that women should be in combat. The women involved in the reported incidents generally did their duty well, but most of the incidents would have been unremarkable if the participants had been men. Men perform well in firefights all the time; the fact that a woman occasionally does so is not terribly strong evidence for integration. Most of the reported incidents were only brief encounters with the enemy, lasting just a few minutes, unlike the intensive battles lasting days or weeks that combat troops have waged in Iraq.

Positive reports about women are relevant only if they are representative. If good performance is more likely to be reported than bad performance, good reports lose much of their persuasive effect, and the press is more likely to report positive stories than negative ones. A Nexis search in the "News,All" library conducted in early 2007 yielded 193 hits for Leigh Ann Hester, the female MP who received a Silver Star for heroism. (A Google search yielded over 13,000 hits.) In contrast, the virtual media blackout on the female helicopter pilot who left her fellow pilot and his crew for dead in Afghanistan (two Nexis hits and two Google hits) has already been mentioned. Reliable judgments about women's performance are possible only if the underlying data are reliable.

The limited value of these isolated anecdotes is illustrated by considering what would happen if the United States had fifteen thousand sixty-year-old men in Iraq and Afghanistan instead of fifteen thousand women. If it did, many of these older men would undoubtedly behave bravely. Would these stories be persuasive evidence that the military should allow sixty-year-olds to enlist? Not at all. The relevant question would be whether the sixty-year-old men are as effective in combat as twenty-year-old men, and few would be (or be expected to be).

Performance of individual women is only part of the story of combat effectiveness. All of the issues about cohesion, pregnancy, sexual problems, prisoner-of-war issues, male protectiveness, and the like exist even if individual women excel at combat. The stories of indiscipline in integrated units in Iraq suggest that we are far from a *Starship Troopers* military, even if we may have a Dizzy Flores or two.

Disparagement of Traditions

A perception of political correctness is also created by abandonment of traditions that are thought to "exclude" women in some way. Of all institutions in the world other than religions, the military is most zealous in guarding its traditions, and even modest tinkering can bring howls from traditionalists. In 2004, for example, Admiral Rempt changed the words of the Naval Academy fight song, "Navy Blue and Gold"—which was adopted in 1923—to make it more "inclusive."[50] Only two small changes were made in the first verse. The first line, "Now college men from sea to sea may sing of colors true," was changed to "Now colleges from sea to sea . . . ," which conjures a decidedly odd mental image. The third line was changed from "For sailor men in battle fair since fighting days of old" to "For sailors brave in battle fair. . . ." Many Naval Academy alumni resented the change, as illustrated by a letter from an alumnus to the superintendent telling him, "It is not your song."

The Naval Academy was not the first service academy to make cosmetic, yet emotionally significant, changes for the sake of inclusion. From the early days of the Air Force Academy, the words "Bring Me Men" in two-foot-tall letters were displayed on a stone portal through which cadets walk on their first day at the Academy. The slogan, described in the *Denver Post* as "one of the most recognizable images in Colorado," was the first line of the poem "The Coming American" by Sam Walter Foss, written in 1894.[51] The first four lines of the poem are:

> *Bring me men to match my mountains,*
> *Bring me men to match my plains;*
> *Men to chart a starry empire,*
> *Men to make celestial claims.*

The words were intended to be inspirational, but in response to the sexual-assault controversy at the Academy it was decided that they sent the wrong message. The aluminum letters were chiseled out of the wall in 2003 to be replaced by something not at the time identified that would "more suitably represen[t]" the co-ed nature of the Academy.

After the announcement that the "Bring Me Men" sign was to come down, Air Force Lieutenant Stephanie Oldham argued in an Internet posting for some appreciation of the context of both the poem and the sign. The speaker in this poem, she said, is not the Air Force Academy, but the Creator. Moreover, she said, "This is a call for those who enter the Academy to strive all their lives to match those mountains," rather than "an attempt to alienate and oppress females in the Air Force."[52] Her plea fell on deaf ears.

Ultimately, what the Academy erected in place of "Bring Me Men" was the Air Force's "core values":

Integrity First
Service Before Self
Excellence in All We Do

These core values were adopted in 1997 during the tenure of Air Force Secretary Sheila Widnall, whose lack of military background shows in the slogan. Unlike the West Point motto "Duty, Honor, Country," or the Navy and Marine Corps' core values of "Honor, Courage, Commitment," there is nothing even vaguely martial about the Air Force values. They are fine aspirations, but they would be more apt as the motto of a commercial bank or the state department of motor vehicles than of a war-fighting organization.

Like the modification of the "Navy Blue and Gold," ultimately this change is relatively trivial, but it is a further signal that the military, a tradition-bound institution, is willing to abandon its traditions for what appears to many to be "political correctness."

. . .

CONCERNS ABOUT DOUBLE standards and political correctness are not necessarily complaints about women themselves but rather about the way the military has responded to their presence, as well as the way that some women have exploited that response. Mistakes in implementation of a policy do not demonstrate that the policy goal is not worthwhile, and many women are themselves concerned about the military's response. There is a sense, however, in which the mistakes the military has made are inevitable, at least as long as its "progress" is measured by how many women it can attract and retain and as long as military leaders allow themselves to be bullied by political pressures into overreaction on "gender issues."

PART VI

SPECIAL PROBLEMS
RESULTING FROM
FEMALE PERSONNEL

In the previous section, a number of threats to cohesion and combat effectiveness were identified that result from the mixing of men and women—male protectiveness, a variety of sexual issues, and double standards. Other problems arise that relate specifically to the sexuality and reproductive biology of women.

All personnel face the risk of suffering abuse at the hands of enemy captors, but women face the special risk of rape. Rape of women is a constant in war, and female prisoners have been sexually abused in both the Gulf War and the Iraq War. This is a problem seldom faced by men. Paradoxically, advocates of women in combat dismiss the risk of rape by the enemy, while at the same time complaining of the high risk of sexual abuse faced by female personnel from their own colleagues.

The other set of problems arises from the reproductive biology of women. One consequence of having many female personnel of reproductive age is that large numbers of military women become pregnant. When they do, they can impose substantial burdens on their units. The fact that so many military women who get pregnant are single means that single motherhood—which is a far greater problem for the military than single fatherhood—is a common phe-nomenon, and it, along with pregnancy, poses substantial obstacles to readiness.

Women also face greater challenges because of menstruation and other hygiene issues. Some women, though not many, are debilitated during portions of their menstrual cycle, and others suffer from performance decline. Field duty and deployments are particularly difficult for women, because of the difficulty of dealing with these issues. All of these problems make field duty and deployments par-ticularly challenging for women. These may not be insurmountable obstacles, but they are obstacles nonetheless, and can hamper unit performance.

17

Rape of Female Prisoners of War

For female soldiers, being raped by the enemy should be considered an occupational hazard of going to war.

—Major Rhonda Cornum[1]

The possibility that the enemy could use threats of sexual abuse of female prisoners as a way of compelling cooperation of male prisoners was discussed in chapter 14. The risk to female personnel extends beyond being used as a prop in prisoner interrogations, however. If women are taken prisoner in substantial numbers and held for a prolonged period, many of them will inevitably be sexually mistreated.

Rape and warfare have gone hand in hand as long as there have been humans, and perhaps even longer. The Old Testament is a compendium of such stories. For millennia, rape and pillage have been the usual consequences of warfare, and in a day when soldiers served without pay, they were actually a form of compensation, hence the adage that "men fight for booty and beauty."[2] Toward the end of World War II, Red Army soldiers were told that German women were theirs by right and were urged to "take them as your lawful prey."[3] Rape as an agent of "ethnic cleansing" by the Serbs was widespread. Thus, the story of war is in very large part a story of rape. Indeed, Susan Brownmiller's influential book *Against Our Will* devotes its longest chapter to war.[4]

One might have thought that advocates for women would resist policies that would increase the probability of rape. Instead, however, they dismiss the risk in a number of ways, using arguments that sometimes border on the bizarre.

ARGUMENT: *The Risk of Rape Is Not That High.*

Some integrationists discount the risk that female prisoners will be raped. Referring to a woman taken prisoner during the Gulf War, Linda Bird Francke asserted that she "was, in fact, safer from sexual abuse in Baghdad than were her fellow female soldiers in the field."[5] Setting aside the comparison with the prisoner's fellow soldiers, there were actually two female prisoners taken in the Gulf War, and at least one of them was sexually abused. The woman referred to by Francke reported that her breasts had been pawed (although she later denied that it had happened),[6] and there were some insinuations that she was raped, despite her repeated claim that she was not.[7] The other woman, Major Rhonda Cornum, reported that she had been digitally penetrated both vaginally and anally but had not been raped because her attacker could not get her flight suit off because of her injuries.[8] Thus, it appears that at least half of the female POWs were subjected to sexual assault.

Prisoner sexual abuse has continued into the current conflict. Although Jessica Lynch had no recollection of the event, Rick Bragg reports in the book telling her story: "The records also show that she was a victim of anal sexual assault. The records do not tell whether her captors assaulted her almost lifeless, broken body after she was lifted from the wreckage, or if they assaulted her and then broke her bones into splinters until she was almost dead."[9]

Two other women, Lori Piestewa—single mother of a four-year-old son and a three-year-old daughter—and Shoshana Johnson—single mother of a two-year-old daughter—were captured that day.[10] The *New York Times* perversely viewed the capture of Shoshana Johnson as good news, serving "as a reminder of how the American military has evolved."[11] Johnson was rescued by Marines after twenty-two days of captivity; Piestewa died in captivity. There have been no public reports that either was sexually abused.

However one counts, the probability of sexual abuse, given recent experience, is high, and we often will not know whether female prisoners have been victimized. Although the public has a legitimate interest in knowing how prisoners are treated, victims also have important privacy interests. Indeed, the Pentagon did not even initially disclose the Gulf War sexual assaults to the Presidential Commission studying sexual integration.[12] The sexual assaults against Rhonda Cornum and Jessica Lynch are known to the public only because they chose to make them so. As for prisoners who choose not to report sexual abuse—or who cannot—we simply do not know. Lori Piestewa, for example, was alive when she was captured, but we do not know whether she was raped before she died. Although sensitivity to privacy concerns is laudable, privacy is not the only relevant value. Knowledge of the risks faced by female prisoners of war is essential to an appropriate weighing of costs and benefits of exposing women to the risk of capture.

ARGUMENT: *Women Are at Greater Risk of Rape from Their Own Side.*

Francke's justification for the surprising argument that POWs were safer than other women in the Gulf is that "at least twenty-five servicewomen were sexually assaulted in the Gulf" compared to only one sexual incident among POWs.[13] Assuming that her figures are correct, that means that twenty-five out of the approximately forty thousand women who served in the Gulf—or *less than one-tenth of 1 percent*—reported being subjected to sexual assault by their own side. The suggestion that POWs, who had rates of sexual abuse of at least 50 percent, were safer than women who faced a less than one-in-a-thousand chance of rape boggles the mind.

ARGUMENT: *Rape Is Really Not That Bad.*

After feminists have been (rightly) arguing for decades that rape is a heinous crime that must be taken seriously, it is surprising to hear them now discount its gravity. Yet Karen Johnson, executive vice president of the National Organization for Women, recently mused publicly about whether it was worse "being raped or being hung by your wrists for days."[14] Imagine if a male general had engaged in such speculation!

Rhonda Cornum's assertion that rape is just "an occupational hazard of going to war" makes it seem the equivalent of black lung to a coal miner or carpal-tunnel syndrome to a secretary. The acceptance of that view is similar to an attitude on display in the United Nations, where "acceptance of rape as a regrettable but unavoidable part of refugee life" led to little being done about it in refugee camps.[15] "What's so terrible about rape?," someone asked, "You don't die from it."

ARGUMENT: *Men Get Raped, Too.*

Another common response to expressions of concern that women prisoners will be subjected to rape is that men can also be subjected to sexual abuse. It is hard to take this argument very seriously. Although male POWs can be subjected to rape, it is relatively uncommon. According to the Presidential Commission, there were no documented cases of male service personnel being sexually abused in Vietnam or in any subsequent conflict.[16] If the enemy held hundreds or thousands of our personnel prisoner, does anyone really believe that female prisoners guarded by men— *enemy* men at that—are no more likely to be sexually exploited than a group of male prisoners?

ARGUMENT: *The Risk of Rape Is Created by Men's Attempts to Protect Women.*

The argument that protectiveness of male prisoners toward their female comrades would cause their captors to repeat their sexual abuse was previously discussed. This argument rests on the incorrect assumption that the enemy's sexual abuse of female prisoners is a means toward the end of obtaining information, rather than an end in itself.

Many erroneously deny that rape has a substantial sexual component, as in the empty slogans "Rape is not about sex, it's about violence" and "Rape is not about sex, it's about power." Joshua Goldstein argues, for example, that the fact that "rapes in wartime apparently bear no relationship to the presence of prostitutes or other available women" shows that "rape is not driven by sexual desire."[17] There is much that is wrong with that argument. First, on the same page that he denies any role for sexual desire, Goldstein notes that "Hirschfeld credits the military brothel system, 'no matter how disgusting,' with reducing the incidence of rape in World War I." Second, the argument assumes that the presence of one sexual outlet eliminates the demand for others. Yet married men frequently have affairs and visit prostitutes.[18] Are we to assume that *their* motives are similarly nonsexual? The widely recognized male interest in sexual variety—a predisposition that no doubt evolved as a consequence of the reproductive benefit associated with having sex with multiple women—implies that many men with one sexual outlet will still desire others.[19]

History no more supports the claim that rape is not about sex than psychology does. After international outcries against widespread rape in Nanking in 1937, the Japanese high command ordered the establishment of "comfort houses" by "luring, purchasing, or kidnaping between eighty thousand and two hundred thousand women," mostly from Korea, but also from elsewhere in Asia.[20] The provision of other sexual outlets to reduce the frequency of rape of local civilians suggests that Japanese leaders did not think that soldiers were raping civilians for military purposes. Indeed, it was largely strategic concerns—worry that widespread rapes would "arouse the antagonism of civilians toward their conquerors"[21]—that led Japanese leaders to take this step.

A look at the profile of rape victims suggests a sexual motive. Although Japanese soldiers in Nanking raped females ranging from children to octogenarians, they had a preference for younger women. Young women disguised themselves as old women to avoid being raped, suggesting that they believed that sexual attractiveness increased the risk of rape. A similar pattern prevailed in the former Yugoslavia. Although the victims ranged in age from seven to sixty-five, "virgins and young women between 13 and 35" were targeted.[22] Japanese and Serb soldiers were motivated by sexual desire no matter how much the victims experienced their abuse as a violent rather than a sexual experience.

ARGUMENT: *Even If They Are Not Raped, Men Are Abused in Other Ways.*

Some argue that male prisoners may also be mistreated, even if the mistreatment of men usually takes a nonsexual form. That is true, but rape is generally considered a more serious imposition than nonsexual assault. Domestic criminal law treats it as such. Indeed, before the Supreme Court held the practice unconstitutional, the death penalty was available in many states for rape.[23]

Captors have a greater incentive to mistreat female prisoners sexually than to mistreat male prisoners nonsexually. Male prisoners may be tortured for instrumental reasons—such as to extract information or punish transgressions—or just for the pleasure of sadistic tormenters. All this is true of women. The sexual motive for rape adds an additional incentive. Imagine a thuggish guard in a POW camp with both male and female sections. He has two options for occupying his spare time. He can beat a male prisoner or rape a female one. Which would he usually choose?

Even in the absence of war and its associated hostilities, incarcerated females are often subjected to sexual exploitation by guards.[24] Many domestic prison systems use female guards to lessen the risk of sexual imposition, and all have procedures in place to attempt to minimize the risk. Perhaps we will someday encounter an adversary as protective of female prisoners as we are, but it is unlikely to be anytime soon.

If rape is driven by misogyny, as often claimed, there is a high likelihood that the "rape culture" of America's enemies will be even more virulent than the one that supposedly exists in the United States.

ARGUMENT: *Women Will Get Raped Even If They Do Not Go to War.*

Another argument that need not detain us is that keeping women out of war zones does not insulate them from the risk of rape, because women in the United States are raped too.[25] True enough, but the fact is irrelevant unless the risk of being raped in the United States is as high as the risk in war. According to FBI crime statistics, the rate of rape in 2005 was 62.5 per 100,000 women.[26] Even assuming substantial underreporting, the domestic rape rate is orders of magnitude lower than the likely rate for rape of female POWs. To suggest that the existence of domestic rape means that we should not worry about the rape of POWs is as nonsensical as an assertion that because men are victims of homicide in peacetime, we should be unconcerned about male combat deaths.

ARGUMENT: *The Enemy's Attempt to Rape Our Troops Will Give Us a Tactical Advantage.*

Perhaps the most bizarre argument is that the propensity of soldiers to rape female enemy combatants actually argues in favor of integration of women into the combat arms. Gerard de Groot argues:

> Extensive studies have cast doubt upon the effectiveness of male soldiers who face female enemies, doubts confirmed by the American experience in Vietnam. American GIs, on encountering female Viet Cong, often reacted not by killing but by attempting to capture and rape. Leaving aside the obvious moral issues, this reaction rendered the soldier less effective and more vulnerable.[27]

The notion that enough enemy soldiers are going to be fumbling with their zippers instead of protecting themselves from the fire of American troops that the United States would gain a tactical advantage by including women in combat units is grotesque, not to mention almost certainly incorrect.

The Risk of Prolonged Captivity

Recent experience with prisoners has caused an unrealistic perception of the risks facing POWs. In Operation Desert Storm and Operation Iraqi Freedom, as well as in smaller conflicts such as in Somalia and Kosovo, only a handful of people were captured, and they were held for a few days or weeks.[28] It will not always be so. The 21 (or so) American POWs taken in the Gulf War pale into insignificance next to the 130,000 POWs in World War II, the 7,000 taken in Korea, or even the 725 in Vietnam. In these longer wars, many prisoners were held for several years.

Lengthy captivity presents a new quality of risk for female POWs. It is one thing to be released after eight days and declare that rape is no big deal. It is quite another to be released after eight years after having born several children by your captors. Such concerns have led Air Force Captain Leslie Christopher to recommend use of a five-year IUD by female personnel, because captured women would probably not have access to their oral contraceptives.[29] Many women would not be able to use the IUD, however, as it is not recommended for women who have not yet had a child or those with a history of either ectopic pregnancy or pelvic inflammatory disease, and it may be dangerous if medical care is unavailable.[30]

THERE IS SOME irony in the simultaneous assertions that women need no special protection from sexual predation by the enemy and that they need special protection from their own comrades. A host of sexual scandals are attributable to sexual integration, and each one seems to be followed by calls for more protection of women. It is only when female personnel are in the hands of the enemy that concerns about their safety seem to abate.

Perhaps the goal of integration of the force is worth the cost of exposing women to the very real risk of rape. But it is a risk that men, for the most part, do not face, and therefore it must be counted as an additional cost of sexual integration.

18

Reproductive Issues:

Pregnancy, Motherhood, and Hygiene

The essence of the military service is the subordination of the desires and interests of the individual to the needs of the service.[1]

—Supreme Court of the United States

Winter 1996: Atlantic Ocean, approximately 125 miles off the coast of Virginia:

The USS *John C. Stennis*, the world's newest nuclear-powered aircraft carrier, is steaming through heavy seas on a postcommissioning "shakedown cruise." Crew members from Helicopter Antisubmarine Squadron Three (the "Tridents") are on "Alert-30" status, meaning that they must be in the air within thirty minutes of an order to fly. The primary mission of the H-60 Seahawk helicopter is antisubmarine warfare, but it has a number of secondary missions, including special operations and combat search-and-rescue. Because of the rough weather, pilots aboard the *Stennis* do not expect to fly tonight.[2]

Suddenly, however, the "bat phone" rings. A sailor aboard the destroyer USS *Hayler* is ill and must be evacuated. The mission to the "night-shrouded, water-tossed destroyer" is a perilous one, and if it could wait until calmer seas and better visibility, it would. The H-60, however, is the sailor's only hope to get to needed medical care. Donning their night-vision goggles, the pilots take off. The *Hayler* is "really rocking and rolling," but they are able to get the patient on board the helicopter, where the flight surgeon stabilizes the patient for the long 125-mile flight to Portsmouth Naval Medical Center where she can receive obstetric care.

May 23, 2003: Aboard the USS Boxer *in the Persian Gulf:* It is exactly three weeks since President George W. Bush announced on board the USS *Abraham Lincoln* that "major combat operations in Iraq have ended." He also warned that there was "difficult work" remaining in Iraq and that military forces would stay until it was done.[3] Aboard the *Boxer*, an amphibious assault ship, the crew remains on a war footing. Most are unaware that the ship will make history tonight.[4]

At 10:58 P.M., the medical staff of the *Boxer* delivers a seven-pound baby boy. When the mother, a thirty-three-year-old Marine staff sergeant, went into labor, she had told the medical staff that she did not know that she was pregnant. Despite nine months of pregnancy, a full-term baby, and a (presumably) nonobese mother, her pregnancy had somehow escaped the notice of both her and her shipmates. After the delivery, the mother and baby are doing fine and are transported to a hospital in Kuwait.

This is the first time that an active-duty service member has given birth on a combat ship in a war zone, although there have been several deliveries aboard other ships since women began serving on ships in 1978. No birth announcement is made by the Pentagon until weeks later when it responds to a query from the *Washington Times*.

MOST OF THE biological differences between men and women described in previous chapters are average differences. Sex differences in reproductive anatomy and physiology, however, are categorical. Only women become pregnant and menstruate, and only women become mothers, which, as most parents know, are not the same thing as fathers.

Pregnancy

Military policy toward pregnancy has evolved in the decades since creation of the All-Volunteer Force. Up until the mid-1970s, pregnancy was automatic grounds for discharge. It no longer is, although it is often the basis for voluntary separation. Policies differ to some extent between the services.

HOW MANY MILITARY WOMEN GET PREGNANT?

Lionel Tiger's explanation for the origins of men's resistance to women as comrades in combat rested in part on the fact that in our ancestral environment large numbers of women would be pregnant or nursing at any time and therefore the missions of men inclined to include women would less likely be accomplished. Today, of course, women have greater control over their pregnancies, so one might suppose that inconvenient pregnancies are no longer a problem. In fact, however, pregnancy has substantial current-day effects on deployability and readiness.

Reliable statistics on military pregnancies are hard to get and are often inconsistent, but a reasonable estimate is that around 10 percent of military women are pregnant at any one time,[5] differing somewhat by branch and rank. Stories about pregnancy do make the press from time to time. From the beginning of the deployment to Bosnia in December 1995 through December 1996, for example, "more than 118 women" were sent back to either Germany or the United States because of pregnancy.[6] That amounts to one woman every three days lost to pregnancy. These pregnancy statistics were said to make the United States a "laughingstock" in the Bosnian press, which claimed that American peacekeepers were breeding like rabbits while ignoring war criminals.

A number of reports of shipboard pregnancies have turned up over the years. When the destroyer tender USS *Acadia* returned from an eight-month deployment during the Gulf War, 36 of the 360 women on board had been transferred off the ship because of pregnancy. Although 22 of them became pregnant after the ship was under way, a Navy spokesman said there were no indications of improper fraternization between men and women on the ship, suggesting that perhaps the women got pregnant on liberty in Hawaii or the Philippines on the way to the Gulf. "These women have a right to get pregnant," sniffed a Navy spokesman. "The conclusion somebody is jumping to is that the *Acadia* is a love boat, and that's not the case." Much to the chagrin of the Navy, however, the "Love Boat" moniker stuck, although one former naval officer has commented that *Acadia* was "about the thirtieth ship" he had heard called the "Love Boat" while in the Navy.[7]

The USS *Eisenhower*, which in 1994 became the first aircraft carrier to have an integrated crew, likewise had a pregnancy problem—thirty-eight in the year following integration and fourteen in the first six months of deployment. Again, a Navy spokesman indicated that there was no indication that the pregnancies had occurred on the ship as opposed to in port.

He could hardly argue that there was no sex going on at all, however, as one pair of enlisted lovebirds—each married to someone else—produced a videotape of themselves having sex on the ship.[8] During a deployment of the aircraft carrier USS *Theodore Roosevelt*, forty-five of the approximately three hundred women who served on it did not deploy or failed to complete the cruise because of pregnancy. Eleven women were flown off the carrier while it was at sea.[9]

A comprehensive medical study of over six thousand female crew members aboard fifty-three ships found an overall pregnancy rate of 19 percent per year.[10] The highest pregnancy rate (27 percent) was on submarine tenders, the class of ships with the largest number of women. Because submarine tenders and destroyer tenders may have crews that are one-fourth to one-third female, the threat to readiness is apparent.

When official data are released, its poor quality—coming from an institution that has close to "total control" over the individual—makes one wonder how much the military wants to know, or at least how much it wants to reveal. The Navy, for example, conducts a periodic Survey of Pregnancy and Parenthood, having released seven such studies since 1988, but the data are of questionable utility. The data come from a mailed survey sent to a random sample of personnel. Participation is voluntary, and the response rate on the last survey (2003) was just 40 percent for women and about 33 percent for men. Although such a response rate might be viewed as acceptably high for some kinds of research, the sensitivity of some of the questions—relating to practicing unprotected sex, sex and alcohol, and the like—as well as the sensitivity of many military women to issues of pregnancy and parenthood, raises doubts about the representativeness of the results.[11]

With the unprecedented use of female personnel in Iraq and Afghanistan, one would think that the military would like to know what their losses are from pregnancy. In fact, a spokesman for Central Command asserted, "We're definitely not tracking it."[12] An Army spokeswoman at the Pentagon said that the Army does release information on how many women choose to leave the service because of pregnancy but that it does not release information on those who leave the war theater, implying that the information is tracked, simply not released to the public. Only "general numbers" are released "to protect the rights of women, soldiers and the organization." The information released suggests that about seventeen hundred women left the Army because of pregnancy in 2003, and over nine hundred left in the first half of 2004.

One wonders how "the rights of women, soldiers and the organization" would be impaired by releasing statistics on the number of women sent home from the theater due to pregnancy. Surely, the rights of *women* and *soldiers* would not be violated by revelation of data containing no identifying information about individuals, so it must be the interest of the "organization" that is being protected. That interest seems to be the military's interest in not being embarrassed.

The Effects of Pregnancy

It is hardly surprising that women at the peak of their reproductive capacity would get pregnant; it would be surprising if none did. At one level, then, one would like simply to say "congratulations" and move on, as Secretary of the Navy Dalton seemed to do in announcing that pregnancy is "compatible with a naval career."[13] If pregnancy interferes with military readiness, however, the analysis must go a little deeper.

As a nation, we are fortunate that when duty calls for the troops, it usually calls overseas. But when overseas deployment is required, the nondeployability rate for women is three to four times the rate for men, the difference being largely due to pregnancy.[14] Once a soldier is confirmed to be pregnant she becomes "nondeployable" and will remain so for up to a year.[15] After deployment, many women must be sent back home because of pregnancy. According to the Pentagon, over 5 percent of all military women deployed during the Gulf War became pregnant, even though most were in the Gulf for far less than a year.[16] Although some studies indicate that the majority of women evacuated from the Gulf were unknowingly pregnant when they arrived, in at least some units the majority conceived in theater.[17]

In the Navy, about 10 percent of women stationed aboard ships are lost to pregnancy each year, and, in the words of a female nurse commander, "We can't do a thing about it."[18] A 1999 study by the Center for Naval Analyses (CNA) reported that "a quarter of women and a tenth of men are lost from ships every year for unplanned reasons." Losses from pregnancy alone were 11 percent, meaning that there were more female losses due to pregnancy than there were male losses altogether and also that there were more female losses due to causes *other than pregnancy* than there were total male losses.[19] Unplanned losses from ships are expensive, as each costs, on average, $12,800. The 2003 Navy survey revealed that approximately the same proportion of women become pregnant while on sea duty as on shore duty.[20]

The CNA study refutes the common argument that the loss of women to pregnancy is balanced by the loss of men due to athletic injuries and misconduct problems.[21] As for sporting injuries, a six-year study of hospital admissions of all active-duty Army personnel found that men were twice as likely as women to be admitted for sports injuries.[22] Still, the rate of male injuries requiring hospitalization was just 38 per 10,000 man-years, a far lower rate than the pregnancy rate. Moreover, the median hospital stay was just three days, compared to the many months of time lost due to each pregnancy. Another distinction between the two kinds of lost time is that sporting activities contribute to both fitness and group cohesion, whereas pregnancy does neither, at least not in militarily useful ways.

The bulk of military pregnancies are unplanned, especially within the junior enlisted ranks. An Army study found that the pregnancies of only 39 percent of junior enlisted soldiers (compared to over 60 percent of those of officers and NCOs) were intended. These figures overestimate the true proportion of planned pregnancies, because the sample included only women who had begun prenatal care and not women who had sought abortions, among whom presumably there is a very high rate of unintended pregnancy. A study of women in the Air Force—the service with the highest proportion of women—found that about 12 percent of women had one or more pregnancies in the study year and that a majority of those pregnancies were unplanned. Similarly, the 2003 Navy survey found that two-thirds of enlisted pregnancies were unplanned (compared with less than one-third for officers).[23]

Pregnancy in the later stages means total absence of the woman—who may or may not be replaced—but even in the earlier stages it results in substantial limitations on a woman's ability to contribute to her unit. In the Army, for example, pregnant soldiers are not transferred to or from overseas commands, and they are exempt from physical training and wearing load-bearing equipment.[24] After twenty weeks, they are exempt from standing at parade rest or at attention for more than fifteen minutes and exempt from weapons training, swimming qualifications, and field duty. Moreover, they are not assigned to duties where nausea, fatigue, or lightheadedness would be hazardous or where they would be exposed to hazardous chemicals. Similar restrictions exist in the Navy, with the added restriction that a woman must be removed from a ship "if the time for medical evacuation of the member to a treatment facility capable of evaluating and stabilizing obstetric emergencies is greater than 6 hours."[25] Regardless of the proximity of medical care, pregnant women may not serve on a ship after they reach twenty weeks.

The limitations on pregnant women can cause special problems. One Army MOS in which there are many women is "fueler" (also known as petroleum supply specialist). Fuelers are responsible for fueling vehicles and are critical to their units. Unfortunately, however, female fuelers are medically restricted from working in that job because of chemical exposure from the date their pregnancy is diagnosed. Therefore, as the Army was preparing for Operation Iraqi Freedom, it had to impose a cap on the number of deployed women who could be allocated to that MOS, and it had to move men from other specialties into the fueler job, creating shortages elsewhere.[26] The increasing use of female medics in Iraq raises similar concerns.[27]

The reduction in value of a pregnant service member is often not captured by time-lost statistics. I asked an active-duty Navy surface-warfare officer about pregnancy statistics and whether pregnancy is a practical problem. His answer:

> Yes. Huge, and . . . you need to watch the data carefully. Pregnancy cases are often just under the general term "medical." The greatest impact on the Sailors is if you have a small shop that requires a certain qualification that has, say, four people in it. If one of them gets pregnant and then can't work due to chemical exposure limitations for pregnant women or the physical demands of the work, the other personnel in the shop have to do the work for her. The way the personnel system is designed though, the pregnant Sailor still counts against their allotment, and no replacement is coming.

A former Navy helicopter pilot told me a similar story. When a woman in the squadron is grounded due to pregnancy, she is "completely useless to everybody," he said, but because she is still there, the squadron is considered to be at full strength. The amount of work has not decreased, however, so other pilots then have to pick up the slack.

Pregnancy sounds like a substantial readiness problem, so why does the military not take it seriously? Certainly, some high-ranking individuals have expressed concern over the effect of pregnancy. Columnist David Hackworth, apparently quoting a classified report that was "slipped to" him, noted the concern of Lieutenant General William Kernan, commander of the Army's XVIII Airborne Corps, who wrote: "My concern is that during these lean manpower years, soldier pregnancies can leave gaping holes in a unit's readiness."[28] For the most part, however, there has been little real discussion of the issue. Even the Chief of Naval Operations's "Guidelines Concerning Pregnant Servicewomen," which contains several pages of the kinds of limitations and restrictions on duties mentioned above, optimistically says at the beginning, "By itself, pregnancy should not restrict tasks normally assigned to servicewomen."

A report prepared by Army Major Merideth Bucher at the Air Command and Staff College of the Air University makes a strong case that pregnancy is a serious problem.[29] She points out that women have nearly four times as much lost time as men, mostly because of pregnancy, and she cites a report from the Center for Army Lessons Learned indicating that in some units at the time of the Gulf War, 18 to 20 percent of female soldiers were nondeployable because of either pregnancy or other physical problems. She also cited the complaint of a battalion commander in the Gulf that one-third of his women could not deploy or were sent home early because of pregnancy, the most common reason for women's evacuation from the Gulf.[30]

Bucher explains why, despite high levels of nondeployability and attrition, the Pentagon has not acknowledged the seriousness of the problem. The Army argues that the numbers do not show a problem in the aggregate. Because at any given moment only approximately 1 percent of the total Army is nondeployable due to pregnancy, the reasoning goes, readiness is not substantially compromised. Ninety-nine percent of force strength is good enough. The problem, Bucher suggests, is that the losses are not uniformly distributed. In all-male units, of course, the percentage loss due to pregnancy is zero, while in units in which women are numerous, 16 or 17 percent of women may be nondeployable, accounting for 6 or 7 percent of unit strength.

It obviously makes little sense just to look at aggregate numbers. One could argue that the Army would still be in pretty good shape if it lost 1 percent of its blood. If each soldier kept 99 percent, that would be true, but if 1 percent of the soldiers lost all their blood and 99 percent lost nothing, that would be a very different story. This is an obvious point, and people in the Pentagon are not stupid. So, why have they not addressed the problem? Merideth Bucher's explanation:

> Army leadership is in a catch 22 position; they must maintain the
> fighting strength and readiness of the force while at the same time

balancing the political issues of a dual-gender Army. It is considered "politically incorrect" or gender-biased to verbalize the problems pregnancies cause our Army, and as a result no one will admit there is a problem.

PREGNANCIES TO AVOID DEPLOYMENT OR OTHER DUTIES

An additional problem beyond understrength units is that pregnancy provides female personnel a potential egress from military service or at least from deployment. Although women no longer have a right to discharge for pregnancy, discharges are available on a discretionary basis.[31] There were widespread and persistent rumors at the outset of the Persian Gulf crisis in 1990 that some women intentionally became pregnant to avoid deployment. For example, four of the twenty-two women in one company scheduled to leave for the Gulf were found to have conceived less than six days before their regiment was deployed.[32] The argument against this being a deliberate act is that women would not get pregnant to avoid deployment because they receive only six weeks of maternity leave.[33] But the critical fact is that if these women did not deploy with their units, they were unlikely to be sent overseas, even if they did report "for duty," and, in any event, they could have elected at that time to leave the Army.

Women's ability to avoid duties creates substantial resentment in the ranks. As Merideth Bucher noted, "Peers and leaders may resent that pregnant soldiers receive full pay and benefits but are exempt from some work, physical training, field exercises, and most importantly, deployments."

Men's resentment that women can avoid deployment in this way is understandable. Any other act by which a service member intentionally incapacitates himself in order to avoid deployment is a court-martial offense.[34] The UCMJ provides that "any person . . . who for the purpose of avoiding work, duty, or service . . . intentionally inflicts self-injury . . . shall be punished as a court-martial may direct." Yet the military does not view intentionally getting pregnant to avoid deployment as any kind of offense at all. The military's reluctance to inquire into a woman's motivations for pregnancy is understandable, but it is not unthinkable that women who become pregnant after receiving orders to deploy might be disciplined.

Intentional pregnancies to avoid deployment have been a problem in the current conflict, although it is usually—but not always—hard to assess a woman's motivations for becoming pregnant. In 2004, the *St. Petersburg*

Times ran a story titled "Get Pregnant, or Get Sent to Iraq."[35] It was a "human interest" story about Cristie Oliver, who was being called back to active duty. She had previously left the Army after having a baby, and she still had a reserve commitment. "They're going to make me leave my baby," Cristie whimpered when she read the notice. The story then recounts Cristie's attempts to become pregnant to avoid deployment. After taking a pregnancy test, she learns the good news: "Congratulations," the clinic assistant told her. "It looks like you're not going to Iraq."

Throughout the entire story there is no indication that attempting to avoid a commitment that she had made to the Army (and the nation) raised an ethical issue. The only sign of disapproval was in a coworker's statement that she was having a baby for the wrong reasons. Letter writers to the newspaper were not so generous. One member of the Army Reserves wrote that the newspaper had "decided to glorify cowardice and moral depravity" and argued that most men and women in the service "face their fears and meet great challenges every day with a high degree of professionalism and morality." The mother of a son about to deploy to Iraq wrote that the story was a "slap in the face" to all of the men and women doing their duty in Iraq.[36]

Single Parenthood

The problems of pregnancy are even greater than the bare numbers suggest because of the large numbers of single parents in the military. The services must face the longer-term issue of how these parents are going to combine the demands of child-rearing and the rigors of a military job. The military and the family are both what sociologists call "greedy institutions."[37] They both suck up commitment, time, and energy. Managing the two is hard enough for married parents, but for single parents the challenges can be overwhelming.

Single Mothers versus Single Fathers

Statistics on the number of single parents in the military are difficult to interpret, because the services sometimes count them inconsistently, often including noncustodial parents. Thus, when it is asserted—as it so frequently is—that there are many more single fathers than single mothers in the service, that statistic masks two things. First, under any view the *proportion* of service members who are single parents is far higher for women, and second, many more female than male "single parents" are actually custodial parents.

Single parenthood is overwhelmingly a "female problem" in the military, and it is a greater problem for enlisted personnel than for officers. The 2003 Navy survey reported that 55 percent of enlisted pregnancies and 33 percent of officers' births were out of wedlock. Siring a child out of wedlock has always been a black mark against an officer. Whether giving birth out of wedlock for a female officer is considered equally negative—or instead just a mark of Murphy Brown–like empowerment—is unclear.

Comparison of the numbers of single mothers and fathers is meaningful only if "single parenthood" means the same thing for mothers and fathers. The 2001 survey made clear that it does not. Respondents were asked about the nature of the custody arrangement—whether it was "sole custody," "joint custody (more than half the time)," or "joint custody (less than half the time)." The difference between mothers and fathers was stark. Of the single mothers, 76 percent had sole custody of the child, whereas only 16 percent of men did. While only 8 percent of single mothers had "joint custody (less than half the time)," 63 percent of fathers did.[38] These are very different parental patterns.

The authors of the 2003 survey apparently decided that too much information was a bad thing. Although it asked the same questions as the 2001 survey about the nature of custody arrangements, the report did not provide the results. Instead, it reported only whether individuals were "single parents" using the definition of whether they had "sole custody or *some version* of joint custody." Naturally, the results did not appear as stark as those in 2001, when the kind of custody arrangement had been revealed. The 2001 survey revealed huge differences between the sexes that are highly relevant to the issue of conflict between parenthood and military service. The failure to report the answers in the 2003 survey appears to have been a deliberate and bad-faith attempt to paper over substantial differences in the circumstances of "single mothers" and "single fathers."

FAMILY CARE PLANS

In order to avoid conflicts between parental responsibilities and military duties, single parents (as well as dual-service couples) are required to file a Family Care Plan Certificate, detailing responsibility for the child.[39] These plans go well beyond simply identifying a babysitter. They must name a person in the local area who agrees to take care of the children at any time, twenty-four hours a day, seven days a week, if the member is called to duty or deployed with no notice. The plan must also identify a person who will provide long-term care in the event that the member is deployed for a significant period of time, assigned to an unaccompanied overseas tour, or assigned to a ship at sea. Both kinds of substitute care providers must sign the plan indicating that they understand and agree to its obligations. The plan must also contain logistical details for transfer of the child, financial arrangements, and the like. Failure to have a valid plan is grounds for administrative separation.

A look at who the service member names as caregiver in the event of deployment highlights the difference between single mothers and fathers. For single fathers, both officers and enlisted, the named caregiver is overwhelmingly the mother, while for single mothers, it is usually a grandparent. This fact suggests another major difference between the sexes: for men, the mother is usually in the picture; for women, the father is usually not.

SINGLE PARENTHOOD AND MILITARY READINESS

The military is often regarded as "family friendly"; indeed, it has been referred to as "a particular mecca for single parents" by one proponent of total sexual integration, because of an array of benefits ranging from free health care to the largest day-care operation in the world.[40] Although in the civilian world, female employment is associated with lower fertility, in the military, fertility levels "are as high if not higher" than those of comparable civilian women.[41] The military knows it has a problem, but it has not figured out what to do about it.

The incompatibility of single parenthood and military service seems obvious and is, in fact, obvious to the services. No branch of the armed forces (other than the National Guard with an appropriate waiver) will allow the enlistment of single parents.[42] Army regulations, for example, state:

> The Army's mission and unit readiness are not consistent with being a sole parent. Persons who are sole parents would be placed in positions, as any other soldier, where they are required at times to work long or unusual hours, to be available for worldwide assignment, and to be prepared for mobilization, all of which would create conflicting duties between children and military requirements for the sole parent.[43]

For much the same reason, the military will not usually accept applicants with military spouses if they have children under eighteen.

The military is very serious about not accepting single-parent enlistees. In order for a single applicant with a child to be eligible for enlistment in the Army, the child must be in the "custody/guardianship of the other parent or another adult." The custody agreement must clearly state that the guardian has "full physical custody and not just a guardianship or oversight role" and that the applicant "does not have physical custody." The applicant is required to certify that his or her intent is not to regain custody after enlistment. An applicant who regains custody in the first term of enlistment will be involuntarily separated for fraudulent enlistment, unless there are special circumstances such as death or incapacity of the custodian.

This is strong stuff, but what happens if applicants properly enlist and then immediately become single parents through pregnancy, divorce, or death of a spouse? The answer is that they become eligible for a panoply of generous benefits, including family housing and health care for the child. This anomaly has led Lieutenant Colonel Carolyn Carroll to argue, in a paper prepared at the Army War College, that enlistees who become single parents during their first term of enlistment—for any reason—should be discharged (honorably).[44]

The problem, as Carroll sees it, is similar to the problem of pregnancy described earlier. Although the Army paints the problem as relatively insignificant because only 7.7 percent of the entire force is made up of single parents, these parents are not randomly distributed through the force. Single parents are disproportionately female and disproportionately first-term enlistees. Carroll concludes that "there is a problem in the Army with single parent soldiers and unit readiness." The precise magnitude of the problem cannot be measured, she says, because the Army does not collect the right kind of data.

The single pregnancy/single motherhood issue is a problem for both the military and the persons involved. Consider the following very sad picture painted for me by an active-duty Navy officer who has had to deal with these issues throughout his career:

> A lot of the 18–20 year old pregnant Sailors are single. In my experience, a very high percentage of them were impregnated by married

Sailors. As a result, they stay single, give birth, and leave the military because they cannot deploy and make child care arrangements.

The math is ugly. I have seen the following many times: Solid, smart, talented 18-year-old joins Navy. Initial training to 1st Command up to 12 months or more. Onboard to pregnancy 6–12 months. Give birth 9 months later. Out of the Navy 3 months after that. With ~3 years of "service" almost nothing has been done to contribute to the Nation's defense. No deployments. No qualifications. Goes back home to her parents. Single. Small child. No skills. No job. No father for her child.

No one likes to talk about this very real problem. We don't hold the sperm donors to account, and neither do the new single mothers.

A huge amount of military resources goes to dealing with these problems. When the commander of the naval base at Pearl Harbor declares that his "first priority is child care,"[45] it might be welcome news to parents, but it does not reassure those who believe that his first priority should be defending the nation.

THE CONFLICT BETWEEN THE BABY AND THE SERVICE CONTRACT

A major difference between the military and the civilian world is that civilian mothers can drop out of the workforce or sometimes reach part-time accommodations with their employers. Many civilian women plan to return to work after a short maternity leave but then find that they are unwilling to be away from their babies. Large numbers of mothers who do return to work cut back on their hours to spend more time with their children.[46]

The conflict with family obligations is orders of magnitude greater in the military. The civilian woman who hates to be away from her baby during the day can usually take solace in the prospect of being reunited with her baby at day's end. The woman who is deployed or assigned an "unaccompanied tour"—such as to Korea, where personnel are stationed for a year without their families—will not ordinarily see her baby again until the deployment is over or until her one-month midtour leave.[47]

This enforced separation of mother from infant can be very difficult. During the Gulf War, a number of Air Force women with children under the age of two—and one assumes women from the other branches—became, in the words of an Air Force psychiatrist, "very vulnerable to stress during the deployment" and were transferred back to the United States.[48]

Elimination of a woman's option to quit work once she has a baby and experiences unexpected feelings may seem hard-hearted, especially when one considers the natural attachment that a mammalian mother feels for her young. The primary demographic of new mothers is young enlistees— often eighteen- to twenty-year-olds—who may be "clueless" about what motherhood will mean to them. To say, "Well, you signed on the dotted line, so tough!" seems heartless, but to say that a woman can exit the military whenever she wants by getting pregnant also creates problems, in both morale and readiness.

An example of the kind of problem that both women and the military face is the case of Emma Cuevas. A Black Hawk helicopter pilot and West Point graduate, Cuevas was denied her request in 1997 to leave the Army three years early when she argued that her pilot duties were interfering with breast-feeding her infant. The Army's position was that it had spent a half-million dollars training her and that she must keep her end of the bargain. She (or more precisely, her infant daughter) brought an unsuccessful suit against the Army. Before it was resolved, however, Cuevas decided that she would rather stay home with her baby than go to work and refused to report for duty. She was sanctioned by a disciplinary board and left the Army. The Army refused to reveal the nature of her discharge or whether she was required to repay the Army for her education, although confidential sources informed the *Army Times* that she would have to pay "some" of the costs.[49]

Stories from Iraq suggest that separation from children is harder on women than men. As a story in the *Christian Science Monitor* reports, "The many mothers here openly mourn missed birthdays, first steps, and bedtime stories, with what seems a greater intensity than the fathers do."[50] The story notes that some women left behind babies as young as a few months old.

EFFECTS ON THE CHILD

It is easy to imagine what the mother is feeling but more difficult to gauge the effects on children. Whether young children are better off being raised at home rather than receiving care from "substitute caregivers" such as day-care centers is obviously a controversial and politically charged issue.

If daily separation from the mother is difficult on the child, as many studies (and common sense) suggest, one must have serious concern about separation of infants from their mothers for many months at a time. Parental deployments are difficult on children, although most children have fathers rather than mothers who deploy. Children with a deployed parent experience elevated levels of depression, for example, with boys and younger children showing the greatest symptoms. A study by Michelle Kelley and colleagues found that although most children cope adequately with separation from their deployed mothers, a subset of children, particularly young ones, seemed more vulnerable to "clinical levels of anxiety, withdrawal, anger, and noncompliance" than children of nondeployed mothers.[51]

Hygiene and Menstruation

Shortly after Newt Gingrich became Speaker of the House in 1994, comments he had made about women in combat while teaching a college class became an occasion for widespread derision. He had said:

> If you talk about being in combat. What does combat mean? If combat means being in a ditch, females have biological problems staying in a ditch for 30 days because they get infections, and they don't have upper body strength. I mean, some do, but they're relatively rare. On the other hand, men are basically little piglets, you drop them in the ditch, they roll around in it, doesn't matter, you know. These things are very real.

So, here we have three propositions, one of which—greater male upper-body strength—should not be controversial. What about the statement that women can get infections staying in a ditch for thirty days and that men do not seem to mind the lack of hygiene? Congresswoman Patricia Schroeder of the House Armed Services Committee indignantly read this statement on the House floor, stating that she was "very, very troubled by the new factual data that seems to be coming out of our new leader." She said that she was unaware that women got infections every thirty days (not, of course, what he said) and that when her male relatives are in ditches "they don't roll around like little piggies."[52]

The factual assertions underlying Gingrich's comments were that living in filthy conditions for prolonged periods of time can lead to infections in women and that men mind less about being dirty. Those are factual issues that Schroeder's sarcasm really did not address, but which will be addressed below.

Finally, the last part of Gingrich's comment and also the last "sound bite":

> On the other hand, if combat means being on an *Aegis* class cruiser managing the computer controls for 12 ships and their rockets, a female again may be dramatically better than a male who gets very, very frustrated sitting in a chair all the time because males are biologically driven to go out and hunt giraffes.

Here, Gingrich is saying that women are better suited for some kinds of combat tasks (this part was often omitted in the press because it did not fit the story line) and that men are more drawn to the physical aspects of warfare. (Presumably, Gingrich did not mean his comment literally, because a fixation on hunting giraffes would similarly preclude men's participation in ground combat.)

It is difficult to understand what was so objectionable about the substance of what Gingrich said, regardless of the quality of his metaphors. Yet he was denounced from the floor of the House, and his remarks made several "worst of 1995" lists.[53] Perhaps the reaction was simply driven by dislike for Gingrich, in which case it is not a very interesting story. Assuming that there actually was some substantive disagreement behind it, however, it is worth considering the merits of his comments.

The part of the story that seemed to anger critics most was the assertion that women would get infections from prolonged exposure to dirty environments. Was Gingrich's statement so ridiculous from a scientific point of view? In an article in the *Journal of the American Academy of Nurse Practitioners* titled "A Military Challenge to Managing Feminine and Personal Hygiene," Diane Wind Wardell and Barbara Czerwinski suggest not. Their article begins: "Hygiene issues affect every woman's life, yet none so profoundly as those women who are in a combat situation."[54]

The women interviewed by Wardell and Czerwinski, who had all previously been deployed, reported "significant problems with privacy, sanitary conditions, facilities, and smells." Vaginal yeast infections and urinary tract infections were commonplace and made worse by promiscuity in the field. The problem is that in the field, sanitary facilities are, well, not very sanitary. The lack of clean facilities was a common complaint, with one woman reporting that she felt "violated" and "pretty much homeless and betrayed." A female sergeant in Iraq commented to a reporter: "We're not like guys. We have to be clean. We need soap and water. You can't live off baby wipes."[55]

Some women's means of coping only made matters worse. Some retained urine and stool and limited their water intake to reduce the number of times they would have to go to the bathroom, but these practices both enhance the risk of infection and decrease work output.[56] Some women wore adult diapers in the field. Not surprisingly, at least one woman commented that women were more concerned about keeping clean than men were.[57]

The authors reported that "female hygiene affected women's attitudes, practice, work, morale and coping" and that management of personal hygiene "was often difficult and consumed a great deal of time." They concluded: "Unmet basic hygiene needs affected morale. Women who felt dirty from being unable to bathe frequently enough to counter the effects of sweating or menses commented on the importance of showers and bathing. They felt this increased the difficulties in coping with the combat environment." They also note that women's hygiene problems have been "closed to discussion" and surrounded by a "code of silence." Gingrich would probably agree.

Menstruation is a challenge for deployed women. Many women experience changes in their periods, and water is not always available to clean with. Women reported a number of problems, "including embarrassment, odor, moodiness, insecurity, and time for managing menses." One woman stated: "You felt you were smelly all the time. That wasn't the case, but women would feel dirty when we were on our period so it was kind of stressful. Those three or four days . . . you are constantly going to the bathroom and cleaning yourself and making sure you are okay." One woman commented that if she had been in combat with the menstrual periods she has now, she would not have been able to cope.

The impairment of performance associated with the menstrual cycle can be serious, especially because many women are reluctant to admit problems. Commander Victoria Voge, a Navy physician, surveyed female Air Force and Army aircrew, asking whether they had noticed a decrease in their flying ability during their menstrual cycle.[58] Only 26 of 299 women (9 percent) reported such a problem. However, 122 women admitted to self-medicating for menstrual problems. Many women reacted with hostility to the question, giving responses like "Get real. How old-fashioned can you get?" or "Shame on you," although another responded, "On tough cramp days, I would rather floss my spine with barbed wire than be asked to do anything." Voge concluded that women's denial "could be seriously detrimental to flight performance," as they seem unwilling to ground themselves out of fear of drawing attention to their inability to perform because of "female-specific problems."

Women report to sick call at much higher rates than men, even excluding gynecologic-related visits. A study of sick-bay use on a submarine tender found that women were six times as likely to visit sick bay as men. On deployment, however, women are often uncomfortable seeking care for "female problems," and in the field, the only health-care provider available for routine care is likely to be an enlisted medic or corpsman whose primary training is in emergency treatment and not primary care for women.[59]

PREGNANCY, SINGLE PARENTHOOD, and hygiene issues make military service, and especially field duty and deployments, considerably more challenging for women than for men. To say, "Sure, it's difficult, but the women managed/will manage" is beside the point. One could as well say that during the Battle of the Bulge G.I.s "managed" one of the coldest winters on record without winter clothing, but they would have been better off—and the war effort would have been better off—if they had had it.[60] In light of Clausewitz's dictum that "everything in war is very simple, but the simplest thing is difficult,"[61] one should be wary of making things more difficult than necessary.

PART VII

MANPOWER ISSUES

Integration of the combat force raises a number of what still are called "manpower issues." Inclusion of women in the combat arms may adversely affect recruiting and retention of both men and women. The appeal to men's masculinity offered by combat service will inevitably diminish, if not disappear, if the combat arms are integrated, reducing the incentive for a young man to join.

Because most women—even military women—do not want to serve in the combat arms, and many would prefer to be excluded from war zones as well, the more equalized the responsibilities between the sexes in and near combat, the less attractive the military is likely to be for the bulk of women.

When people speak of "allowing" women to serve in combat, they almost always add "if they want to." Yet, if these positions are opened up to women for the sake of equality, equality may demand that men and women actually be treated the same. If women were eligible for ground combat and a draft were reinstated, women probably could not legally be excluded from the draft.

Because many of the problems that flow from integration result from mixing the sexes, some have advocated segregation of men and women in basic training and even in operational combat units. Mixed-sex basic training has two primary flaws. First, because of sex differences in physical capacity, it is difficult, if not impossible, to provide physical training that is appropriate for both men and women. Second, mixing the sexes in training leads to indiscipline, and drill sergeants must spend much of their time simply policing the sexes.

All-female operational units, however, are impractical. Most women would be unwilling to go into combat with only "sisters" and no "brothers." Such units would also magnify the effect of sex differences in strength and temperament in ways detrimental to combat effectiveness, and they would tend to lack cohesion over time.

In the debate over integration, analogies are often made to racial discrimination in the military and sexual discrimination in the civilian workplace. Attempts to end those forms of discrimination faced many of the same arguments now raised against sexual integration of the military, advocates argue, yet both forms of discrimination were eliminated to good effect. Such analogies are misguided. Racial segregation in the military was not based on militarily relevant differences between the races. In contrast, biological differences between the sexes make them quite differently suited for combat.

19

Recruiting, Retention, and Conscription:
Is a Fully Integrated Military Attractive to Either Men or Women?

Many Army women are puzzled when they see feminists in the media pushing to open up combat roles to women, because they are unaware of any military women who are interested in such roles.

Laura Miller[1]

Integration of women into the combat arms is likely to have a substantial impact on the nature of the force. It may affect the kind of men who join and the willingness of men to remain once in. Subjecting women to the same kinds of combat obligations that military men have always lived under may also adversely affect recruiting and retention of women.

You Have to Get Men in the Door

Throughout the ages, men have joined the military both to test and to prove their manhood, attracted by its traditionally masculine life. In an era in which the armed forces rely on volunteers, eliminating that source of attraction to the men upon whom it depends may have negative effects on the military's ability to field a sufficient number of troops.

The services have periodically had difficulty attracting enough recruits, in part because of the booming civilian economy and the smaller cohort of eighteen- to twenty-two-year-olds.[2] Given the current orientation of military recruiting, which is primarily to compete on civilian-labor-market terms, these difficulties are not surprising. When the military is perceived as just another job, it lacks the special attributes that have traditionally attracted young recruits. It may not be a coincidence that the Marine Corps—the most "masculine" of the services, the only service to retain sex-segregated basic training, and the service accused of being the most "disconnected" from civilian society—is the one service that has consistently met its recruiting goals.

Integration of the combat arms would decrease not only the appeal of the combat arms themselves but also the appeal of the military in general. If society in general is uneasy having women fight its battles, a man in a support position facilitating a woman's doing that fighting while he remains safe would likely feel an emotion stronger than uneasiness.

And You Want the Right Ones

Sexual integration may affect not just the numbers of men who join; it may also negatively affect which men join. If the masculine appeal is eliminated, then a greater proportion of men entering the service are likely to be drawn by the pay, health benefits, or educational opportunities. One major criticism of the volunteer force is that it has substituted an occupational orientation for an institutional orientation; it has come to compete with the civilian sector in civilian terms.[3] Thus, there is substantial focus on compensation competitive with the civilian sector and training that will have value outside the military. The problem was recognized almost a quarter century ago by sociologists Mady Wechsler Segal and David Segal, who observed that military recruiting strategies have attracted "young people who in fact think of their service as a job, and tend not to think of war-fighting as a part of that job."[4] A survey of Army women revealed that a bare third believed that the central mission of the Army is to fight wars.[5] Diminishing the sense of "warrior spirit" that is associated with the military would predictably enhance the shift toward an occupational orientation.

Many integrationists object to recruitment aimed at the people who would probably be the most able fighters. Thus, slogans such as "The Marine Corps is looking for a few good men" and "Kiss your momma goodbye" (Army National Guard) are to be avoided because they play on "men's insecurities about their masculinity."[6] Instead, proponents presumably approve of such advertisements as a television commercial for the Army National Guard that showed a woman helping a man over an obstacle course. While this kind of advertisement may appeal to some women, it seems unlikely to appeal to many men and especially not to the kind of men one would like to send into battle.

You Also Have to Get the Men to Stay

Perhaps the leading cause of dissatisfaction among military men—at least prior to the current wars—was a profound change in the culture of the military, some but not all of which was due to sexual integration. As the Center for Strategic and International Studies reported, "Unmet expectations for a challenging and satisfying military lifestyle were identified as a larger issue in nearly every focus group," with the greatest concern about sexual integration being voiced by less senior personnel.[7] Stephanie Gutmann put it well. At the beginning of the last decade, she says, the services "threw away the mystique, the one thing that gave them an edge over the civilian economy with which they now find themselves in competition." She continued:

> Without all those intangibles, without the monastery, stripped of its aggressive "we kill people and break stuff" nature, military service becomes.the corporation at its dreary, petty, soul-killing worst, or just another civil service job—a place of low pay, dim lighting, crummy furniture, ugly buildings, piles of paperwork, and a sort of sexless, exhausted male/female rapport.[8]

These changes are the result of a military culture that attempts to suppress many of its masculine attributes in order to provide a more welcoming environment for women, but in the process diminishes the satisfactions that men formerly found in the military.

Although the Presidential Commission found that majorities of all subgroups surveyed reported that the assignment of women to combat positions would not significantly affect their likelihood of remaining in the military, substantial minorities indicated that it would. Thirty-nine percent of Marines and 25 percent of Army personnel—hardly trivial segments—reported that it would decrease their likelihood of remaining in the service. Another survey found that many Army and Air Force pilots believed that the military is not worthwhile as a career because of political considerations.[9]

The influence of men's wives on their decisions whether to remain in the military should not be underestimated, nor should the influence of wives' concern about threats to their marriage posed by their husbands' working with female colleagues, especially during months of absence during deployment.[10] Unlike the civilian world, in which husbands usually come home from work every day, military men often end up bunking with their female colleagues for extended periods. Some may say that the wives should just "get over it," but many do not, and their concerns carry substantial weight when their husbands must decide whether to sign on for another tour.

Few Women Are Interested in Serving in Combat

As the quotation from Laura Miller at the outset of the chapter suggests, few women are actually interested in serving in ground-combat positions, and if no allowance is made for sex, even fewer would be qualified for them. In the aftermath of the Gulf War, only 15 percent of Army women surveyed expressed a desire to occupy combat positions. Other surveys have revealed similar numbers. Despite the fact that most Army women think women should be allowed to volunteer for ground combat, Laura Miller found that few of them would actually do so themselves. Only 11 percent of enlisted women, 13 percent of NCOs, and 14 percent of officers said that they would volunteer, which suggests that at most 2 percent of the force consists of women who would be willing to volunteer for combat, but only some fraction of that number would actually be qualified.[11]

Countries that have opened ground-combat specialties to women—such as Belgium, Canada, Denmark, the Netherlands, Norway, and Spain[12]— have been unable to attract significant numbers of women.[13] Canada's experience may illustrate women's general level of interest. In 1989, the Canadian Human Rights Commission ordered the Canadian Forces to integrate women fully into the forces (with the exception of submarines). In 1989, there were forty-eight women (and 12,700 men) in combat positions. By 1997, there were sixty-six women (and 10,450 men). Because of this glacial pace, the army implemented a $1.5 million advertising campaign to attract women to infantry, armor, artillery, and combat engineering. Its goal was to recruit two thousand new soldiers, including five hundred women, for combat arms in the ensuing twelve to eighteen months. In the event, the army was able to enlist ninety women, of whom approximately half graduated. Undeterred by the military's difficulty in attracting women, the Canadian Defence Minister announced his desire to boost the representation of women in combat units to 50 percent, although he declined to specify how he intended to do so other than by abolishing "attitudes," "skepticism," "barriers," and "well-intended concerns."[14]

If few women are interested in combat, then one might argue that their inclusion would not have a major effect on either the culture or the effectiveness of combat arms. However, many of the costs discussed in this book must be incurred as long as even a few women serve. Sexual issues, problems of double standards and political correctness, male protectiveness, and the like must be dealt with whether women make up 2 percent or 50 percent of the relevant force. Moreover, if experience is any indicator, the services would not accept, or be allowed to accept, the fact that only very small numbers of women would enter combat specialties. Indeed, the small number itself would be viewed as evidence that the services were not creating a welcoming environment for women. The superintendent of the Naval Academy recently announced his desire to raise the percentage of women to 20 percent, presumably in order—in the cant of the quota business—to create a "critical mass" of women.[15] If it really takes 20 percent women to create a critical mass, there is little likelihood that a critical mass could ever be achieved in the ground-combat arms.

Combat Eligibility May Drive Women Away

Full integration into combat specialties may have the opposite effect of that intended on women's willingness to serve in the military. Many women may be less inclined to join if by doing so they expose themselves to involuntary assignment to combat units or combat zones. Even if service is entirely voluntary, opening combat positions to women may put pressure on career-oriented women to serve in combat, even if they would rather not.

In the early days of the wars in Iraq and Afghanistan, many women were placed "in harm's way" who never expected to be. The older sister of Shoshana Johnson, who was captured along with Jessica Lynch, said that her sister had joined the Army to train as a chef and never expected to face danger. "It never crossed our mind that she'd be right up in the front lines," Johnson's sister said.[16] The mother of a female soldier scheduled to deploy to Iraq wrote to *USA Today*, "She does not want to be involved in a combat position as a result of supplying troops—and neither do most of her fellow female soldiers in the unit. She did not sign up for this combat-type role and is very upset about the situation in Iraq."[17]

There are undoubtedly more women who would be discouraged from a military career by the possibility of required combat service than would be attracted by that same possibility. If all female soldiers were at the same combat risk as all male soldiers, recent recruitment statistics suggest that the military could not hope to keep its female numbers anywhere near current levels. Between 2000 and 2005, the percentage of female Army recruits dropped from 22 percent to 17 percent, although the Army has continued to meet most of its enlistment targets, including its 2006 target of eighty thousand new recruits.[18] A 2004 study conducted for the Army indeed found that women now see exposure to combat as a substantial deterrent to military service.[19] Thus, opening more positions to women may have made the military more attractive to some women, while simultaneously making it less attractive to others. Judging from the reduction in female enlistments, there are more women in the latter category than in the former. It already costs more to recruit women than men, and that differential is likely to increase with greater combat risks.

Should Women Be Assigned Involuntarily to Combat Positions?

Surveys show that most military women think that if women are to serve in combat it should be wholly voluntary. A study of Air Force pilots found that over half of the women surveyed believed that "any pilot should have a choice as to whether or not to fly in combat."[20]

Laura Miller found little support among Army women for complete "equality."[21] She found that while 78 percent of enlisted personnel, 72 percent of NCOs, and 70 percent of officers favored voluntary combat service for women, only 6 percent, 4 percent, and 14 percent, respectively, favored women being treated just like men (the remainder were satisfied with the status quo). Thus, those favoring equality of treatment with men were outnumbered by ratios of 16 to 1, 24 to 1, and 6 to 1, respectively. According to Kate O'Beirne, surveys by the Army Research Institute since 1993 consistently found that 85 to 90 percent of female enlisted soldiers were opposed to being assigned combat roles on the same involuntary basis as male soldiers. The Army's response, she says, was to quit asking women their opinion about serving in combat in 2001.[22]

The real test of equality is whether women would have the same obligation to serve in combat that men do. Although men in the military have substantial say in the selection of their MOS, they can be assigned wherever they are needed. To provide women choices in assignments that men do not have—for example, to send them to war zones only if they volunteer to be sent—would cause substantial morale problems, not to mention creating a logistical nightmare if large numbers of individuals in a unit slated for deployment were allowed to "opt out" at the last minute.

What About the Draft?

As of this writing, there are no serious plans to revive the draft. Despite claims during the 2004 election campaign that the Bush administration had a secret plan to do so, the only initiative in Congress to implement a draft had been proposed by antiwar Democrats who hoped that revival of the draft would sap support for the war. Nonetheless, some argue that the United States actually needs a draft to satisfy its manpower needs.[23]

If a draft were to resume, allowing women to opt in to ground-combat specialties would substantially increase the likelihood that women would be drafted and placed involuntarily in combat units. When Congress reinstated draft registration in 1980 in response to the Soviet invasion of Afghanistan, only men were required to register because the primary need would be for combat troops if an emergency arose. In 1981, the Supreme Court rejected a claim by male plaintiffs who argued that requiring men but not women to register violated the "equal protection of the laws."[24] The Court emphasized its traditional deference to Congress in military matters and accepted that the purpose of registration "was to prepare for a draft of combat troops." Even "assuming that a small number of women could be drafted for noncombat roles," the Court reasoned, Congress was entitled to conclude that it was not "worth the added burdens of including women in draft and registration plans." (The plaintiffs had not challenged the exclusion of women from combat.)

Whether the Supreme Court would decide a challenge to a male-only draft today as it did in 1981 is unclear in light of changes in women's military participation and subsequent legal developments. In 1981, the percentage of women in the military was just half what it is today. The higher the proportion of women in the military, the less likely their exclusion from the draft would be deemed legitimate. Moreover, the intensity of the scrutiny the Court gives sex-based classifications has arguably increased.[25] Nonetheless, the Court will probably continue to defer to Congress and the military in maintaining a male-only draft. The Department of Defense continues to view the exclusion of women from direct ground combat as a justification for excluding them from draft registration,[26] and the Court would be disinclined to overrule that judgment.

The Court's deference would likely evaporate, however, if ground-combat positions were opened to women on a voluntary basis. Under such circumstances, the political branches would have made the judgment that women are fit for ground combat. It is one thing for the government to decline to draft women because women are ineligible to hold the combat positions that the draft is intended to fill. It is quite another to say that both men and women may volunteer for combat positions but only men can be forced into them. Although some proponents of opening combat positions to women also support the drafting of women, should there be a draft,[27] most who favor allowing women in combat positions favor it only for women who want to serve. They should understand that if they get their way, they are increasing the likelihood that women will have to serve in combat even if they *don't* want to serve.

Some may argue that if women are qualified, there is no reason to exclude them from the draft, even if far fewer women than men would actually be qualified. Such a contention overlooks a critical distinction between a volunteer military and a conscripted one. A volunteer military can require applicants to prove they are qualified. If you want in, for example, it can require that you prove you can do twenty push-ups. A draft-based military cannot do that, however, because draftees typically would rather not serve. Everyone is capable of *not* doing twenty push-ups. A system of conscription, therefore, requires people to prove they are *not* qualified, in order to avoid service. As people who lived through the draft era can attest, that system put a lot of men in uniform who were not suited to it, but one cannot run a draft for highly motivated people. Instead, entry requirements typically turn on objective criteria that cannot be faked, such as height, weight, and absence of readily discernible disqualifying conditions. In other words, the military is going to be drafting a lot of women who do not want to serve and who would not be viewed by friends and family as qualified to serve.

FROM A MANPOWER PERSPECTIVE, the assumption that expanding the pool of potential personnel necessarily increases the resulting strength of the military is simply wrong. If opening combat positions to women makes the military less attractive to women, the military will thereby be weakened. If opening combat jobs to women makes the military less attractive to men, the military will be weakened even more. To say "we can't run a military without women" is rhetoric. To say "we can't run a military without men" is not rhetoric at all; it is reality.

20

Should the Sexes Be Separated?
Sex-Segregated Training and Operational Units

The present organizational structure in integrated basic training is resulting in less discipline, less unit cohesion and more distraction from the training programs.

—Federal Advisory Committee on Gender-Integrated Training and Related Issues[1]

Because many of the problems accompanying the entry of women into combat (and in the military more generally) result from mixing the sexes, one set of potential solutions entails separating men and women. Two distinct approaches are possible. The first is to segregate the sexes during basic training but to fully integrate them thereafter; the second is to maintain sexually segregated operational units.

Basic Training

Perhaps nowhere are the problems and perils of sexual integration more apparent than in the issue of whether the sexes should go through basic training together, a question that has been studied extensively and has yielded conflicting recommendations from blue-ribbon panels. Under current practice, Army Basic Combat Training (BCT) is sexually integrated, although because of the skewed sex ratio, most male recruits do not actually experience sexually integrated training. Those training for infantry do not go to BCT but rather to Infantry Training Brigade (ITB), which is for men only. Air Force Basic Military Training (BMT) and Navy boot camp are sexually integrated, but, again, because of the sex ratio not all men train with women. Alone among the services, the Marines have never had integrated boot camp.

Those arguing for separating the sexes highlight sex differences in physical performance that make unified training under a single performance standard unrealistic. If the sexes train together under the same standards, training of men must be relaxed, because a regimen that challenges most men will cause most women to fail, a situation that would be perceived as unacceptable to many. Conversely, a training regimen that could be completed by many women would not challenge most men. Moreover, the social issues that arise from combining the sexes are a distraction from training at a time when the military's norms of discipline have not yet been internalized.

The argument in favor of integrated training is that the military is a sexually integrated organization, and the sexes need to learn to work together. The slogan is that you should "train as you fight." Cohesion is enhanced when individuals share a grueling experience together, and separating the sexes makes women perpetual "outsiders" who will not be trusted by their male comrades.

The dilemma posed by these conflicting arguments, neither of which is absurd on its face, is no doubt responsible for the military's vacillation. The Army trained the sexes together in the late 1970s but abandoned integrated training in the early 1980s because men were being held back and women were not able to excel.[2] It reinstated integrated training in 1994.

The conflicting pressures are also reflected in opposing recommendations of two commissions assigned to consider the question of integrated training. The first was created by the secretary of defense and headed by former senator Nancy Kassebaum Baker. It unanimously recommended in 1997 that the sexes be separated in basic training in all services because integrated training resulted in "less discipline, less unit cohesion, and more distraction from the training program." The secretary of defense rejected that recommendation, however,[3] asserting that the Joint Chiefs of Staff opposed the move because it violated the "train as you fight" precept.

The second study was commissioned by Congress and chaired by Anita K. Blair.[4] In 1999, it recommended, by a bare majority, that the status quo be maintained—that is, that integrated training be retained in the Army, Navy, and Air Force, and segregated training be continued in the Marines. Five of the nine members supported the recommendation, one voted against, and three abstained. The abstentions were prompted by concern that the majority was not devoting sufficient attention to the negative aspects of integrated training, especially, as noted by Commissioner Charles Moskos, "the overwhelming consensus among trainers that something is seriously flawed in gender-integrated training."

SEXUAL INTEGRATION CHANGES THE NATURE OF TRAINING

One of the principal reasons for the traditional rigor of basic training is that cohesion is enhanced when individuals have shared a particularly grueling experience. Much of that rigor has been eliminated, in part because of sexual integration. Navy recruits have been told that it does not matter how fast they cover the "confidence course," because the point is "just to have a good time." A reassuring orientation video tells them that "physically, anybody can get through boot camp" and that it is "O.K. to cry."[5] Men leave basic training disappointed that it was not the challenge they thought it would be.

Much of the competitive aspect of basic training of necessity must be eliminated if men and women are to be trained together. According to Anita Blair, recruits in Navy boot camp run in formation, with the slowest runners setting the pace.[6] In the Air Force, trainees run around a track for thirty minutes, but they can maintain their own pace. The Army separates runners into ability groups, but women tend to end up in the two slowest groups. Many female recruits condemned this "tracking" as sexism, arguing that there should just be a single minimum pace and people should be judged on a pass-fail basis.

The watering down of training for noncombat troops in the 1990s had unfortunate results in Iraq, as these troops tended to perform poorly when they began facing combat situations.[7] Although support troops have since been given more combat training, anyone hoping for rigor has reason for disappointment. Today, almost as a parody of Stephanie Gutmann's book title *The Kinder, Gentler Military*, Army drill sergeants are told to "yell less and mentor more." The drill sergeant attitude "you better meet my standard or else" has been replaced by "I am going to do all I can to assist you in meeting the Army standard." Drill sergeants formerly ordered overweight soldiers to skip desserts and sodas, but today they are forbidden to give this order. The *Wall Street Journal* describes a drill sergeant ordering his recruits to attention and the recruits rising "slowly and unevenly."[8] The drill sergeant, "sounding more let down than angry," asks the recruits, "Could we all just stand up together? It would look so much nicer." Finding that too many recruits were being injured in training, the Army has reduced the amount of running that trainees do by more than 60 percent.

Many both inside and outside the Army are worried about the softness of the training. "If the privates can't handle the stress of a drill sergeant yelling at them," one drill sergeant asked, "how will they handle the stress of bullets flying over their head?" A recent column in the *Army Times* by a Marine captain supports the view that Army basic training lacks rigor.[9] He had attended the basic-training graduation of a friend at Fort Jackson, South Carolina, and saw little in the way of "military bearing" and "no pride in what should have been a life-changing event for these young adults." He suggested that if the Army is training as it fights, it "is training soldiers for a pillow fight, not a war."

One might fairly ask whether these changes have been made in order to get the best out of men and women or whether they were designed to get the best out of women—or simply to get women out of basic training successfully—without concern about their effect on the training of men.

SEX DIFFERENCES IN MOTIVATION

Numerous studies have shown that different techniques are effective in motivating males and females. Men respond better to harsh discipline and criticism; women respond better to positive motivation. Competition tends to motivate men; it tends to demotivate women. Failure tends to make men work harder; it tends to make women quit.[10] The tendency of women not to persist after failure is especially acute when tasks are defined as favoring men,[11] as are most military tasks. Although it might be a good strategy for motivating women, no serious person can believe that the way to motivate young men is to tell them that a task is an easy one that anyone can do and that it is "O.K. to cry." Telling a man that a task is easy saps all incentive for doing it, as there is little reward for success at an "easy" task but much stigma in failure. The rewards for a difficult task, in contrast, are large, and there is far less stigma in failing.

The Marine Corps has found that the traditional male drill-instructor model does not work well for women. According to the female commander of the female training battalion at Parris Island, South Carolina, "males and females learn differently and we communicate differently," a fact that will come as no surprise to sports coaches.[12] As Tony DiCicco, coach of the 1999 Women's U.S. World Cup soccer team, put it, "Male and female athletes respond differently to criticism, separation from their families, and personal relationships within the team."[13] Thus, different training methods are needed, even to achieve the same goals. Not only do female Marine recruits tend not to be comfortable with the traditional form of training, female drill instructors tend not to be comfortable in the traditional drill-instructor role.

There is a deeper reason than antifemale animus that drill sergeants traditionally exhorted their recruits by calling them "ladies" and otherwise challenging their masculinity. By succeeding, the man has gone some way toward proving his manhood. That kind of motivation does not work well for women, however, so it has largely been discontinued. Lieutenant General Claudia Kennedy, who later made headlines with her sexual harassment accusation against a fellow general, declared that basic training was "a safe and intensely supervised experience."[14] When the female head of the Great Lakes Naval Training Center boot camp refers to recruits as "the youngsters in our care," you know that, in the words of one observer, "this is not your father's navy."[15] Her declaration mirrors that of General Kennedy, who began speeches introducing the "Consideration of Others" program with the boast, "This is not your father's army anymore!" as if abandonment of tradition would enhance respect for, and attachment to, military institutions.

THE COSTS OF SEXUALLY INTEGRATED TRAINING OUTWEIGH THE BENEFITS

Both integrated and segregated training have their costs, and both kinds of costs are a consequence of sexual integration. The challenge for the military is to train males and females in such a way as to get the best out of both of them and at the same time create conditions that allow them later to participate in cohesive units. If the primary purpose of basic training is to create a self-identity as a "warrior," to instill military discipline, and to whip recruits into physical condition, such a result seems more likely to be achieved through segregated training.

Sex-Segregated Combat Units

Another potential solution to the "train as you fight" dilemma is to retain sex-segregated training but to form sex-segregated operational units as well. Writing in the journal *Foreign Affairs*, Francis Fukuyama argued that the principal obstacle to effective use of women in the military comes from mixing the sexes. Those women who have the ability to participate in combat could do so in all-female units, he suggested, avoiding the problems of integration. Others have made similar arguments, pointing out that most women in the Soviet army during World War II served in all-female units.[16]

Service in sexually segregated units would eliminate a number of the problems related to group cohesion. Such a course would tend to reduce the sexual jealousy and frustration that result from inclusion of women within the group, as well as the negative emotional response from men to their inclusion. Problems of double standards being applied, at least within the unit, would disappear.

Is it realistic to envision all-female combat units? They would create logistical problems but perhaps no greater than the problems created by units formerly made up of Nisei or blacks. A further question, though, is whether one could find many women willing to participate in battle without being surrounded by large numbers of men. A study by Leora Rosen and her colleagues found that female soldiers are even less likely than male soldiers to want to work with women, a sentiment also expressed by female Dutch peacekeepers in the Balkans.[17] Another question is whether the American people—assuming that they could overcome their reluctance to send women into combat at all—would be willing to send their daughters into combat without their sons being there to protect them.

All-female units would also tend to magnify individual sex differences. In a unit with only a few women, average psychological sex differences may get swamped by the large numbers of men. That does not mean that they will not matter, only that their effects will not be so noticeable. If the unit is all female, however, these differences will be observable on a gross level and be even more likely to become critical to unit effectiveness.

Finally, there is reason to doubt that all-female groups would exhibit the same kind of cohesion that men's groups exhibit. As we have seen, women are not as good as men at working with people they do not like.

They tend to take disagreements personally and hold grudges more than men do, a pattern that begins in childhood. A study of Dutch peacekeepers found that women "complained that women like to fight more than men do; that women never forgive or forget [and] that they are very jealous of each other."[18] One female soldier complained that "women are very often turning against each other," and another characterized the problem as "more women, more arguments." A male Navy officer told me that he had suggested to a female officer friend that perhaps all-female ships were the solution to the persistent problems caused by sexual integration. She laughed and said that she would not want to serve on an all-female ship, as it would be too "cliquish." For a variety of reasons, then, all-female units do not appear to be a practical option.

Why Comparisons to Some Other Forms
of Discrimination Are Unpersuasive

The main argument for the integration of women in the armed forces must be the same as it was for blacks: Does it make for a more effective military? The bottom line is that blacks and whites are essentially interchangeable soldiers. But when physical differences and privacy concerns matter—and they do—men and women are not.

—Charles Moskos[1]

Objections to women in combat are commonly met with two arguments comparing the combat exclusion to other kinds of discrimination. The first is that these objections are similar to objections to racial integration and no more worthy of accommodation. The second equates resistance to women in combat to resistance to women's participation in the civilian workplace. Proponents of both arguments contend that those resisting change in the past were wrong and that integration was highly successful. Thus, they argue, the same would be true for sexual integration in the military.

Although perhaps superficially appealing, these arguments do not withstand more than a moment's reflection. Few would argue that segregation of sports teams by sex is the moral equivalent of segregating them by race, and the fact that society has concluded that racially segregated bathrooms were an abomination says nothing about whether sexually segregated bathrooms should be abolished. Maybe they should be, but the argument is not won simply by equating race and sex. Similarly, the fact that many civilian occupations have been sexually integrated does not answer the military question. Military combat presents very different issues from most civilian occupations. In fact, if the civilian comparison is appropriate, it is apt to point out that the more a civilian occupation has in common with combat, the less integrated it tends to be.

The Racial Analogy

Unlike sexual segregation, racial segregation in the military had nothing to do with the biology of race, which is real, and everything to do with the social meaning placed upon race. That social meaning is also "real," of course, but, as history has shown, it is also reasonably amenable to social change. Despite arguments of some feminists to the contrary, however, sex is not just a social construct, and meaningful sex differences exist wholly independent of what we think about them.

If race and sex distinctions are really equivalent, one might have expected sexual integration of the military to occur even more smoothly than racial integration. Racial integration occurred six years prior to the landmark *Brown v. Board of Education* case of 1954, which outlawed racial segregation in public schools, and it occurred despite what was often substantial hostility and suspicion between the races. Rather than being "ahead of the curve," as the military was with racial integration, however, sexual integration took place against a backdrop of a recent history of profound changes in women's role in society. The All-Volunteer Force was instituted in 1973 at the conclusion of the Vietnam War, and the service academies were opened to women in 1976. These events occurred a decade after sex discrimination in employment had been outlawed by the same law that had prohibited racial discrimination. The principle of equal pay for equal work was by then well accepted, and the idea that women should be widely barred from jobs solely because of their sex was a decidedly minority view.

Despite the seemingly more receptive social climate, the military has had less success in fostering acceptance of women than it had in increasing mutual acceptance between the races.[2] Skepticism about women in the military continues to be widespread today, even though the enlistee of today was born a decade after the service academies were opened to women and was a young child when images of military women serving in the first Gulf War were widely broadcast. Indeed, most military personnel *retiring* today have spent their entire careers in a sexually integrated military. Nonetheless, controversy abounds.

Unlike the experience with racially integrated units—where service in such units tended to increase racial acceptance—experience working with women often does not significantly increase men's acceptance of them. According to a 1990 poll, for example, while 45 percent of male midshipmen entering the Naval Academy felt women did not belong, 38 percent of seniors also felt the same way.[3] Early studies found that negative attitudes toward women actually increased over time.[4]

Invocation of the racial analogy is a favored stratagem of those who seek to paper over the weaknesses of their own case. The central orientation of the civil rights struggles of the second half of the last century was to right the colossal and inarguable injustices visited on blacks. Attempts to co-opt the arguments of that fight for other purposes are both rhetorically lazy and intellectually dishonest. Advocates for sexual integration need to make their own case, rather than simply "piggybacking" on the case for racial integration.

The Civilian-Workplace Analogy

Some see in the arguments concerning women in the military shades of arguments concerning women in the professions and in other traditionally male occupations. After all, it was sometimes said that women should not be lawyers because they are insufficiently aggressive to be litigators, and that including women in law partnerships could disrupt the relationship among lawyers, and so forth. The military is just the latest, and perhaps the last, example of such specious reasoning, the argument goes, which is based upon men's desire to keep the "good jobs" for themselves and "perpetuate an all-male preserve and career advantages."[5] According to the National Organization for Women, for example, "the exclusion of women from combat in the modern military is a fraud only to perpetuate a second class status of women in the military."[6] It takes more than assertion, however, to make it so.

The argument that the combat exclusion reflects a desire of men to keep the "good jobs" for themselves is implausible. Although it is perfectly understandable, for example, that male candidates for aviation positions might resent competition from female candidates for purely selfish reasons, self-interest does not explain why their instructors, who are not in competition with the women, might also judge women lacking.

Self-interest also cannot explain why Congress has been a willing accomplice all these years. Why was a Congress that was willing to eliminate "male privilege" through the Nineteenth Amendment to the Constitution giving women the right to vote, the Equal Pay Act, Title VII of the Civil Rights Act of 1964, Title IX of the Educational Amendments of 1972, the Equal Rights Amendment to the Constitution (ultimately rejected in the states), the Civil Rights Act of 1991, the Violence Against Women Act, and a host of other laws intended to benefit women, so determined to stand up for male interests by retaining the combat exclusion? Is it because congressmen believe that service in the military is more important to the maintenance of "male privilege" than, say, the right to vote or the right to employment throughout the civilian economy? In retaining the exclusion for "direct ground combat" but permitting the opening up of shipboard and aviation positions, were policymakers motivated by a belief in the superiority of the job of infantry rifleman over the job of fighter pilot or aircraft-carrier commander? It seems unlikely.

If anything, it is women rather than men who are seeking "the good jobs." Many of the men who served in Vietnam, for example, may not have thought that their job was so good. Women were not much interested in the "good job" of combat service until the draft was abolished and the grubby memories of Vietnam had been replaced by the afterglow of the clean and relatively bloodless (for the coalition) victory in the Gulf War and until the military began trying to make itself attractive in civilian terms. Even after the Gulf War, most of the clamoring was not to get women into the infantry. After all, when the killing starts, a disproportionate number of infantrymen die.[7] If men were clamoring to *include* women in the infantry, one imagines that they would be denounced as selfish for trying to get women killed so that they would not have to die themselves.

Rather than attempting to integrate the infantry, pressure to include women in combat focused primarily on high-prestige jobs such as aviation—truly the "good jobs." Yet far more women could potentially benefit by opening up the infantry in light of the vastly more plentiful infantry positions. Nonetheless, there has been far less sentiment to place women in such pedestrian (literally) positions.

Most of the civilian occupations in which women have had the greatest difficulty finding acceptance bear certain similarities to the military. Contrary to those who think that male resistance is a method of maintaining a male monopoly on high-prestige jobs, the common attribute is not status but physical danger. Policemen, for example, like men in the military, have been reluctant to work with women. Although many studies have found that female police officers are effective, and in some contexts—notably defusing potentially violent domestic situations—more effective than men, many male police officers still hold strongly negative attitudes toward female officers on patrol. Indeed, a study of the Los Angeles Police Department found that men's attitudes toward policewomen became more negative after they worked together.[8] The reason for these persistent negative views is that male officers simply do not feel they can depend on women in those relatively infrequent circumstances when confrontations turn violent.[9]

The same concern about female colleagues exists in firefighting. Kate O'Beirne quotes an official at the New York State Fire Academy commenting frankly on the inclusion of women in the ranks: "They're accepted because they have to be accepted, not because they are considered to be equal in their abilities. The men have to say, 'Yes, there are women who can do the job and I wouldn't mind trusting my safety to a female the same way I would to a male.' "[10]

But they do not believe it, just as many police officers do not believe it, and just as many soldiers do not believe it. A female sergeant—who left the Army after fourteen years—told the *Sacramento Bee* that her tour in Iraq convinced her that even though women were fully capable of serving in combat they should not serve in integrated units, because a "sense of unity" is not possible. "It's hard to do your job to your fullest capability when you're thought of as less than what I wanted to be—a soldier." A survey at the Air Force Academy found that 40 percent of cadets, both male and female, believed that physical and psychological differences between the sexes meant that women would *never* be completely accepted in the military. Twenty percent of male cadets said that women should not even be at the Academy. The longer they were there, the more cynical male cadets were about policies to ensure that women are treated "equally."[11] As anthropologist Anna Simons has noted, "No matter how much women might feel they deserve to 'belong,' their acceptance by men is not up to them."[12]

Women have achieved such widespread acceptance in high-status professions such as law and medicine because these occupations are physically safe. In positions involving physical danger, men are reluctant to trust their lives to their female colleagues. This explanation may not resonate with many who have not worked in dangerous occupations, which may be why sexual integration in the military made such great strides once the top civilian leadership consisted of men and women—including the president and secretary of defense—who had not themselves served in the military.[13]

Is Age Discrimination a More Apt Analogy?

The combat exclusion for women in many ways resembles less the discrimination against blacks in the military than it does the exclusion of older people. The exclusion of blacks was based on prejudice against a group that did not differ biologically from the nonexcluded groups in militarily relevant ways. The exclusion of women, like the exclusion of older people, is based (at least in large part) on group generalizations that rest not just on societal attitudes but on biological fact.

Why is it that the military will refuse to allow a fifty-year-old man to enlist, even if he is strong, healthy, and possesses skills that the military wants? There are, after all, many fifty-year-old men who are stronger, smarter, more disciplined, and more aggressive than many of today's undisciplined nineteen-year-olds of either sex,[14] whom the military is eager to have. In most ways, the argument for inclusion of older men is stronger than the argument for including women. Most fifty-year-old men are stronger than most twenty-year-old women. Older men can probably partake of the bonds of comradeship with young men better than can women of any age. To be sure, older men are likely to get injured more often and have more health problems than younger men, but the same is true of young women. Older men would probably be less inclined to enlist than younger men, but again the same is true of young women. Older men are more averse to physical risk than younger men, but that also does not distinguish them from women.

Most people do not find the military's age rules morally problematic, and bars on women are no more so. Although debating points may be scored by invoking spurious analogies, such rhetorical devices do not advance the goals of reasoned argument.

22

Conclusion

We are afraid to put men to live and trade each on his own private stock of reason; because we suspect that this stock in each man is small, and that the individuals would be better to avail themselves of the general bank and capital of nations, and of ages. . . . Your literary men, and your politicians, and so do the whole clan of the enlightened among us, essentially differ in these points. They have no respect for the wisdom of others; but they pay it off by a very full measure of confidence in their own.

—Edmund Burke[1]

As Lord Moran observed, "the art of command is the art of dealing with human nature."[2] Building a military worth commanding similarly requires that one deal realistically with the raw material of human nature. Individuals with the necessary qualities must be selected, trained, and deployed, but the process requires more than an atomistic focus on individual traits, as soldiers must be formed into groups that will function effectively. Both the selection of individuals and their formation into groups require a keen understanding of human nature, including comprehension of the fact that the "nature of human nature" differs between the sexes. We can pretend that these differences do not exist, but we ignore them at our peril. The Roman poet Horace wrote of the difficulty of "fighting Mother Nature":

> Drive Nature forth by force, she'll turn and rout
> The false refinements that would keep her out.[3]

The military can attempt to drive out the elements of human nature that make integration of combat units so difficult, but in the end, nature will exact a heavy toll.

The quotation from Edmund Burke's *Reflections on the Revolution in France* set forth at the outset of the chapter should remind us to guard against an arrogance that convinces us that we are the first society wise enough to recognize that men and women are interchangeable in combat roles, given that mankind's vast experience with warfare has been to the contrary. There are often very good reasons for traditions that have built up over millennia, and despite our often-undeserved faith in our own powers of reasoning, we may not fully understand those reasons. Although Oliver Wendell Holmes's observation that "it is revolting to have no better reason for a rule of law than so it was laid down in the time of Henry IV"[4] is relevant, so also is his aphorism that "a page of history is worth a volume of logic."[5] The experience of the millennia is that men, not women, should serve as the community's combatants. The claim of some to have a "better idea" should be evaluated cautiously, given that we are still dealing with the same raw material of human nature as our ancestors were.

A Future *Starship Troopers* Combat Force?

Perhaps sometime in the distant future, combat will not require strength—or perhaps even killing. Combatants may set their *Star Trek*–like phasers on "stun" and do battle at a distance, largely eliminating the physical demands of combat. Perhaps the uniform of the future will contain "nanomuscles" that replace the need for human muscle. But that day is not yet here.

In the future, perhaps mixing the two sexes in their peak reproductive years and placing them in conditions of forced intimacy will not result in the host of sexual problems seen in today's military. Accomplishing that goal will require more than social change, however, as chemical means might have to be employed to eliminate sexual desire during the period of military service. If so, a return to conscription is inevitable. Young patriots may be willing to do much for their country, but being gelded—even temporarily—is not on the list for most.

Maybe society can change so that men no longer feel an obligation to protect women. Early training of boys that they should be as rough with girls and as willing to get into fights with them as with boys may help in this regard. The Violence Against Women Act will have to be repealed, or at least renamed, and we should discourage the display of such obviously problematic messages as "There Is No Excuse for Violence Against

Women." The desensitization to violence against women that occurs in the Air Force's SERE training could be extended broadly, so that it would be taught not only throughout the entire military but also as a required course in high school. Perhaps abolition of the urge to protect women will result in the military's elimination of the many double standards adopted for just that purpose.

With enough indoctrination, boys may come to learn that there is nothing inherently masculine about combat—that the noble warrior is as likely to be female as male. They may discover that the field of battle is a place to prove that one is a "real man" *or* a "real woman" and the two terms, unlike today, will have largely the same meaning. Men will no longer seek military service to prove their masculinity. They can do it instead to prove their "personhood"—if they have any doubts about it, but few probably will.

Perhaps someday men will look upon females as their complete equals as combat compatriots, bonding with their "sisters" as they do with their "brothers." This would require, as preconditions, that all of the previously mentioned changes have been effectuated to give men and women the equal footing that is necessary for cohesive combat units. But it would also require a change deep inside of men—inside their DNA—to enable women to trigger the same emotional bonding reaction that men do today in all-male groups organized for violence.

Unless these obstacles can be overcome—and there is good reason to think that they cannot—sexual integration of combat forces must be seen as posing a significant threat to national security.

Who Should Bear the Burden of Proof?

As every lawyer knows, assignment of the burden of proof can be important, if not outcome-determinative, in many controversies. Who bears the burden of proof on the question of integration of women into combat positions? Must proponents of placing women in combat prove that they will not harm combat effectiveness, or must opponents prove that they will? Needless to say, partisans on both sides would like to impose the burden on their opponents.

One basis for assigning the burden of proof is to impose it on the party making an unusual or facially implausible claim. Proponents of women in combat generally believe that the sexes are largely identical and that the claim of intractable biological differences is implausible and attributable to the same kind of irrational prejudice that excluded blacks from the military. Opponents, on the other hand, tend to believe that differences between the sexes are more likely to be innate and that it is the assumption of interchangeability that is improbable. They rest their argument in part on the almost universal cultural pattern of relying on men for warfare, in addition to the many physical and psychological sex differences for which there is compelling evidence of biological origins.

Another basis for assigning the burden of proof is the perceived cost of error. If the costs of error are asymmetrical, the party advocating the position that would result in the greater harm if wrong should, all else being equal, bear the burden. The primary cost of erroneous exclusion of women from combat would be to deprive a relatively small number of women of that opportunity, which would not only cut off a desired job choice but also, integrationists argue, limit women's prospects for promotion. They also identify the "stigma" of second-class citizenship as a cost, although the magnitude of that cost is subject to substantial debate. Against the cost of erroneous exclusion must be weighed the cost of erroneously including women in combat units. If the arguments against integration are erroneously rejected, the resulting reduction in military effectiveness caused by less able soldiers and less cohesive combat units will be measured in human lives and in a reduction in military power. Thus, asymmetry in the costs of error seems to argue for placing the burden of proof on those favoring integration.

Asymmetry in the costs of error is responsible for a distinctive feature of the debate over integration: integrationists are almost universally unwilling to admit the possibility of being wrong. I do not mean to imply that they are necessarily more wedded to their views than I am to mine. What I mean is that the structure of their argument precludes acknowledgment of the possibility of error. To the question "What if you're wrong?" I reply, "I don't think I am wrong, but if I am, some women will be unfairly excluded from combat, and the military will be deprived of their services; that is a risk, but one I think worth running." To that same question, integrationists reply, "I'm not wrong, period," as few have the courage to say, "I don't think I am wrong, but if I am, some people will die unnecessarily, and national security may be impaired; that is a risk, but one I think worth running."

As is obvious from the foregoing, the decision of where to assign the burden of proof is so intimately tied up with the substantive merits of the question that discussing it at length as a procedural matter is fruitless. It is worthwhile, however, to keep in mind the relevant questions: Which position represents the more unusual or implausible claim, and which carries with it the greater harm if wrong?

Costs and Benefits of Integrating Combat Units

This book has identified a number of costs of full integration of the military. Inclusion of women creates a segment of the military that is physically weaker, more prone to injury (both physical and psychological), less physically aggressive, able to withstand less pain, less willing to take physical risks, less motivated to kill, less likely to be available to deploy when ordered to, more expensive to recruit, and less likely to remain in the service even for the length of their initial contracts. Women are placed in units with men who do not trust them with their lives and who do not bond with them the way that they do with other men. The groups into which they are introduced become less disciplined and more subject to conflict related to sexual jealousy and sexual frustration, and men receive less rigorous training because of their presence. Officers and NCOs must divert attention from their central missions to cope with the "drama" that sexual integration brings, and they must reassign physical tasks (or do them themselves) because women cannot get them done fast enough, if at all. Men who have traditionally been drawn to the military because of its appeal to their masculinity now find that the military tries to cure them of it to make the environment more comfortable for women.

All of these factors act together to weaken the military's ability to wage war. A reduction in military effectiveness reduces the country's ability to achieve its strategic objectives in the event of conflict and potentially creates reluctance to intervene militarily when it is strategically advisable. Moreover, concern about female casualties may discourage action in circumstances in which male casualties would be viewed as "acceptable." Undue emphasis on limiting casualties, it should be understood, is just another form of military weakness.[6] These are the costs of sexual integration, and they are substantial ones.

Against these potentially heavy costs, what are the corresponding benefits *to the military* from sexual integration? Other than a few minor ones, I must confess that I find them difficult to identify. This is not to suggest that there are not many outstanding women in today's military or that military women are less dedicated or professional than men in the military. But unless they are *more* outstanding, on average, than the men who would hold their positions were they not there (and *some* no doubt are), then no matter how good they are—and no matter how much the nation's citizens should be grateful for their service—they cannot count as a benefit of integration per se, since against the gain from their service must be balanced the corresponding loss of someone else's.

Two kinds of benefits are potentially available to the military from sexual integration. The first is an increase in the pool from which the services may draw. Although the rhetoric of integrationists suggests that women "double" the recruiting pool, that contention would be meaningfully true only if women were as likely to serve as men. In fact, sexual integration of the military has increased the pool by only 15 to 20 percent. That is not nothing, but it is far from double. As for expansion of the potential pool of *combat* volunteers, integration of the combat arms would increase the available pool by perhaps 1 to 2 percent at most. That is not nothing, but it is almost nothing.

How important is this moderate expansion of the pool by 15 or 20 percent for the military generally? The argument that "we couldn't run a military without women" suggests that it is critical, but is it? In fact, it would not be particularly difficult to muster a military that had *no* women (other than nurses), although that is not what I am advocating. The active forces of the United States today stand at 1.4 million, of whom 200,000 are women, out of a population of 300 million. At the time of the Gulf War, the active force was 2.1 million strong, and about 230,000 were women.[7] At the end of World War II (with a U.S. population less than half what it is today),[8] there were 12 million Americans in uniform, and about 280,000 of them were women.[9] Could the United States really not increase the male contingent of today's military by 200,000 to make up for the loss of women? That would still be almost a half million fewer men than were in the active forces during the Gulf War. If the country lacks that capacity, it is in a very precarious position militarily and, presumably, on the brink of a draft. The ongoing conflicts in Iraq and Afghanistan, coupled with tensions with Iran, North Korea, and farther out, perhaps China or even Russia, have led for calls to expand the armed forces. If the well is already dry, however, that is not an option.

The other potential benefit that sexual integration may bring to the military—in addition to sheer numbers—is the possibility that women *as women* contribute something special. One inarguable benefit of some sexual integration comes from female nurses. With the labor pool of nurses being less than 5 percent male, simple numbers dictate the use of women. Moreover, most would agree that women bring something special to nursing generally and to military nursing specifically. As Richard Holmes has written, male soldiers respond well to female nurses in part because they satisfy a "need for female affection, as opposed to mere sexual gratification." Eliminating female nurses from the military is, needless to say, not on anyone's agenda.

Beyond nursing, however, do women bring anything to the military distinctively as a product of their sex? Use of women in Iraq has been important in order to interact with and search female Iraqis, but there is no requirement that these women be military women or even that they be American, although using military women unquestionably enhances flexibility. This task, however, occupies only a handful of women.

Navy Secretary Richard Danzig, in a talk to senior female Navy officers in the late 1990s, suggested that the "something special" women bring is their "sensitivity"[10] (although not everyone would agree that a more sensitive military is a better military). Secretary Danzig's latching on to sensitivity suggests that despite his strong support for women in the military—he was favorably disposed toward integration of submarines, for example[11]—he could think of little *distinctively* valuable about their contribution.

Other benefits identified by integrationists, such as sexual equality and promotional opportunities, inure to (a few) women rather than to the military as an institution. The number of women who are both interested and physically qualified (assuming an absence of "sex norming" of qualification standards) is likely to be minuscule, however, at least for ground-combat positions.

How Would We Learn If Integration Was a Mistake?

One might suggest that we experiment with sexual integration of ground-combat forces and make a decision based upon the results of the experiment. Although that argument might sound reasonable at first blush, experiments are helpful only if they are likely to produce useful data. The question, therefore, is whether accurate information about women's performance would be forthcoming if they did not perform as well as men.

There is every reason to be skeptical about the quality of the data that would make its way to the public.

The Defense Department and the military have shown a consistent unwillingness to disclose information that reflects poorly on women. We have seen that the Army will not release data on the number of women evacuated from Iraq because of pregnancy, purportedly "to protect the rights of women, soldiers and the organization," and that information on strength issues is not disclosed because it can be used as an argument against integration. Moreover, the frequent "spin" on episodes thought to reflect poorly on either integration efforts or on women—such as the Kara Hultgreen incident and the crying truck drivers in Panama—makes it very difficult to draw conclusions in which one might have confidence.

For the "great experiment" to be declared a failure, the nation's military and civilian leaders would have to acknowledge their sacrifice of the lives of the nation's sons and daughters in a misguided pursuit of their vision of "gender justice." There is little in the history of this nation or any nation that makes such an admission likely, at least until there is a tragedy of immense proportions that is so clearly and unambiguously a consequence of sexual integration that it cannot be denied. The ingenuity displayed by supporters of integration in blaming everything but integration for its adverse results—whether leadership, training, men, equipment, generation gaps, and the like—makes it likely that no failure will ever be unambiguous. A person courageous enough to say that the emperor has no clothes is likely to have something in common with the emperor when he is stripped of his uniform. Regardless of actual performance, then, the experiment will almost certainly be labeled a success.

The Lack of Positive National-Security Arguments for Integration

A consistent feature of the women-in-combat debate is the dearth of positive national-security arguments in its favor. No one argues, for example, that the solution for victory in Iraq and Afghanistan is to increase the number of women or that eliminating the combat exclusion would unleash the whirlwind on America's enemies. The question generally argued is whether introducing women into combat units would harm the effectiveness of those units. Strikingly absent is any claim that women would make combat units more effective. This book has suggested myriad ways, however, in which women would make these units less effective, and there is little to balance the scales in the other direction.

The overwhelming focus of integrationists has been the argument for equal rights rather than national security. An individual-rights approach is hardly surprising among civilian feminists, many of whom who are unsympathetic to the military and its goals, anyway. It is more disturbing coming from military women, such as the female helicopter pilot in Iraq who asked: "Why should I not be allowed to do something I want to do because some guy lying on a couch watching TV feels uncomfortable seeing me dragged through the street?"[12] Perhaps one answer to that question is: "Because if his reaction is representative, public support for the war will be more difficult to maintain, and the bad guys can exploit that fact by targeting female personnel." One might respond, depending upon one's view of the current conflicts, that diminished public support for these particular wars is a good thing, but these are effects that will be felt in both "good" and "bad" wars, and one's views on integration should not turn on opinions about the wisdom of a particular war.

The question "why should I not be allowed to do something I want to do because . . . ?" comes in infinite varieties depending on the kind of unit. The blank can be filled in with:

- "Men do not feel comfortable with me in their rifle squad."
- "Men do not feel comfortable having to defecate in front of me; I'm willing to defecate in front of them."
- "Men might feel motivated to protect me; I didn't ask them to."
- "Men might think of me in a sexual way; I'm not interested in them."
- "I may not be able to carry my full weight."
- "In a combat situation, I probably couldn't carry one of my injured comrades out of a kill zone."
- "I am more likely to return home with PTSD."
- "My presence will cause conflict among the men; that's their problem, not mine."
- "I may get pregnant and leave my unit in the lurch."
- "Men might not trust me in a combat situation; they should."

Ultimately, the argument almost always comes down to placing self-actualization over military effectiveness—putting individual interest above the common good.

The individual-rights argument tends to distract the focus from where it should be—not on individuals but on groups and on the mission. If a woman is not strong enough to do her part, that is not just her problem. It is everyone's problem, not just everyone in her unit but everyone in whose name the war is being prosecuted. Moreover, combat forces are not simply collections of individuals bringing only their own individual characteristics to the battle. The strength of the wolf really is the pack, and although group dynamics are more difficult to measure than physical traits, they are often more important. Anything that diverts focus from the mission or weakens the unit's ability to function as a harmonious whole endangers the mission and human life.

Where Do These Arguments Take Us?

What changes flow from the observations in this book? First, something like the "risk rule" should be reinstated, excluding women not only from combat positions but also from positions presenting a substantial risk of combat or capture. This rule would have obvious implications for the war going on now in Iraq. Taking seriously the argument that most of Iraq is a combat zone and that most personnel there face combat risks, the number of positions that women could hold would be substantially reduced. Combat risks in some areas may be relatively low, so judgments would have to be made and lines would have to be drawn. However, women would not be performing tasks such as convoy security. Needless to say, adoption of the risk rule would preclude expansion of women into the combat positions from which they are currently barred, such as infantry, armor, artillery, and submarines.

The exclusion of women from combat aviation should also be reinstated. Ultimately, combat aviation crews may end up fighting for survival on the ground. Moreover, when aircraft are hit by fire from either the ground or the air, physical strength can become a critical factor in maintaining control. Although there have been no American pilots killed in air-to-air combat since Vietnam, we cannot count on future enemies burying their airplanes in the sand before a war even begins. Aerial combat must therefore continue to be part of the pilot's repertoire, and for a variety of reasons discussed in chapter 4, there is reason to think that few women will be able to perform at the level of men. Pilots flying over enemy territory face a serious risk of being shot down and captured, as we saw in Vietnam, and it is in the national interest not to have women taken prisoner, even if individual women are willing to take the risk.

Women should also be barred from warships. Problems of pregnancy and sexual relations and the impact on cohesion that they can have pose a substantial threat to military effectiveness. In war and peace, but especially in war, all hands must be prepared to pitch in and perform the highly physical task of damage control. Women's lack of upper-body strength puts the entire ship's crew at risk. Although we have not faced a serious naval power in combat since World War II, we may in the future, and the problems will become even more serious.

There may be other positions that should be closed as well. A number of the problems identified in this book plague support units as well as combat units. Judgments should be made about whether it makes sense for them to be open to both sexes, using military effectiveness as the benchmark. The decision to include women should not be made, as the head of the Army Diversity Office has argued, to allow the Army "to progress even further toward work-force diversity,"[13] or, as Secretary of Defense Les Aspin said in announcing the integration of some positions in the early nineties, because it is perceived as "the right thing to do."[14] It is the right thing to do only if it does not damage the ability of the military to satisfy its mission. The military must be understood for what it is—a warfighting institution. The fact that it creates career opportunities for large numbers of people is a beneficial side effect of having a military, but that is not its purpose.

Because of changes that the military, especially the Army, has made already—integrating women into positions closer and closer to combat, sometimes in apparent violation of Department of Defense policy—some short-term costs would have to be incurred to implement these suggestions. Any departure from the status quo has transition costs, of course. The argument that "we've put them there, so now we need them there" rests solely on the demands of the near term and not on a long-term view of what is best for the military and the country. Women were phased into these positions, and they can be phased out.

Testifying before the 1992 Presidential Commission, a Gulf War mechanized infantry commander captured an important point: "This is not Olympic diving. We do not get extra credit for adding an extra degree . . . of difficulty."[15] Many of the problems identified in this book add several degrees of difficulty to the already challenging tasks facing combat units. One can argue that each of the problems can be worked around—but not solved—with "leadership and training." Even if that were so, and the claim seems far-fetched, wouldn't that leadership and training be better devoted to increasing the killing power of the military?

The nation depends upon the military to preserve its liberty and security. To weaken the military's ability to do so in order to benefit a small number of women who desire combat service is an ill-advised trade. To weaken the military to make a "statement" about equality—particularly at a time when we face enemies with far more primitive views of sexual equality than even a complete exclusion of women from the military would represent—is little short of lunacy.

Notes

Chapter 1: Introduction

1. Hanson, 1999, p. 273.
2. *Starship Troopers,* 1997.
3. *G.I. Jane,* 1997.
4. Official U.S. Navy SEAL Information Web site.
5. IMDb, n.d.
6. Reid, 2004; Tan, 2006; Icasualties.org.
7. Gavin, 1997; Binkin, 1993, p. 4.
8. Jontz, 2005.
9. Harrell and Miller, 1997.
10. Holm, 1992, p. 439.
11. Presidential Commission, 1992; Moskos, 1995/1996.
12. Harrell and Miller, 1997, pp. 2–4.
13. Binkin, 1993, p. 52.
14. Scarborough and Curl, 2005.
15. Eberhart, 2005.
16. Addis, 1994, pp. 3–4.
17. Peach, 1996, p. 165.
18. DEOMI, 2006, pp. 8, 40.
19. Tan, 2006; Icasualties.org.
20. Fainaru, 2005; Sisk, 2004.
21. Waller, 1995.
22. Dunnigan and Nofi, 1999, pp. 161, 241.
23. CNN Newsmaker, 1991.
24. Leahy, 1991.
25. Stout, 1998.
26. Bowman, 2006, p. 118.

Part I: Sex Differences and Their Origins

1. Fausto-Sterling, 1992, p. 207.
2. Orwell, 1945, p. 379.

Chapter 2: Physical Sex Differences in Size, Strength, and Speed: Separating Fact from Myth

1. http://www.isteve.com/gendrgap.htm. Reprinted from Sailer and Seiler, 1997.
2. Shapiro, 2003.
3. Vanden Brook, 2006.
4. Cohen, 1988.
5. Pheasant, 1983; Reilly, Zedeck, and Tenopyr, 1979; Morrow and Hosler, 1981.

6. Brainard and Burmaster, 1992.
7. Cheuvront, Moffatt, and DeRuisseau, 2002.
8. Bjorntorp, 1991.
9. Francke, 1997, p. 248.
10. Goldstein, 2001, p. 160.
11. Cheuvront et al., 2005.
12. Cheuvront, Moffatt, and DeRuisseau, 2002.
13. Ibid.
14. Smoll and Schutz, 1990; Jacklin, Snow, and Maccoby, 1981.
15. Glenmark et al., 1994.
16. Thomas and French, 1985.
17. Lunn and Kimura, 1989; Jardine and Martin, 1983.
18. Kolakowski and Malina, 1974; Thieme, 1997.
19. Knapik et al., 1980, p. 1089.
20. Bishop, Cureton, and Collins, 1987.
21. Daniels et al., 1982.
22. Harman et al., 1997.
23. Associated Press, January 30, 1996.
24. Solaro, 2006, p. 269.
25. Browne, 1995, p. 1019.
26. Angier, 1992.
27. Sailer and Seiler, 1997.
28. Burfoot and Post, 1992; Seiler, De Koning, and Foster, 2007.
29. Janofsky, 1991.
30. Holden, 2004.
31. Knapik et al., 2001; Amoroso, Bell, and Jones, 1997.
32. Deitch et al., 2006; Hewett, Myer, and Ford, 2006.
33. Ministry of Defence (UK), 2002, pp. B3, B5.
34. Solaro, 2006, p. 272.

Chapter 3: Sex Differences in Mind: Separating Fact from Myth Again

1. Alexander, 1979, p. 241.
2. Williams and Best, 1990, pp. 77–78.
3. Jussim, McCauley, and Lee, 1995.
4. Marcusson and Oehmisch, 1977.
5. Morrongiello and Dawber, 1998.
6. Morrongiello and Rennie, 1998.
7. Byrnes, Miller, and Schafer, 1999, p. 378.
8. Hillier and Morrongiello, 1998.
9. Bureau of Labor Statistics, 2003; Toscano and Windau, 1998.
10. Veevers and Gee, 1986.
11. Gregersen and Berg, 1994; Simons-Morton, Lerner, and Singer, 2005.
12. Torrance and Ziller, 1957.
13. Johnson, 1996.
14. Carnegie Hero Fund Commission, 2006.
15. Fessler, Pillsworth, and Flamson, 2004.
16. Nagy et al., 2001; Arrindell, 1999; Cornelius and Averill, 1983; Fetchenhauer and Buunk, 2005; Campbell, 2006.
17. Fazackerley, 2006.
18. Smith and Torstensson, 1997.
19. Bendyna et al., 1996; Lerner et al., 2003.
20. Zivotofsky and Koslowsky, 2005.
21. Archer, 1991; Eagly and Steffen, 1986, p. 320.
22. Rushton et al., 1986; Feingold, 1994.
23. Boulton, 1993.
24. Archer, 2004.
25. Fox and Zawitz, 2006.
26. U.S. Department of Justice, 2003, 1999.
27. Campbell and Muncer, 1994.
28. Mazur and Booth, 1998, p. 353.
29. Maccoby, 1998.
30. Browne, 2002, pp. 35–49.
31. Maccoby and Jacklin, 1974, p. 215; Geary, 1998, pp. 98–105.
32. Baron-Cohen and Wheelwright, 2004; Archer, 2004.
33. Zeanah, 1989; Amato and Booth, 1996.
34. Browne, 2002, pp. 42–44.
35. Singer et al., 2006.
36. Rushton et al., 1986.
37. BBC News, April 7, 2005.
38. Riley et al., 1998.
39. Aloisi and Bonifazi, 2006.
40. Fillingim, 2003.
41. Craft, Mogil, and Aloisi, 2004.
42. Huston et al., 1981.
43. Carnegie Hero Fund Commission, 2001.
44. Browne, 2005, 2006a.
45. Halpern, 2000.
46. Browne, 2002, pp. 55–66.
47. Voyer, Voyer, and Bryden, 1995; Hegarty and Waller, 2005; Silverman et al., 2000.

Chapter 4: How Did Sex Differences Come About? Pure Socialization, or Do Hormones Play a Role?

1. Cohen-Bendahan, van de Beek, and Berenbaum, 2005, p. 377.
2. Colapinto, 2000, pp. xiii, 12, 25, 56–61, 65, 68, 75, 131; Diamond and Sigmundson, 1997.
3. Lytton and Romney, 1991.
4. Serbin et al., 2001; Servin, Bohlin, and Berlin, 1999.
5. Williams, 1989, p. 11; Benenson, Philippoussis, and Leeb, 1999.
6. Campenni, 1999; Fisher-Thompson, 1993.
7. Williams and Best, 1990.
8. Williams and Meck, 1991; Gaulin, FitzGerald, and Wartell, 1990; Lacreuse et al., 1999.
9. Alexander and Hines, 2002.
10. Maccoby, 1987, p. 235.
11. Fausto-Sterling, 1992, p. 199.
12. Eagly and Wood, 1999; Wood and Eagly, 2002.
13. Breedlove, 1994.
14. Cohen-Bendahan, van de Beek, and Berenbaum, 2005, p. 356.
15. Berenbaum and Snyder, 1995.
16. Helleday et al., 1993; Berenbaum and Resnick, 1997.
17. Hines et al., 2003; Berenbaum, 1999.
18. Hines et al., 2002.
19. Udry, Morris, and Kovenock, 1995.
20. Grimshaw, Sitarenios, and Finegan, 1995.
21. Van Bokhoven et al., 2006.
22. Archer, 2006.
23. Aluja and Torrubia, 2004.
24. King, De Oliveira, and Patel, 2005.
25. Orengo et al., 2002; Kyomen et al., 1999.
26. Bröder and Hohmann, 2003.
27. Fillingim, 2003; Craft, Mogil, and Aloisi, 2004.
28. Randy Thornhill, 2005, personal communication.
29. Udry, 2000.
30. Goldstein, 2001, p. 246.

Chapter 5: Evolutionary Origins of Sex Differences: The "Why" Question

1. Ratchnevsky, 1991, p. 153.
2. Ibid., pp. 67, 152, 164.
3. Zerjal et al., 2003; Keegan, 1993, p. 205.
4. Darwin, 1871, Vol. I, p. 256.
5. Cronin, 1991, p. 234.
6. Geary, 2007.
7. Trivers, 1972, p. 141; Geary, 2002.
8. Clutton-Brock, 1991.
9. Buss, 1994.
10. Smuts, 1995, p. 5.
11. Betzig, 1986, 1993.
12. Chagnon, 1988.
13. Hawkes, 1991.
14. Hrdy, 1999, p. 112; Low, 1992.
15. Nyborg, 1994.
16. Wilson and Daly, 1985.
17. Campbell, 1999.
18. Hrdy, 1999, pp. 485–490.
19. Baron-Cohen, 2003.
20. Alcock, 2000; Wright, 1999.
21. Levin, 1987, p. 66
22. Murdock, 1932, p. 200; 1971, p. 19.

Part II: Modern Warfare

1. Keeley, 1996; LeBlanc, 2003; Wrangham and Peterson, 1996.
2. Keeley, 1996, pp. 89–92.
3. Pantano, 2006, p. 84.

Chapter 6: The Nature of Modern Warfare

1. Wheeler, 1978, p. 44.
2. Marshall, 1947, p. 19.
3. Fick, 2005, p. 134.
4. Lonsberry, 2004.
5. Snopes.com, 2005.
6. Addis et al., 1994, p. xv.
7. De Groot, 1995, p. 259; *New York Times*, 2003a.
8. Herr, 1977, p. 94.
9. *Sunday Times* of London Insight Team, 1982, pp. 259–260; Bishop and Witherow, 1982, p. 133.
10. Dunn, 2004.

11. Smith, 2005.
12. Beeston and Grey, 2004.
13. Cosner, 2003.
14. Anderson, 1997; Federal Advisory Committee on Gender-Integrated Training and Related Issues, 1997, pp. 16, 18.
15. Department of the Army, 2005, pp. 1–6.
16. Palmer, Wiley, and Keast, 1948, pp. 212–213.
17. Ellis, 1980, p. 296.
18. Ambrose, 1997, p. 274.
19. Stokesbury, 1988, p. 60.
20. Estep, 1991, p. 170.
21. Dunnigan, 2003, p. 546.
22. Gutmann, 2000, p. 54.
23. Dunnigan, 2003; Shanker, 2004.
24. Murray and Scales, 2003, p. 169.
25. Smith, 2001.
26. Ministry of Defence, 2002, p. B3.
27. Donnelly, 2006.
28. Pantano, 2006, p. 200.
29. Schechter, 2004.
30. Gutmann, 2000, pp. 244–262.
31. Dunnigan, 2003, p. 315.
32. Presidential Commission, 1992, p. 74.
33. Baldwin, 1998a.
34. McMichael, 2001.
35. Peniston, 2006, pp. 143, 150–151, 156, 223.
36. Peach, 1996, p. 185 n. 26.
37. Sensing, 2003.
38. U.S. General Accounting Office, 1993, pp. 24–25.
39. Gutmann, 2000, p. 15.
40. Williams, 2005, p. 90.
41. Castaneda, 2006; Exum, 2006.
42. Bowden, 1999, p. 215.
43. Gray, 2005, p. 16.
44. Stokesbury, 1988.
45. Moniz, 2005.
46. Colimore, 2006.
47. Eller, 2005.
48. Jones, 1997.
49. Devilbiss, 1996, pp. 198, 201.
50. Miller and Moskos, 1995, pp. 625–631.
51. Sion, 2006.

3. Osborn, 2001, pp. 108–132, 251–254; Larson, 2002; Dejevsky, 2001; Turnbull, 2003.
4. Binkin, 1993, p. 40.
5. Shields, Curry, and Nichols, 1990, p. 21.
6. Garrison, 1994.
7. Dejevsky, 2001.
8. Zucchino, 2004, pp. 287–288.
9. McConnell, 1985, pp. 49–50, 147, 156, 226.
10. Congressional Medal of Honor Society, 1985, pp. 309–313.
11. O'Grady, 1995.
12. Mills, 1992.
13. Wilcox, 1996, pp. 3–4; Spick, 1988, p. 152.
14. Spick, 1988, p. ii.
15. Dunnigan, 2003, p. 139.
16. Spick, 1988, pp. 28, 157–158.
17. Hilton and Dolgin, 1991, p. 95.
18. Fry and Reinhardt, 1969, pp. 485–486.
19. Wilcox, 1996, pp. 165–166.
20. Voge and King, 1997a, p. 884.
21. Hartman and Secrist, 1991, p. 1084; Carretta, Perry, and Ree, 1996, p. 21; Spick, 1988, pp. vi, 63.
22. Jones and Endsley, 1996, pp. 507–508.
23. Carretta, Perry, and Ree, 1996, p. 21.
24. Endsley and Bolstad, 1994, p. 244; Boer, 1991, p. 103.
25. Carretta, 1997a.
26. Carretta, 1997b.
27. Carretta, Perry, and Ree, 1997, p. 28.
28. Boyd, Patterson, and Thompson, 2005.
29. Dunnigan, 1993, p. 156.
30. Spick, 1988, pp. vi–vii.
31. Wilcox, 1996, p. 44.
32. Hartman and Secrist, 1991, p. 1084.
33. Wilcox, 1996, p. 67.
34. Stockdale, 1995, p. 105.
35. Wilcox, 1996, p. 6.
36. Lambeth, 2002.
37. Kernan, 2005, p. 120.

Chapter 7: The "Special Case" of Aviation

1. Shields, Curry, and Nichols, 1990.
2. Wilcox, 1996, pp. 37–38.

Chapter 8: War as a Traditionally Masculine Pursuit

1. Kipling, 1890.
2. D'Andrade, 1966, pp. 174–204.

3. Turney-High, 1971, p. 161.
4. Lewis and Clark, 1805, entry of October 13, p. 111; Connolly and Anderson, 1987, p. 24; Baron, 1974a, 1974b.
5. Stouffer et al., 1949, p. 131.
6. Sion, 2001.
7. Egbert et al., 1957, cited in Binkin, 1993, p. 39; Egbert, 1954, p. 47; Watson, 1978, p. 49.
8. Gimbel and Booth, 1996.
9. Van Creveld, 2001; Goldstein, 2001, p. 19.
10. Goldstein, 2001, p. 22; Alpern, 1998, p. 38; Van Creveld, 2001, p. 116.
11. Goldstein, 2001, pp. 79–81.
12. Van Creveld, 1992; 2001, pp. 19, 185.
13. Van Creveld, 2001, pp. 140–142.
14. Goldstein, 2001, pp. 22, 65.
15. Van Creveld, 2001, pp. 140–148, 228.
16. Jones, 1997.
17. Abrams, 1993; Addis, 1994, p. 17; Morris, 1996, pp. 660, 701, 751.
18. Scales, 2005, p. 15.
19. Morris, 1996, p. 746.
20. Watson, 1978, pp. 244–245.
21. Morris, 1996, p. 751 (emphasis added).

Chapter 9: What Men Fear

1. Slim, 1957, p. 5.
2. Keegan, 1976, p. 297.
3. Ellis, 1976; Keegan, 1998.
4. Dollard, 1944, pp. 18–19; Holmes, 1985, p. 142; Stouffer et al., 1949, pp. 131–132.
5. McPherson, 1997, pp. 78–79.
6. Sledge, 1981, p. 19; Murphy, 1949, pp. 80–81.
7. Holmes, 1985, pp. 142–143.
8. Bartone and Kirkland, 1991, pp. 395–396.
9. Browne, 2002, pp. 35–49.
10. Keegan, 1993, p. 226.
11. Kunich, 1995.
12. Wright, 2004, p. 57.
13. Marshall, 1947, p. 149.
14. Dunnigan, 2003, p. 330.
15. Fick, 2005, p. 28.
16. Dollard, 1944, pp. 18–19; Holmes, 1985, p. 222.

17. Caputo, 1977, p. 288.
18. Marshall, 1947, p. 78.
19. Eibl-Eibesfeldt, 1979, p. 100; Chang, 1998, pp. 56–58.
20. Marshall, 1947, pp. 50–63.
21. Spiller, 1988; Smoler, 1989.
22. Spiller, 1988; RUSI Panel, 2001, p. 49 (Remarks of David Rowland).
23. Eibl-Eibesfeldt, 1979, pp. 122–125.
24. Holmes, 1985, pp. 361, 366.
25. RUSI Panel, 2001, p. 46 (Remarks of Allan Davis).
26. Marshall, 1947, p. 153.
27. Runciman, 1998, p. 740.
28. Ozkaptan, 1994, p. 236.
29. Keegan, 1976, p. 71; Spick, 1988, p. 3; Smith, 1983b, pp. 34–35.
30. Watson, 1978, p. 220.
31. Stein, Walker, and Forde, 2000.
32. Moniz, 2005.
33. Rosen, et al., 1999.
34. Kilner, 2002.
35. O'Connor et al., 2003; Zimmer and Minkovitz, 2003.
36. Scharnberg, 2005.
37. Umberson, 1992.
38. Meo, 2006.
39. Tyson, 2003.
40. Reed, 2005.
41. Morgan, 2004.
42. Fainaru, 2005.
43. Aristotle, 350 BC, p. 67; Miller, 2000, p. 252.
44. Morris, 1996, p. 751.
45. Marlowe, 1983, p. 192.
46. Dinter, 1985, p. 50; Middlebrook, 1978, pp. 335–336.
47. Voge and King, 1997a, p. 884.
48. Stouffer et al., 1949, pp. 208–209.
49. Conant, 2004; Jacoby, 2004.
50. Chase, 2004.
51. Conant, 2004; McHugh, 2004.
52. Mitchell, 1998, pp. 197–198.
53. Ambrose, 1997, p. 113.
54. Marshall, 1947, p. 61.
55. Braun, Wiegand, and Aschenbrenner, 1991, p. 55.
56. Richardson, 1978, p. 95. Also Bartone and Kirkland, 1991, p. 394; Dinter, 1985, p. 126.
57. Binkin, 1993, p. 39.
58. Moskos, 1970, p. 154.

Chapter 10: Why Men Love War

1. Gray, 1959, p. 28.
2. Goldstein, 2001, p. 253.
3. Hanson, 1999, pp. 148, 151, 161–162, 173–174, 182, 234.
4. Holmes, 1985, p. 171; Henderson, 1985, p. 164.
5. Fick, 2005, p. 368; Exum, 2004, p. 233.
6. Holmes, 1985, p. 274; Farago, 1964, p. 486.
7. Stokesbury, 1981, p. 34; Murphy, 1949, pp. 7–8; Sledge, 1981, p. 5.
8. Kernan, 1994, p. 130; Hynes, 1988, p. 180.
9. Sajer, 1967, p. 333.
10. Caputo, 1977, p. 81.
11. Wright, 2004, p. 11.
12. Karnow, 1997, p. 480.
13. Dunnigan and Nofi, 1999, p. 65.
14. Fussell, 1996, p. 171.
15. Stiehm, 1982, p. 371.
16. Fick, 2005, pp. 28, 50.
17. Exum, 2004, p. 9; Scales, 2005, p. 10.
18. Hynes, 1997, p. 23.
19. Dunnigan, 2005.
20. Wright, 2004, p. 5.
21. Hanson, 1999, p. 164.
22. Carrington, 1965/2006, p. 259.
23. Estep, 1991, p. 5; Fick, 2005, p. 261; Wright, 2004, p. 349.
24. Churchill, 1897, p. 116; Wright, 2004, p. 306.
25. Downs, 1978, p. 149.
26. Bourke, 1999, pp. 18–21; Schmitt, 2005, p. A12.
27. Broyles, 1984, p. 61; Hemingway, 1936; Coughlin and Kuhlman, 2005, p. 12.
28. Wright, 2004, p. 182.
29. Fick, 2005, p. 368.
30. Gray, 1959, p. 150.
31. Kernan, 1994, p. 93; Gray, 1959, p. 61.
32. Wright, 2004, p. 2.
33. Keegan and Holmes, 1985, p. 267; Bowden, 1999, p. 254; Wright, 2004, pp. 252, 266.
34. Wright, 2004, p. 105.
35. Gray, 1959, p. 63.
36. Bargh et al., 1995.
37. Wilson and Daly, 1997.
38. Berglund, 1993.
39. Purrfect Angelz, 2006; Martineau and Wiegand, 2006.
40. Jensen, Clark, and Snider, 2003.
41. Wright, 2004, p. 21.
42. Ibid., pp. 21–22.
43. Exum, 2004, p. 34.

Chapter 11: The Bond of Brothers: All for One and One for All

1. Shakespeare, *Henry V,* act 4, sc. iii.
2. Keegan, 1976; Hibbert, 1978.
3. Hanson, 2001, p. 292.
4. Xenophon, ~380 BC, p. 64; Heinl, 1966, p. 196.
5. Stouffer, 1949, pp. 192–241; Daddis, 2004.
6. Du Picq, 1880, p. 54.
7. Moran, 1966, p. 4.
8. Dunnigan, 2003, p. 521.
9. Wong et al., 2003.
10. Fritz, 1996.
11. Holmes, 1985, p. 374.
12. Caputo, 1977, p. 230.
13. Marshall, 1947, p. 42; Henderson, 1985, p. 107.
14. George, 1971; Gal, 1986; Henderson, 1985, p. 3.
15. Turney-High, 1971, p. ix (Foreword by David C. Rapoport); Bartov, 1992, pp. S36–S37.
16. Caputo, 1977, p. xvii; Hynes, 1988, p. 77.
17. Henderson, 1985, p. 300.
18. Lowry, 2005; *Washington Times,* 2006; Heidt, 2006.
19. Phillips, 2005; Neuman, 2007.
20. Moskos, 1970, pp. 145–146.
21. Solaro, 2006, p. 298.
22. Geary and Flinn, 2002.
23. Henderson, 1985, p. 18; Luddy, 1994.
24. Henderson, 1985, p. 18; Savage and Gabriel, 1976, p. 372 n. 14; Holmes, 1985, p. 262.
25. Josefowitz and Gadon, 1989, p. 22.
26. Pershing, 2006.
27. Josefowitz and Gadon, 1989, p. 25.
28. Stockdale, 1995, pp. 25–26.
29. Marshall, 1947, p. 154; Carrington, 1965/2006, pp. 98–99.
30. Murphy, 1949.
31. Wray, 1987, p. 51; Ambrose, 1997, p. 277.
32. Manchester, 1979, p. 391.

33. Kellett, 1982, p. 45; Buss and Portnoy, 1967.
34. Gal, 1983; Gal and Gabriel, 1982.
35. Goodacre, 1953, pp. 177–179.
36. Henderson, 1985, p. 75; Watson, 1978, pp. 116–117.
37. Manning and Fullerton, 1988; Solomon, Mikulincer, and Hobfoll, 1986; Ingraham and Manning, 1980.
38. Henderson, 1985, p. 334.
39. Manning, 1991, p. 456.
40. Greer, 1999.
41. Binkin, 1993, p. 40.
42. Grice and Katz, 2005, pp. vii, 1.
43. Presidential Commission, 1992, p. 71.
44. Center for Strategic and International Studies, 2000.
45. Manning, 1991, p. 456.
46. Kier, 1998.
47. Siebold, 1999, p. 6.
48. Mullen and Copper, 1994; National Defense Research Institute, 1993, pp. 291–294.
49. Watson, 1978, p. 114.
50. Lipsyte, 1992.
51. MacCoun, Kier, and Belkin, 2005.
52. Gray, 1959, p. 40.
53. Manning and Fullerton, 1988, p. 504.
54. Presidential Commission, 1992, p. c-86.
55. Henderson, 1985, pp. xviii, 22, 107.
56. Catignani, 2004; Scales, 2005, p. 16.
57. Bourne, 1970, p. 42.
58. Holmes, 1985, p. 90.
59. Rosen et al., 1996; Rosen and Martin, 1997.
60. Rosen, Bliese, et al., 1999, pp. 377–382.
61. Rosen, Knudson, and Fancher, 2003.
62. U.S. General Accounting Office, 1993; Miller, 1997, p. 48.
63. Center for Strategic and International Studies, 2000.
64. Harrell and Miller, 1997, p. 99.
65. Presidential Commission, 1992, pp. 29, 66.
66. Harrell and Miller, 1997, p. 92.
67. Presidential Commission, 1992, p. 26.
68. Voge and King, 1997b.
69. Miller, 1997, p. 43.
70. Presidential Commission, 1992, p. 29.
71. Shields, Curry, and Nichols, 1990, pp. 21, 32.

Chapter 12: *Who Men Follow: Leadership and Followership in Combat*

1. Bradley, 1981.
2. Manchester, 1979, pp. 234–237.
3. Marshall, 1947, p. 168; Watson, 1978, p. 436.
4. Stouffer, 1949, p. 117; McMichael, 2001.
5. Henderson, 1985, pp. 113, 133.
6. Manning, 1991, p. 457.
7. Calvert, 1995, pp. 229–230.
8. Sledge, 1981, pp. 40, 140–141.
9. Kellett, 1982, p. 599; Dinter, 1985, p. 56; Grinker and Spiegel, 1945, p. 25.
10. Frost, Fiedler, and Anderson, 1983; Dixon, 1976, p. 217; Smith, 1983a; Dunnigan, 2003, p. 290.
11. Grinker and Spiegel, 1945, pp. 46–47.
12. Henderson, 1985, p. 113.
13. Caputo, 1977, p. 187; Hanson, 1999, p. 279.
14. Gray, 1959, p. 13.
15. Atwater et al., 1999.
16. Eagly, Karau, and Makhijani, 1995; Eagly, Makhijani, and Klonsky, 1992; Rice, Bender, and Vitters, 1980; Tiger, 1969, pp. 57, 74.
17. Jeanquart-Barone and Sekaran, 1994; Eagly and Karau, 2002.
18. Atwater, Carey, and Waldman, 2001.
19. Boldry, Wood, and Kahsy, 2001.
20. Boyce and Herd, 2003.
21. Eagly and Karau, 1991.
22. Eagly and Johnson, 1990.
23. Eagly, Makhijani, and Klonsky, 1992; Eagly and Carli, 2004.
24. Shils, 1951, p. 65 n. 60; also Dinter, 1985, p. 56; Dixon, 1976, pp. 216–217.
25. Rice, Bender, and Vitters, 1980.
26. Watson, 1978, pp. 160–161.
27. Mitchell, 1998.
28. Rice, Yoder, and Adams, 1984.
29. Banerjee and Hart, 2004; Sloan and Barry, 2004; Conant, 2004; Hudson, 2004; Huntley, 2004; Worth, 2004.
30. Leonard, 2004.
31. Taguba, 2004; Serrano and Mazzetti, 2005; White, 2005.
32. De Bertodano, 2004; Marzullo, 2004.
33. De Bertodano, 2004; BBC News, 2004.
34. Karpinski, 2005; Stannard, 2005.

35. Leibovich, 2006.
36. Greyhawk, 2006; Icasualties.org.
37. Taylor, 1977.
38. Bartone and Kirkland, 1991.
39. Reeder, 1994, p. 233.
40. Baucom, 1985.
41. Nicholson, 1998, p. 146.
42. Holliday, 2004.

Chapter 13: The Evolved Nature of Male Bonding: Is Men's Aversion to Female Comrades in Arms Intractable?

1. McPeak, 1992, pp. 78–79.
2. Tiger, 1969, pp. 75, 126–131.
3. Martin and Fabes, 2002.
4. Maccoby, 1998; Fagot, 1985; Maccoby, 1990.
5. Campbell, 1999, p. 208.
6. Savin-Williams, 1979.
7. Pettit et al., 1990; Benenson, 1999; Savin-Williams, 1979; Benenson and Schinazi, 2004.
8. Fagot, Rodgers, and Leinbach, 2000; Geary et al., 2003.
9. Kirshnit, Ham, and Richards, 1989.
10. Martin and Fabes, 2002, p. 443.
11. Browne, 2002, pp. 46–47.
12. Maccoby, 1998, pp. 39–40.
13. Benenson and Schinazi, 2004, p. 329.
14. Dobson and Iredale, 2006.
15. Tyson, 2003.
16. David Geary, 2006, personal communication.
17. Hrdy, 1981, p. 130.
18. Fisher, 1999, pp. 43–44; Campbell, 2006.
19. Williams, 2005, pp. 88–89, 91.
20. Benenson and Alavi, 2004.
21. Butovskaya et al., 2000.
22. Geary and Flinn, 2002.
23. Brown, 1991, pp. 48, 137.
24. Mead, 1949, p. 7.
25. D'Andrade, 1966.
26. Tiger, 1969, pp. 193–197.
27. Preuschoft and van Schaik, 2000.
28. Low, 1992; Wrangham and Peterson, 1996.
29. Low, 2000, p. 194.
30. Fisher, 1999, p. 44.

31. Tiger, 1969, pp. 42, 100.
32. Farthing, 2005.
33. Binkin, 1993, p. 43.
34. Johnston, 1999, p. 179.
35. Browne, 2006b.
36. Howland, 2006.
37. Cottrell, Neuberg, and Li, 2007, p. 227.
38. Browne, 2002, p. 62.
39. Haselton and Funder, 2006, p. 31.
40. Berkun and Meeland, 1958.
41. Cottrell and Neuberg, 2005, p. 771.
42. Messick and Kramer, 2001, pp. 98, 103–104.
43. Tversky and Kahneman, 1974.
44. Haselton and Buss, 2000.
45. Haselton and Funder, 2006.
46. Öhman and Mineka, 2001.
47. Epstein, 1994.
48. Solaro, 2006, pp. 130, 140, 331, 345–348.
49. Gabriel and Savage, 1978, pp. 43, 183; Holmes, 1985, pp. 329–330.
50. Holmes, 1985, pp. 320, 330.
51. Ibid., p. 329.
52. Miller, 1997, p. 39.
53. Wright, 2004, pp. 68–69, 120, 268.
54. Anderson, 1976, pp. 189–190.

Part V: Threats to Cohesion and Effectiveness Arising from Mixing the Sexes

1. Clausewitz, 1832, p. 140.

Chapter 14: Who Men Protect: Women and Children First

1. Kipling, 1896.
2. Eaton and Haas, 1994.
3. Phillips, 2002; Gribble, n.d.
4. Burg, 1997; Oceans Africa, 2006.
5. Shaw, 2002, pp. 136, 139, 202, 205.
6. Stiglmayer, 1994.
7. Carpenter, 2003, pp. 662, 682, 687; also Carpenter, 2005.
8. Felson, 2000, p. 92.
9. Kersten, 2001.
10. Mathewes-Green, 1996.
11. Anderson and Oppat, 1999.
12. Kristof, 2003.
13. Bowman, 2006, p. 33.

14. Presidential Commission, 1992, p. c-86.
15. U.S. General Accounting Office, 1993, p. 25.
16. Holmes, 1985, pp. 194–195.
17. Dalrymple, 2007.
18. Moss, 2005; Dominus, 2006.
19. Scarborough, 2004b.
20. Linderman, 1997, p. 159.
21. Mason, 1983, pp. 309–310.
22. Filkins, 2006.
23. Ursano et al., 1985.
24. Watson, 1978, p. 266.
25. *Larry King Live,* 2007.
26. McGlohn, King, Butler, and Retzlaff, 1997; Voge and King, 1997a; Voge and King, 1997b.
27. Francke, 1997, p. 89.
28. Jones, 1999; Palmer and Thornhill, 2003.
29. Kerber, 1993, p. 125.
30. Francke, 1997, p. 91.

27. Burnham et al., 2003.
28. Holmes, 1985, p. 95.
29. Schogol, 2006; Dunnigan, 2004b.
30. Jowers, 2006.
31. Dunnigan, 2004b.
32. Browne, 2007.
33. Scarborough, 1994b.
34. Scarborough, 1994c; PBS, n.d.
35. Scarborough, 1996b.
36. Scarborough, 1997a.
37. Lewthwaite, 1996.
38. Spinner and Priest, 1997.
39. Sciolino, 1997b; Gibbs, 1997.
40. *New York Times,* 1997a.
41. Sciolino, 1997a.
42. Vistica and Thomas, 1997.
43. Young, 1999; Goodyear, 1999.
44. Olson, 2006b.
45. Olson, 2006a.
46. Vogel, 2006.
47. Kelly, 2006c.
48. Sion, 2001, p. 16.

Chapter 15: Sexual Relationships and Attraction

1. Van Hooff and Van Schaik, 1994, p. 317.
2. Flinn, 1997, p. 246.
3. Simons, 1997, pp. 184–185.
4. Kellett, 1982, p. 43.
5. Binkin, 1993, p. 44.
6. Harrell and Miller, 1997, pp. 81–82.
7. Gutmann, 2000, pp. 229–230.
8. Scarborough, 2000.
9. Kates, 2005.
10. Martineau and Wiegand, 2005b.
11. Williams, 2005, pp. 18, 21.
12. Barry and Thomas, 1997.
13. Gutmann, 1997.
14. Coleman, 1991, p. A7.
15. Williams, 2005, pp. 18–19.
16. Morris, 1996, pp. 756–757.
17. Lieberman, Tooby, and Cosmides, 2003.
18. Bleske-Rechek and Buss, 2001.
19. Filmsite.org, n.d.
20. Williams, 2005, pp. 13–14; Sion, 2001, pp. 16–17.
21. Simons, 2001b, p. 95.
22. *New York Times,* 2003a.
23. *New York Times,* 2006; 2004; 2003c; 2003b; 2000; 1997b.
24. Corbett, 2007.
25. Solaro, 2006, p. 330.
26. Webb, 1979, p. 144.

Chapter 16: Double Standards and Political Correctness

1. Gutmann, 2000, p. 23.
2. Grinker and Spiegel, 1945, p. 47; Little, 1964, p. 218.
3. Harrell and Miller, 1997, pp. 77–81.
4. U.S. General Accounting Office, 1995; U.S. Department of the Navy, 1997.
5. Gutmann, 2000, p. 260.
6. Scarborough, 2001; 2003b.
7. Harrell and Miller, 1997, pp. 80–81; Miller, 1997, p. 47.
8. Harrell and Miller, 1997, pp. 42, 47.
9. Gutmann, 2000, p. 35.
10. Mitchell, 1998, pp. 204–206; Miller, 1997, p. 45.
11. Mitchell, 1998, pp. 204–206.
12. Miller, 1997, pp. 46–47.
13. Williams, 2005, p. 20.
14. Washington, 2005.
15. Harrell and Miller, 1997, pp. 85–86.
16. Williams, 2005, pp. 93, 103.
17. Jaffe, 2006.
18. Morris, 1996, p. 738.
19. Miller, 1997, p. 74.
20. Ibid., p. 73; Federal Advisory Committee on Gender-Integrated Training, 1997, pp. 10, 18.

21. Compart, 1997.
22. Office of the Inspector General, 1993, p. 42.
23. Scarborough, 1994d.
24. United Press International, 1993; Scarborough, 1993.
25. Office of the Inspector General of the Department of Defense, 2004.
26. Kelly, 2006b; Countervailing Force, 2006.
27. Brown, 1999.
28. Gandt, 1997, p. 36.
29. Presidential Commission, 1992, p. 50; Gandt, 1997, p. 34.
30. Pruden, 1995; Corry, 1995.
31. Mitchell, 1998, pp. 288–302; Garrison, 1995a, 1995b; Blazar, 1997.
32. Vistica, 1997, pp. 393–394.
33. Voge and King, 1997a, p. 881.
34. Blair, 1999.
35. Miller, 1997, p. 48.
36. Scutro, 2006.
37. Kelly, 2006a.
38. Olson, 2006c.
39. CDR Salamander, 2006.
40. Newman, 1997.
41. Scarborough, 1997b.
42. Donnelly, 1998.
43. Miller, 1998, p. 40.
44. Smith, 2001.
45. Tyson, 2005.
46. Miller, 1998, p. 41.
47. Jordan, 2002; Perry, 2002.
48. Lubold and Curtis, 2002.
49. CNN Live Today, 2001a; 2001b.
50. Kelly, 2004.
51. Emery, 2003.
52. Oldham, 2003.

Chapter 17: Rape of Female Prisoners of War

1. Gordon, 1992.
2. Turney-High, 1971, p. 151.
3. Holmes, 1985, pp. 389–390.
4. Brownmiller, 1975, pp. 31–113.
5. Francke, 1997, p. 96.
6. Sciolino, 1992.
7. Nantais and Lee, 1999, p. 186.
8. Francke, 1997, pp. 98–99.
9. Bragg, 2003, p. 96.
10. Reid, 2003; Hockstader, 2003.
11. *New York Times,* 2003a.
12. Jolidon, 1992.
13. Francke, 1997, p. 96.
14. Hermann, 2003.
15. Cohen, 2000, p. 74
16. Presidential Commission, 1992, p. c-46.
17. Goldstein, 2001, p. 363.
18. Monto and McRee, 2005.
19. Palmer and Thornhill, 2003; Buss, 1994.
20. Chang, 1998, pp. 52, 91–96.
21. Tanaka, 1999, p. xi.
22. Niarchos, 1995, p. 658.
23. Francke, 1997, pp. 252–253; *Coker v. Georgia,* 433 U.S. 584 (1977).
24. U.S. General Accounting Office, 1999.
25. Peach, 1996, p. 170.
26. Federal Bureau of Investigation, 2006.
27. De Groot, 1995, p. 259.
28. U.S. Department of Veterans Affairs, 2006.
29. Christopher, 2004, pp. 14, 18–19.
30. Fact Sheet: Mirena.

Chapter 18: Reproductive Issues: Pregnancy, Motherhood, and Hygiene

1. *Goldman v. Weinberger,* 475 U.S. 503, 507 (1986) (internal quotation marks omitted).
2. Scarborough, 1996a; Hook, 1996.
3. DeYoung, 2003.
4. Scarborough, 2003a.
5. Military Operational Medicine Research Program, 1999.
6. Smucker, 1997.
7. Baldwin, 1998b.
8. Priest, 1995.
9. Bowman, 1999.
10. Garland, Garland, and Gorham, 2000.
11. Uriell and White, 2005.
12. Scarborough, 2004a.
13. Scarborough, 1995.
14. Presidential Commission, 1992, p. 20; Bucher, 1999.
15. Bucher, 1999.
16. Gertz, 1996.
17. Ritchie, 2001; Hanna, 1992.
18. Book, 2001.
19. Garcia, 1999.

20. Uriell and White, 2005, pp. 52, 54.
21. Peach, 1996, p. 170; Francke, 1997, p. 251.
22. Lauder et al., 2000.
23. Borsay-Trindle and Pass, 1991; Clark, Holt, and Miser, 1998; Robbins et al., 2005; Uriell and White, 2005, p. 56.
24. Binkin, 1993, pp. 28–29.
25. Chief of Naval Operations, 2003.
26. Carroll, 2005.
27. Tyson, 2005.
28. Hackworth, 1998.
29. Bucher, 1999.
30. Ryan-Wenger and Lowe, 2000.
31. Richter, 1999.
32. Fields, 1990.
33. Wheelwright, 1994, p. 130.
34. Uniform Code of Military Justice, § 915, art. 115 (2000); Mitchell, 1998, p. 154.
35. LaPeter, 2004.
36. Kingsley, 2004; Davis, 2004.
37. Segal, 1986.
38. Uriell, 2004, p. 5.
39. Powers, 2006a.
40. Francke, 1997, p. 139.
41. Lundquist and Smith, 2005.
42. Powers, 2006b.
43. Army Regulation AR 601–210, § 2–10, 2005.
44. Carroll, 2005.
45. Gutmann, 2000, p. 130.
46. Browne, 2002, pp. 86–87.
47. Ritchie, 2001.
48. Nordheimer, 1991.
49. Thompson, 1997; Adde, 1997a.
50. Tyson, 2003.
51. Jensen, Martin, and Watanabe, 1996; Kelley et al., 2001.
52. Seelye, 1995.
53. Roberts, 1995; Brotman, 1995; Hurst, 1995; *Los Angeles Times*, 1995; Goodman, 1995.
54. Wardell and Czerwinski, 2001.
55. Tyson, 2003.
56. Lowe and Ryan-Wenger, 2003.
57. Wardell and Czerwinski, 2001.
58. Voge, 1996.
59. Omicinski, 2001; Lowe and Ryan-Wenger, 2003.
60. Ambrose, 1997, pp. 212, 258.
61. Clausewitz, 1832, p. 138.

Chapter 19: Recruiting, Retention, and Conscription: Is a Fully Integrated Military Attractive to Either Men or Women?

1. Miller, 1998, p. 33.
2. Myers, 1999a.
3. Moskos, 1988.
4. Segal and Segal, 1983, p. 240.
5. O'Beirne, 1997.
6. Benecke and Dodge, 1990, p. 245 and n. 195.
7. Center for Strategic and International Studies, 2000.
8. Gutmann, 2000, p. 277.
9. Presidential Commission, 1992, p. c-113; Voge and King, 1997a, p. 883.
10. Hertz, 1996; Voge and King, 1997a.
11. Enloe, 1994, pp. 81, 95; Binkin, 1993, p. 47; Scarborough, 1998; Miller, 1998, p. 47.
12. Valpolini and Sculte, 1999.
13. Presidential Commission, 1992, pp. 26, c-21.
14. Thompson, 1999; Canadian Newswire, 1997; Hobson, 1999; Canadian Newswire, 1999.
15. Stiehm and Olson, 2006.
16. O'Beirne, 2006, p. 118.
17. Shureb, 2005.
18. White, 2005; Scarborough, 2006.
19. White, 2005.
20. McGlohn, et al., 1997, p. 5.
21. Miller, 1997, p. 43.
22. O'Beirne, 2006, p. 117.
23. Carter and Glastris, 2005.
24. *Rostker v. Goldberg*, 453 U.S. 57 (1981).
25. *United States v. Virginia*, 518 U.S. 515 (1996).
26. U.S. General Accounting Office, 1998; Selective Service System, 1998.
27. Solaro, 2006, p. 347.

Chapter 20: Should the Sexes Be Separated? Sex-Segregated Training and Operational Units

1. Federal Advisory Committee on Gender-Integrated Training and Related Issues, 1997, p. 15.
2. Blair, 1999; Anderson, 1997.

3. Federal Advisory Committee on Gender-Integrated Training, 1997; Priest, 1998.
4. Congressional Commission on Military Training and Gender-Related Issues (Blair Commission), 1999.
5. Thompson, 1997b.
6. Blair, 1999.
7. Dunnigan, 2003.
8. Jaffe, 2006.
9. Gibbs, 2006.
10. Miller, 1985.
11. Geary, 1998, p. 187.
12. Millard, 1995; also Fuentes, 1997.
13. Shipley, 1999.
14. Gutmann, 2000, p. 44.
15. Johnson, 1997.
16. Fukuyama, 1998; Dinter, 1985, p. 45.
17. Rosen et al., 1996, p. 550; Sion, 2001.
18. Sion, 2001, pp. 18–19.

Chapter 21: Why Comparisons to Some Other Forms of Discrimination Are Unpersuasive

1. Moskos, 1998.
2. Moskos and Butler, 1996.
3. Francke, 1997, p. 187.
4. DeFleur, Gillman, and Marshak, 1978; Priest, Vitters, and Prince, 1978, p. 218.
5. Benecke and Dodge, 1990, pp. 232–233; Francke, 1997, p. 23.
6. National Organization for Women, 1990.
7. Ellis, 1980, p. 158; Dunnigan and Nofi, 1999, p. 3.
8. Balkin, 1988, p. 30; Craig and Jacobs, 1985.
9. Martin, 1980, pp. 90–96.
10. O'Beirne, 2006, p. 138.
11. Martineau and Wiegand, 2005a; Dunnigan, 2003.
12. Simons, 2001a.
13. Gutmann, 2000, p. 119.
14. Maze, 1999.

Chapter 22: Conclusion

1. Burke, 1790, pp. 87–88.
2. Moran, 1966, p. 183.
3. Horace, 21 BC, p. 101.
4. Holmes, 1897, p. 469.
5. *New York Trust Co. v. Eisner*, 256 U.S. 345, 349 (1921).
6. Eikenberry, 1996.
7. Sirica, 1990.
8. http://www.census.gov/popest/archives/1990s/popclockest.txt.
9. Holm, 1992, p. 100.
10. Philpott, 1999.
11. Myers, 1999b.
12. Tyson, 2003.
13. Reyes, 2006, p. 2.
14. Scarborough, 1994a.
15. Presidential Commission, 1992, p. 65.

Bibliography

Abrams, K. (1993). Gender in the military: Androcentrism and institutional reform. *Law and Contemporary Problems*, 56:217–241.

Adde, N. (1997). Cuevas let go from Army: Breast feeding Black Hawk pilot must repay education funds. *Army Times*, October 27, p. 8.

Addis, E. (1994). Women and the economic consequences of being a soldier. In Addis, E., Russo, V. E., and Sebesta, L. (eds.), *Women Soldiers: Images and Realities*, pp. 3–27. New York: St. Martin's Press.

Addis, E., Russo, V. E., and Sebesta, L. (1994). Introduction. In Addis, E., Russo, V. E., and Sebesta, L. (eds.), *Women Soldiers: Images and Realities*, pp. xi–xxiv. New York: St. Martin's Press.

Alcock, J. (2000). Misbehavior: How Stephen Jay Gould is wrong about evolution. *Boston Review*, April/May.

Alexander, G. M., and Hines, M. (2002). Sex differences in response to children's toys in nonhuman primates (*Cercopithecus aethiops sabaeus*). *Evolution and Human Behavior*, 23:467–479.

Alexander, R. D. (1979). *Darwinism and Human Affairs*. Seattle: University of Washington Press.

Aloisi, A. M., and Bonifazi, M. (2006). Sex hormones, central nervous system and pain. *Hormones and Behavior*, 50:1–7.

Alpern, S. B. (1998). *Amazons of Black Sparta: The Women Warriors of Dahomey*. New York: New York University Press.

Aluja, A., and Torrubia, R. (2004). Hostility-aggressiveness, sensation seeking, and sex hormones in men: Re-exploring their relationship. *Neuropsychobiology*, 50:102–107.

Amato, A, and Booth, A. (1996). A prospective study of divorce and parent-child relationships. *Journal of Marriage and the Family*, 58:1356–1365.

Ambrose, S. E. (1997). *Citizen Soldiers: The U.S. Army from the Normandy Beaches to the Bulge to the Surrender of Germany: June 7, 1944—May 7, 1945.* New York: Simon & Schuster.

Amoroso, P. J., Bell, N. S., and Jones, B. H. (1997). Injury among female and male army parachutists. *Aviation, Space, and Environmental Medicine,* 68:1006–1011.

Anderson, C. R. (1976). *The Grunts.* San Rafael, CA: Presidio Press.

Anderson, J. H. (1997). *Boot Camp or Summer Camp? Restoring Rigorous Standards to Basic Training.* Heritage Foundation Backgrounder No. 1157.

Anderson, S., and Oppat, S. (1999). Young hero praised for aid to victim of prank. *Ann Arbor News,* September 8, p. A1.

Angier, N. (1992). 2 experts say women who run may overtake men. *New York Times,* January 7, p. C31.

Archer, J. (1991). The influence of testosterone on human aggression. *British Journal of Psychology,* 82:1–28.

———. (2004). Sex differences in aggression in real-world settings: A meta-analytic review. *Review of General Psychology,* 8:291–322.

———. (2006). Testosterone and human aggression: An evaluation of the challenge hypothesis. *Neuroscience and Biobehavioral Reviews,* 30:319–345.

Aristotle. (350 BC). *Politics* (Jowett, B., trans.). New York: Dover.

Arrindell, W. A. (1999). Disgust sensitivity and the sex differences in fears to common indigenous animals. *Behaviour Research and Therapy,* 37:273–280.

Associated Press. (1996). Women can train to lift like men, study finds. January 30.

Atwater, L. E., Carey, J. A., and Waldman, D. A. (2001). Gender and discipline in the workplace: Wait until your father gets home. *Journal of Management,* 27:537–561.

Atwater, L. E., Dionne S. D., Avolio, B., Camobreco, J. F., and Lau, A. W. (1999). A longitudinal study of the leadership development process: Individual differences predicting leader effectiveness. *Human Relations,* 52:1543–1562.

Baldwin, J. D. (1998a). *Women in Combat.* May 17, http://yarchive.net/mil/women_in_navy.html.

———. (1998b). *Women in Combat.* May 24, http://yarchive.net/mil/women_in_navy.html.

Balkin, J. (1988). Why policemen don't like policewomen. *Journal of Police Science and Administration,* 16:29–38.

Banerjee, N., and Hart, A. (2004). Inquiry opens after reservists balk in Baghdad. *New York Times,* October 16, p. A1.

Bargh, J. A., Raymond, P., Pryor, J. B., and Strack, F. (1995). Attractiveness of the underling: An automatic power→sex association and its consequences for sexual harassment and aggression. *Journal of Personality and Social Psychology,* 68:768–781.

Baron, R. A. (1974a). Sexual arousal and physical aggression: The inhibiting influence of "cheesecake" and nudes. *Bulletin of the Psychonomic Society,* 3:337–339.

———. (1974b). The aggression-inhibiting influence of heightened sexual arousal. *Journal of Personality and Social Psychology,* 30:318–322.

Baron-Cohen, S. (2003). *The Essential Difference: The Male and Female Brain and the Riddle of Autism.* New York: Penguin.

Baron-Cohen, S., and Wheelwright, S. (2004). The empathy quotient: An investigation of adults with Asperger syndrome or high functioning autism and normal sex differences. *Journal of Autism and Developmental Disorders,* 34:163–175.

Barry, J., and Thomas, E. (1997). Shifting lines: After cracking down on an adulterous female pilot, the brass shields an adulterous male general. *Newsweek,* June 16, p. 32.

Bartone, P. T., and Kirkland, F. R. (1991). Optimal leadership in small army units. In Gal, R., and Mangelsdorff, A. D. (eds.), *Handbook of Military Psychology,* pp. 393–409. New York: John Wiley and Sons.

Bartov, O. (1992). The conduct of war: Soldiers and the barbarization of warfare. *Journal of Modern History,* 64(Suppl.):S32–S45.

Baucom, D. R. (1985). The professional soldier and the warrior spirit. *Strategic Review*, Fall, pp. 57–66.

BBC News. (2004). Iraq abuse "ordered from the top." June 15, http://news.bbc.co.uk/2/world/americas/3806713.stm.

———. (2005). Women feel pain more than men: Women are bigger wimps than men when it comes to pain, research suggests, contrary to the popular notion that the reverse is true. http://news.bbc.co.uk/July4/2/1/hi/health/4641567.stm.

Beeston, R., and Grey, S. (2004). Backlash fear after British kill 28 fighters. *Times* (London), May 17.

Bendyna, M. E., Finucane, T., Kirby, L., O'Donnell, J. P., and Wilcox, C. (1996). Gender differences in public attitudes toward the Gulf War: A test of competing hypotheses. *Social Science Journal*, 33:1–22.

Benecke, M. M., and Dodge, K. S. (1990). Military women in nontraditional job fields: Casualties of the armed forces' war on homosexuals. *Harvard Women's Law Journal*, 13:215–250.

Benenson, J. F. (1999). Females' desire for status cannot be measured using male definitions. *Behavioral and Brain Sciences*, 22:216–217.

Benenson, J. F., and Alavi, K. (2004). Sex differences in children's investment in same-sex peers. *Evolution and Human Behavior*, 25:258–266.

Benenson, J. F., Philippoussis, M., and Leeb, R. (1999). Sex differences in neonates' cuddliness. *Journal of Genetic Psychology*, 160:332–342.

Benenson, J. F., and Schinazi, J. (2004). Sex differences in reactions to outperforming same-sex friends. *British Journal of Developmental Psychology*, 22:317–333.

Berenbaum, S. A. (1999). Effects of early androgens on sex-typed activities and interests in adolescents with congenital adrenal hyperplasia. *Hormones and Behavior*, 35:102–110.

Berenbaum, S. A., and Resnick, S. M. (1997). Early androgen effects on aggression in children and adults with congenital adrenal hyperplasia. *Psychoneuroendocrinology*, 22:505–515.

Berenbaum, S.A., and Snyder, E. (1995). Early hormonal influences on childhood sex-typed activity and playmate preferences: Implications for the development of sexual orientation. *Developmental Psychology*, 31:31–42.

Berglund, A. (1993). Risky sex: Male pipefishes mate at random in the presence of a predator. *Animal Behaviour*, 46:169–175.

Berkun, M., and Meeland, T. (1958). Sociometric effects of race and of combat performance. *Sociometry*, 21:145–149.

Betzig, L. (1986). *Despotism and Differential Reproduction: A Darwinian View of History*. New York: Aldine.

———. (1993). Sex, succession, and stratification in the first six civilizations: How powerful men reproduced, passed power on to their sons, and used power to defend their wealth, women, and children. In Ellis, L. (ed.), *Social Stratification and Socioeconomic Inequality*, Vol. 1, pp. 37–74. Westport, CT: Praeger.

Binkin, M. (1993). *Who Will Fight the Next War?: The Changing Face of the American Military*. Washington, DC: Brookings Institution.

Bishop, P., Cureton, K., and Collins, M. (1987). Sex difference in muscular strength in equally trained men and women. *Ergonomics*, 30:675–687.

Bishop, P., and Witherow, J. (1982). *The Winter War: The Falklands*. London: Quartet Books.

Bjorntorp, P. (1991). Adipose tissue distribution and function. *International Journal of Obesity*, 15:67–81.

Blair, A. K. (1999). *Gender-Integrated and Gender-Segregated Training*, Testimony Before the House Armed Services Committee, March 17, http://www.au.af.mil/au/awc/awcgate/congress/99=03=17blair.htm.

Blazar, E. (1997). Wing of fate: What went wrong–IG report details mistakes in rushing women onto carriers. *Navy Times*, July 14, p. 4.

Bleske-Rechek, A., and Buss, D. M. (2001). Opposite-sex friendship: Sex differences and similarities in initiation, selection, and dissolution. *Personality and Social Psychology Bulletin*, 27:1310–1323.

Boer, L. C. (1991). Spatial ability and orientation of pilots. In Gal, R., and Mangelsdorff, A. D. (eds.), *Handbook of Military Psychology*, pp.103–114. New York: John Wiley and Sons.

Boldry, J., Wood, W., and Kahsy, D. A. (2001). Gender stereotypes and the evaluation of men and women in military training. *Journal of Social Issues*, 57:689–705.

Book, E. G. (2001). Military women: 200,000 and counting. *National Defense*, October, pp. 14–15.

Borsay-Trindle, L. A., and Pass, C. M. (1991). Unplanned pregnancy among active-duty Army females as a readiness issue. *Military Medicine*, 156:82–86.

Boulton, M. J. (1993). Aggressive fighting in British middle school children. *Educational Studies*, 19:19–39.

Bourke, J. (1999). *An Intimate History of Killing: Face to Face Killing in 20th Century Warfare*. New York: Basic Books.

Bourne, P. G. (1970). *Men, Stress, and Vietnam*. Boston: Little, Brown.

Bowden, M. (1999). *Black Hawk Down*. New York: Atlantic Monthly Press.

Bowman, J. (2006). *Honor: A History*. New York: Encounter Books.

Bowman, T. (1999). Women on submarines: Navy secretary says it's coming: ROTC crews trying it out. *Seattle Times*, June 28, p. A4.

Boyce, L. A., and Herd, A. M. (2003). The relationship between gender role stereotypes and requisite military leadership characteristics. *Sex Roles*, 49:365–378.

Boyd, J. E., Patterson, J. C., and Thompson, B. T. (2005). Psychological test profiles of USAF pilots before training vs. type aircraft flown. *Aviation, Space, and Environmental Medicine*, 76:463–468.

Bradley, O. N. (1981). Leadership. *Parameters*, 11(3):2–7.

Bragg, R. (2003). *I Am a Soldier, Too: The Jessica Lynch Story*. New York: Alfred A. Knopf.

Brainard, J., and Burmaster, D. E. (1992). Bivariate distributions for height and weight of men and women in the United States. *Risk Analysis*, 12:267–275.

Braun, P., Wiegand, D., and Aschenbrenner, H. (1991). The assessment of complex skills and of personality characteristics in military services. In Gal, R., and Mangelsdorff, A. D. (eds.), *Handbook of Military Psychology*, pp. 37–61. New York: John Wiley and Sons.

Breedlove, S. M. (1994). Sexual differentiation of the human nervous system. *Annual Review of Psychology*, 45:389–418.

Bröder, A., and Hohmann, N. (2003). Variations in risk-taking behavior over the menstrual cycle: An improved replication. *Evolution and Human Behavior*, 24:391–398.

Brotman, B. (1995). One step forward, one back: The year of any woman brought out the best in us, and the worst. *Chicago Tribune*, December 31, p. C1.

Brown, D. (1999). Danzig seals midshipman's expulsion. *Navy Times*, June 21, p. 17.

Brown, D. E. (1991). *Human Universals*. New York: McGraw-Hill.

Browne, K. R. (1995). Sex and temperament in modern society: A Darwinian view of the glass ceiling and the gender gap. *Arizona Law Review*, 37:971–1106.

———. (2002). *Biology at Work: Rethinking Sexual Equality*. New Brunswick, NJ: Rutgers University Press.

———. (2005). Women in science: Biological factors should not be ignored. *Cardozo Women's Law Journal*, 11:509–528.

———. (2006a). Evolved sex differences and occupational segregation. *Journal of Organizational Behavior*, 27:143–162.

———. (2006b). Sex, power, and dominance: The evolutionary psychology of sexual harassment. *Managerial and Decision Economics*, 27:145–158.

———. (2007). Military sex scandals from Tailhook to the present: The cure can be worse than the disease. *Duke Journal of Gender Law & Policy*, 14:749–789.

Brownmiller, S. (1975). *Against Our Will: Men, Women and Rape.* New York: Simon & Schuster.

Broyles, W. (1984). Why men love war. *Esquire*, November, pp. 55–65.

Bucher, M. A. (1999). *The Impact of Pregnancy on U.S. Army Readiness.* AU/ACSC/016/ 1999–04. Air Command and Staff College, Air University.

Bureau of Justice Statistics. (1997). *Sex Differences in Violent Victimization, 1994.* U.S. Department of Justice, NCJ-1645, http://www.ojp.usdoj.gov/bjs/pub/pdf/sdvv.pdf.

Bureau of Labor Statistics. (2003). *Fatal Occupational Injuries by Worker Characteristics and Event or Exposure, All United States, 2002,* http://www.bls.gov/iif/oshwc/cfoi/ cftbo186.pdf.

Burfoot, A., and Post, M. (1992). Battle of the sexes. *Runner's World*, April, p. 40.

Burg, B. R. (1997). "Women and children first": Popular mythology and disaster at sea, 1840–1860. *Journal of American Culture*, 20(4):1–9.

Burke, C. (1996). Pernicious cohesion. In Stiehm, J. H. (ed.), *It's Our Military, Too!: Women and the U.S. Military*, pp. 205–219. Philadelphia: Temple University Press.

Burke, E. (1790). *Reflections on the Revolution in France.* Oxford: Oxford University Press.

Burnham, T. C., Chapman, J. F., Gray, P. B., McIntyre, M. H., Lipson, S. F., and Ellison, P. T. (2003). Men in committed, romantic relationships have lower testosterone. *Hormones and Behavior*, 44:119–122.

Buss, A. H., and Portnoy, N. W. (1967). Pain tolerance and group identification. *Journal of Personality and Social Psychology*, 6:106–108.

Buss, D. M. (1994). *The Evolution of Desire: Strategies of Human Mating.* New York: Basic Books.

Butovskaya, M., Verbeek, P., Ljungberg, T., and Lunardini, A. (2000). A multicultural view of peacemaking among young children. In Aureli, F., and de Waal F. B. M. (eds.), *Natural Conflict Resolution*, pp. 243–252. Berkeley: University of California Press.

Byrnes, J. P., Miller, D. C., and Schafer, W. D. (1999). Gender differences in risk-taking: A meta-analysis. *Psychological Bulletin*, 125:367–383.

Calvert, J. F. (1995). *Silent Running: My Years on a World War II Attack Submarine.* New York: John Wiley and Sons.

Campbell, A. (1999). Staying alive: Evolution, culture, and women's intrasexual aggression. *Behavioral and Brain Sciences*, 22:203–252.

———. (2006). Sex differences in aggression: What are the psychological mediators? *Aggression and Violent Behavior*, 11:237–264.

Campbell, A., and Muncer, S. (1994). Sex differences in aggression: Social representation and social roles. *British Journal of Social Psychology*, 33:233–240.

Campenni, C. E. (1999). Gender stereotyping of children's toys: A comparison of parents and nonparents. *Sex Roles*, 40:121–138.

Canadian Newswire. (1997). Army calls for more women to sign up for combat. *Toronto Star*, December 19, p. A33.

———. (1999). Eggleton wants a few (more) good women. February 26, p. 24.

Caputo, P. (1977). *A Rumor of War.* New York: Henry Holt.

Carnegie Hero Fund Commission. (2001). *Carnegie Hero Fund Commission Cites U.S. Terror Responders as "Heroes of Civilization,"* http://www.carnegiehero.org/awardees_ 911.php.

———. (2006). *Requirements for a Carnegie Medal,* http://www.carnegiehero.org/ nominate.php.

Carpenter, R. C. (2003). "Women and children first": Gender, norms, and humanitarian evacuation in the Balkans 1991–1995. *International Organization*, 57:661–694.

———. (2005). "Women, children and other vulnerable groups": Gender, strategic frames and the protection of civilians as a transnational issue. *International Studies Quarterly*, 49:295–334.

Carretta, T. R. (1997a). Group differences on U.S. Air Force pilot selection tests. *International Journal of Selection and Assessment*, 5:115–127.

————(1997b). Male-female performance on U.S. Air Force pilot selection tests. *Aviation, Space and Environmental Medicine*, 68:818–823.

Carretta, T. R., Perry, D. C., Jr., and Ree, M. J. (1996). Prediction of situational awareness in F-15 pilots. *International Journal of Aviation Psychology*, 6:21–41.

Carrington, C. (1965/2006). *Soldier from the Wars Returning*. Barnsley, UK: Pen and Sword.

Carroll, C. (2005). The need to change Army policies toward single parents and dual military couples with children. *USAWC Strategy Research Project*. Carlisle Barracks, PA: U.S. Army War College.

Carter, P., and Glastris, P. (2005). The case for the draft. *Washington Monthly*, March.

Castaneda, A. (2006). Now troops have body armor and they shun it as "too heavy." *New York Sun* (AP), March 27.

Catignani, S. (2004). Motivating soldiers: The example of the Israeli Defense Forces. *Parameters*, 34(3): 108–121.

CDR Salamander. (2006). LT Black's court-martial: Unintended consequences. January 25, http://cdrsalamander.blogspot.com/2006/01/lt-blacks-court-martial-unintended.html.

Center for Strategic and International Studies. (2000). *American Military Culture in the Twenty-First Century*. Washington, DC: CSIS Press.

Chagnon, N. A. (1988). Life histories, blood revenge, and warfare in a tribal population. *Science*, 239:985–992.

Chang, I. (1998). *The Rape of Nanking: The Forgotten Holocaust of World War II*. New York: Basic Books.

Chase, C. (2004). Montana guardsmen finish mission other unit refused in Iraq. *Daily Inter Lake* (Kalispell, MT), October 22.

Cheuvront, S. N., Carter, R., DeRuisseau, K. C., and Moffatt, R. J. (2005). Running performance differences between men and women. *Sports Medicine*, 35:1017–1024.

Cheuvront, S. N., Moffatt, R. J., and DeRuisseau, K. C. (2002). Body composition and gender differences in performance. In Wolinksy, I., and Driskell, J. A. (eds.), *Nutritional Assessment of Athletes*, pp. 177–200. Boca Raton, FL: CRC Press.

Chief of Naval Operations. (2003). *Guidelines Concerning Pregnant Servicewomen*, Section 103(b). OPNAVINST 6000.1B. Washington, DC: Department of the Navy.

Christopher, L. A. (2004). *Women in War: Operational Issues*. Department of the Air Force, Report No. CI04–351, Wright Patterson AFB, Ohio.

Churchill, W. S. (1897). *The Story of the Malakand Field Force: An Episode of Frontier War*. Aegypan Press.

Clark, J. B., Holt, V. L., and Miser, F. (1998). Unintended pregnancy among female soldiers presenting for prenatal care at Madigan Army Medical Center. *Military Medicine*, 163:444–448.

Clausewitz, C. von. (1832). *On War*. (Howard, M., and Paret, P., trans.). New York: Alfred A. Knopf.

Clutton-Brock, T. H. (1991). *The Evolution of Parental Care*. Princeton, NJ: Princeton University Press.

CNN Live Today. (2001a). Interview with U.S. Marine. December 24, Transcript No. 122423CN.V75.

————. (2001b). Merry military Christmas from Kandahar. December 24, Transcript No. 122424CN.V75.

CNN Newsmaker. (1991). Transcript #50, March 2.

Cohen, J. (1988). *Statistical Power Analysis for the Behavioral Sciences* (2nd ed.). Hillsdale, NJ: Lawrence Erlbaum.

Cohen, R. (2000). "What's so terrible about rape?" and other attitudes at the United Nations. *SAIS Review*, Summer/Fall, pp. 73–77.

Cohen-Bendahan, C. C. C., van de Beek, C., and Berenbaum, S. A. (2005). Prenatal sex hormone effects on child and adult sex-typed behavior: Methods and findings. *Neuroscience and Biobehavioral Reviews*, 29:353–384.

Colapinto, J. (2000). *As Nature Made Him: The Boy Who Was Raised as a Girl*. New York: HarperCollins.

Coleman, M. (1991). Unplanned pregnancy. *Military Medicine*, 156(12):A7–A10.

Colimore, E. (2006). Iraq raises stakes for female troops. *Philadelphia Inquirer*, May 15, p. 1.

Compart, A. (1997). New standard: Don't look, don't touch. *Navy Times*, December 8, p. 10.

Conant, E. (2004). Fast chat: Amber McClenny. *Newsweek*, December 27, p. 12.

Congressional Commission on Military Training and Gender-Related Issues (Blair Commission). (1999). *Statement and Status Report*, http://www.au.af.mil/au/awc/awcgate/congress/99-03-17commission1.htm.

Congressional Medal of Honor Society. (1985). *Above and Beyond: A History of the Medal of Honor from the Civil War to Vietnam*. Boston: Boston Publishing Co.

Connolly, B., and Anderson, R. (1987). *First Contact: New Guinea's Highlanders Encounter the Outside World*. New York: Viking Press.

Corbett, S. (2007). The women's war. *New York Times Magazine*, March 18.

Cornelius, R. R., and Averill, J. R. (1983). Sex differences in fear of spiders. *Journal of Personality and Social Psychology*, 45:377–383.

Corry, J. (1995). The death of Kara Hultgreen. *American Spectator*, June.

Cosner, K. J. (2003). Special Forces soldier receives Silver Star for Afghanistan combat. *Special Warfare*, August.

Cottrell, C. A., and Neuberg, S. L. (2005). Different emotional reactions to different groups: A sociofunctional threat-based approach to "prejudice." *Journal of Personality and Social Psychology*, 88:770–789.

Cottrell, C. A., Neuberg, S. L., and Li, N. P. (2007). What do people desire in others? A sociofunctional perspective on the importance of different valued characteristics. *Journal of Personality and Social Psychology*, 92:208–231.

Coughlin, J., and Kuhlman, C. (2005). *Shooter: The Autobiography of the Top-Ranked Marine Sniper*. New York: St. Martin's Press.

Countervailing Force. (2006). Duke on the Severn: Lamar Owens testimonial immunity. *The Countervailing Force*, July 22, http://pcrevolt.blogspot.com/2006_07_01_archive.html.

Craft, R. M., Mogil, J. S., and Aloisi, A. M. (2004). Sex differences in pain and analgesia: The role of gonadal hormones. *European Journal of Pain*, 8:397–411.

Craig, J. M., and Jacobs, R. R. (1985). The effect of working with women on male attitudes toward female leadership. *Basic and Applied Social Psychology*, 6:61–74.

Cronin, H. (1991). *The Ant and the Peacock: Altruism and Sexual Selection from Darwin to Today*. Cambridge: Cambridge University Press.

Daddis, G. A. (2004). Understanding fear's effect on unit effectiveness. *Military Review*, July/August, pp. 22–27.

Dalrymple, T. (2007). No way to treat a lady. *Wall Street Journal*, March 31, p. A10.

D'Andrade, R. G. (1966). Sex differences and cultural institutions. In Maccoby, E. E. (ed.), *The Development of Sex Differences*, pp. 174–204. Stanford, CA: Stanford University Press.

Daniels, W. L., Wright, J. E., Sharp, D. S., Kowal, D. M., Mello, R. P., and Stauffer, R. S. (1982). The effect of two years' training on aerobic power and muscle strength in male and female cadets. *Aviation, Space, and Environmental Medicine*, 53:117–121.

Darwin, C. (1871). *The Descent of Man and Selection in Relation to Sex*. London: Murray.

Davis, C. (2004). A slap in the face of war families. *St. Petersburg Times*, September 26, p. 2P.

De Bertodano, H. (2004). My army life: Lonely, restless and afraid. *Times* (London), August 13, p. 4.

De Groot, G. J. (1995). Women warriors. *Contemporary Review*, 266:257–260.

———. (1999). More blessed are these peacekeepers: Testosterone flows too freely when the job is left to male soldiers, says a historian of women in the military. *Toronto Star,* July 25.

DeFleur, L. B., Gillman, D., and Marshak, W. (1978). Sex integration of the U.S. Air Force Academy: Changing roles for women. *Armed Forces and Society,* 4:607–622.

Deitch, J. R., Starkey, C., Walters, S. L., and Moseley, J. B. (2006). Injury risk in professional basketball players: A comparison of Women's National Basketball Association and National Basketball Association athletes. *American Journal of Sports Medicine,* 34:1077–1083.

Dejevsky, M. (2001). Spy crew feared they were "seconds from death." *The Independent* (London), April 14, p. 14.

DEOMI (Defense Equal Oportunity Management Institute) (2006). *Annual Demographic Profile of the Department of Defense and U.S. Coast Guard FY 2005.* Research Directorate, Patrick AFB, FL, Statistical Series Pamplet No. 06–1.

Department of the Army. (2005). *Field Manual 3–23.30: Grenades and Pyrotechnic Signals.* Washington, DC: Headquarters, Department of the Army.

Devilbiss, M. C. (1996). To fight, to defend, and to preserve the peace: The evolution of the U.S. military and the role of women within it. In Stiehm, J. H. (ed.), *It's Our Military, Too!: Women and the U.S. Military,* pp. 195–202, Philadelphia: Temple University Press.

DeYoung, K. (2003). Bush proclaims victory in Iraq: Work on terror is ongoing, President says. *Washington Post,* May 2, p. A1.

Diamond, M., and Sigmundson, H. K. (1997). Sex reassignment at birth: Long-term review and clinical implications. *Archives of Pediatric and Adolescent Medicine,* 151:298–304.

Dinter, E. (1985). *Hero or Coward: Pressures Facing the Soldier in Battle.* London: Frank Cass.

Dixon, N. F. (1976). *On the Psychology of Military Incompetence.* London: Jonathon Cape.

Dobson, R., and Iredale, W. (2006). Office queen bees hold back women's careers. *Sunday Times* (London), December 31.

Dollard, J. (1944). *Fear in Battle.* New York: AMS Press.

Dominus, S. (2006). The war's deadliest day for U.S. women. *Glamour,* May.

Donnelly, E. (1998). Testimony of Elaine Donnelly before the House National Security Subcommittee on Personnel, March 17, http://armedservices.house.gov/comdocstestimony/105thcongress/3–17–98donnelly.htm.

———. (2006). Statement to the House Subcommittee on National Security, Emerging Threats, and International Relations. *Hearings on Sexual Assault and Violence Against Women in the Military and at the Academies,* June 27.

Downs, F. (1978). *The Killing Zone: My Life in the Vietnam War.* New York: W. W. Norton.

Dunn, T. N. (2004). Army's fearless five. *Sun,* July 5.

Dunnigan, J. (2003). Feminization can kill in combat. *Strategy Page,* October 11, http://www.strategypage.com/dls/articles2003/20031011.asp.

———. (2004a). No sex for 21st century soldiers. *Strategy Page,* October 2, http://www.strategypage.com/dls/articles2004/200410223.asp.

———. (2004b). Sexual paradise lost. *Strategy Page,* November 19, http://www.strategypage.com/dls/articles2004/2004111923.asp.

———. (2005). The real reasons women aren't in the infantry. *Strategy Page,* April 18, http://www.strategypage.com/dls/articles2005/20054172330.asp.

Dunnigan, J. F. (2003). *How to Make War: A Comprehensive Guide to Modern Warfare in the Twenty-first Century* (4th ed.). New York: Harper Paperbacks.

Dunnigan, J. F., and Nofi, A. A. (1999). *Dirty Little Secrets of the Vietnam War.* New York: St. Martin's Press.

Du Picq, A. (1880). *Battle Studies* (Greely, J. N., and Cotton, R. C., trans., 1920). Whitefish, MT: Kessinger Publishing.

Eagly, A. H. (1995). The science and politics of comparing women and men. *American Psychologist,* 50:145–158.

Eagly, A. H., and Carli, L. L. (2004). Women and men as leaders. In Cianciolo, A. T., Sternberg, R. J., and Antonakis, J. (eds.), *The Nature of Leadership in the New Millennium,* pp. 279–301. Thousand Oaks, CA: Sage.

Eagly, A. H., and Johnson, B. T. (1990). Gender and leadership style: A meta-analysis. *Psychological Bulletin,* 108:233–256.

Eagly, A. H., and Karau, S. J. (1991). Gender and the emergence of leaders: A meta-analysis. *Journal of Personality and Social Psychology,* 60:685–710.

———. (2002). Role congruity theory of prejudice toward female leaders. *Psychological Review,* 109:573–598.

Eagly, A. H., Karau, S. J., and Makhijani, M. G. (1995). Gender and the effectiveness of leaders: A meta-analysis. *Psychological Bulletin,* 117:125–145.

Eagly, A. H., Makhijani, M. G., and Klonsky, B. G. (1992). Gender and the evaluation of leaders: A meta-analysis. *Psychological Bulletin,* 111:3–22.

Eagly, A. H., and Steffen, V. J. (1986). Gender and aggressive behavior: A meta-analytic review of the social psychological literature. *Psychological Bulletin,* 100:309–330.

Eagly, A. H., and Wood, W. (1999). The origins of sex differences in human behavior: Evolved dispositions versus social roles. *American Psychologist,* 54:408–423.

Eaton, J. P., and Haas, C. A. (1994). *Titanic: Triumph and Tragedy* (2nd ed.). New York: W. W. Norton.

Eberhart, D. (2005). Did GI Jane policy allow Bin Laden to escape? *NewsMax,* June 2005, p. 46, http://www.newsmax.com/archives/articles/2005/4/18/122306.shtml.

Egbert, R. L. (1954). Profile of a fighter. *Infantry School Quarterly,* October, pp. 46–51.

Egbert, R. L., Meeland, T., Cline., V. B., Forgy, E. W., Spickler, M. W., and Brown, C. (1957). *Fighter I: An Analysis of Combat Fighters and Nonfighters.* Technical Report 44 (Presidio of Monterey, CA: U.S. Army Leadership Human Research Unit), pp. iii, cited in Binkin, 1993, p. 39.

Eibl-Eibesfeldt, I. (1979). *The Biology of Peace and War: Men, Animals, and Aggression.* New York: Viking Press.

Eikenberry, K. W. (1996). Take no casualties. *Parameters,* 26(2): 109–118.

Eller, R. D. (2005). Women in combat. *Army Times,* July 4, p. 52.

Ellis, J. (1976). *Eye-Deep in Hell: Trench Warfare in World War I.* New York: Pantheon.

———. (1980). *The Sharp End: The Fighting Man in World War II.* New York: Scribner's.

Emery, E. (2003). AFA ends "Bring Me Men" era. *Denver Post,* March 30, p. B7.

Endsley, M. R., and Bolstad, C. A. (1994). Individual differences in pilot situation awareness. *International Journal of Aviation Psychology,* 4:241–264.

Enloe, C. H. (1994). The politics of constructing the American woman soldier. In Addis, E., Russo, V. E., and Sebesta, L. (eds.), *Women Soldiers: Images and Realities,* pp. 81–110. New York: St. Martin's Press.

Epstein, S. (1994). Integration of the cognitive and the psychodynamic unconscious. *American Psychologist,* 49:709–724.

Estep, J. (1991). *Company Commander: Vietnam.* Novato, CA: Presidio Press.

Evans, D. (2001). *Emotion: The Science of Sentiment.* Oxford: Oxford University Press.

Exum, A. (2004). *This Man's Army: A Soldier's Story from the Front Lines of the War on Terrorism.* New York: Gotham Books.

———. (2006). All dressed up with no way to fight. *New York Times,* January 14, p. A15.

Fabes, R. A., Martin, C. L., and Hanish, L. D. (2003). Young children's play qualities in same-, other-, and mixed-sex peer groups. *Child Development,* 74:921–932.

Fact Sheet: Mirena: The Levonorgestrel-Releasing Intrauterine System, http://www.mirena-us.com/pdf/MirenaPressRoom.FactSheet.pdf.

Fagot, B. I. (1985). Beyond the reinforcement principle: Another step toward understanding sex role development. *Developmental Psychology,* 21:1097–1104.

Fagot, B. I., Rodgers, C. S., and Leinbach, M. D. (2000). Theories of gender socialization. In Eckes, T., and Trautner, H. M. (eds.), *The Developmental Social Psychology of Gender,* pp. 65–89. Mahwah, NJ: Lawrence Erlbaum Associates.

Fainaru, S. (2005). Silver Stars affirm one unit's mettle: Women play key roles in combat near Baghdad. *Washington Post,* June 26, A1.

Farago, L. (1964). *Patton: Ordeal and Triumph.* New York: Ivan Obolensky.

Farthing, G. W. (2005). Attitudes toward heroic and nonheroic physical risk takers as mates and as friends. *Evolution and Human Behavior,* 26:171–185.

Fausto-Sterling, A. (1992). *Myths of Gender: Biological Theories About Women and Men* (2nd ed.). New York: Basic Books.

Fazackerley, A. (2006). Female lecturers more likely to "freeze." *Times Higher Education Supplement,* June 24, p. 1.

Federal Advisory Committee on Gender-Integrated Training and Related Issues. (1997). *Final Report to the Secretary of Defense,* Kassebaum Baker Committee, http://www.defenselink.mil/pubs/git/report.html.

Federal Bureau of Investigation. (2006). Forcible rape. *Crime in the United States.* Uniform Crime Reporting Program. Washington, DC: U.S Department of Justice, http://www.fbi.gov/ucr/05cius/offenses/violent_crime/forcible_rape.html.

Feingold, A. (1994). Gender differences in personality: A meta-analysis. *Psychological Bulletin,* 116:429–456.

Felson, R. B. (2000). The normative protection of women from violence. *Sociological Forum,* 15:91–116.

Fessler, D. M. T., Pillsworth, E. G., and Flamson, T. J. (2004). Angry men and disgusted women: An evolutionary approach to the influence of emotions on risk-taking. *Organizational Behavior and Human Decision Processes,* 95:107–123.

Fetchenhauer, D., and Buunk, B. P. (2005). How to explain gender differences in fear of crime: Towards an evolutionary approach. *Sexualities, Evolution and Gender,* 7:95–113.

Fick, N. (2005). *One Bullet Away: The Making of a Marine Officer.* Boston: Houghton Mifflin.

Fields, S. (1990). Life in the co-ed tents. *Washington Times,* December 13, p. G1.

Filkins, D. (2006). U.S. says 2 bodies retrieved in Iraq were brutalized. *New York Times,* June 21, p. A1.

Fillingim, R. B. (2003). Sex-related influences on pain: A review of mechanisms and clinical implications. *Rehabilitation Psychology,* 48:165–174.

Filmsite.org. (n.d.). *When Harry Met Sally,* http://www.filmsite.org/when.html.

Fischer, D. V. (2005). Strategies for improving resistance training adherence in female athletes. *Strength and Conditioning Journal,* 27:62–67.

Fisher, H. (1999). *The First Sex: The Natural Talents of Women and How They Are Changing the World.* New York: Random House.

Fisher-Thompson, D. (1993). Adult toy purchases for children: Factors affecting sex-typed toy selection. *Journal of Applied Developmental Psychology,* 14:385–406.

Flinn, K. (1997). *Proud to Be: My Life, the Air Force, the Controversy.* New York: Random House.

Fox, J. A., and Zawitz, M. W. (2006). *Homicide Trends in the United States.* U.S. Department of Justice, Office of Justice Programs, Bureau of Justice Statistics, http://www.ojp.usdoj.gov/bjs/pub/pdf/htius.pdf.

Francke, L. B. (1997). *Ground Zero: The Gender Wars in the Military.* New York: Simon & Schuster.

Fritz, S. G. (1996). "We are trying . . . to change the face of the world"—ideology and motivation in the Wehrmacht on the eastern front: The view from below. *Journal of Military History,* 60:683–710.

Frost, D. E., Fiedler, F. E., and Anderson, J. W. (1983). The role of personal risk-taking in effective leadership. *Human Relations,* 36:185–202.

Fry, G. E., and Reinhardt, R. F. (1969). Personality characteristics of jet pilots as measured by the Edwards Personal Preference Schedule. *Aerospace Medicine,* 40:484–486.

Fuentes, G. (1997). Softening a tough road. *Navy Times-Marine Corps Edition,* December 1, p. 14.

Fukuyama, F. (1998). Women and the evolution of world politics. *Foreign Affairs,* September/October, pp. 24–40.

Fussell, P. (1996). *Doing Battle: The Making of a Skeptic.* Boston: Little, Brown.

Gabriel, R. A., and Savage, P. L. (1978). *Crisis in Command: Mismanagement in the Army.* New York: Hill & Wang.

Gal, R. (1983). Courage under stress. In Breznitz, S. (ed.), *Stress in Israel,* pp. 65–91. New York: Van Nostrand Reinhold.

———. (1986). Unit morale: From a theoretical puzzle to an empirical illustration: An Israeli example. *Journal of Applied Social Psychology,* 16:549–564.

Gal, R., and Gabriel, R. A. (1982). Battlefield heroism in the Israeli Defence Forces. *International Social Science Review,* 57:232–235.

Gandt, R. (1997). *Bogeys and Bandits.* New York: Viking Press.

Garcia, F. E. (1999). *Women at Sea: Unplanned Losses and Accession Planning.* CRM 98–182. Alexandria, VA: Center for Naval Analyses.

Garland, F. C., Garland, C. F., and Gorham, E. D. (2000). A model of expected occurrence of adverse pregnancy outcomes aboard U.S. Navy ships. *Military Medicine,* 165:691–697.

Garrison, B. (1994). One size jet doesn't fit all: Modifications are needed for some women aviators. *Navy Times,* November 11, p. 34.

———. (1995a). Internal report confirms Hultgreen's error. *Navy Times,* April 3, p. 3.

———. (1995b). Female aviator's flying in question: Squadronmate of Hultgreen subject of investigation aboard carrier. *Navy Times,* July 3, p. 10.

Gaulin, S. J. C., FitzGerald, R. W., and Wartell, M. S. (1990). Sex differences in spatial ability and activity in two vole species. *Journal of Comparative Psychology,* 104:88–93.

Gavin, L. (1997). *American Women in World War I: They Also Served.* Niwot, CO: University Press of Colorado.

Geary, D. C. (1998). *Male, Female: The Evolution of Human Sex Differences.* Washington, DC: American Psychological Association.

———. (2002). Sexual selection and sex differences in social cognition. In McGillicuddy-De Lisi, A. V., and De Lisi, R. (eds.), *Biology, Society, and Behavior: The Development of Sex Differences in Cognition,* pp. 23–53. Greenwich, CT: Ablex/Greenwood.

———. (2007). An evolutionary perspective on sex differences in mathematics and the sciences. In Ceci, S. J., and Williams, W. (eds.), *Sex Differences in Mathematics and Science.* Washington, DC: American Psychological Association.

Geary, D. C., Byrd-Craven, J., Hoard, M. K., Vigil, J., and Numtee, C. (2003). Evolution and development of boys' social behavior. *Developmental Review,* 23:444–470.

Geary, D. M., and Flinn, M. V. (2002). Sex differences in behavioral and hormonal response to social threat: Commentary on Taylor et al. (2000). *Psychological Review,* 109:745–750.

George, A. L. (1971). Primary groups, organization, and military performance. In Little, R. W. (ed.), *Handbook of Military Institutions,* pp. 293–318. Beverly Hills, CA: Sage.

Gertz, B. (1996). Dozens of GIs in Bosnia pregnant: Army bans booze, doesn't curb sex. *Washington Times,* July 18, p. A1.

Gibbs, A. C., and Wilson, J. F. (1999). Sex differences in route learning by children. *Perceptual and Motor Skills,* 88:590–594.

Gibbs, J. (2006). Soft serve: In recruit-coddling Army, lower standards are starting to show. *Army Times,* December 11, p. 46.

Gibbs, N. (1997). Wings of desire: The Air Force's star female pilot finds herself enmeshed in a tale full of passion and lies. *Time,* June 2, p. 28.

G.I. Jane. (1997). Hollywood Pictures.

Gimbel, C., and Booth, A. (1996). Who fought in Vietnam? *Social Forces,* 74:1137–1157.

Glenmark, B., Hedberg, G., Kaijser, L., and Jansson, E. (1994). Muscle strength from adolescence to adulthood: Relationship to muscle fibre types. *European Journal of Applied Physiology and Occupational Physiology,* 68:9–19.

Goldsmith, T. H. (1991). *The Biological Roots of Human Nature: Forging Links Between Evolution and Behavior.* New York: Oxford University Press.

Goldstein, J. S. (2001). *War and Gender: How Gender Shapes the War System and Vice Versa.* Cambridge: Cambridge University Press.

Goodacre, D. M., III. (1953). Group characteristics of good and poor performing combat units. *Sociometry,* 16:168–179.

Goodman, E. (1995). And the winners of this year's Equal Rites Award are. . . . *Boston Globe,* August 27, p. 71.

Goodyear, C. (1999). Air Force set to try Travis pilot over affair: Accused captain could get 27 years in prison. *San Francisco Chronicle,* February 12, p. A21.

Gordon, G. (1992). Rape risk goes with the job says girl POW: Ordeal of soldier abused by Iraqis. *Daily Mail* (London), June 10, p. 10.

Gouchie, C., and Kimura, D. (1991). The relationship between testosterone levels and cognitive ability patterns. *Psychoneuroendocrinology,* 16:323–334.

Gray, C. S. (2005). How has war changed since the end of the cold war? *Parameters,* 35(1):14–26.

Gray, J. G. (1959). *The Warriors: Reflections of Men in Battle.* New York: Harper and Row.

Greer, T. H. (1999). The rifle company: Cohesion through competition. *Infantry,* September/December, pp. 35–38.

Gregersen, E. (1982). *Sexual Practices: The Story of Human Sexuality.* New York: F. Watts.

Gregersen, N. P., and Berg, H. Y. (1994). Lifestyle and accidents among young drivers. *Accident Analysis and Prevention,* 26:297–303.

Greyhawk. (2006). Death before dishonor. *Mudville Gazette,* February 6, http://www.mudvillegazette.com/archives/004141.html.

Gribble, J. (n.d.). The wreck of HM Transport Birkenhead. *The Cape Odyssey.* Reprinted at http://www.overberginfo.com/content/view/367/467.

Grice, R. L., and Katz, L. C. (2005). *Cohesion in Military and Aviation Psychology: An Annotated Bibliography and Suggestions for U.S. Army Aviation.* United States Army Research Institute for the Behavioral and Social Sciences, Technical Report 1166.

Grimshaw, G. M., Sitarenios, G., and Finegan, J. K. (1995). Mental rotation at 7 years: Relation with prenatal testosterone levels and spatial play experiences. *Brain and Cognition,* 29:85–100.

Grinker, R. R., and Spiegel, J. P. (1945). *Men Under Stress.* Philadelphia: Blakiston.

Gurian, M. (1999). *A Fine Young Man.* New York: Putnam.

Gutmann, S. (1997). Sex and the soldier. *The New Republic,* February 24, p. 18.

———. (2000). *The Kinder, Gentler Military: Can America's Gender-Neutral Fighting Force Still Win Wars?* New York: Scribner.

Hackworth, D. H. (1998). Americans depending on TV news miss big story about national readiness. *Sun Sentinel* (Fort Lauderdale), December 3, p. 17A.

Halpern, D. F. (2000). *Sex Differences in Cognitive Abilities* (3rd ed.). Mahwah, NJ: Lawrence Erlbaum.

Hanna, J. H. (1992). An analysis of gynecological problems presenting to an evacuation hospital during Operation Desert Storm. *Military Medicine,* 157:222–224.

Hanson, V. D. (1999). *The Soul of Battle: From Ancient Times to the Present Day: How Three Great Liberators Vanquished Tyranny.* New York: Free Press.

———. (2001). *Carnage and Culture: Landmark Battles in the Rise of Western Power.* New York: Doubleday.

Harman, E., Frykman, P., Palmer, C., Lammi, E., Reynolds, K., and Backus, V. (1997). *Effects of a Specifically Designed Physical Conditioning Program on the Load Carriage and Lifting Performance of Female Soldiers.* USARIEM Technical Report T98–1. Fort Detrick, MD: U.S. Army Medical Research and Materiel Command.

Harrell, M. C., and Miller, L. L. (1997). *New Opportunities for Military Women: Effects Upon Readiness, Cohesion, and Morale.* Santa Monica, CA: RAND.

Hartman, B. O., and Secrist, G. E. (1991). Situational awareness is more than exceptional vision. *Aviation, Space, and Environmental Medicine,* 62:1084–1089.

Haselton, M. G., and Buss, D. M. (2000). Error management theory: A new perspective on biases in cross-sex mind reading. *Journal of Personality and Social Psychology,* 78:81–91.

Haselton, M. G., and Funder, D. C. (2006). The evolution of accuracy and bias in social judgment. In Schaller, M., Simpson, J. A., and Kenrick, D. T. (eds.), *Evolution and Social Psychology,* pp. 15–37. New York: Psychology Press.

Hausmann, M., Slabbekoorn, D., Van Goozen, S. H. M., Cohen-Kettenis, P. T., and Güntürkün, O. (2000). Sex hormones affect spatial abilities during the menstrual cycle. *Behavioral Neuroscience,* 114:1245–1250.

Hawkes, K. (1991). Showing off: Tests of an hypothesis about men's foraging goals. *Ethology and Sociobiology,* 12:29–54.

Hegarty, M., and Waller, D. (2005). Individual differences in spatial abilities. In Shah, P., and Miyake, A. (eds.), *The Cambridge Handbook of Visuospatial Thinking,* pp. 121–169. New York: Cambridge University Press.

Heidt, M. (2006). In the presence of greatness. *Blackfive,* October 13, http://www.black-five.net/main/2006/10/in_the_presence.html.

Heinl, R. D., Jr. (1966). *Dictionary of Military and Naval Quotations.* Annapolis, MD: Naval Institute Press.

Helleday, J., Edman, G., Ritzen, E. M., and Siwers, B. (1993). Personality characteristics and platelet MAO activity in women with congenital adrenal hyperplasia (CAH). *Psychoneuroendocrinology,* 18:343–354.

Hemingway, E. (1936). On the blue water: A Gulf Stream letter. *Esquire,* April p. 31.

Henderson, W. D. (1985). *Cohesion: The Human Element in Combat.* Washington, DC: National Defense University Press.

Hernandez, N. (2006). No penalty for Midshipman Owens: Found guilty of two non-rape charges. *Washington Post,* July 22, p. B1.

Herr, M. (1977). *Dispatches.* New York: Vintage.

Herrmann, A. (2003). Question of servicewomen in war zones arises. *Chicago Sun-Times,* April 3, p. 8.

Hertz, R. (1996). Guarding against women? Responses of military men and their wives to gender integration. *Journal of Contemporary Ethnography,* 25:251–284.

Hewett, T. E., Myer, G. D., and Ford, K. R. (2006). Anterior cruciate ligament injuries in female athletes: Part 1, mechanisms and risk factors. *American Journal of Sports Medicine,* 34:299–311.

Hibbert, C. (1978). *Agincourt* (2nd ed.). New York: Dorset.

Hillier, L. M., and Morrongiello, B. A. (1998). Age and gender differences in school-age children's appraisals of injury risk. *Journal of Pediatric Psychology,* 23:229–238.

Hilton, T. F., and Dolgin, D. D. (1991). Pilot selection in the military of the free world. In Gal, R., and Mangelsdorff, A. D. (eds.), *Handbook of Military Psychology,* pp. 81–101. New York: John Wiley and Sons.

Hines, M., Fane, B. A., Pasterski, V. L., Mathews, G. A., Conway, G. S., and Brook, C. (2003). Spatial abilities following prenatal androgen abnormality: Targeting and mental rotations performance in individuals with congenital adrenal hyperplasia. *Psychoneuroendocrinology,* 28:1010–1026.

Hines, M., Golombok, S., Rust, J., Johnston, K. J., Golding, J., and the Avon Longitudinal Study of Parents and Children Study Team. (2002). Testosterone during pregnancy and gender role behavior of preschool children: A longitudinal, population study. *Child Development,* 73:1678–1687.

Hobson, S. (1999). Canada struggles to meet combat arms quotas. *Jane's Defence Weekly,* June 23.

Hockstader, L. (2003). Ex-POW's family accuses Army of double standard on benefit. *Washington Post,* October 24, p. A3.

Holden, C. (2004). An everlasting gender gap? *Science,* 305:639–640.

Holliday, B. (2004). Born leaders. *Something Ventured,* May 21, http://www. bctechnology.com/statics/bh-may2104.html.

Holm, J. (1992). *Women in the Military: An Unfinished Revolution* (rev. ed.). Novato, CA: Presidio Press.

Holmes, O. W., Jr. (1897). The path of the law. *Harvard Law Review,* 10:457–478.

Holmes, R. (1985). *Acts of War: The Behavior of Men in Battle.* New York: Free Press.

Hook. (1996). HS-3 rockin' and rollin' in Stennis. *The Hook: Journal of Carrier Aviation,* Summer, pp. 40–41.

Horace (21 BC). Epistle to Aristius Fuscus. *The Satires, Epistles, and Art of Poetry* (2006), pp. 101–102. Lenox, MA: Hard Press.

Howland, J. (2006). Trust cf. loyalty. *USNA-At-Large,* March 28, http://groups.yahoo.com/group/USNA-At-Large/message/6208.

Hrdy, S. B. (1981). *The Woman That Never Evolved.* Cambridge, MA: Harvard University Press.

———. (1999). *Mother Nature: A History of Mothers, Infants, and Natural Selection.* New York: Pantheon.

Hudson, J. (2004). Top officer relieved of duties amid convoy probe. *Clarion-Ledger* (Jackson, MS), October 22, p. 1A.

Huntley, D. (2004). Convoy chief removed: Rock Hill–based reservist commanded group that didn't go. *Charlotte Observer,* October 22, p. 4A.

Hurst, C. (1995). Say what? Great howlers of 1995. *Toronto Star,* December 30, 1995, p. A1.

Huston, T. L., Ruggiero, M., Conner, R., and Geis, G. (1981). Bystander intervention into crime: A study based on naturally occurring episodes. *Social Psychology Quarterly,* 44:14–23.

Hynes, S. (1997). *The Soldiers' Tale: Bearing Witness to Modern War.* New York: Allen Lane.

———. (1988). *Flights of Passage: Reflections of a World War II Aviator.* New York: Frederic C. Beil; Annapolis, MD: Naval Institute Press.

IMDb. (n.d.). *Memorable Quotes from G.I. Jane,* http://www.imdb.com/title/tt0119173/quotes.

Ingraham, L. H., and Manning, F. J. (1980). Psychiatric battle casualties: The missing column in a war without replacements. *Military Review,* 60(8):18–29.

Jacklin, C. N., Snow, M. E., and Maccoby, E. E. (1981). Tactile sensitivity and muscle strength in newborn boys and girls. *Infant Behavior and Development,* 4:261–268.

Jacoby, M (2004). Revolt in the ranks in Iraq. *Salon,* October 16, http://dir.salon.com/story/news/feature/2004/10/16/soldiers/index.html.

Jaffe, G. (2006). Marching orders: To keep recruits, boot camp gets a gentle revamp. *Wall Street Journal,* February 15, p. A1.

Janofsky, M. (1991). Coaches concede that steroids fueled East Germany's success in swimming. *New York Times,* December 3, p. B15.

Jardine, R., and Martin, N. G. (1983). Spatial ability and throwing accuracy. *Behavior Genetics,* 13:331–340.

Jeanquart-Barone, S., and Sekaran, U. (1994). Effects of supervisor's gender on American women's trust. *Journal of Social Psychology,* 134:253–254.

Jensen, K., Clark, M., and Snider, M. (2003). 100 reasons to toast Bob Hope. *USA Today,* May 29, p. 6D.

Jensen, P. S., Martin, D., and Watanabe, H. (1996). Children's response to parental separation during Operation Desert Storm. *Journal of the American Academy of Child and Adolescent Psychiatry,* 35:433–441.

Johnson, D. (1997). New messages sent at Navy boot camp: A focus on treating all recruits better. *New York Times,* March 17, p. A10.

Johnson, R. C. (1996). Attributes of Carnegie medalists performing acts of heroism and of the recipients of those acts. *Ethology and Sociobiology,* 17:355–362.

Johnston, V. S. (1999). *Why We Feel: The Science of Human Emotions.* New York: Perseus.

Jolidon, L. (1992). Sexual assaults of female POWs withheld from panel. *USA Today,* June 11, p. 4A.

Jones, D. E. (1997). *Women Warriors: A History.* Washington, DC: Potomac.

Jones, D. G., and Endsley, M. R. (1996). Sources of situation awareness errors in aviation. *Aviation, Space, and Environmental Medicine,* 67:507–512.

Jones, O. D. (1999). Sex, culture, and the biology of rape: Toward explanation and prevention. *California Law Review,* 87:827–941.

Jontz, S. (2005). Marine raid breaks gender barrier. *Stars and Stripes,* May 4.

Jordan, B. (2002). A helo's deadly stall: Report details the events that brought down a Super Stallion. *Marine Corps Times,* August 19, p. 10.

Josefowitz, N., and Gadon, H. (1989). Hazing: Uncovering one of the best-kept secrets of the workplace. *Business Horizons,* May, pp. 22–26.

Jowers, K. (2006). Paying the price: Patronizing prostitutes just got more costly. *Army Times,* January 30, p. 4.

Jussim, L. J., McCauley, C. R., and Lee, Y-T. (1995). Why study stereotype accuracy and inaccuracy? In Lee, Y-T, Jussim, L. J., and McCauley, C. R. (eds.), *Stereotype Accuracy: Toward Appreciating Group Differences,* pp. 3–28. Washington, DC: American Psychological Association.

Karnow, S. (1997). *Vietnam: A History* (2nd ed.). New York: Penguin.

Karpinski, J. (2005). What went wrong at Abu Ghraib. *San Francisco Chronicle,* April 7, p. B9.

Kates, B. (2005). Out of control at Camp Crazy! Female soldiers dress down and get dirty for mud romps. *New York Daily News,* February 5, p. 29.

Keegan, J. (1976). *The Face of Battle.* New York: Viking Press.

———. (1993). *A History of Warfare.* New York: Alfred A. Knopf.

———. (1998). *The First World War.* New York: Alfred A. Knopf.

Keegan, J., and Holmes, J. (1985). *Soldiers: A History of Men in Battle.* New York: Viking Press.

Keeley, L. H. (1996). *War Before Civilization: The Myth of the Peaceful Savage.* New York: Oxford University Press.

Keen, M. (1984). *Chivalry.* New Haven, CT: Yale University Press.

Kellett, A. (1982). *Combat Motivation: The Behavior of Men in Battle.* Boston: Kluwer Nijhoff.

Kelley, M. L., Hock, E., Smith, K. M., Jarvis, M. S., Bonney, J. F., and Gaffney, M. A. (2001). Internalizing and externalizing behavior of children with enlisted Navy mothers experiencing military-induced separation. *Journal of the American Academy of Child and Adolescent Psychiatry,* 40:464–471.

Kelly, E. (2004). Academy changes its tune. *Capital* (Annapolis, MD), May 18, p. A1.

———. (2006a). Academy professor unfairly targeted for sex comments? *Capital* (Annapolis, MD), January 14, p. A1

———. (2006b). Judge blasts prosecution in Owens' trial. *Capital* (Annapolis, MD), July 14, p. A1.

———. (2006c). Naval Academy grads take up Owens' cause. *Capital* (Annapolis, MD), October 6, p. B1.

Kerber, L. K. (1993). "A constitutional right to be treated like . . . ladies": Women, civic obligation, and military service. *University of Chicago Law School Roundtable,* 1993: 95–128.

Kernan, A. (1994). *Crossing the Line: A Bluejacket's World War II Odyssey.* Annapolis, MD: Naval Institute Press.

———. (2005). *The Unknown Battle of Midway: The Destruction of the American Torpedo Squadrons.* New Haven, CT: Yale University Press.

Kersten, K. (2001). Mixed-sex wrestling is a step back from equality and sense. *Star Tribune* (Minneapolis), January 17.

Kier, E. (1998). Homosexuals in the military: Open integration and combat effectiveness. *International Security*, 23(2):5–39.

Kilner, P. (2002). Military leaders' obligation to justify killing in war. *Military Review*, 82(2):24–31.

Kimura, D. (1999). *Sex and Cognition*. Cambridge, MA: MIT Press.

King, J. A., De Oliveira, W. L., and Patel, N. (2005). Deficits in testosterone facilitate enhanced fear response. *Psychoneuroendocrinology*, 30:333–340.

Kingsley, K. (2004). Share the stories of soldiers who fulfill military duties. *St. Petersburg Times*, September 26, p. 2P.

Kipling, R. (1890). The Ballad of the King's Jest. In Kipling, R., *Complete Verse: Definitive Edition* (1989), pp. 245–248. New York: Anchor Books.

———. (1896). Soldier an' Sailor Too. In Kipling, R., *Complete Verse: Definitive Edition* (1989), pp. 431–433. New York: Anchor Books.

Kirshnit, C. E., Ham, M., and Richards, M. H. (1989). The sporting life: Athletic activities during early adolescence. *Journal of Youth and Adolescence*, 18:601–615.

Knapik, J. J., Canham-Chervak, M., Hauret, K., Hoedebecke, E., Laurin, M. J., and Cuthie, J. (2001). Discharges during U.S. Army basic training: Injury rates and risk factors. *Military Medicine*, 166:641–647.

Knapik, J. J., Wright, J. E., Kowal, D. M., and Vogel, J. A. (1980). The influence of U.S. Army Basic Initial Entry Training on the muscular strength of men and women. *Aviation, Space, and Environmental Medicine*, 51:1086–1090.

Kolakowski, D., and Malina, R. M. (1974). Spatial ability, throwing accuracy and man's hunting heritage. *Nature*, 251:410–412.

Kristof, N. D. (2003). A woman's place. *New York Times*, April 25, p. A31.

Kunich, J. C. (1995). Drumming out ceremonies: Historical relic or overlooked tool? *Air Force Law Review*, 39:47–56.

Kyomen, H. H., Satlin, A., Hennen, J., and Wei, J. Y. (1999). Estrogen therapy and aggressive behavior in elderly patients with moderate-to-severe dementia: Results from a short-term, randomized, double-blind trial. *American Journal of Geriatric Psychiatry*, 7:339–348.

Lacreuse, A., Herndon, J. G., Killiany, R. J., Rosene, D. L., and Moss, M. B. (1999). Spatial cognition in rhesus monkeys: Male superiority declines with age. *Hormones and Behavior*, 36:70–76.

Lacreuse, A., Verreault, M., and Herndon, J. G. (2001). Fluctuations in spatial recognition memory across the menstrual cycle in female rhesus monkeys. *Psychoneuroendocrinology*, 26:623–639.

Lambeth, B. S. (2002). Kosovo and the continuing SEAD challenge. *Aerospace Power Journal*, 16(2):8–22.

LaPeter, L. (2004). Get pregnant, or get sent to Iraq. *St. Petersburg Times*, September 19, p. 1A.

Larkin, J. E., and Pines, H. A. (2003). Gender and risk in public performance. *Sex Roles*, 49:197–210.

Larry King Live. (2007). Iranian hostage crisis. CNN, March 28, http://transcripts.cnn.com/transcripts/0703/28/lkl.01.html.

Larson, J. (2002). The China syndrome: Shane Osborn discusses crash of US EP-3 and detainment in China. *Dateline NBC*, May 27.

Lauder, T. D., Baker, S. P., Smith, G. S., and Lincoln, A. E. (2000). Sports and physical training injury hospitalizations in the Army. *American Journal of Preventive Medicine*, 18(3S):118–128.

Leahy, P. (1991). *Remarks.* 137 Cong. Rec. S11432 (daily ed., July 31).

LeBlanc, S. A. (2003). *Constant Battles: The Myth of the Peaceful, Noble Savage.* New York: St. Martin's Press.

Leibovich, L. (2006). Have the deaths of some female soldiers in Iraq been covered up? *Salon,* January 30, http://www.salon.com/mwt/broadsheet/2006/01/30/karpinski/index.html.

Leonard, M. (2004). Abuse raises gender issues: Women soldiers' role is debated. *Boston Globe,* May 16, p. A17.

Lerner, J. S., Gonzalez, R. M., Small, D. A., and Fischhoff, B. (2003). Effects of fear and anger on perceived risks of terrorism: A national field experiment. *Psychological Science,* 14:144–150.

Levin, M. (1987). *Feminism and Freedom.* Somerset, NJ: Transaction Publishers.

Lewis, M., and Clark, W. (1805). *Original Journals of the Lewis and Clark Expedition,* Vol. 3 (Thwaites, R. G., ed., 1904).

Lewthwaite, G. A. (1996). Army heeds the lessons of Tailhook: Quick response averts suspicion of cover-up. *Baltimore Sun,* November 18, p. 1A.

Lieberman, D., Tooby, J., and Cosmides, L. (2003). Does morality have a biological basis? An empirical test of the factors governing moral sentiments relating to incest. *Proceedings of the Royal Society of London (B),* 270:819–826.

Linderman, G. F. (1997). *The World Within War: America's Combat Experience in World War II.* New York: Free Press.

Lipsyte, R. (1992). Backtalk: Equity, plus or minus. *New York Times,* November 15, sec. 8, p. 9.

Little, R. W. (1964). Buddy relations and combat performance. In Janowitz, M., *The New Military: Changing Patterns of Organization,* pp. 195–223. New York: Russell Sage.

Lonsberry, B. (2004). Something that didn't make the news, http://lonsberry.com/writings.cfm?story=1400&go=4.

Los Angeles Times. (1995). Editorial: A few words on 1995. December 25, p. E1.

Low, B. S. (1992). Sex, coalitions, and politics in preindustrial societies. *Politics and the Life Sciences,* 11:63–80.

———. (2000). *Why Sex Matters: A Darwinian Look at Human Behavior.* Princeton, NJ: Princeton University Press.

Lowe, N. K., and Ryan-Wenger, N. A. (2003). Military women's risk factors for and symptoms of genitourinary infections during deployment. *Military Medicine,* 168: 569–574.

Lowry, R. (2005). Sgt. Rafael Peralta, American hero. *National Review,* January 11.

Lubold, G., and Curtis, R. (2002). Helo crash recovery required guts, ingenuity. *Marine Corps Times,* January 14, p. 114.

Luddy, J. F. (1994). The warrior cult: Why women cannot be a part. *Marine Corps Gazette,* 78(12):55–57.

Lundquist, J. H., and Smith, H. L. (2005). Family formation among women in the U.S. military: Evidence from the NLSY. *Journal of Marriage and the Family,* 67:1–13.

Lunn, D., and Kimura, D. (1989). Spatial abilities in preschool-aged children. Research Bulletin No. 681, University of Western Ontario, Department of Psychology. Cited in Hall J. A. Y. and Kimura, D. (1995), Sexual orientation and performance on sexually dimorphic motor tasks, *Archives of Sexual Behavior,* 24:395–407.

Lytton, H., and Romney, D. M. (1991). Parents' differential socialization of boys and girls: A meta-analysis. *Psychological Bulletin,* 109:267–296.

Maccoby, E. E. (1987). The varied meanings of "masculine" and "feminine." In Reinisch, J. M., Rosenblum, L. A., and Sanders, S. A. (eds.), *Masculinity/Femininity: Basic Perspectives.* New York: Oxford University Press.

———. (1990). Gender and relationships: A developmental account. *American Psychologist,* 45:513–520.

———. (1998). *The Two Sexes: Growing Up Apart, Coming Together.* Cambridge, MA: Belknap Press.

Maccoby, E. E., and Jacklin, C. N. (1974). *The Psychology of Sex Differences.* Stanford, CA: Stanford University Press.

McConnell, M. (1985). *Into the Mouth of the Cat: The Story of Lance Sijan, Hero of Vietnam.* New York: W. W. Norton.

McCormick, C. M., and Teillon, S. M. (2001). Menstrual cycle variation in spatial ability: Relation to salivary cortisol levels. *Hormones and Behavior,* 39:29–38.

MacCoun, R. J., Kier, E., and Belkin, A. (2005). Does social cohesion determine motivation in combat? An old question with an old answer. *Armed Forces and Society,* 32:1–9.

McGlohn, S. E., Callister, J. D., King, R. E., and Retzlaff, P. D. (1997). *Female and Male Air Force Student Pilots: Attitudes Toward Mixed-Gender Squadrons, Career Issues, and Combat Flying.* United States Air Force, Armstrong Laboratory, Aerospace Medicine Directorate, AL/AO-TR-1997–0096.

McGlohn, S. E., King, R. E., Butler, J. W., and Retzlaff, P. D. (1997). Female United States Air Force (USAF) pilots: Themes, challenges, and possible solutions. *Aviation, Space, and Environmental Medicine,* 68:132–136.

McHugh, J. (2004). No court-martials in convoy incident. *Army Times,* December 20, p. 19.

McMichael, W. H. (2001). To save the Cole. *Navy Times,* March 5.

McPeak, M. (1992). Testimony before the Military Personnel and Compensation Subcommittee and the Defense Policy Panel of the House Armed Services Committee, July 29 and 30. *Gender Discrimination in the Military,* H201–1, 60–540 MC. Washington, DC: U.S. Government Printing Office.

McPherson, J. M. (1997). *For Cause and Comrade: Why Men Fought in the Civil War.* New York: Oxford University Press.

Manchester, W. (1979). *Goodbye Darkness: A Memoir of the Pacific War.* Boston: Little, Brown.

Manning, F. J. (1991). Morale, cohesion, and esprit de corps. In Gal, R., and Mangelsdorff, A. D. (eds.), *Handbook of Military Psychology,* pp. 453–470. New York: John Wiley and Sons.

Manning, F. J., and Fullerton, T. D. (1988). Health and well-being in highly cohesive units of the U.S. Army. *Journal of Applied Social Psychology,* 18:503–519.

Marcusson, H., and Oehmisch, W. (1977). Accident mortality in childhood in selected countries of different continents, 1950–1971. *World Health Statistical Report,* 30:57.

Marlowe, D. H. (1983). The manning of the force and the structure of battle: Part 2—men and women. In Fullinwider, R. K., *Conscripts and Volunteers: Military Requirements, Social Justice, and the All-Volunteer Force.* Totowa, NJ: Rowman and Allanheld.

Marshall, S. L. A. (1947). *Men Against Fire: The Problem of Battle Command in Future War.* New York: William Morrow.

Martin, C. L., and Fabes, R. A. (2002). The stability and consequences of young children's same-sex peer interactions. *Developmental Psychology,* 37:431–446.

Martin, S. E. (1980). *Breaking and Entering: Policewomen on Patrol.* Berkeley: University of California Press.

Martineau, P., and Wiegand, S. (2005a). Women at war. *Sacramento Bee,* March 6, p. 1A.

———. (2005b). Scarred survivors. *Sacramento Bee,* March 8, p. A1.

———. (2006). Show's not so "purrfect" for female forces in Iraq. *Sacramento Bee,* March 12, p. A1.

Marzullo, T. (2004). Abused prisoners and gender-based promotions. MensNewsDaily.Com, May 4, http://www.mensnewsdaily.com/archive/m-n/marzullo/2004/marzullo050404.htm.

Mason, R. (1983). *Chickenhawk.* New York: Viking Press.

Mathewes-Green, F. (1996). Men protecting women. NPR, *All Things Considered,* October 9, www.frederica.com/writings/men-protecting-women.html.

Maze, R. (1999). Survey: Recruits aren't tough anymore/quality down, say 65% of Navy people polled. *Navy Times,* October 4, p. 8.

Mazur, A., and Booth, A. (1998). Testosterone and dominance in men. *Behavioral and Brain Sciences,* 21:352–397.

Mead, M. (1949). *Male and Female: A Study of the Sexes in a Changing World.* New York: Morrow Quill.

Meo, N. (2006). Women who kill with guns and blades. *The Times* (London), April 1, p. 46.

Messick, D. M., and Kramer, R. M. (2001). Trust as a form of shallow morality. In Cook, K. (ed.), *Trust in Society*, pp. 89–117. New York: Russell Sage.

Middlebrook, M. (1978). *The Kaiser's Battle*. New York: Penguin.

Military Operational Medicine Research Program. (1999). *Health and Performance Research for Military Women: The 1994 Defense Women's Health Research Program* (DWHRP94). MOMRP Fact Sheet Number 9, USAMRMC.

Millard, L. (1995). Differences in coaching behaviors of male and female high school soccer coaches. *Journal of Sport Behavior*, 19:19–31.

Miller, A. A. (1985). Developmental study of the cognitive basis of performance impairment after failure. *Journal of Personality and Social Psychology*, 49:529–538.

Miller, L. L. (1997). Not just weapons of the weak: Gender harassment as a form of protest for Army men. *Social Psychology Quarterly*, 60:32–51.

———. (1998). Feminism and the exclusion of Army women from combat. *Gender Issues*, 16(3):33–64.

Miller, L. L., and Moskos, C. (1995). Humanitarians or warriors? Race, gender, and combat status in Operation Restore Hope. *Armed Forces and Society*, 21:615–637.

Miller, W. I. (2000). *The Mystery of Courage*. Cambridge, MA: Harvard University Press.

Mills, H. L., Jr. (1992). *Low Level Hell: A Scout Pilot in the Big Red One*. Novato, CA: Presidio Press.

Ministry of Defence (United Kingdom). (2002). *Women in the Armed Forces*. Report by the Employment of Women in the Armed Forces Steering Group.

Mitchell, B. (1998). *Women in the Military: Flirting with Disaster*. Washington, DC: Regnery.

Moniz, D. (2005). Female amputees make clear that all troops are on front lines. *USA Today*, April 28, p. 1A.

Monto, M. A., and McRee, N. (2005). A comparison of the male customers of female street prostitutes with national samples of men. *International Journal of Offender Therapy and Comparative Criminology*, 49:505–529.

Moran, Lord. (1966). *Anatomy of Courage* (2nd ed.). London: Constable.

Morgan, D. (2004). Deploying to Iraq? Lessons from an infantry company commander. *Infantry*, 93(1):28–32.

Morris, M. (1996). By force of arms: Rape, war, and military culture. *Duke Law Journal*, 45:651–781.

Morrongiello, B. A., and Dawber, T. (1998). Toddlers' and mothers' behaviors in an injury-risk situation: Implications for sex differences in childhood injuries. *Journal of Applied Developmental Psychology*, 19:625–639.

Morrongiello, B. A., and Rennie, H. (1998). Why do boys engage in more risk taking than girls? The role of attributions, beliefs, and risk appraisals. *Journal of Pediatric Psychology*, 23:33–43.

Morrow, J. R., and Hosler, W. W. (1981). Strength comparisons in untrained men and trained women athletes. *Medicine and Science in Sports and Exercise*, 13:194–197.

Moskos, C. (1970). *The American Enlisted Man: The Rank and File in Today's Military*. New York: Russell Sage.

———. (1988). Institutional and occupational trends in armed forces. In Moskos, C. C., and Wood, F. R. (eds.), *The Military: More than Just a Job?*, pp. 15–26. Washington, DC: Pergamon-Brassey's.

———. (1990). Army women. *Atlantic Monthly*, August, pp. 70–78.

———. (1995/1996). *Women in the Military* (book review). *Armed Forces and Society*, 22:316–318.

———. (1998). The folly of comparing race and gender in the Army. *Washington Post*, January 4, p. C1.

Moskos, C., and Butler, J. S. (1996). *All That We Can Be: Black Leadership and Racial Integration the Army Way*. New York: Basic Books.

Moss, M. (2005). Hard look at mission that ended in inferno for 3 women. *New York Times,* December 20, p. A1.

Mullen, B., and Copper, C. (1994). The relation between group cohesiveness and performance: An integration. *Psychological Bulletin,* 115:210–227.

Murdock, G. P. (1932). The science of culture. *American Anthropologist,* 34:200–215.

———. (1971). Anthropology's mythology. *Proceedings of the Royal Anthropological Institute of Great Britain and Ireland,* 1971:17–24.

Murphy, A. (1949). *To Hell and Back.* New York: Grossett & Dunlap.

Murray, W., and Scales, R. H., Jr. (2003). *The Iraq War.* Cambridge, MA: Belknap Press.

Myers, S. L. (1999a). Drop in recruits pushes Pentagon to new strategy. *New York Times,* September 27, p. A1.

———. (1999b). New debate on submarine duty for women. *New York Times,* November 15, p. A1.

Nagy, E., Loveland, K. A., Kopp, M., Orvos, H., Pal, A., and Molnar, P. (2001). Different emergence of fear expressions in infant boys and girls. *Infant Behavior and Development,* 24:189–194.

Nantais, C., and Lee, M. F. (1999). Women in the United States military: Protectors or protected? The case of prisoner of war Melissa Rathbun-Nealy. *Journal of Gender Studies,* 8:181–191.

National Defense Research Institute (1993). *Sexual Orientation and U.S. Military Personnel Policy: Options and Assessment.*

National Organization for Women. (1990). *National Board Policy: Women in the Military,* http://www.now.org/issues/military/policies/wim.html.

Neuman, J. (2007). Bush awards medal of honor to Marine killed in Iraq: Cpl. Jason Dunham is recognized for saving two servicemen's lives by throwing himself on an insurgent's grenade. *Los Angeles Times,* January 12, p. A9.

New York Times. (1997a). Editorial: Trent Lott's military mind. May 21, p. A22.

———. (1997b). Editorial: The harassment of female troops. September 13, sec. 1, p. 22.

———. (2000). Editorial: Charges of harassment by a general. April 7, p. A22.

———. (2003a). Editorial: The pinking of the armed forces. March 24, p. A14.

———. (2003b). Editorial: The Air Force Academy scandal. March 28, p. A16.

———. (2003c). Editorial: Protecting female cadets. July 26, p. A12.

———. (2004). Editorial: Confronting rape in the military. March 12, p. A20.

———. (2006). Editorial: Scandal at the Coast Guard Academy. July 2, sec. 4, p. 9.

Newman, R. J. (1997). Army Sex Ed 101: Lessons from racial integration could ease gender wars. *U.S. News & World Report,* August 11, pp. 50–52.

Niarchos, C. N. (1995). Women, war, and rape: Challenges facing the International Tribunal for the former Yugoslavia. *Human Rights Quarterly,* 27:649–690.

Nicholson, N. (1998). How hardwired is human behavior? *Harvard Business Review,* 76(4):134–147.

Nordheimer, J. (1991). Women's role in combat: The war resumes. *New York Times,* May 26, sec. 1, p. 1.

Nyborg, H. (1994). *Hormones, Sex, and Society: The Science of Physicology.* Westport, CT: Praeger.

O'Beirne, K. (1997). Bread and circuses. *National Review,* November 24.

———. (2006). *Women Who Make the World Worse.* New York: Sentinel.

Oceans Africa. (2006). Shark Cage Diving, http://www.oceansafrica.com/cagediving.htm.

O'Connor, D. B., Archer, J., Hair, W. M., and Wu, F. C. W. (2001). Activational effects of testosterone on cognitive function in men. *Neuropsychologia,* 39:1385–1394.

O'Connor, T. G., Heron, J., Golding, J., Glover, V., and the ALSPAC Study Team. (2003). Maternal antenatal anxiety and behavioural/emotional problems in children: A test of a programming hypothesis. *Journal of Child Psychology and Psychiatry,* 44:1025–1036.

Office of the Inspector General. (1993). *The Tailhook Report.* Department of Defense. New York: St. Martin's Press.

Office of the Inspector General of the Department of Defense. (2004). *Report Summary: Evaluation of Sexual Assault, Reprisal, and Related Leadership Challenges at the United States Air Force Academy,* Report No. IPO2004C003.

Official U.S. Navy SEAL Information Web site. Introduction to Naval Special Warfare, http://www.sealchallenge.navy.mil/seal/introduction.aspx.

O'Grady, S. (1995). *Return with Honor.* New York: Doubleday.

Öhman, A., and Mineka, S. (2001). Fears, phobias, and preparedness: Toward an evolved module of fear and fear learning. *Psychological Review,* 108:483–522.

Oldham, S. (2003). "Bring me men," a proud Air Force Academy heritage. *Talking Proud,* March 28, http://www.talkingproud.us/Eagle032803.html.

Olson, B. (2006a). Navy trial in rape case: Mids' quarterback to face most serious form of court-martial. *Baltimore Sun,* April 29, p. 1B.

———. (2006b). Mid tells jury of rape in her dorm: Defense attacks credibility, says Navy QB had consensual sex. *Baltimore Sun,* July 12, p. 1A.

———. (2006c). Ex-academy instructor cleared at hearing: Officer receives no punishment for "crude" remarks. *Baltimore Sun,* September 2, p. 1A.

Omicinski, J. (2001). Study: Navy women visit sick bay more often than men. *Navy Times,* February 1.

Orengo, C., Kunik, M. E., Molinari, V., Wristers, K., and Yudofsky, S. C. (2002). Do testosterone levels relate to aggression in elderly men with dementia? *Journal of Neuropsychiatry and Clinical Neurosciences,* 14:161–166.

Orwell, G. (1945). Notes on nationalism. In Orwell, S., and Angus, I. (eds.), *As I Please, 1943–1945: The Collected Essays, Journalism & Letters of George Orwell,* pp. 361–380, New York: Harcourt Brace.

Osborn, S. (2001). *Born to Fly: The Untold Story of the Downed American Reconnaissance Plane.* New York: Broadway Books.

Ozkaptan, H. (1994). Determinants of courage. In Holz, R. F., Hiller, J. H., and McFann, H. H. (eds.), *Determinants of Effective Unit Performance: Research on Measuring and Managing Unit Training Readiness,* pp. 233–253. Alexandria, VA: U.S. Army Research Institute for the Behavioral and Social Sciences.

Palmer C. T., and Thornhill R. (2003). Straw men and fairy tales: Evaluating reactions to *A Natural History of Rape. Journal of Sex Research,* 40:249–255.

Palmer, R. R., Wiley, B. I., and Keast, W. R. (1948). *United States Army in World War II, The Army Ground Forces: The Procurement and Training of Ground Combat Troops.* Washington, DC: Department of the Army.

Pantano, I. (2006). *Warlord: No Better Friend, No Worse Enemy.* New York: Threshold Editions.

PBS. (n.d.). Frontline: The Navy Blues: Punishment after Tailhook '91, http://www.pbs.org/wgbh/pages/frontline/shows/navy/tailhook/disc.html.

Peach, L. J. (1996). Gender ideology in the ethics of women in combat. In Stiehm, J. H. (ed.), *It's Our Military, Too!: Women and the U.S. Military,* pp.156–194. Philadelphia: Temple University Press.

Peniston, B. (2006). *No Higher Honor: Saving the USS* Samuel B. Roberts *in the Persian Gulf.* Annapolis, MD: Naval Institute Press.

Perry, T. (2002). Soil-clogged engines blamed for fatal Afghan helicopter crash. *Los Angeles Times,* August 7, p. 23.

Pershing, J. L. (2006). Men and women's experiences with hazing in a male-dominated elite military institution. *Men and Masculinities,* 8:470–492.

Pettit, G. S., Bakshi, A., Dodge, K. A., and Coie, J. D. (1990). The emergence of social dominance in young boys' play groups: Developmental differences and behavior correlates. *Developmental Psychology,* 26:1017–1025.

Pheasant, S. T. (1983). Sex differences in strength: Some observations on their variability. *Applied Ergonomics,* 14:205–211.

Phillips, D. W. (2002). *The Birkenhead Drill.* San Antonio, TX: The Vision Forum.

Phillips, M. M. (2005). *The Gift of Valor: A War Story.* New York: Broadway Books.

Philpott, T. (1999). Full speed ahead. *Washingtonian,* July, p. 89.

Powell, M., and Ansic, D. (1997). Gender differences in risk behaviour in financial decision-making: An experimental analysis. *Journal of Economic Psychology,* 18: 605–628.

Powers, R. (2006a). What about the children?, http://usmilitary.about.com/cs/genfamily/a/familycare.htm.

———. (2006b). Single parents, http://usmilitary.about.com/od/joiningthemilitary/a/enl-standards_3.htm.

Presidential Commission on the Assignment of Women in the Armed Forces. (1992). *Women in Combat: Report to the President.* McLean, VA: Brassey's (US).

Preuschoft, S., and van Schaik, C. P. (2000). Dominance and communication: Conflict management in various social settings. In Aureli, F., and de Waal, F.B.M. (eds.), *Natural Conflict Resolution,* pp. 77–105. Berkeley: University of California Press.

Priest, D. (1995). Navy punishes two for sex aboard ship: Male sailor showed tape to co-workers. *Washington Post,* March 19, p. A13.

———. (1998). Defense chief opposes separating sexes in basic training. *Washington Post,* June 9, p. A9.

Priest, R. F., Vitters, A. G., and Prince, H. T. (1978). The first co-ed class at West Point: Performance and attitudes. *Youth and Society,* 10:205–224.

Pruden, W. (1995). Sex, lies, videotape and the U.S. Navy. *Washington Times,* April 14, p. A4.

Purrfect Angelz. (2006). *The Purrfect Angelz,* http://www.purrfectangelz.com/introduction.htm.

Ratchnevsky, P. (1991). *Genghis Khan: His Life and Legacy.* New York: Blackwell.

Reed, C. L. (2005). War stress heavier on women. *Chicago Sun-Times,* May 8, p. 4

Reeder, R. P. (1994). *Born at Reveille: Memoirs of an American Soldier* (rev. ed.). Quechee, VT: Vermont Heritage Press.

Reid, T. (2004). Women in war zone at same risk as men. *The Times* (London), May 29, p. 22.

Reid, T. R. (2003). Lori Piestewa, a mother, a Hopi and a "hero," is 1st American woman to die in Iraq War. *Washington Post,* April 6, p. A30.

Reilly, R. R., Zedeck, S., and Tenopyr, M. L. (1979). Validity and fairness of physical ability tests for predicting performance in craft jobs. *Journal of Applied Psychology,* 64:262–274.

Reyes, A. D. (2006). *Strategic Options for Managing Diversity in the U.S. Army.* Military Fellow Research Report. Washington, DC: Joint Center for Political and Economic Studies, http://www.jointcenter.org/publications1/publication-PDFs/TonyReyes.pdf.

Rice, R. W., Bender, L. R., and Vitters, A. G. (1980). Leader sex, follower attitudes toward women, and leadership effectiveness: A laboratory experiment. *Organizational Behavior and Human Decision Processes,* 25:46–56.

Rice, R. W., Yoder, J. D., and Adams, J. (1984). Leadership ratings for male and female military cadets. *Sex Roles,* 10:885–901.

Richardson, F. M. (1978). *Fighting Spirit: A Study of Psychological Factors in War.* London: Leo Cooper.

Richter, P. (1999). Exodus of female recruits signals trouble for military. *Los Angeles Times,* November 29, p. A1.

Riley, J. L., Robinson, M. E., Wise, E. A., Myers, C. D., and Fillingim, R. B. (1998). Sex differences in the perception of noxious experimental stimuli: A meta-analysis. *Pain,* 84:181–187.

Ritchie, E. C. (2001). Issues for military women in deployment: An overview. *Military Medicine,* 166:1033–1037.

Robbins, A. S., Chao, S. Y., Frost, L. Z., and Fonseca, V. P. (2005). Unplanned pregnancy among active duty servicewomen, U.S. Air Force, 2001. *Military Medicine,* 170:38–43.

Roberts, J. (1995). The envelope, please: Best and worst of 1995. *San Francisco Chronicle,* December 31, p. 7.

Rosen, L. N., Bliese, P. D., Wright, K. A., and Gifford, R. K. (1999). Gender composition and group cohesion in U.S. Army units: A comparison across five studies. *Armed Forces and Society,* 25:365–386.

Rosen, L. N., Durand, D. B., Bliese, P. D., Halverson, R. R., Rothberg, J. M., and Harrison, N. L. (1996). Cohesion and readiness in gender-integrated combat service support units: The impact of acceptance of women and gender ratio. *Armed Forces and Society,* 22:537–553.

Rosen, L. N., Knudson, K. H., and Fancher, P. (2003). Cohesion and the culture of hyper-masculinity in U.S. Army units. *Armed Forces and Society,* 29:325–351.

Rosen, L. N., and Martin, L. (1997). Sexual harassment, cohesion, and readiness in U.S. Army support units. *Armed Forces and Society,* 24:221–244.

Rosen, L. N., Wright, K., Marlowe, D., Bartone, P., and Gifford, R. K. (1999). Gender differences in subjective distress attributable to anticipation of combat among U.S. Army soldiers deployed to the Persian Gulf during Operation Desert Storm. *Military Medicine,* 164:753–757.

Runciman, W. G. (1998). Greek hoplites, warrior culture, and indirect bias. *Journal of the Royal Anthropological Institute,* 4:731–751.

Rushton, J. P., Fulker, D. W., Neale, M. C., Nias, D. K., and Eysenck, H. J. (1986). Altruism and aggression: The heritability of individual differences. *Journal of Personality and Social Psychology,* 50:1192–1198.

RUSI Panel (2001). Morale in the armed forces. *RUSI Journal,* April, pp. 46–53.

Ryan-Wenger, N. A., and Lowe, N. K. (2000). Military women's perspectives on health care during deployment. *Women's Health Issues,* 10:333–343.

Sailer, S., and Seiler, S. (1997). Track and battlefield. *National Review,* December 31.

Sajer, G. (1967). *The Forgotten Soldier.* Washington, DC: Brassey's (US).

Savage, P. L., and Gabriel, R. A. (1976). Cohesion and disintegration in the American Army: An alternative perspective. *Armed Forces and Society,* 2:340–376.

Savin-Williams, R. C. (1979). Dominance hierarchies in groups of early adolescents. *Child Development,* 50:923–935.

Scales, R. H. (2005). Urban warfare: A soldier's view. *Military Review,* 85(1):9–18.

Scarborough, R. (1993). Tailhook witness told lies: Navy, IG knew, still sought trial. *Washington Times,* July 23, p. A1.

———. (1994a). Aspin announces rules for women in ground combat. *Washington Times,* January 14, p. A3.

———. (1994b). Navy judge says Kelso lied in Tailhook probe: Rebukes admiral, dismisses last 3 cases. *Washington Times,* February 9, p. A1.

———. (1994c). Politics blamed for flaws in Tailhook probe, cases. *Washington Times,* February 18, p. A3.

———. (1994d). Tailhook report barred at civil trial: Pentagon probe "not trustworthy." *Washington Times,* September 6, p. A1.

———. (1995). Navy shifts stance on pregnancy: It's now "compatible," but not as a way of ducking duty. *Washington Times,* February 8, p. A4.

———. (1996a). Carrier's "shakedown cruise" turns into maternity mission. *Washington Times,* August 26, p. A3.

———. (1996b). Army trainees accuse instructors of rape, harassment. *Washington Times,* November 8, p. A3.

———. (1997a). Sex-abuse hot lines' value questioned: Gone too far? Cohen wonders. *Washington Times,* June 16, p. A4.

———. (1997b). Pentagon study excises references to pregnancy, readiness. *Washington Times,* November 7, p. A3.

———. (1998). Women in arms say no thanks to combat. *Washington Times,* September 29, p. A1.

————. (2000). Military policing of sexes eats time. *Washington Times,* January 18, p. A1.

————. (2001). Marines' training runs probed: Compulsory jog canceled after female officer complains. *Washington Times,* July 9, p. A1.

————. (2003a). Marine had baby on ship in war zone. *Washington Times,* June 11, p. A1.

————. (2003b). Probe finds Southern Command staff runs reasonable: Pentagon investigators report that they see no "gender discrimination." *Washington Times,* August 22, p. A3.

————. (2004a). Pregnant troops leave the war: Central Command not counting. *Washington Times,* June 16, p. A1.

————. (2004b). Zarqawi targets female soldiers: Terrorists told to kidnap U.S. women. *Washington Times,* July 1, p. A1.

————. (2006). Military will meet '06 recruiting goal: Army credits perks, relaxed rules. *Washington Times,* September 14, p. A3.

Scarborough, R., and Curl, J. (2005). Despite pressure, Bush pledges "no women in combat." *Washington Times,* January 12, p. A1.

Scharnberg, K. (2005). Stresses of battle hit female GIs hard: VA study hopes to find treatment for disorder. *Chicago Tribune,* March 22, p. C1.

Schechter, E. (2004). Anything boys can do . . . *Jerusalem Post,* January 29, p. 22.

Schmitt, E. (2005). General is scolded for saying, "It's fun to shoot some people." *New York Times,* February 4, p. A12.

Schogol, J. (2006). Patronizing a prostitute is now a specific crime for service members. *Stars and Stripes* (Mideast edition), January 7.

Schooley, R. L., McLaughlin, C. R., Matula, G. J., Jr., and Krohn, W. B. (1994). Denning chronology of female black bears: Effects of food, weather, and reproduction. *Journal of Mammalogy,* 75:466–477.

Sciolino, E. (1992). Female P.O.W. is abused, kindling debate. *New York Times,* June 29, p. A1.

————. (1997a). Air Force chief has harsh words for pilot facing adultery charge. *New York Times,* May 22, p. A1.

————. (1997b). Pilot facing adultery charge agrees to a general discharge. *New York Times,* May 23, p. A1.

Scutro, A. (2006). Foul comments: Academy instructor's remarks land him in court-martial. *Navy Times,* January 30, p. 8.

Seelye, K. Q. (1995). Gingrich's "piggies" poked. *New York Times,* January 19, p. A20.

Segal, M. W. (1986). The military and the family as greedy institutions. *Armed Forces and Society,* 13:9–38.

Segal, M. W., and Segal, D. R. (1983). Social change and the participation of women in the American military. *Research in Social Movements,* 5:235–258.

Seiler, S., De Koning, J. J., and Foster, C. (2007). The fall and rise of the gender difference in elite anaerobic performance 1952–2006. *Medicine & Science in Sports & Exercise,* 39:534–540.

Selective Service System. (1998). *Why Women Aren't Required to Register,* http://www.sss.gov/women.htm.

Sensing, D. (2003). Israeli military closes the door on ground combat for women. *One Hand Clapping,* October 20, http://www.donaldsensing.com/2003/10/israeli-military-closes-door-on-ground.html.

Serbin, L. A., Poulin-Dubois, D., Colburne, K. A., Sen, M. G., and Eichstedt, J. A. (2001). Gender stereotyping in infancy: Visual preferences for and knowledge of gender-stereotyped toys in the second year. *International Journal of Behavioral Development,* 25:7–15.

Serrano, R. A., and Mazzetti, M. (2005). General demoted over prison scandal: Janis Karpinski of the Army Reserve failed to supervise Abu Ghraib guards in Iraq, officials say. *Los Angeles Times,* May 6, p. A20.

Servin, A., Bohlin, G., and Berlin, L. (1999). Sex differences in 1-, 3-, and 5-year-olds' toy choice in a structured play-session. *Scandinavian Journal of Psychology,* 40:43–48.

Shakespeare, W. *Henry V,* act 4, scene iii.

Shanker, T. (2004). With eye on Iraq, Army pushes revamped basic training. *New York Times,* August 3, p. A13.

Shapiro, L. (2003). Sorenstam misses the cut: Historic outing against men at Colonial ends. *Washington Post,* May 13, p. A1.

Shaw, D. W. (2002). *The Sea Shall Embrace Them: The Tragic Story of the Steamship Arctic.* New York: Free Press.

Shields, P. M., Curry, L., and Nichols, J. (1990). Women pilots in combat: Attitudes of male and female pilots. *Minerva Quarterly,* 8:21–35.

Shils, E. A. (1951). The study of the primary group. In Lerner, D., and Lasswell, H. D. (eds.), *The Policy Sciences,* pp. 44–69. Stanford, CA: Stanford University Press.

Shipley, A. (1999). The man behind the U.S. women. *Washington Post,* July 7, p. D1.

Shureb, L. (2005). Daughter's safety. *USA Today,* June 1, p. 9A.

Siebold, G. L. (1999). The evolution of the measurement of cohesion. *Military Psychology,* 11:5–26.

Silverman I., Choi, J., Mackewn, A., Fisher, M., Moro, J., and Olshansky, E. (2000). Evolved mechanisms underlying wayfinding: Further studies on the hunter-gatherer theory of spatial sex differences. *Evolution and Human Behavior,* 21:201–213.

Simons, A. (1997). *The Company They Keep: Life Inside the U.S. Army Special Forces.* New York: Free Press.

———. (2001a). The author replies. *Parameters,* 31(3):158–159.

———. (2001b). Women in combat units: It's still a bad idea. *Parameters,* 31(2):89–100.

Simons-Morton, B., Lerner, N., and Singer, J. (2005). The observed effects of teenage passengers on the risky driving behavior of teenage drivers. *Accident Analysis and Prevention,* 37:973–982.

Singer, T., Seymour, B., O'Doherty, J. P., Stephan, K. E., Dolan, R. J., and Frith, C. D. (2006). Empathic neural responses are modulated by the perceived fairness of others. *Nature,* January 18, pp. 466–469.

Sion, L. (2001). "The weakest link": Women in two Dutch peacekeeping units. *Minerva: Quarterly Report on Women and the Military,* 19(3/4):3–26.

———. (2006). "Too sweet and innocent for war"? Dutch peacekeepers and the use of violence. *Armed Forces and Society,* 32:454–474.

Sirica, J. (1990). More minorities serving in Gulf: Growth in black, female ranks. *Newsday,* December 20, p. 15.

Sisk, R. (2004). Bronze Star hers after ambush: Courageous move saves 11. *New York Daily News.* December 26, p. 40.

Sledge, E. B. (1981). *With the Old Breed at Peleliu and Okinawa.* Novato, CA: Presidio Press.

Slim, W. (1957). *Courage and Other Broadcasts.* London: Cassell.

Sloan, R., and Barry, E. (2004). In defense of their soldiers: Relatives of reservists who refused to deliver fuel in Iraq last week are hitting airwaves, presenting a challenge for the U.S. military. *Los Angeles Times,* October 19, p. A10.

Smith, M. (2001). Tests for Army women "watered down." *Daily Telegraph* (London), March 26, p. 1.

———. (2005). "I bayoneted people. It was me or them." *Daily Telegraph* (London), March 18, p. 3.

Smith, R. B. (1983a). Why soldiers fight: Part I. Leadership, cohesion and fighter spirit. *Quality and Quantity,* 18:1–31.

———. (1983b). Why soldiers fight: Part II. Alternative theories. *Quality and Quantity,* 18:33–58.

Smith, W. R., and Torstensson, M. (1997). Gender differences in risk perception and neutralizing fear of crime. *British Journal of Criminology,* 37:608–634.

Smoler, F. (1989). The secret of the soldiers who didn't shoot. *American Heritage,* 40(2): 36–45.

Smoll, F. L., and Schutz, R. W. (1990). Quantifying gender differences in physical performance: A developmental perspective. *Developmental Psychology*, 26:360–369.

Smucker, P. (1997). Pregnant troops make U.S. laughingstock of Bosnia: Gender-relations
classes target problem. *Washington Times*, November 4, p. A1.

Smuts, B. 1995. The evolutionary origins of patriarchy. *Human Nature*, 6:1–32.

Snopes.com. (2005). *Urban Legends Reference Pages*, http://www.snopes.com/politics/military/
chontosh.asp.

Solaro, E. (2006). *Women in the Line of Fire: What You Should Know About Women in the
Military*. Emeryville, CA: Seal Press.

Solomon, Z., Mikulincer, M., and Hobfoll, S. E. (1986). Effects of social support and battle intensity on loneliness and breakdown during combat. *Journal of Personality and
Social Psychology*, 51:1269–1276.

Spick, M. (1988). *The Ace Factor: Air Combat and the Role of Situational Awareness*.
Annapolis, MD: Naval Institute Press.

Spiller, R. (1988). S. L. A. Marshall and the ratio of fire. *RUSI Journal*, 133(Winter):63–71.

Spinner, J., and Priest, D. (1997). Women Say Army Agents Bullied Them: 5 Allege Investigators Urged Sex Accusations. *Washington Post*, March 12, p. A14.

Stannard, M. B. (2005). Many shared blame in Abu Ghraib: Ex-prison overseer accepts her
role but says others involved. *San Francisco Chronicle*, April 2, p. A7.

Starship Troopers. (1997). Tristar Pictures and Touchstone Pictures.

Stein, M. B., Walker, J. R., and Forde, D. R. (2000). Gender differences in susceptibility to
posttraumatic stress disorder. *Behaviour Research and Therapy*, 38:619–628.

Stiehm, J., and Olson, B. (2006). For Navy women, sailing has gotten smoother. *Baltimore
Sun*, July 5, p. 1A.

Stiehm, J. H. (1982). The protected, the protector, the defender. *Women's Studies International Forum*, 5:367–376.

Stiglmayer, A. (1994). The war in the former Yugoslavia. In Stiglmayer, A. (ed.), *Mass Rape:
The War Against Women in Bosnia-Herzegovina*, pp. 1–34. Lincoln: University of
Nebraska Press.

Stockdale, J. B. (1995). *Thoughts of a Philosophical Fighter Pilot*. Stanford, CA: Hoover
Institution Press.

Stokesbury, J. L. (1981). *A Short History of World War I*. New York: William Morrow.

———. (1988). *A Short History of the Korean War*. New York: William Morrow.

Stouffer, S. A., Lumsdaine, A. A., Lumsdaine, M. H., Williams, R. M., Jr., Smith, M. B.,
et al. (1949). *The American Soldier* Vol. II: *Combat and Its Aftermath*, Princeton, NJ:
Princeton University Press.

Stout, D. (1998). Cohen upholds mixed training in the military. *New York Times*, June 9, p. A16.

Sunday Times of London Insight Team. (1982). *War in the Falklands: The Full Story*. New
York: Harper & Row.

Taguba, A. M. (2004). *Article 15–6 Investigation of the 800th Military Police Brigade*,
http://www.npr.org/iraq/2004/prison_abuse_report.pdf.

Tan, M. (2006). By the numbers: Who's fighting. *Army Times*, December 11, pp. 14–16.

Tanaka, Y. (1999). Introduction. In Henson, M. R. (ed.), *Comfort Women: A Filipina's Story
of Prostitution and Slavery Under the Japanese Military*, pp. vii–xxii. Lanham, MD:
Rowman & Littlefield.

Taylor, M. D. (1977). Military leadership: What is it? Can it be taught? In *Distinguished
Lecture Series*, Spring 1977, pp. 84–93. Washington, DC: National Defense University
(reprinted in Lester, R. I., and Morton, A. G. (eds.). (2001). *Concepts for Air Force
Leadership*, Air University Press, Maxwell AFB, Alabama, http://www.au.af.mil/au/
awc/awcgate/au–24/taylor.pdf.

Thieme, H. (1997). Lower Paleolithic hunting spears from Germany. *Nature*, 385:807–810.

Thomas, J. R., and French, K. E. (1985). Gender differences across age in motor performance: A meta-analysis. *Psychological Bulletin*, 98:260–282.

Thompson, A. (1999). Military slammed over women's role. *Toronto Star*, February 20, p. 1.

Thompson, M. (1997a). A call to nurse. *Time,* February 24, p. 32.

————. (1997b). Boot camp goes soft: Empathetic drill sergeants make basic training easier, but the recruits may not be ready for war. *Time,* August 4, p. 20.

Tiger, L. (1969). *Men in Groups.* New York: Random House.

Torrance, E. P., and Ziller, R. C. (1957). Risk and life experience: Development of a scale for measuring risk-taking tendencies. *Research Report AFPTRC-TN–57–23,* Randolf Air Force Base, San Antonio, TX, Crew Research Laboratory, Air Force Personnel and Training Research Center, cited in Jobe, J., Holgate, S. H., and Scrapansky, T. A. (1983). Risk taking as motivation for volunteering for a hazardous experiment. *Journal of Personality,* 51:95–107.

Toscano, G. A., and Windau, J. A. (1998). Profile of fatal work injuries in 1996, in Bureau of Labor Statistics, *Compensation and Working Conditions,* Spring, pp. 37–45.

Trivers, R. L. (1972). Parental investment and sexual selection. In Campbell, B. G. (ed.), *Sexual Selection and the Descent of Man,* pp. 136–179. Chicago: Aldine.

Turnbull, J. (2003). Lt. Shane Osborn: Looking at a miracle. *Naval Aviation News,* 85(6):20.

Turney-High, H. H. (1971). *Primitive War: Its Practice and Concepts* (2nd ed.). Columbia: University of South Carolina Press.

Tversky, A., and Kahneman, D. (1974). Judgment under uncertainty: Heuristics and biases. *Science,* 185:1124–1131.

Tyson, A. S. (2003). The expanding role of GI Jane. *Christian Science Monitor,* April 3, p. 1.

————. (2005). For female GIs, combat is a fact: Many duties in Iraq put women at risk despite restrictive policy. May 13, p. A1.

U.S. Department of Justice. (1999). *Assessing the Accuracy of State Prison Statistics,* Office of Justice Programs, Bureau of Justice Statistics.

————. (2003). *Census of State and Federal Correctional Facilities, 2000.* Office of Justice Programs, Bureau of Justice Statistics.

U.S. Department of the Navy. (1997) *Policy on Sexual Harassment,* SecNavInst. 5300.26C.

U.S. Department of Veterans Affairs. (2006). *Fact Sheet: VA Benefits for Former Prisoners of War.* Office of Public Affairs, Washington, DC.

U.S. General Accounting Office. (1993). *Operation Desert Storm: Lessons Learned in the Deployment of Women in the Military,* GAO/NSIAD-93-93.

————. (1995). *DOD Service Academies: Update on Extent of Sexual Harassment,* GAO/NSIAD-95-58.

————. (1998). *Gender Issues: Changes Would Be Needed to Expand Selective Service Registration to Women,* GAO/NSIAD-98-199.

————. (1999). *Women in Prison: Sexual Misconduct by Correctional Staff,* GAO/GGD-99-104.

Udry, J. R. (2000). Biological limits of gender construction. *American Sociological Review,* 65:443–457.

Udry, J. R., Morris, N. M., and Kovenock, J. (1995). Androgen effects on women's gendered behaviour. *Journal of Biosocial Science,* 27:359–368.

Umberson, D. (1992). Gender, marital status and the social control of health behavior. *Social Science and Medicine,* 34:907–917.

United Press International. (1993). Tailhook defendant rails at accusers. July 16.

Uriell, Z. A. (2004). *Pregnancy and Parenthood: Results of the 2001 Survey.* NPRST-AB–04–03. Millington, TN: Navy Personnel Research, Studies, and Technology, Bureau of Naval Personnel.

Uriell, Z. A., and White, S. L. (2005). *Results of the 2003 Pregnancy and Parenthood Survey.* NPRST-AB–05–2. Millington TN: Navy Personnel Research, Studies, and Technology, Bureau of Naval Personnel.

Ursano, R. J., Wheatley, R. D., Carlson, E. H., and Rahe, A. J. (1985). The prisoner of war: Stress, illness and resiliency. *Psychiatric Annals,* 17:532–535.

Valpolini, P., Sculte, H., and Lewis, J. A. C. (1999). Women warriors. *Jane's Defence Weekly,* June 23, pp. 24–26.

Van Bokhoven, I., et al. (2006). Salivary testosterone and aggression, delinquency, and social dominance in a population-based longitudinal study of adolescent males. *Hormones and Behavior,* 50:118–125.

Van Creveld, M. (1992). Women of valor: Why Israel doesn't send women into combat. *Policy Review,* 62(Fall):65–67.

———. (2001). *Men, Women and War.* London: Cassell.

Vanden Brook, T. (2006). Army makes way for older soldiers. *USA Today,* August 1, p. 1A.

Van Hooff, J. A. R. A. M., and Van Schaik, C. P. (1994). Male bonds: Affiliative relationships among nonhuman primate males. *Behaviour,* 130:309–337.

Veevers, J. E., and Gee, E. M. (1986). Playing it safe: Accident mortality and gender roles. *Sociological Focus,* 19:349–360.

Vistica, G. L. (1997). *Fall from Glory: The Men Who Sank the U.S. Navy.* New York: Touchstone.

Vistica, G. L., and Thomas, E. (1997). Sex and lies. *Newsweek,* June 2, p. 26.

Voge, V. M. (1996). Self-reported menstrual concerns of U.S. Air Force and U.S. Army rated women aircrew. *Military Medicine,* 161:614–615.

Voge, V. M., and King, R. E. (1997a). Interpersonal relationship and prisoner of war concerns of rated military male and female aircrew. *Aviation, Space, and Environmental Medicine,* 68:879–885.

———. (1997b). Women in combat: Concerns of U.S. Air Force and U.S. Army rated male and female aircrew. *Military Medicine,* 162:79–81.

Vogel, S. (2006). Superintendent faulted over rape case e-mails. *Washington Post,* July 7, p. B4.

Voyer, D., Voyer, S., and Bryden, M. P. (1995). Magnitude of sex differences in spatial abilities: A meta-analysis and consideration of critical variables. *Psychological Bulletin,* 117:250–270.

Waller, D. (1995). All hands on deck: A successful experiment of men and women aboard the U.S.S. *Eisenhower. Time,* April 17, p. 36.

Wardell, D. W., and Czerwinski, B. (2001). A military challenge to managing feminine and personal hygiene. *Journal of the American Academy of Nurse Practitioners,* 13:187–193.

Washington, K. (2005). Women in combat. *Army Times,* July 4, p. 52.

Washington Times. (2006). Editorial: Nobles and knaves. October 21, p. A12.

Watson, P. (1978). *War on the Mind: The Military Uses and Abuses of Psychology.* New York: Basic Books.

Webb, J. (1979). Women can't fight. *Washingtonian,* November, p. 144.

Wheeler, R. (1978). *Sherman's March: An Eyewitness History of the Cruel Campaign That Helped End a Crueler War.* New York: Thomas Y. Crowell.

Wheelwright, J. (1993). "It was exactly like the movies!" The media's use of the feminine during the Gulf War. In Addis, E., Russo, V. E., and Sebesta, L. (eds.), *Women Soldiers: Images and Realities,* pp. 111–134. New York: St. Martin's Press.

White, J. (2005). Steady drop in black Army recruits: Data said to reflect views on Iraq war. *Washington Post,* March 9, p. A1.

Wilcox, R. K. (1996). *Wings of Fury: From Vietnam to the Gulf War: The Astonishing True Stories of America's Elite Fighter Pilots.* New York: Pocket Books.

Williams, C. L. (1989). *Gender Differences at Work: Women and Men in Nontraditional Occupations,* Berkeley: University of California Press.

Williams, C. L., and Meck, W. H. (1991). The organizational effects of gonadal steroids on sexually dimorphic spatial ability. *Psychoneuroendocrinology,* 16:155–176.

Williams, J. E., and Best, D. L. (1990). *Measuring Sex Stereotypes: A Multination Study* (rev. ed.). Newbury Park, CA: Sage.

Williams, K. (2005). *Love My Rifle More Than You: Young and Female in the U.S. Army.* New York: W. W. Norton.

Wilson, M., and Daly, M. (1997). Life expectancy, economic inequality, homicide, and reproductive timing in Chicago neighbourhoods. *British Medical Journal,* 314:1271–1274.

———. (1985). Competitiveness, risk taking, and violence: The young male syndrome. *Ethology and Sociobiology*, 6:59–73.

Wong, L., Kolditz, T. A., Millen, R. A., and Potter, T. M. (2003). *Why They Fight: Combat Motivation in the Iraq War*. Strategic Studies Institute, U.S. Army War College, http://www.carlisle.army.mil/ssi/pdffiles/PUB179.pdf.

Wood, W., and Eagly, A. H. (2002). A cross-cultural analysis of the behavior of women and men: Implications for the origins of sex differences. *Psychological Bulletin*, 128: 699–727.

Worth, R. F. (2004). Army punishes 23 for refusing convoy order. *New York Times*, December 7, p. A12.

Wrangham, R., and Peterson, D. (1996). *Demonic Males: Apes and the Evolution of Human Violence*. Boston: Houghton Mifflin.

Wray, J. D. (1987). Replacements back on the road at last. *Military Review*, 67:46–53.

Wright, E. (2004). *Generation Kill: Devil Dogs, Iceman, Captain America and the New Face of American War*. New York: Putnam.

Wright, R. (1999). The accidental creationist: Why Stephen Jay Gould is bad for evolution. *New Yorker*, December 13, pp. 56–65.

Xenophon. (~380 BC). *Anabasis: March Up Country* (W. H. D. Rouse, trans., 1947). Ann Arbor: University of Michigan Press.

Young, S. (1999). S.D. captain's love tale could end in jail. *Argus Leader* (Sioux Falls, SD), April 18, p. 1A.

Zeanah, C. H. (1989). Adaptation following perinatal loss: A critical review. *Journal of the American Academy of Child and Adolescent Psychiatry*, 28:467–480.

Zerjal, T. et al. (2003). The genetic legacy of the Mongols. *American Journal of Human Genetics*, 72:717–721.

Zimmer, K. P., and Minkovitz, C. S. (2003). Maternal depression: An old problem that merits increased recognition by child healthcare practitioners. *Current Opinion in Pediatrics*, 15:636–640.

Zivotofsky, A. Z., and Koslowsky, M. (2005). Gender differences in coping with the major external stress of the Washington, D.C., sniper. *Stress and Health*, 21:27–31.

Zucchino, D. (2004). *Thunder Run: The Armored Strike to Capture Baghdad*. New York: Atlantic Monthly Press.

Index

PERMISSIONS

Epigraph for Chapter 2: Excerpt from article by Steve Sailer and Stephen Seiler. Reprinted by permission of the authors. See endnote for full citation.

Epigraph for Chapter 3: Quotation by Richard D. Alexander. By permission of the author. See endnote for full citation.

Epigraph for Chapter 4: Excerpt from article by Celina Cohen-Bendahan et al. By permission of the publisher. See endnote for full citation.

Epigraphs for Chapter 6: Excerpt from *One Bullet Away: The Making of a Marine Officer* by Nathaniel Fick. Copyright © 2005 by Nathaniel Fick. Reprinted by permission of Houghton Mifflin Company. All rights reserved.

Excerpt from article by Bob Lonsberry. By permission of the author. See endnote for full citation.

Epigraphs for Chapter 7: Excerpt from article by Patricia M. Shields et al. By permission of the publisher. See endnote for full citation.

Excerpt from *Wings of Fury* by Robert K. Wilcox. Copyright © 1996 by Robert Wilcox. Reprinted with permission of Pocket Books, a division of Simon & Schuster Adult Publishing Group.

Epigraph for Chapter 9: Excerpt from *The Face of Battle* by John Keegan. Copyright © John Keegan, 1976. Used by permission of Viking Penguin, a division of Penguin Group (USA) Inc.

Epigraph for Chapter 12: Excerpt from an article by Omar Bradley. By permission of the publisher. See endnote for full citation.

Epigraphs for Chapter 15: Excerpt from article by Jan A. R. A. M. Van Hooff et al. By permission of the publisher. See endnote for full citation.

Excerpt from *Proud to Be* by Kelly Flinn. Copyright © 1997 by Kelly J. Flinn. Used by permission of Random House, Inc.

Epigraph for Chapter 16: Quotation by John Hillen. By permission of the author.

Epigraph for Chapter 19: Excerpt from article by Laura L. Miller. By permission of the publisher. See endnote for full citation.

Epigraph for Chapter 21: Excerpt from article by Charles Moskos. By permission of the author. See endnote for full citation.